The Author and his Book

CW00371521

David Northcroft spent the earlier part of his boyhood in Worcestershire and Susse[...]
became exciseman at Cragganmore Distillery, Ballindalloch, Banffshire, he was moved up to [...]
has seen no reason to live anywhere else ever since.

He attended Aberlour High School, followed by degrees at the Universities of Aberdeen, Cambridge and a doctorate at Stirling. His career has been in education, firstly as a teacher of English at Aberdeen Grammar School, then as a member of staff at Aberdeen College of Education (later Northern College). By the time of his early retirement he was Vice Principal.

He has divided the happy years since then between helping to look after his five granddaughters (no grandsons!) and researching in, first, Scottish school education and latterly in oral history, where he has concentrated on building up an archive of personal reminisces from North-east folk. In November 2010, he brought out what was planned to be the first of four volumes which draw upon these recollections: *Grampian Lives, 1900-1950* (Leopard Press). This was followed by two further volumes in his 'Lives' series: *Grampian Lives, 1950-2000* (2010) and *Aberdeen Lives – Work and Play* (2013). The quartet is now completed by this volume, *Aberdeen Lives: War and Peace*. He is also responsible for three earlier books: *Scots at School* (Edinburgh University Press, 2003); *North-east Identities and Scottish Schooling* (Aberdeen University Press, 2005); *A Most Honourable Profession: the graduation speeches of James Scotland* (Aberdeen University, 2009).

He has lived in Muchalls for over 50 years. He is married to Kathleen and they have two sons: Jonathan, who as Football Correspondent to the *Sunday Times* resides in Leicester and is forced to watch Man U and Chelsea rather than the Dons, and then Mat, who is both a Primary school teacher and was for 10 years a Grade 1 referee but has now returned to his earlier love, the Highland League. Mat, Elaine and his three North-east granddaughters – Erin, Abby and Rachael – also live round the corner in Muchalls and together with the recently arrived wee Leicester cousins, Ishbel and Cora, are all five of them a constant source of wonderment and delight.

While the bulk of the interviews which fill this volume were conducted by David Northcroft, some dozen of them were the work of Ken McHardy, who describes himself as the product of both a 'toonser' and a 'teuchter'. He was born in Fonthill Maternity Home in 1955, first lived in a tenement in Causewayend and then grew up in Kincorth, starting school there. He moved on to Aberdeen Grammar School at the age of nine where, in 1967, he first encountered his – then – young English teacher, David Northcroft. Ken went on to study Medicine at Aberdeen University and a career as a diabetes specialist in the city, with an interest in research and training, followed.

Aberdeen Lives: War and Peace purports to offer a collective portrait of the shape and texture of daily life in the city of Aberdeen, as experienced by folk who have spent formative years there. The personal recollections which appear in this book are extracted from the recorded words of some of the 500 people David Northcroft has interviewed over the last 18 years. Usually these interviews have been made in the subjects' own homes and been conducted in an informal, conversational style. The selection of witnesses – commonly derived from word-of-mouth recommendation or from newspaper letters and stories – has been guided by the ambition to cover a representative range of places, social backgrounds and occupations.

This present volume focuses on the wartime, family, community and arts life of Aberdeen in the 20th century. In this respect it acts as the companion to the 2017 *Aberdeen Lives: Work and Play* and as a complement to the author's earlier pair of Grampian Lives books, which concentrated on the region's rural and coastal experiences.

Readers are invited to get in touch with observations and further memories – at davidjnorthcroft@gmail.com or telephone 01569 730621.

Published in October, 2019

Copyright © David Northcroft

The right of David Northcroft to be identified as author of this book has been asserted
under the Copyright, Designs & Patents Act 1988

All rights reserved. No part of this publication may be reproduced, stored in a retrieval system, or transmitted,
in any form or by any means, electronic, mechanical, photocopying, recording or otherwise,
without the prior permission of the copyright holder.

A catalogue record for this book is available from the British Library

ISBN 978-1-9162614-0-2

Design and typesetting by Leopard Press
LePress@btconnect.com

Printed and bound in Scotland by
Robertsons, Forfar

Published by Leopard Press
Auld Logie, Pitcaple, Inverurie, Aberdeenshire AB51 5EE

ABERDEEN LIVES

Aberdeen at War and Peace

Volume 2: 1901–2000

David Northcroft

LEOPARD PRESS

DEDICATION

To Kathleen and to Cora. The first and the latest of the wonderful women in my life.

ACKNOWLEDGEMENTS

No book can ever be produced without the assistance and support of others – in the case of *Aberdeen Lives* that has been especially so.

While the great majority of the photographs which illustrate the reminiscences in the pages that follow have been provided by the speakers themselves – people who have trustingly allowed me access to precious family collections – I must thank a number of other helpers. Some 17 images have been purchased from Aberdeen Journals and here I must thank Gary Thomas and Kirsty Smith for effecting this business in such a friendly and helpful manner. Similarly Norman Adams of the City Council has been helpful in supplying a pair of images of Lord Provost Barney Crockett.

A number of individuals have been supportive in a variety of ways, either by establishing contacts with likely interviewees, by the detection and provision of photographs, or by readily answering specific queries. They are Chris and Heather Anstock; Pat and Alistair Brown; the late Irene Bryce; Brian Butler; Ron Caie; Bob Cooper; David Hartley; Gloria Hay; Rosy Long; George Masson; Lesley Milne; Gavin Morrice; Pauline Ord; Alison Sharman of the University's Elphinstone Institute; Carol Strang; Sandy Watson. In addition thanks are due to the Aberdeen Medico-Chirurgical Society for the supply of the two portraits of Sir Dugald Baird and of Sir Alexander Ogston.

Brian Watt has, once again, generously opened up his extraordinary collection of old postcards for me to plunder. He is the author of two Richard Stenlake publications *Old Stonehaven* and *Old Newtonhill and Muchalls*.

Even more important has been the enthusiastic and collaborative help unstintingly offered me by my old Aberdeen Grammar School pupil and Balmoral Cricket Club team mate (and occasional run out partner), Ken McHardy. His contribution is explained in the 'About the Author' section, but I would wish here to add the extent to which it has been a real pleasure to have enlisted his assistance in the composition of *Aberdeen Lives*: not only has he uncovered some dozen valued interviewees but he has also proved to be a ferociously vigilant proof reader. Many, many thanks, Ken.

Once more I must also offer up hearty thanks to Lindy Cheyne and to Ian Hamilton of the Leopard Press, whose genial and inspiring co-operation has exceeded the normal bounds of professional assistance. Not only have they performed their customary skilled and creative task in editing and laying out the presentation of *Aberdeen Lives,* they have been fine folk to have worked with.

I would dearly like to thank my family for being just that – my family, an unfailing source of life-giving support. The names of this incomparable set of North-east and North-east related people are Kathleen, Jonathan, Mat, Elaine, Jan, and young Erin, Abby, Rachael, Ishbel and Cora.

But above all else, my gratitude belongs to all the City and North-east folk who have opened up their memories to me. Once I had exhausted the circle of my own relatives and friends I became dependent upon the willingness of complete strangers to welcome me into both their homes and their lives, there to ply me with fly cups, home bakes and their own very human stories. The names which appear in this book confirm the truth that the city of Aberdeen and its rural and coastal hinterland contain some of the finest people you could hope to meet anywhere. I hope that they will accept this further volume as my repeated tribute to them.

Cover Photographs

FRONT: Union Street is the common thread which, for the last 200 years, has run through all Aberdonians' lives. Nowadays their cry is that 'it is not what it was'. This photograph, taken from the collection of Brian Watt, shows the city's main thoroughfare, during the Edwardian era, when its reputation as one of Britain's finest main streets was unchallenged.

Notes

The words which appear in this book are taken from transcripts of recordings of the recollections offered by the named contributors to it. In each case, scripts were sent back to the speakers for their own amendments before an agreed version was arrived at. The accounts set out in what follows are selected extracts: the typical interview lasted some 90 minutes and yielded over 4,000 words. Editing has occurred but has been kept to the minimum necessary to smooth out repetition and hesitations and also so as to produce a narrative flow.

Witnesses spoke in their own dialects and accents. As these ranged along a continuum of usage rather than falling into any distinct 'Standard English' / 'Doric' / 'City Spik' category – often within the one interview – the decision has been made to render their words in the one universally recognised Standard form, excepting emphatic instances, usually of reported direct speech.

The location names that are added to each speaker's name refer to the locations focussed on in their interviews, not to birth or current living places. The names which appear are as given to me and in the case of women these have usually been their married rather than maiden forms.

Many more interviewees have given themselves to my oral history project than I have been able to squeeze into this volume. I hope they will not take their omission as being enforced by anything other than a simple exigency of space. My great discovery in researching this book is that everyone – and especially in our socially rich North-east – has a worthwhile story to tell, whether I have found room for it or not.

Sadly, but inevitably, given their age range, some of my witnesses have subsequently died. As, however, it has been impossible to ascertain exact dates and circumstances, the decision has been made to give the date of birth only.

Every effort has been made to trace the provenance of the photographs used in this book. If, nevertheless, any outstanding examples are uncovered, then the copyright holder is invited to contact the author.

FOREWORD

Aberdeen Lives: a City to be Proud of?

'Aberdeen looks so different from anywhere else. Granite buildings. Imposing on a grey day, sparkling silver in the sun. Even in the city, you smell the sea. Classic architecture, deep shadows. The grit and the glint. Glimmer. Permanence. '
When we want something done, we want it done well. Careful judgement. Genuine. It is what it is. Honesty. Realness. Genuinely warm people- quietly confident with a proud spirit.'

– WALL POSTER AT ABERDEEN AIRPORT.

It is doubtful if any reader - if such a person there be - will be able to recall exactly what they were doing on Monday September 3 1956 - but I can. I passed that dreamy late summer's day seated in a deck chair, watching the second day's play at Hove County Cricket Ground as my team Sussex laid waste to some mediocre Lancashire bowling.

Tuesday September 4 1956 was to be frighteningly different. Twenty-four hours later I found myself some 550 miles to the north in the very strange city of Aberdeen, apprehensively wondering what my future in this far distant place could possibly hold.

The background to this personal drama can be briefly explained. I was 14 years old, the son of a Custom and Excise officer who had been working at the Newhaven docks - but who had now won a transfer to Cragganmore Distillery, Ballindalloch, Banffshire, there to take up the post of Exciseman. So here I was, alighting from the overnight sleeper at the Joint Station with a couple of hours to put in before the connecting journey to Craigellachie Junction and onward to my new home in unknown, impossibly far-away Banffshire.

We decided to walk up Bridge Street to have a look at this Aberdeen. The spectacle that hit me at the traffic lights corner was one that has possessed my memory these six decades since. There, stretching out on either side, was a mile-long valley of stately glittering granite, full of proud shop frontages and picture houses, its broad pavements thick with pedestrian bustle and its highway graced with green tramcars swishing up and down in either direction. Before me was a dramatic glen of garden and of mature foliage, fringed by church dome and spires. And yes, the sun was shining.

It all spoke to me of a self-assured integrity, of an urbanity that I immediately knew would become my home city and a place with which I would enrich my native southern identity.

This immediate sense of belonging was not to be disappointed. Over the coming years I settled in Speyside, got my Highers at Aberlour High School, then attended Aberdeen University, graduated, built up a career in education in the city, married a local girl and raised our family within its environs.

And now, some 63 years on and a long time retired, I am, with this volume, coming to the completion of a 20-year long project of oral history, one that, at the turn of this century, began with an interview of that notable North-east lad o'pairts, James Michie, son of a farm labourer, graduate in Modern Languages, teacher, innovative Director of Education, weekly golfer, follower of the Dons, vivid raconteur and energetic champion of the Doric.

That afternoon in James's home in Morningfield Road was the first on a trail that has since covered 500 interviewees from the North-east, including 200 in the city itself, each of them contributing their own rich store of personal memories of daily life as it has been experienced in our region over the whole stretch of a century.

To a large extent I would like to offer this, the published fruits of all that record of North-east folk, as the fulfilment of a covenant first entered into on that September day back in 1956. For, in the long years since, I have been content to embrace City and Shire as my own heart-felt destination, a place in which to settle, to grow, to and to pass on my own memories to the next generation of Aberdonians.

The outcome has been three - and now a fourth - book in what has become a quartet of North-east 'Lives'. In my more grandiose moments I like to think of this collected effort as my own homage to a region and to its city - a complementary pair that I have long since come to engage with as my home - and to the full life it has given me and to the friends and the family I have developed here.

Ah, but Aberdeen is not what it was… it's a cry that has greeted me time and again of late. When its inhabitants proffer this verdict what they seem to be denouncing is the machinations of the Council, the degradation of its centre, and the disappearance of all those proudly independent stores that had so impressed that 14-year old back in 1956, all to be replaced by the shabby scatterings of charity and betting shops and of boarded up frontages. The cinemas have now fled to an anonymous multiplex site and the sleek green trams, which so captivated my boyhood self, have long since met a fiery end.

Well, yes, there is truth in all this - our city has not been immune to the city-centre erosion that has afflicted other British towns. But it is a lament that substitutes appearances for the inner character. When people decry the vegetation poking out of the guttering and the rotted window frames atop Union Street, the jams at the Haudagain, the brutalising blocks of glass and stone of Marischal Square, the delays to the refurbishment of the Art Gallery and to Union Terrace Gardens, and all the rest of it, what they are really doing is to focus on the fabric and to miss the soul that ever lies within.

But then, self-deprecation has always been a well-recognised trait of the Aberdonian character - 'a built-in reticence', Dianne Morrison says (page 359) and 'a reticence to brag about what Aberdeen's good at and what we do well'. Or as, Jenny Shirreffs adds in the same 'Community' chapter, 'Oh, we're so very good at moaning!'

Yet both of these witnesses are life-long natives of the city and wouldn't dream of moving away from it. And why? The answer is simple: it's because of the people. As Dianne goes on to claim, 'There is still a community feel to Aberdeen. I don't feel that I am just another person, another ant, but that I belong somewhere.'

And Jenny Shirreffs draws our attention to the extraordinary diversity of the post-war city, of the willingness of people from all over the globe to choose to make this the place in which to refashion their lives and to bring up their young.

So, it is perhaps to the in-comers that we should turn to affirm the enduring appeal of Aberdeen. Look through the chapter, 'Incomers and Ex-Pats', which details their reactions, and share in Meg Forbes's tribute to the hard-working sacrifices that the 'ordinary' Aberdonian makes to ensure that the next generation will enjoy the better career that economic circumstances denied themselves - a contrast, she says, to the attitudes she had left behind in Denny - or in the Northern Irishman, John Dunn's, gratitude for Aberdeen's offering him a 'secure ethos' and for the absence of the social divisions and sectarianism to be encountered in so many other UK centres.

Then there are the experiences of those who have come to us from overseas - the real test of any community's moral substance. Read of the warm generosity that welcomed Nepalese Prasanna Gautam's, arrival on a chilly, rain-swept night and which convinced him that this northern city was the place in which to further his medical career. And then go on to follow the Karachi reared Izhar Khan's dealings with his renal patients at Foresterhill: 'I have come to admire their character… I would say that North-east folk are more stoical and resilient than most; that they keep their feelings to themselves and are loath to express pain or grief'.

His fellow Asian immigrant, Tauqeer Malik - once son of a Pakistani farmer but now a successful Grades cricketer, businessman and Councillor - simply sums it all up with: 'I am very grateful for the way in which

Aberdeen people have taken me to their hearts….I would say that Aberdeen people are the very best!'

It is an accolade that this in-comer author can only echo. My oral history project - leading to the compilation of this Aberdeen Lives, has amply reinforced what I already knew about the people of my adopted North-east and of Aberdeen. To listen to the life- stories of some 500 of its folk has been to immerse myself, not only in the records of these others, but also to become deeply aware of the integrity and sheer genuineness that has infused them. Everywhere, I have encountered a warm yet unaffected hospitality, a willingness to reach out to the stranger. And sitting there, in their own homes; drinking in the personal stories, recounted with such straightforward modest fidelity, I have been invariably enheartened by the degree to which, without exception, there has been revealed the will to draw upon an ingrained work-ethic and to replicate the grounded good sense that is their birthright alongside an abiding social responsibility and the commitment to engage with their home environment so as to make the very best of themselves and thus be able to hand on an ever better life to the next generation.

To, in short, sustain the moral inheritance of their native place and to ensure that *Aberdeen Lives* is not simply a noun but is also to be read as an active verb.

'Aberdeen- a city to be proud of?' Time to change that punctuation mark; yes most certainly: 'Aberdeen is a City to be proud of!'

– David Northcroft. September 2019.

Sadly, some of my witnesses are no longer with us. But others – and not always the younger ones – live on. Here is Beryl Booth on the last day of September 2019, celebrating her 100th birthday, surrounded by family and friends. Daughter Beryl Mackenzie is to her left and son Bruce is to her first right.

CONTENTS

A proper upbringing

Health and welfare

Different worlds

CHURCH, MOSQUE, FAITH AND BELIEF

The teachers' viewpoint

Some university experiences

A ladder of opportunity

The Scottish system

SOME NOTABLE LIVES – 2

INCOMERS AND EX-PATS

Aberdonians abroad

The new Aberdonians

THE ARTS 278

Visual arts

Lure of the stage and power of the arts

Making music

IN TIME OF WAR:

The World Wars

Remembrance Day: Portlethen November 2018.

Cookney remembers
its fallen.
November 2018.

ECHOES OF THE FIRST WORLD WAR

A tale of two communities

The loss of life in the First World War was such that almost no communities were left untouched by the general slaughter. Almost all, but not quite, for there were a few that were fortunate enough to emerge with all its combatants still alive when peace was finally declared in November 1918.

One such was the small fishing village of Muchalls, situated on the Kincardineshire coast some 10 miles south of Aberdeen. But three miles away, inland, the farming community of Cookney suffered grievously – its war memorial lists some 30 names.

There was, apparently, some ill-feeling, even enmity towards Muchalls after the war: why did they all survive when we have lost so many!

There can be no War Memorial at Muchalls; instead the villagers decided to erect a Peace Memorial, which stands on a mound by the railway line – the date '1919' refers to the Treaty of Versailles which brought peace with Germany.

Information supplied by Colin Johnston.

Muchalls celebrates
the peace.

Aberdeen played a full part

Aberdeen played its full part in the war effort. When war was declared in August 1914, there was a massive rush to enlist. One of them was my great uncle, Alex. He reported to the recruitment office (just off Golden Square, in Crimon Place)

Recruits off to the Front, being bade farewell at Aberdeen Joint Station.

and joined the Artillery. He was required to report to Duthie Park the next day in a suit and carrying a broomstick. This was to be his 'rifle'. He told of the embarrassment of being followed by groups of young lads, jeering at them as they all practised marching up and down in the park.

Then came the day when they were ordered to march out of the park, along Riverside, then across the Bridge of Dee, along the South Deeside Road to Milltimber Brae and then back along North Deeside Road, via Mannofield, to the Duthie Park. By this time, they were all in agony; they had not been issued with proper boots and they were limping along in their best shoes, creaking and groaning with the effort. But then came a transformation. At the wall which runs along Mannofield Reservoir, there appeared a small group of Gordon pipers, tuning up their instruments. For the final two miles back to Duthie Park they felt as if they were floating on air; such was the power of the bagpipes.

Aberdeen lost 5,000 to the First World War. My great uncle survived but never really opened up about the experience; it would seem it was all too terrible to discuss in peacetime. What I did get out of him was his answer to my question as to what was the most vivid memory he carried with him from his time at the Front. It was simply, and without a moment's hesitation, 'the noise'. The constant bombardment, especially standing next to the guns as they were being fired, and the cries and the shrieks were overwhelming.

Then there was the gas. He described watching the clouds of gas looming towards

The Gordon Highlanders parade through Culter, August 1914.

Old comrades in arms: Tom Rearrie (centre), taken in his workshop with a set of German visitors. The man with his arm round him is Ala Niedermeier, who was once a member of the Hitler Youth and fought against the Russians in 1945. The three younger men are Colin Johnston's Bavarian pals, on a visit to Scotland.

them like a great white jellyfish, preceded by a sweet, sickly smell. It was reckoned that if you did have that smell in your nose and mouth then it was too late. My great uncle Alex was a victim of a gas attack at Hill 60, near Ypres. He was informed by a doctor that he could only expect to survive for another five years; in the event, he lived till he was into his late eighties and that on 40 fags a day.

One of my best witnesses has been Tom Rearrie, a tailor, originally from a farm near Newmachar, who lived into his 90s. In his early days, he'd been a horseman on the farm, but changed careers to become an apprentice tailor in Newburgh, later moving to Newmachar.

Tom joined up, fought through nearly the whole campaign and survived. He had the huge advantage, he claimed, of only being five feet tall. That was priceless in the trenches when those of normal height would have to remember to duck down so as to avoid the German snipers.

Tom talks of all those young English officers who, at six feet tall, were fine specimens of manhood. Yet so many of them lost their lives and in the most undignified circumstances imaginable. They would visit the latrines, crouch down to do their business but then, on rising up again, would stand upright so as to pull their trousers up, with the result that 'bang!', a sniper would pick them off just like that. The Germans would watch for the tell-tale sign of steam rising up from the latrine and that would be that. This was where the kilted soldiers had the advantage; their dress, Tom claimed, was ideal both for fornication and for defecation – though not necessarily in that order!

Tom had a brother who was at the Front with him. One day they both had to seek cover in a shell hole. But they were running out of water and becoming desperate. They noticed a small stream nearby but to get to it would mean the exposure of breaking cover. They spun a coin to see who should go and Tom lost. He duly crept down to the stream and as he did so heard 'Bang!'. His brother had received a hit and was blown to smithereens, never to be seen again.

With the war over, Tom returned to the North-east, married and raised a family. But for the next 10 years he could never get a satisfactory night's sleep. Horrific memories came back to him in recurrent nightmares.

During the war he did once get some leave. At that time, he was still living with his parents on their farm near Ellon. He travelled by train almost all the way home from Flanders Field, still in his uniform and carrying his rifle and pack. When he reached Aberdeen, he discovered there were no trains running out to Ellon, so he marched all the

Julian the tank at
the Castlegate.

16 miles there on foot in his filthy uniform, with the mud of the Somme on him. When
he finally approached home, his sister, who was looking out of the window, shouted out in
excitement, 'Tom's here!'. His mother came to the door, took one look at her dirty,
stinking son and pronounced, 'Ye're nae comin into ma hoose in that state! Git oot ti the
pigsty an clean yersel up!' So that was his hero's welcome.

Tom Rearrie's experiences must have been typical of many other North-east lads. The
region certainly played its part. The area round Turriff suffered the largest percentage of
deaths in the whole of the UK. Then there were the exploits of 'Julian the Tank'. Six
tanks were sent around the country as part of the effort to raise money for the war. The
idea was for passers-by to throw sixpenny pieces into a special wire cage perched on top
of the tank. Aberdonians gave with such generosity that the city was allowed to keep one
of the tanks after the war. For years it stood up on the Broad Hill before it was broken
up for scrap at the start of the Second World War. The special 'path' up which Julian
travelled to his lofty perch can still be clearly seen, just behind the Beach Ballroom.

When the British entered the war in August 1914, they were up against a formidable
and well-prepared enemy. The country had concentrated its strength on the Navy and
was content to maintain a comparatively small army for 'peacekeeping' in the Empire. It
was no more than 160,000 regulars up against a German army of 2,000,000.

Colin Johnston b.1948. Aberdeen. Interviewed 2016.

During his time as History teacher at the Bridge of Don and Hazlehead academies,
Colin Johnston led a number of pupil groups on visits to the First World War battle sites.
He has made an extensive study of the war, focussing on first-hand recollections
and nearly 40 years of travelling to Flanders Field.

Julian the tank on its
perch at the Broad Hill.

Our teacher had three brothers killed at the same time in World War I

The telegraph boy was worn out

One of the teachers we had at Victoria Road had had three brothers killed at the same time in World War I and this was the main event of her life. She had been in the house on what was an infamous day for Gordon Highlanders as such vast numbers got wiped out and she said that by night time, the telegraph boy was absolutely worn out with going up and down the road taking telegrams to people. So she was very driven about peace and had worked for the League of Nations in Turkey in her youth and was very keen that everyone would make a contribution [to society] and that you would always do your best.

Barney Crockett. b.1953. Victoria Road School. Interviewed 2016.

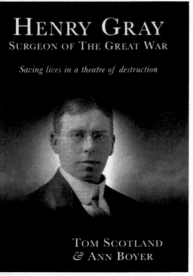

HENRY GRAY
SURGEON OF THE GREAT WAR

Saving lives in a theatre of destruction

TOM SCOTLAND
& ANN BOYER

The cover page to Tom Scotland's biography of Sir Henry Gray.

Aberdeen's unsung medical hero

It was while I was researching the role and development of Surgery in the First World War that I first came across the name of Henry Gray. As I found out more about him, I realised that here was an Aberdonian who had played a huge but now largely forgotten part in the treatment of the wounded at the front.

Henry Gray studied Medicine at the University of Aberdeen. He graduated in 1895 and then became Sir Alexander Ogston's house surgeon. Ogston had made his name by discovering the existence of the staphylococcus, the principal cause of surgical wound infections, and also through his introduction of anti-septic surgery to Aberdeen. He had also been instrumental in the founding of the Royal Army Medical Corps in 1898.

After spending a year as Ogston's house surgeon, Henry Gray went to Germany to further his studies in surgery before returning to the position of assistant surgeon at Aberdeen Royal Infirmary. In 1904 he was appointed consultant surgeon. Over the following 10 years he worked as the sort of general all-purpose surgeon that was commonly employed in those days. He had to take on anything and everything, from appendectomies and hysterectomies to bowel and orthopaedic operations.

He built up a strong reputation as the surgeon who was ready to take on very difficult cases which had been turned away by others as hopeless. Nevertheless, he was no more than a standard practitioner, albeit an outstanding one, doing routine general work. So when war broke out, he immediately volunteered for service at the Front.

He was initially sent to be a consultant surgeon in charge of a group of base hospitals in Rouen where the Army hospitals were situated, well back from the front line. His work showed him that despite a well-equipped hospital set-up, men were dying at an alarming rate from overwhelming wound infections caused by the organisms responsible for gas gangrene. Surgeons were still using the methods that had been employed during the Second Boer War (1899-1902) – but that war had been fought in the dry conditions of the Veldt whereas the France and Flanders campaign was taking place amidst the mud and wet of a lowland area.

One of the problems in ensuring any successful treatment of the wounded was the fact that the battle fields were situated in agricultural fields that had been thoroughly manured and were therefore packed full of dangerous bacteria and, especially, clostridium perfringens, the organism responsible for gas gangrene. High explosive shellfire had spread fragments of shell casing and created multiple filthy contaminated wounds which had allowed the entry of bacteria. In such circumstances speed was of the essence. By the time the wounded had been entrained back to the base hospitals the deadly infections had set in and the cases had become past treatment.

Gray realised that the only way to prevent this was through a swift application of radical surgery aimed at removing all dead tissue – skin, bone, flesh, as well as foreign material driven into the wound. He was the first to write up the new approach and to move to institute, not only the methods of complete excision of devitalised and contaminated tissue, but of shifting the centre of treatment to as close to the Front as possible so as to avoid delay. Casualty clearing stations, which could be reached relatively quickly by ambulance wagon convoys, became the location for urgent limb and life-saving surgery.

One of his innovations was in the treatment of compound fractures of the femur. The standard approach had been simply to make a splint out of a Lee Enfield rifle, but this was proving to be a crude and unstable one. The result was that by the time the patient came to the operating theatre, his fracture would have been subject to constant moving about, with bone grinding against bone; he would have lost an excessive amount of blood as a result of poor splintage and be in great pain and in no condition to withstand the rigours of early wound excision.

When he was Consulting Surgeon to the British Third Army in 1917, Gray ensured that all femoral fractures were immobilised using a Thomas Splint, which stabilised the

Can any good thing come out of Aberdeen? The distinguished surgeon, Sir Alexander Ogston. (IMAGE BY KIND PERMISSION OF ABERDEEN MED-CHI SOCIETY).

> Gray's innovations had the result that the mortality rate of femoral fractures dropped from around 80% to 15%.

fracture much more effectively. Patients were transferred immediately to casualty clearing stations specialising in the management of femoral fractures. Thanks to effective splintage, blood loss was considerably less, with the result that they arrived in good clinical condition and fit to undergo radical limb and life-saving surgery. Gray's innovations had the result that the mortality rate of femoral fractures dropped from around 80% to 15%.

But despite the fact that Gray came to be regarded as the best operating surgeon at the Front there were difficulties in his gaining due acceptance. His was an impulsive and dictatorial temperament; with his patients and with younger surgeons he was unfailingly considerate, but with his senior peers he could be abrupt and dismissive. Never one to suffer fools gladly, he upset many of those around him. He earned the reputation of being difficult and this was a trait which was to cost him dearly later on.

There was – as always in the medical profession – the matter of professional jealousy. The consequence was that though he emerged from the war with honours and a knighthood, his re-entry into civilian life was never going to be a smooth one. He had bruised too many feelings for that.

So he returned to Aberdeen in 1919 and back to his routine work at ARI, as somebody far short of a hero. His recognition as one of the great medical figures of the First World War also suffered from the prevailing peace time determination to put all that behind themselves. Yet the war had been a period of dramatic advances in surgery, when under the pressure of working out new treatments for such areas as plastic, orthopaedic and neuro surgery, a range of exciting innovations had been effected. Gray had been in the thick of it and yet he was now expected simply to resume his career as if nothing had changed.

Another issue was that Aberdeen was regarded in medical circles as a parochial backwater; Edinburgh was seen as the great Scottish centre, while the London medical establishment had little time for this difficult Aberdonian. Day by day, Gray might be showing himself in the ARI operating theatres to be a superlative surgeon, but by doing all this 500 miles north of where all the important stuff was naturally held to be happening, that counted for little.

That is why when, out of the blue, an offer came to emigrate to Canada and to take up an apparently prestigious position as Surgeon-in-Chief to the Royal Victoria Hospital in Montreal, he jumped at the chance.

One of the attractions of the Montreal post was the lure of a university chair. But the move turned out to be a disastrous one. He became embroiled in some vicious university in-fighting; his own manner as an intemperate incomer meant that he became sucked into a power struggle between Sir Arthur Currie, Principal and Vice-Chancellor of McGill University, and Sir Henry Vincent Meredith, president of the Royal Victoria Hospital. His personal reputation became unfairly besmirched.

Yet he couldn't return to Aberdeen as a failure, so he had no alternative but to stick it out. He saw out his career in Canada in comparative obscurity, doing private work. He collapsed with a heart attack and died when he was 67. The body was cremated and, as far as I can tell, there is no memorial either here or across the Atlantic.

These days Gray is a forgotten figure in the city of his birth. In many respects you could describe him as a typical Aberdonian of his era: he was possessed of clear-cut, definite views, was extremely capable in a practical sense, was quick to take offence and even quicker to express regret, was somewhat grumpy and off-putting and, above all, was exceptionally industrious.

He was the victim of his own personality, of circumstances, of the general post-1918 desire to consign the war and all its dreadful experiences into the past and of professional rivalry and jealousies. But it is difficult not to conclude that he was also the victim of geography. Take the reputation of the man he first trained under in Aberdeen, Sir Alexander Ogston. By any fair reckoning this was a most distinguished figure, one who had done invaluable work in the field of sepsis and the adaptation of Lister's theories to surgery. On the Continent his work was well received, but it is no accident that he was forced to give his first paper to a German audience. After all, as the editor of the British Medical Journal commented, 'Can any good thing come out of Aberdeen?'

Thomas (Tom) Scotland. Flanders. Interviewed 2016.

For further information see *War Surgery 1914-18*, edited by Thomas Scotland and Steven Heys, 2013 [Helion & Co.] and also *Henry Gray, Surgeon of the Great War, saving lives in a theatre of destruction,* by Tom Scotland and Ann Boyer. [Capercaillie Books, Edinburgh, 2015]

On leave: David Allan poses in front of his Aberdeen home.

THE SECOND WORLD WAR
– on land and in the air

North Africa, Salerno and the rest – four years on the front line

I t was when I was serving on the south coast that I made my error of one day noticing this poster on the wall which offered us the chance to apply for something 'different and interesting'. I put my name down and that's when I found myself learning the Morse code that would send me to years of front-line service.

We were then given three months of training in wireless operation and the use of the Morse code. To begin with I almost always came last in the tests; I found it so difficult to pick up. But finally, it clicked and once I'd got hold of it I became a real expert. Then I was called up to go abroad and that's where I served for the next three and a half years. I was in Egypt, in Palestine, in Beirut, in Greece and then I took part in the invasion of Italy, landing at Salerno.

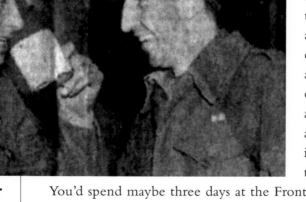

Home on leave for a few days' respite: Gunner Allan (right) at a canteen in Aberdeen.

You'd spend maybe three days at the Front, then be taken back for 10 days before returning; it was reckoned that three days of such intense fighting at the Front was all a man could be expected to stand at any one time. You were under fire almost constantly. Of course, it was frightening – anybody who tells you differently is either lying or they weren't there. Some men actually turned tail and ran off, but I never did. You just learned how to stand your ground. It's what you had to do.

While we were in North Africa, Churchill came out to inspect the troops at Tunis. We were all lined up and instructed to give him three mighty cheers. Well, there we were standing for a whole hour in the sweltering sun, getting more and more thirsty and fed up. Then along came a water-carrying truck, 'At last!' we thought, 'time for a drink!' But no, the truck was there to lay the dust so that Churchill wouldn't get any discomfort from it. So, when he did appear, and the officers called for three cheers, we just let out a round of booing. There he was sitting in his truck, just like a slab of white marble with a cigar in his hand.

I was in the Salerno landings for the liberation of Italy. We had to fight our way up north, up towards Rome. But the Germans made a stand at Monte Cassino; they took over the monastery and used it as their garrison. It took us six months to get through. We were shelled each day and there were American planes overhead dropping bombs. The loss of life was horrific; we called the place Murder Mile.

The only time I ever landed up in hospital was through hypothermia in Italy. Rain or shine, snow or sun we just had to get on with it; this might be sunny Italy but believe me, it could be perishing cold during those winter nights. And we had no real meals either. No cooks up on the front line, just tins of corned beef. You couldn't light a fire for warmth or for cooking in case the Germans spotted it.

We did have a high old time of it on leave in Cairo. 'Three days in Cairo' – I could

100 today! David Allan celebrates his centenary, March 2019.

In North Africa

tell you a few stories about that! Once I was telling an old lady in the Abbeyfield residences here about those days and she remarked, 'Three days in Cairo – I expect that gave you the chance to visit all the museums!'. Well, not exactly – I became more familiar with Shepherd's Hotel than any museum!

Rome was just as wild too. You daren't leave your vehicle because if you did then you'd come back to find nothing but the chassis left; the engine, the tyres, the bodywork would all have been stripped. Then there were all these young men going around and telling you, 'You want? Nice meal, and very nice sister!'.

When you are in the war, at the Front, time of day doesn't really exist – there are only two times: night and daylight. We never carried watches. You had to carry your kit at all times. Where you are is where you sleep. You would roll out a groundsheet and cover yourself with a blanket. If it rained you could fold the groundsheet over you so as to make a sort of tent. In the desert you simply slept under the stars. Soon any life you had beforehand comes to seem unreal. After a while I never thought of Aberdeen – I never thought I'd ever see it again. My folks back home didn't hear from me for two years – all they got was a pre-printed card with the words 'I am well' on it. You lived in the day and didn't think of any future or the past.

My essential task was to keep the wireless equipment going. You'd go up in advance of the front line with an officer who would carry out a reconnaissance and then give orders back to the artillery as to where and when to fire. My job was to translate these orders into Morse code messages. I could do 30 words a minute; you could say I was there to act as the officer's mobile phone. We would dig ourselves into some sort of foxhole and the shells would come whizzing over us as we lay there. It was like being in the middle of a shooting gallery. The noise and the smoke were unbearable, but you just had to keep going.

We were landing men and equipment at Salerno – armoured cars. We were to rendezvous on the beach. We piled into the cars but then heavy machine gun fire opened up on us. We got over to a viaduct for some shelter. The Major decided to see what the situation was so he clambered up an embankment – there was a rattle of gunfire and he staggered back dead. A great pity – he was a lovely man, one of the very best. We put his body into the car and drove back as fast as we could. Our despatch rider, Taffy Robertson, was with us on his motorbike. Another hail of bullets and Taffy was no more.

Later I was informed that I'd been mentioned in despatches. There was an item in the paper which went: 'By the King's order, the name of David G Allan, the King's Artillery, is published in the *London Gazette* of the 29th November 1945 and is mentioned in despatches for distinguished service'. I later got hold of a copy of this *London Gazette* expecting to read a wee bit about myself and what my distinguished service had consisted of, but, no, all that appeared was my bare name. So that's what being 'mentioned in despatches'; means – the bare mention and nothing else!

I came through the whole war almost without a scratch; all I suffered were sores on my hands and body. I always maintained that I had two guardian angels to look over me:

My folks back home didn't hear from me for two years – all they got was a pre-printed card with the words 'I am well' on it.

In Greece, combatting the guerrillas: David Allan is second right.

my mother and my eldest sister.

I never really hated the enemy. In North Africa we had taken so many of them prisoner and I quickly discovered that they were just like me and you – simply men who'd been ordered to do something that wasn't of their making. It's politicians who make war, not the ordinary people. Really, all that slaughter, it was just senseless. But while you're in it you just have to keep going. You're there, for better or for worse, and there's nothing else but just keep at it and see it through.

David Allan, b.1919. North Africa and Salerno. Interviewed 2014.

Survival was the luck of the draw

I was called up at the start of September, 1939, two days before the start of the war. We had three weeks in Aberdeen. Then we were told we would be going to Cove; that's great we all thought: we'll be able to get home every night. But it was Cove in Hampshire!

We were attached to the 51st Highland Division which went over to France in January 1940. We were lucky because we got out as the Germans invaded.

In 1943 I was flown into Burma. We lost a lot of fellows there. I had malaria three times and typhus fever. When I came home, I was eight stone and looked like a Chinaman. We were now part of the 36th British Division and flown into Makele. There we moved down through the villages and the jungle, down to the Irrawaddy. We crossed the river in December 1943. The Royal Engineers, a unit from the Hardgate, Aberdeen, took us over in rafts.

I was a nursing orderly, part of a Medical Corps. Whether you survived or not was the

The young serviceman George Fraser, little knowing what awaited him in Burma.

A late life picture of George with wife Alma who was his regular correspondent all the time he was in Burma.

My uncle came back from a prisoner of war camp completely insane.

luck of the draw. Many days I assumed I would never see Aberdeen again. We lost a few in France when we were dive bombed by a Jerry plane. The galling thing was that later that German pilot crashed and we had to tend him – the bugger who had bombed us all and, here we were, looking after him! Although I was a stretcher-bearer in Burma, we all had to carry weapons. We were up against the Japanese and the Geneva Convention meant nothing to them.

I was 19 when the war started; I was demobbed in 1946, six-and-a-half years later. I had survived.

George Fraser. b. 1919. Burma Star. Interviewed 2006.

He spent the whole night screaming

A colleague tells the following story: 'In 1945, my uncle came back from a Japanese prisoner of war camp and he was completely insane – destroyed and screaming.' We lived in a tiny two-bedroomed flat – my mum and dad and two teenage girls. My mum just said that our uncle was going to have to sleep in our bedroom. There was nowhere else willing to take him. So we had this poor man who spent the whole night screaming and having nightmares in the same bedroom as two teenage girls.

Barney Crockett b.1953. Footdee. Interviewed 2016.

I was confident I would get through

I was enlisted into the Seventh Battalion and sent down to the south of England. We were preparing for D-day, though none of us were ever told that. We were loaded into these Liberty boats and were crammed together on the deck. We were lined up on deck and the Commander told us we were to go over to France. We approached the shore with shells whizzing over our heads being fired by the Royal Navy. We were then loaded onto the landing crafts. You had to clamber on as best you could, holding on to a rope with the sergeant's warning ringing in our ears, 'Remember if you fall in, we're not stopping for you,'.

Once we got to the beach we went up to the main road and then across a field. We were a group of about 20. I was always confident that I would get through all right, though I had no reason to think that way. I guess I was too young and too naïve to realise just how dangerous it all was. But some of us did fall under the German gunfire. When I landed, I had looked down and seen a body floating in the water and that did give me a turn. It was at that point that you realised that you really were in a war and that people were going to get killed. But I also knew that whatever you did you couldn't stop, and that you just had to keep going.

Jim Glennie- second top right with mug in hand- is among this group digging in just after the D-Day landings.

Our object was to take the port of Le Havre. Corporal Swan ordered us to advance and take as much ammunition with us as we could manage. Shells were coming over – the 'Moaning Minnies' we called them. Corporal Swan was by my side and that's when he got a bullet through his cheek. He went down like a log. He'd been hit by a German sniper – it could easily have been me, but the sniper preferred to aim at the officer rather than an unpromoted squaddie like me. I called for the stretcher bearers and they took him away.

We were doing our best to make progress when some German tanks arrived. We dived into a ditch and that's when I got shot. I got a couple of wounds, to my elbow and to my right arm. The Germans took me off in an ambulance to a hospital where I was operated on by a British doctor, who had been captured earlier. Then the next day I was taken off in an ambulance. I was stowed on the top bunk and as we were jolting along, I could hear the RAF strafing us. 'Just my luck to be killed by my own side,' I thought.

As long as you didn't attempt anything rash then the Germans would be content to keep you as a prisoner, but any attempt at an escape would be fatal. In the hospital there were a pair of guys and they did go for it. They hid themselves in the laundry but were discovered and then taken outside and shot.

I was taken to this large prison camp near Leipzig – Stalag IVB. My right arm made a good recovery – that British doctor had done a good job. The camp was close to a benzene factory. This was continually getting bombed and we were given the task of filling in all the bomb craters. But we were in some danger from all these air raids, of being killed by our own RAF.

Stalag IVB was a huge camp, holding some 18,000 prisoners, all kept in a series of large huts. We were showered and our clothes were deloused. During my whole time there I only got three showers. All you got was a dirty towel and a bucket of cold water. Conditions were austere but not brutal. We had a fair amount of freedom to fill in the

The portal to Stalag IVB.

We noticed how worn our German warders' uniforms were compared to ours and how they would feel the quality in ours quite longingly.

days as best we could. We played football and held concert parties. We received Red Cross parcels and these always contained cigarettes, so these became our currency, a situation which suited me as a non-smoker. Entry to a concert was one fag, as was a haircut and a toothbrush. It was important to keep yourself clean and not to let your standards drop – that was vital for morale.

For exercise you would take a walk around the perimeter of the camp and for food we only got one meal a day, at tea time, which consisted of little more than watery cabbage or pumpkin soup, plus a small block of bread to be shared among seven prisoners.

We were treated reasonably well – no brutality or beatings. But it was noticeable that if an SS guard was present the other German warders wouldn't speak to us, but as soon as he was gone, they would be quite friendly. They would ask us about conditions back in the UK and we would exaggerate just how well off the people were there with plenty of food. We noticed how worn their uniforms were compared to ours and how they would feel the quality in ours quite longingly.

We never considered trying to make an escape. We knew we would be shot if we tried. We had a wireless smuggled into one of the huts and every night someone would come round, shut the door to our hut and give us the latest news. From this we knew that victory was getting nearer and nearer and all we had to do was to hang on.

At the end of the war things began to break down and the Germans lost control. We were all marched out; the Germans were afraid that the advancing Russian troops would get to them. We didn't really know where we were going and had to live off the land as best we could. We had to sleep by the roadside.

Our march was an increasingly disorganised affair. It was clear that the German corporal hadn't a clue as to where we should be going. One day we marched through this wood and the very next day found ourselves marching through it all over again. We were going round in circles. One day we came up against this large prison-like building. The German corporal went through its door and then came out another one soon after. 'About turn!' he ordered us. We had been trying to get into Colditz but Colditz was full up. After that our German guards just disappeared and we were on our own.

We came to this small village. The Canadians among us said, 'Well, we're not going to sleep rough tonight,'. So we went up to the largest house in the place and the Canadians knocked at the door. A lady came out and was told, 'We give you one hour to get out,'. She immediately shot down the road, but soon came back with another woman who spoke perfect English. 'Yes, lads, you can have a bed tonight,' she told us. We slept in comfort and the next day were given breakfast even though it was obvious they had little for themselves. These ladies were our enemies, but they were giving us hospitality because they were more afraid of the advancing Russians than they were of us.

We set off again and then some Yanks came driving by. They stopped, 'You guys want a lift? Then jump in and come with us.' Soon we were bowling down the autobahn. We had the road more or less to ourselves and made good progress.

We ended up in this town on the German-French border and that's where the

Americans stopped us. 'Where are you guys going?' They took us in for the night. The following day we were taken in a lorry to an American base, showered and fed, handed American uniforms and treated to some great food.

Soon we were flying home. I was taken back to the south of England where we had our American uniforms swapped for British ones.

And here I still am at the age of 90. There's not many of us left now. At our last reunion meeting only 16 turned up. For our 71st anniversary of the D-day landings, the Queen's Gallery, Buckingham Palace commissioned portraits of 12 of the surviving veterans. I had my portrait done by the artist, Carl Randall, sitting in my chair, dressed up and wearing my medals. 'The Last of the Tide' they've called the collection. We were invited to the Palace; I was presented to Prince Charles and Camilla and they were most pleasant to talk to.

I have also been presented to the Duke of Edinburgh. He asked me how I had got my medals. 'Prisoner of War, sir,' I told him. 'Prisoner of War, eh? Humph! Humph!' he replied and passed on.

James (Jim) Glennie. b. 1925 D-Day landings and Stalag IVB. Interviewed 2015.

The presentation to Prince Charles and Camilla, Queen's Gallery, 2015. Jim Glennie second right.

Chatting to Prince Charles, his portrait in the background.

BUCKINGHAM PALACE

The Queen and I offer you our heartfelt sympathy in your great sorrow.

We pray that your country's gratitude for a life so nobly given in its service may bring you some measure of consolation.

George R.I.

J. Watson, Esq.

The message of condolence from Buckingham Palace.

The fateful telegram arrives. News of the loss in action of Wendy Bradford's great uncle Harry.

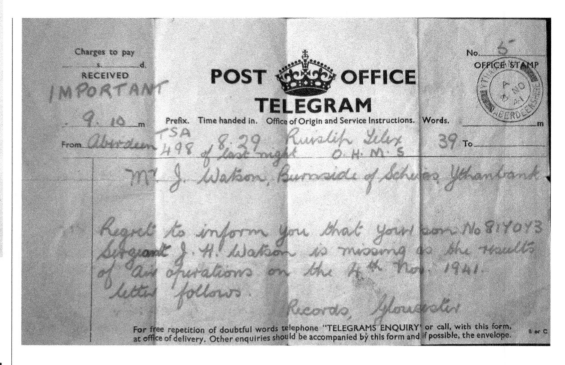

Burma campaign medals – (left–right): the 39-45 Star; the Burma Star; the Defence Medal; the War Medal.

The telegram boy turned into their road

My granda was in a tank and spent time in India and Burma with the Gordon Highlanders and the Armoured Corps. He remembered getting off the boat and that they were all in their military regalia. They hadn't really been doing anything for months and it was roasting hot. Their officer had said to them, "We're the Gordon Highlanders. We'll march." So off they went and they lasted a couple of miles before they were all keeling over because it was so hot and they were all dressed up.

And he got into trouble when he was in his tank; I remember him telling me that he had his ear defenders on but he would always keep one up and one down and he got a row for not having both of them down at the same time. He said, "What if a sniper tried to shoot me? At least with one ear I'd hear the bullet ricochet off the tank." But he always felt the senior people didn't listen to the practical aspects of trying to keep alive.

Granda was one of five. They'd stayed in a farm on Ythanbank and his mother, my great-grandmother, would listen for the boy coming past on his motor bike and would hope every day that he'd carry on past the end of their road with his telegrams. But one day the bike turned up her road and she knew they were going to get bad news. Granda's older brother, Harry, had been killed. Harry was in the RAF and got shot down over the

English Channel. He was only in his twenties and the eldest son and so would have been expected to take over the farm.

Wendy Bradford. b. 1972. The Gordon Highlanders. Interviewed 2016.

My brother was lost in action

My brother was lost in the war. He'd joined the RAF and was brought down on a mission. It broke our hearts. He and a pal were playing tennis in the Duthie Park when his call up papers arrived. I ran all the way there to give them to him. 'You're to go!', I shouted out. His whole crew perished. He was buried in Holland in a local cemetery where they keep a special plot for the burial of British airmen. The locals there are anxious to keep the memory alive and each May the school children walk down and plant flowers on the graves.

How we learned of the death was this: a telegram came to the house, 'Missing, presumed dead'. But we were actually down in London, hoping to see Bob there. It was a neighbour who passed on the news to us. So we had to return home. The only consolation we had was that his body was discovered, so at least we knew for certain what had happened and where his resting place would be. But it was a truly traumatic experience. We all became ill afterwards: my mother developed heart trouble and I lost my voice for a while. Bob had been just 22.

Bob had been a wireless operator and rear gunner – what was known as a 'Tail end Charlie' – and had been on a mission over Germany in a Stirling Bomber. The year was 1942. The plane was brought down over the North Sea. The crew all perished and were found still sitting upright in their seats, for all the world like passengers on a bus. They had been drowned.

Helen Hendry. b. 1921. The RAF. Interviewed 2013.

Wendy Bradford's grandfather – middle of the back row – serving in Burma in WW2.

Helen Hendry's brother Bob Ritchie as a member of the Dyce Auxiliary Air Force, 1938.

Martha Alexander (centre) with sister Aileen and brother David around the time in the war when the family moved to a new house in Auchinyell Gardens.

He dipped his wings to let her know he was safe

When we lived in Auchanyell during wartime, every bit of ground was in vegetables; they speak about a healthy diet now, but I think we got the healthy diet because my mother just used to go out and pull the vegetables. But the one thing we wouldn't eat was lettuce, limp lettuce, and she used to put sugar on it to get us to eat it.

There was a squadron at Dyce and their planes used to fly over our houses; the girl two up from us was going out with one of the pilots and she used to count the planes out and she'd hear them coming back and she'd start counting – but he'd dip his wings as he flew over to let her know that he was back safe.

My dad worked in the slaughterhouse. Twice he went to join up and they wouldn't let him. They said, 'No. Your job's more important.' My dad took a lot of stick from my aunties because their men were all away at the war. My mum had been a net braider and she persuaded the firm she'd worked with to let her do the nets at home. The woman upstairs' son was killed in the war and, obviously, the woman went to pieces. But my mother then taught her to be a net braider and the woman always maintained that that's what helped to take her mind off the loss of her son.

One of the poignant things that came up was when my mother was asked to do camouflage nets for the tanks; one of my uncles was a Tank Commander. When Uncle Mac came home, he turned to drink; they maintained that it was to try and forget his troop's tanks that had been blown out under them, yet he was safe. My Aunt, his wife, never knew where Mac had been posted.

Out of the blue she got a letter from a priest in Eindhoven, Holland, saying – it never mentioned soldiers in the group of men at his church – that one of the gentlemen sang *Ave Maria* and she knew that was my uncle as he was a singer. That was the only way she knew where he was, from that priest.

He couldn't mention tanks or things like that; he had to dress it up, so his message got through to let my Auntie Nora know where he was. But all my uncles and aunts were in the services: Geddes was Army, Johnnie was Army, Margaret was Navy – they were all in the services and luckily, they all came home safely. The size of the family, it was a wonder that none of them perished during the war.

Martha Alexander. b. 1937. Auchinyell. Interviewed 2015.

German police sent me into forced labour

I was born in Silesia, Poland, in 1926. In 1939 we were invaded by the Germans and became an occupied land. I was very patriotic and had developed a hatred for the Germans. I made a comment that I hoped they would lose the war just as they had the first one and it was overheard and reported. The German police sent me into forced labour.

Some of the devastation at Aachen during the latter part of WW2, where William Pyka was sent by the Germans to 'clear up the mess'.

You were under constant fear. You could be brutally treated. When you walked in the street, you were liable to get a kick and be pushed off into the gutter, if you weren't wearing a swastika. The Jews were marked out by a star and had to stay in the gutter.

I was sent to work on a farm. I escaped. They caught me. I was sent straight to prison. I was interrogated at two in the morning – 'Why did you escape? Who were your contacts?'

But while I was at that prison, they asked for volunteers to work in the garden and I went to that. There I had a lucky break. We were under a high-ranking officer who wore a black uniform and a swastika. One day I picked up an apple in the garden and was seen. He summoned me – trouble! But he took me into the kitchen and ordered the housekeeper, 'A plate of soup for the boy,'. Every day the same thing: a plate of soup in the kitchen. One day the housekeeper told me that it was because he had lost a son in a car accident and that the son had looked like me.

Later I was taken by the guards for further interrogation. They tied me down onto a couch, stripped me to my bare back and wet it. Then they went to the fire, took some hot coals and began to apply them to my back: 'Now, talk!' At that point the officer came in and immediately ordered them to stop. A guardian angel was looking over me, I'm sure.

I had been brought up in the Roman Catholic Church. But till then it had only been a traditional thing; there was no depth to my faith. But now I found it. I had looked death in the face and been saved. My faith has stayed with me ever since.

After the gardening, I got a job as an understudy in a textile factory, working in the office. I used to listen to the BBC at lunchtimes when all the others had gone. One day I was at the radio and the words, 'Hier ist London' had just come on when the manager entered: 'Was ist das?' I told him I was listening to a German station from Krakow. I was taken to a police station, marched onto a train and sent to Germany. I was put into a group whose job it was to clear up the debris left by air raids and the ground fighting.

You lived off your nerves. If you were in bed and heard a knock at the door you would be shaking.

One job was to go to the airstrips after an RAF raid and get them re-tarmacked ready for use within 12 hours.

Then in September 1944 we were put in lorries and driven off to Holland. We were told nothing but could hear the noise of explosions and artillery fire all around us. In the morning we arrived at Arnhem. There was a bridge over the street with a tank collapsed onto it. Our job was to remove the bodies and to clear a way through the debris. We were removing bodies by the dozen; some of the remains just had to be squashed down into barrels. It was sickening work; I didn't eat for 48 hours afterwards.

Then I was sent to Aachen. The place was besieged and our job was to clear a way for the Germans through the debris. One morning I was looking out of the windows when there was a shout of 'Heraus! Heraus!' The Germans ran off, without waiting for us. We decided to stay put and take cover in a cellar. We could see the American troops in front of us but we knew the Germans were behind us; we were stuck in no-man's land. We were a motley crew – Poles, Czechs, French. I became the leader. We waved a shirt as a white flag and ran towards the Americans. We made it; we were checked out and accepted. I was given a Sten gun and told to watch over the German POWs – I could be useful as a translator.

We went to the POW camp at Cherbourg. From there I volunteered for the Polish Army in Britain and eventually landed up here, in Scotland.

At the time you simply lived off your nerves. If you were in bed and heard a knock at the door you would be shaking. Even now when I enter a strange room, I look for two doors; I can only sit in a restaurant with my back to the wall, looking outwards. In the office, if anyone tries to walk behind me, I have to tell them not to – I must see them at all times.

William Pyka. b.1926. Poland and Holland. Interviewed 2005.

THE SECOND WORLD WAR
– at sea

That put a stop to the looting

Then in May 1940 the war erupted. The British once again fell for Jerry's invasion trick: he made as if to go through Belgium but actually sent the main German forces through Luxembourg and swept all before him. The British were caught in the triangle at Dunkirk, being bombed and strafed from the air. But I had been given a little six-wheeler and me and a few others managed to creep round the coast till we got to the port of St Nazaire. Everything was in chaos and you could live off the land as you went. You'd come across a deserted NAAFI and you'd go in and help yourself to food and petrol and keep going.

When we got to St Nazaire the Navy was in control and, believe me, they were the top dog then, not the RAF. We felt we were in good hands and so it proved. I found myself at the quayside in the dead of night with this naval commander. Men were waiting to make their getaway by ship and were having to dump lots of equipment and provisions there and then. Some of the locals were coming in to loot them but he quickly saw to that. 'Just see him off!', he ordered and the Froggie [sic] was shot dead just like that. That put a stop to the looting, I can tell you. Then he ordered me to drop everything except for my rifle and climb up a rope ladder onto this old tramp steamer that would take me over to Plymouth. I had to leave my kitbag on the quayside; it was packed with fags, so no doubt Jerry got some rich pickings.

Alexander (Alec) Milne. b. 1914. St Nazaire. Interviewed 2009.

Adventurous to the point of foolishness

The sight that really shook me was the spectacle of dozens of dead German bodies simply stuffed into the bunkers

My apprenticeship was interrupted by war service. I didn't actually need to go because I was in a reserved occupation, but with my two older brothers already serving in the Navy, I decided I just couldn't stay at home away from all the action. So I decided to do my bit and join up. I didn't tell my employers what was happening and slipped off down to Glasgow to sign up.

I was put into the Merchant Navy. I was sent up to Perth and put onto this troop ship which was going to take us up to Thurso and on to Scapa Flow. *The Jericho* it was called. At Thurso we were embarked onto the ferry boat *St Ola* and then on to Orkney. I had to report to an ammunition ship, *SS Adjutant* – a small 10,000-ton flat-bottomed old boat – and that's where I was for months on end, at anchor; our task was to refuel the ships of the fleet that would come to us for fresh guns and ammunition. I hardly ever got ashore and saw no real action – not the exciting mission I had imagined when I joined up.

Then as D-Day approached – not that we were told what was happening – we were ordered to sail down the west coast, on our way to Japan – or so they told us. We had to make our way through mine fields, but as a flat-bottomed vessel we were relatively safe.

Finally, we were ordered to lay at anchor off the Normandy coast. This was the D-day landings and our task was to lay there offshore ready to refuel the ships of the fleet and the landing craft. I can't say I saw much in the way of action: not only were we kept away from the actual invasion, but for three days it was so foggy that you could scarcely make out where you were. It was quite scary because you had to rely on sound and all you could hear was the eerie noise of other boats' bells, without really being able to identify them clearly. You kept hearing noises of things coming up to the sides and you never knew whether it was the enemy or a mine about to go off.

Once the invasion forces had cleared the beaches we were allowed to step ashore. We were quite free as members of the Merchant Navy, not being subject to military discipline.

We were at complete liberty to wander about along the beaches and pop into the cafés. The sight that really shook me was the spectacle of dozens of dead German bodies simply stuffed into the bunkers, waiting to be dealt with once the fighting permitted.

We were all so young – just about 19/20 or so – and quite adventurous to the point of foolishness, so we used to take spare boxes of ammunition up to the cliff tops and then throw them down to see if they exploded. They never did – they needed to be primed for explosion, I suppose, so it was all a bit tame. But we were young, away from home, in the middle of a great war and that was our idea of excitement.

Just this last week we've been watching the 70th anniversary D-day celebrations from the Normandy beaches. It's all rather poignant and although my own role in it all wasn't exactly the height of glamour, I could still feel a wee bit of pride that I was a part of it all.

Charles (Charlie) Leiper, b. 1925. Normandy. Interviewed 2014.

At work on the Mulberry Harbour

B eing a skilled engineer, my father's task in the war was to assist with the preparations and the setting up of the floating harbour – the 'Mulberry'. In the months leading up to the invasion he was up in the Faroes training. He wasn't present at the actual landings, but once the bridgehead had been secured he came in with the floating harbour which was to act as a landing stage for the equipment and the provisions that the Army needed. He was at what became 'Gold' Beach at Arromanches.

He was also at a small town in Normandy near Lisieux; we've been there since and it strikes you nowadays as a very pleasant peaceful spot, but in 1944 it was the scene of some very heavy fighting which reached massacre proportions. He was commended for his prompt and brave actions during the establishment of the harbour. We have a letter upstairs from his

The Mulberry floating port in action.

Charles Gray's commanding officer, puts on record his appreciation of the part played by him in developing the Mulberry Floating Port.

Margaret Mann's father (Charles Gray) in the uniform of a Royal Engineer.

JOHN COWAN & LINN,
CIVIL ENGINEERS.

WILLIAM LINN, A.M.INST.C.E.
R.J.P.COWAN B.Sc. A.M.INST. C.E.

121 WEST REGENT STREET,
GLASGOW, C.2. 28th December, 1945

No. 2033065 W.O. 11 C.Gray. Royal Engineers

C.S.M. Gray was posted to my Company in February 1944 when we were forming the special Port Floating Equipment Company for building the "Mulberry pre-fabricated harbour.

Gray was put in charge of the Workshops and Motor Transport Section of the Company and he very rapidly got this section into shape and showed most excellent organising powers as well as high technical ability.

Gray landed in Normandy on 7th June 1944 and his behaviour under fire in the first days was first-class - he was steady and utterly reliable under all conditions.

During the construction and maintenance of Mulberry B he was in charge of the electrical and mechanical equipment of fourteen spud pierheads (Lobnitz design - 200 ft long by 60ft wide) and a large shore based workshop. During the heavy storm of 19th, 20th, and 21st June he was invaluable and did terrific work in emergency repairs and was one one of the men to whom most of the credit must go for the survival of "Mulberry B" from the storm that wrecked the other Mulberry

In short Gray is a most excellent chap; he is an Aberdeen Scot - shrewd, hard working, clever with his head and his hands, has an all-round knowledge of engineering, and has the rare ability to get men to work hard for him and to get the best out of them. He is also a very decent, clean living man.

I have a very high opinion of this soldier and will be very glad at any time to furnish further information about him.

He is probably the most useful fellow I have met in the Army.

Lieutenant Colonel.

Commanding Officer which praises him for the way in which he and few others, when a storm blew up, didn't hesitate to dive in to secure the pontoons which had broken away from each other in the foul weather.

On another occasion when the unit was in dire need of a generator, he got into his jeep and went off looking for one. He spotted a generator which was lying on its side in a ditch. It was an American one and presumably had been accidentally tipped over and was now awaiting its rescue by the American forces. But my father simply decided to requisition it and thus saved the day for his own unit.

That was what he was like, my dad – a very resourceful person who could get you out of any fix. After the war he would borrow a car to take us all on holiday. But as petrol was rationed, buying at the pumps could be tricky, so he simply filled up half a dozen jerry cans with some fuel that he had managed to acquire from contacts and tied them to the back of the car and that is how we managed our journeys with a smelly set of petrol cans sloshing around us all. It never occurred to us that we were travelling around in a mobile bomb!

Margaret Mann. b. 1941. Normandy landings. Interviewed 2015.

The magazine was claustrophobic

I n the Navy I was in the catering – with being an apprentice baker. I was up in Russia and then in the Med on a carrier; I spent almost a year-and-a-half out there. And, of course, you doubled up during the war and as well as catering I was in the magazine. I'd been to a fire-fighting course in Rosyth and when I joined the carrier they said as I'd done the course I'd work in the magazine. They said 'It's voluntary,' but I said 'Aye okay. I'll volunteer'.

One of the things about the magazine was claustrophobia; you were battened down and couldn't get out. You were covered in asbestos hoods and goggles – anti-flash gear. You spent hours and hours doing that and a lot couldn't stand the job; that's why it was voluntary. Your air was rationed; there was just an ordinary intake fan on the weather deck. There's a guy who said, 'Action Stations', then he switched it on, filled the magazine for a few minutes, and then it was put off again. It was off more than it was on. Any fire near the fan if it's on, even a small bit of flame, would mean fire getting into the magazine and that was one way you could be wiped out. They wouldn't open the magazine as it was full of shells and explosives – so the crew in the magazine was kept battened down.

James (Jim) Butler b. 1923. Russia. Interviewed 2015.

Jim Butler at 96, some 70 years after escaping Hitler's navy.

Unsung heroes kept the country going

W hen the war started, I decided to do my bit for the country and joined up in the Merchant Navy. There was no record of seafaring in the family – my father worked at the power station at Millburn Street – but a couple of my mates had already got into the Navy and the sight of them at home on leave in their uniforms stirred something within me.

My first thought was the Royal Navy, but I was informed that I was too young for that. So it was suggested I try the Merchant Navy.

My first voyage was on a brand-new ship, the *Empire Homer,* which sailed out of Greenock. The vessel had been built at Greenock, had done its trials and was now due to join a convoy, whether to sail to Russia or the States was never made clear. But in the event that didn't matter for the ship ran ashore in heavy seas on the island of Sanday just at the southern tip of the Hebrides. The ship was a complete loss and yet its paint was hardly dry. We managed to get ashore, and the Isle of Barra lifeboat picked us up a couple of days later.

I then got a spot of survivors' leave before I had to go back to the pool in Glasgow. There I was told to join Number 38 ship which was to be part of a convoy. I remember the lashing rain as we were taken out on a small boat and helped on board. The boat turned out to be a Norwegian vessel, the *Vilna.*

The crew was almost entirely Norwegian and there were only three other Brits, but

From Deck Boy to Ship's Master: Gordon Brown in full skipper's uniform.

The ill-fated *Empire Homer* goes down on its maiden voyage off the island of Sandray.

there was a lot of English spoken and we all got on well enough.

So, anchors away and off across the Atlantic. The first foreign port I ever saw was New Orleans, where the *Vilna* had to go into dry dock for maintenance. Then it was back across the Atlantic again, this time to Freetown in Sierra Leone. That's where I joined the *Fort Fraser* and sailed on it along the west coast of Africa before landing at Durban and then up the east coast to Port Said. That's where we shed our cargo – it was now 1941/42 and the push at El Alamein was on.

Altogether it was a 14-month trip. The *Vilna* was a typical 7,000-ton tramp steamer which carried grain, timber, stores for the Army, ammunition and general cargo. It was the sort of boat which acted as a common or garden transport work horse – not glamorous, but part of a vital lifeline that kept the country going during those war years.

After that I was all over the world – West Indies, India, China, South Africa and so on. Another boat I was on was the *Teeswood* which ran into rough seas off the Kent coast; as the waves hit us the cargo shifted and the boat was tipped upside down. Fortunately, the Dungeness lifeboat managed to get to us after no more than 90 minutes in the water and we were all saved, all except the cook who suffered a heart attack and died.

So I had quite an eventful war. I was shipwrecked twice and got frozen while on the Russian convoys. In 1943 my boat was torpedoed in the Indian Ocean by a German U-boat and I was three days in an open boat before we got picked up by one of the British India Company ships and taken ashore in Bombay. Another time I was on a tanker that ran ashore at Alderney in the Channel Islands. On the Russian convoy we got regular attacks from German seaplanes acting as dive bombers.

Although I might originally have preferred the Royal Navy, I think the Merchant one suited me better. Things were much less formal and stuffy, with none of the fiddling and farting about you get in Her Majesty's Royal Navy. When I joined, we were classed as civilians, no uniform, just a badge with 'MN' on it. We were never the glamorous service but, really, it was us that kept the country going during those war years. I know we had a reputation as being the dumping ground for naughty boys since our crews came from all

An extract from **Gordon Brown's packed log book,** showing a few of the many vessels he served on.

sorts of backgrounds, some of which were quite dubious. A lot of them had had difficult domestic origins – the Doctor Barnardo's homes gave us many of our men, for example. We were an unsung lot and our effort was never fully recognised. I mean how many people realise that during the war no fewer than 317 convoys sailed from here to Russia?

The crews came from all over – Arabs, Somalis, Liverpudlians, men from Cardiff, Shetland – any Merchant Navy crew would be a real international mix. We were like long-distance lorry drivers, travelling the roads of the seas at a steady 10 knots an hour, day after day. But seeing new places, being constantly on the move, was a way of life which suited me. I wouldn't be home for very long before my mother would remark, 'Look, you've only been back 10 minutes yet I can see you're just itching to be off again,'. You'd be home for a fortnight, you'd hit the dance halls, meet a girl, have a brief fling, then away once more. To begin with there would be romantic letters going to and fro, but these would soon peter out and you'd be single and fancy free once more.

That suited me in my younger days, before I settled down and got married – and that wasn't until I was 38 years of age. I was very keen on the ladies you see. Just after the war, we made a number of runs to Hamburg and believe me, the German women proved to be most affable. A tin of Nestlé's coffee or a box of fags and the world was your oyster. It was the same in Russia.

The security at Murmansk was tight, but the ladies there were anything but. For those Arctic trips you had to wear inch-and-half thick woollen overalls; I met up with one Russian girl who was so intrigued by my uniform that all she seemed to want to do was to get inside it, along with me.

Another highlight was a Liberty boat trip to New York. This gave me the bonus of a six-week shore leave and the opportunity to see the sights – Empire State Building, Coney Island and a big welcome at the Ivy Club where the ladies proved to be most hospitable. I hit it off with a Swiss Jewish woman called Hilda and we had some fantastic times together. She was up for anything, I can tell you. One of the most memorable nights of my life was being with her – well it was like one of those film scenes where the couple are making love on a sultry evening on the roof of a New York skyscraper. We made a real concerto together, she on the clarinet, me playing my trumpet…

Gordon Brown. b 1925. The Merchant Navy. Interviewed 2016.

After the war, Gordon Brown continued his Merchant Navy career. Having started as a deckhand boy, he rose up through the ranks to become a Ship's Master, retiring after 42 years at sea.

At home in Portlethen celebrating his 90th birthday.

Children were brought up to be seen and not heard. It was a case of — the saying up here was - 'little juggies, big luggies'. I can remember my mother pulling the beret over Nancy's ears because she was saying something that she didn't want Nancy to hear.

– Gladys Morrice. b. 1920

FAMILY LIFE

Last Lunch for the Leopard 'family': The Leopard magazine production team and regular contributors – (front row, left to right) – Eva Robertson, Margaret Hardie, Buff Hardie, Lindy Cheyne, Ian Hamilton, Esma Shepherd, Robbie Shepherd, Grace Simpson. Back row – Keith Thomson, Simon McPhun, Judith McPhun, Corrie Cheyne, Norman Harper, Mark Chalmers, John Fiddes, June Fiddes, J. Derrick McClure, John Duff, Walter Miller, Alison Harper.

LIFE WAS HARD

It's long since been knocked down

I was born in the Gilcomston area – a slum. My father had his war pension and my mother worked as a cook at the High School for Girls. Things were hard. There was a fish merchant, John Ritchie, who kept open all hours and used to give out hot roes to us kids. At the bottom of the street there was another fish shop, where you could get fish at fourpence the pound. Then there was old Aggie who stayed in a slum cottage in the middle of Baker Street. She had an old fashioned boiler, which she would stoke up with coal, and sell fish at twopence a go. These people kept the poor folk going all through the '20s and '30s.

The general rule was large families; they all lived off their pennyworth of fish and chips. It was all desperately poor: poor clothing; poor diets; poor living accommodation. At Skene Square School, you'd see classes full of kids with grey suits and tackety boots, handed out by the Corporation, and with their hair cropped short. There was a social stigma attached to all this; you'd notice kids with faces covered with gentian violet blue because of skin conditions. You didn't mix with them.

I was an only child and that helped. So, I always got plenty food. You paid tenpence a pound for stew; one shilling for steak. I had a happy childhood.

I started married life in a small cottage behind Baker Street – long since knocked down. For water you had to use a pump at the porch and carry a pail up the stairs. Three other tenants had to share this.

Alex Booth b. 1921. Gilcomston. Interviewed 2004.

Living in a Baker Street cottage was tough but family life was good. Alec and Beryl Booth with their first born, Beryl, 1946.

Early childhood during the Depression

My early childhood was during the Depression years and there was a lot of unemployment. My father had spells when all he could do was sign on at the Broo. He felt his position badly. I remember my Aunt Alice, who had the job as cashier at Woolworth's, complaining once at the amount of income tax she had to fork out and my father remarking, 'Well, I wish I earned enough money to pay income tax'.

On another occasion, when my mother had at last been able to buy a new coat and was showing it off, Auntie Alice commented, 'Yes, a nice coat – but what a pity you've not got a nice new pair of shoes to go with it.' My father just bristled.

He was very church oriented and refused to allow a Sunday paper in the house. He was also a socialist. The minister would visit and there would ensue these ding dong arguments about the economic situation. Life turned out hard for him. When I told him my ambition to become a teacher he would remark sadly, 'The only way that can happen, Margaret, is if there's a change of government.' And of course, after the war there was – but he never lived to see it.

When the war came he was able to go back into the shipyards, but he fell between two boats and then took Weil's disease. He was in hospital for a while; I remember going to

Among the crowd at St Fittick's Kirk, celebrating Coronation Day, 1937. The young Margaret Donald is to be glimpsed beneath the left corner of the flag.

With father and mother at the Glasgow Empire exhibition, 1938.

The grandparents Smith and Auntie Mina in the Duthie Park.

A rare example of Margaret sitting on the fence. Taken at home at Craig Place.

see him and taking this little box of sweeties – and then dropping them just as we were entering the ward, the sweeties box crashing to the floor and disturbing the peace and hush of the hospital.

Then when I was 12 he died suddenly. He used to come home for his lunch, but this day didn't turn up; I was sent down to the harbour to look for him and was told he had left to go home right enough. But he'd gone wandering along the cliffs at Cove, had fallen into the sea and been drowned. I remember the police coming to the door to tell my mother and how she just collapsed, whoosh, just like that.

Margaret Donald. b. 1929. Craig Place, Torry. Interviewed 2014.

My mother was a bastard

My mother's grandmother used to work as a cleaner up at Gray's School of Architecture. She had a daughter who used to go with her to the work; she would have been about 18 at this time. She fell in with one of the students and got in the family way. She bore a daughter of her own and this was my mother. After the birth the father would have nothing to do with her; he did provide some financial support till my mother reached 16, but this was all done through a solicitor.

All this meant that my mother was born and grew up a bastard. In those days to be born out of wedlock carried a stigma and my mother was resentful of the way in which the children at her school would taunt her and ask where her daddy was. Even in old age this bitterness never left her. She became worried that the Government would take away her money and property when she died; she could never escape the thought that she had had to go through life a bastard.

William Booth b. 1914. Frederick Street. Interviewed 2007.

The real driving force in the household

My mother came from what you'd term the respectable, aspirational working class. She was the real driving force in the household. She was a very clever woman who had done well at school, had passed the Qualifying Exam and gone on to the Central School. She was destined, both by ability and ambition, to take her Highers and then proceed to University and into a worthy middle class job. But then, when she was 13, her mother died and so her father removed her from the school so as to look after the family. She became the substitute mother.

Anyway, my mother did go to evening classes, got qualifications and then took up the post of bank clerkess in the Bank of Scotland – the very first female to occupy that position in the whole country. But, as was the way then, as soon as she got married she gave up her work to become a full time housewife.

You've got to note my birth date – 1929, the year of the Wall Street crash and the beginning of a decade of cruel unemployment. Our situation was made worse by the fact that my father was a vehicle body builder. This was a skilled job for which he'd served an apprenticeship and for a time it had given him a good steady living. In the '20s, carriages, cars, even buses were still being assembled by hand, but then assembly line methods of mass production came in and so his position became insecure. The pattern developed of summer work but being laid off each winter. The first time this happened was a shock, but the second year my mother had saved up during the summer months and that was the budgetary method of it from then on. We managed to get by: father had his own allotment plot and he would take homer jobs on the black market – but it did mean that every penny counted.

Ours was a fairly typical tenement flat of its era. It had only the two rooms and no bathroom; the lavatory was on the landing and had to be shared. Space was at a premium; I actually had to share the one bedroom with my sister and that remained the situation until I was 25 years of age. Our father did fix up a sort of curtained partition, but even at the time I considered this to be something of an odd situation, one that I was embarrassed about – and even now I find it awkward to testify to the sleeping arrangements I had to endure till I was well past adolescent status.

Ralph Dutch. b. 1929. Urquhart Street. Interviewed 2014.

I was blessed with a loving family

Our family lived at Rosemount House which sounds very grand but wasn't. Although the house had given the district its name, by our time it had been divided into six flats.

I was blessed with a loving family. By the time I was born, my sister Jessie was 15, Kathleen was 13 and my brother Adam was 11. They teased me about being 'the mistake'.

My father was a psychiatric nurse at Cornhill and my mother had also been one. I

Two new parents: Ralph Dutch with wife Mary and their first born, Susie.

Something to celebrate: 'I'm not sure about this one. Possibly it was when the Queen popped by on her way to Balmoral and kindly stood me a drink'.

Rosalind Cheyne.

A complex, creative individual, my mother lived into her 90s and was an adored and adoring grandmother.

have warm memories of my father. I loved to climb up on his knee when he came back from work, still in his uniform. There would sometimes be a bar of chocolate hidden under his hankie in his top pocket for me to find. This would be cut into pieces for us all to share. He was the sort of man everyone turned to for help. If any of our neighbours suffered an injury they would come to our door to have their wounds dressed.

My mother had a harrowing childhood. She became an orphan under the most awful circumstances. She was one of five children and the family lived at Birse, where her father, George Littlejohn, was a landscape gardener. Her early life was happy, but then her father contracted TB and died at only 38. So my grandmother was a widow with five children to bring up. She set to and converted the back of their cottage into a laundry and took in washing.

But four or five years later she fell pregnant and living in such a rural, strictly Presbyterian community this was regarded as shameful. She received poison pen letters and became an object of scandal. When the baby was very young, she sent my mother – then only 13 – to fetch the salts of lemon, a sort of bleaching agent. She drank it down and died a horrible death. The baby, Philip, was christened over his mother's open coffin. She was buried in Birse Kirkyard but there is no stone to mark the spot.

The family was scattered. My mother was sent to a farm down the road. She had been attending Aboyne Higher Grade School and was a good scholar. When she joined the farmer's family he promised the headmaster she would be allowed to continue her education, but he only wanted her as a skivvy to look after his three children. She was soon pulled out of the school.

The house itself was broken up, plundered in fact. My mother watched the roup from the farmyard down the road and watched all the locals walking off with their belongings. The cat, Topsy, was taken away under the arm of the local fishmonger, a fact which gave her some consolation since she reckoned the cat would at least be well fed. The worst moment came when she saw a man carrying the brass fender that her mother had polished so lovingly and which had the words, 'Home Sweet Home' engraved on it.

But the headmaster put in a word for my mother and she was able to leave the farm and join the home of Colonel Lilburn at Coull House. She was taken on as a trainee nurse-governess to the family's two boys and was very well treated. When my mother reached 17, Mrs Lilburn told her, 'You can't do this for the rest of your life. You need a proper training.' And that's how my mother became a nurse.

But these early experiences left their mark on her. There was a streak of bitterness and anger which she could never quite shake off. My mother was a complex, creative individual, one who could alternate between affection and a spikey aloofness.

She lived into her 90s and was an adored and adoring grandmother. It was as if, in her old age, she could now leave all her anger and frustrations behind and settle down to enjoy the family she had created.

Rosalind (Lindy) Cheyne. b. 1943. Rosemount House. Interviewed 2016.

The young Gladys Morrice, with her mother, Violet Kerr, daughter Diane and son Gavin in Union Street, 1949

Gladys aged 96 at a Westhill group's celebration of the Queen's 90th birthday, April 2016.

People seemed to be poor but proud

My father was the youngest of his family, a big family, who all did well – but he, like an idiot, ran away to the war. Although he'd been a Robert Gordon's College boy, he never really picked up on that and we were quite poor. For a while my father was unemployed and my mother told me that she got 18 shillings (unemployment benefit). Okay, things were much cheaper but you still had rent to pay, you still had coal to buy.

Mother used to tell me that she had two dresses for me and she washed one every night and ironed it dry and everybody said, 'Oh, you keep your bairn right bonny'. Little did they know I had only two frocks. At that time, the people of Aberdeen seemed to be very proud. It was a different society to what it is today. Today it's 'I'm entitled: I can get this, I can get that'. Then, they wouldn't have let you know they were poor.

And another place the Scottish pride came in: my grandmother would have said to my mother, 'Now are you alright, Violet? Have you got a loaf of bread?' And Mother would say, 'I've a whole loaf not even started.' And she said to me when I grew up, 'If I hadn't had a heel of bread in the house, I wouldn't have told her. I would have pretended that I was well off.' That was the way of them then.

Gladys Morrice. b. 1920 King Street. Interviewed 2016.

My younger brother, Bertie, slept in one of the drawers — that was his bed.

Father took baby mice to the City Council

My granny used to stay in Albion Street which is now part of the Beach Boulevard; she lived in a little cottage there. My mother had four children, two boys – Charlie and Bertie, my sister Elsa and me. We lived in two little attics, above my granny's cottage. We needed more room; my younger brother, Bertie, slept in one of the drawers – that was his bed. I have many memories of living in this house, one being when my father came home and found these little baby mice. They were pink; there were four of them and he took them up in a matchbox to Aberdeen City Council to show them we needed to get out of that house.

Kathleen Porter (nee Hay). b. 1932 Albion Street. Interviewed 2016.

My mother was a wonderful woman

I was born in 1951. My first years were spent in West North Street. I was an only child. My mother did bear a brother, but he died just two weeks after birth. The birth certificate and the death certificate are no more than a fortnight apart.

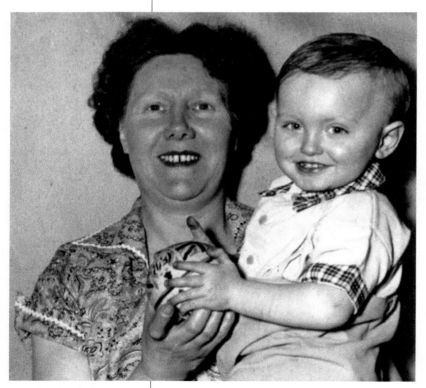

A wonderful woman: The young Cliff Milne with his mother, Flo, 1954/55.

My mother was a wonderful woman and very good looking too. My father worked at the harbour at the fish and he head-hunted my mother. She worked at Pirie Appleton's and he used to hang around outside there so he could see her when she came out after her shift. To begin with she wanted nothing to do with him, but he gradually wore her down. She had lovely blonde hair and had been well sought after by others, but he was the one whose persistence got the prize.

My father was quite a good laugh and good company. He worked as a fish manager; he was street wise, got on well with everyone he met. As money was pretty tight, my parents had to settle for a top floor flat, one with no running water and only an outside toilet. There were only two outside toilets for the whole block. I have vivid memories of using them on freezing cold winter nights. You'd go into the toilet with only a candle and a comic for company. You'd sit there freezing, made worse by the fact that the toilet had a gap beneath its door – often the wind would come whistling under it and blow the candle out, leaving you in pitch darkness.

Watch that knife!
Cliff Milne's father among the filleters, at work at the Fish Market.

This was the situation when I came on the scene in 1951. I was a small baby at birth, no more than three pounds. My father was still in the fish trade and good at his job; he was responsible for buying at the fish auctions and got on well with people. My mother was a cleaner at Marischal College. She would start at six in the morning and continue till 10. This meant that I had to be left in the house myself as both parents were out at their work. My mother would dash back during her tea break at eight to check up on me and the next door neighbour would look in past to check on me; back in those days the doors were always open – that was the norm.

Once I was old enough to walk my father would take me over to the Spital to visit my granny and aunt, where they had a large house. Then my mother would come and fetch me after her work.

Clifford Milne. b. 1951. West North Street. Interviewed 2018.

Their dream was a house of their own

My granny brought up a huge family in Torry – there were 13 of them. Before we left there, my oldest auntie, who looked after my granny, and my youngest auntie also lived with us – so where we all stayed or slept is a mystery, in a house that must have been like an accordion. There were just no houses to be had.

In front of the 'new house': Alex Rae, far right, aged 10, with 47 Longwalk Road, Mastrick, in the background. He is with some of their new neighbours: David and John Neill and Marlene and Graeme Stewart.

Enjoying the sunshine of Mastrick. Alex's mother, Grace (left) and Auntie Norma taking some sun, mid-1950s

Various aunties through the town stayed with various relatives. My other granny, my father's mother, had part of her family staying with her because it wasn't until the start of building Kincorth and Mastrick in the 1950s that the likes of us had a house of our own.

When it happened it was fantastic. We were in the very first road to be built in Mastrick after the war, Long Walk. If you see it now the buildings go on for miles but at that time it was just fields. The roads soon marched back further and further west.

It was a revelation having a house to ourselves; it was fantastic. That would have been in '53, I was six, when we moved up there. I was told by my mother it was a right struggle money-wise. My father came home from the forces as a Sergeant Major, and then worked for Barry, Hendry & Cook as an engineer. My mother worked as well, and there was only me – but she said they had to think long and hard about whether to take the house or not. It was their dream to get a house of their own, but even then they had to worry about paying the rent for it.

Alex Rae. b. 1947 Mastrick. Interviewed 2016.

SIMPLE PLEASURES

Putting on the style

W e stayed in Jopp's Lane, a street with a grain warehouse across the road. I grew up with the smell of grain and of horses in my nostrils – and the cooing of the pigeons attracted by the grain.

The Jopper was an interesting place. Part of the house was given over to my grandfather's store room, a real treasure trove – he appeared to deal in things. He kept a trap and pony, which we all used to pile upon. One of my abiding images is of him coming along Jopp's Lane with a heap of children gleefully piled up behind him on this small trap. I loved my grandfather. My grandmother, on the other hand, was a very formidable woman – quite a different personality altogether.

The pair of them were as poor as church mice, but they had extraordinary airs about themselves. They were theatre people; in those days in Aberdeen the theatre was a centre of Edwardian style: people went there and put on vast social affectations. They would speak in the grand manner all the time.

But it was all very faded. I remember how my grandmother would take me down to Lipton's to purchase her special tea. This would be made up into a packet according to her very own mixture. I remember how all the assistants would jump to it in order to get it absolutely right. She was a very imposing figure, who seemed to be about 10 feet tall, with a great scarf wound round her long neck. She expected the whole world to do her bidding. She was very much the great lady – but it was all fantasy, really. In actuality, they were desperately poor.

William (Bill) Ord. b. 1929. Jopp's Lane. Interviewed 2003.

Today's style: Two shots of Jopp's Lane during the week when the Nuart Festival visited the street, 2019.

Grandfather and grandmother were theatre people; they would speak in the grand manner all the time.

The infant Bill at the Victoria Park with cousins Rosalie and Kathleen.

The two-year-old Bill with Teddy.

Scooters could be ridden in Union Street as well as indoors in Rose Street. Brother Gordon in action.

The largest indoor play area in Aberdeen

I spent my boyhood in Rose Street – very much a city centre loon. In those days this position, just off Union Street, was an excellent place in which to grow up. It was comparatively quiet and had a neighbourly feel to it – we seemed to be surrounded by friendly people. There were parks within easy walking distance and in the school summer holidays, I would gather with pals from round about to walk up Esslemont Avenue then down Watson Street to the Westburn Park and spend hours and hours playing cricket. We had complete freedom to wander through the streets in this way and I had no shortage of friends to do this with- school pals, boys from my Life Boys and later Boys Brigade company, and others from the homes all around us.

Our home was in a large tenement which had a distinctive configuration. We were in number 51 and this was joined to next door 53, which, in its turn, was joined to 55. There were five flats in 51 and 53 and two in 55. Fifty-one and 53 shared a common back garden and, best of all, a large drying loft which we had the run of – the largest indoor playroom in the whole of Aberdeen. This was where we lads could gather to play darts, to enjoy feasts and to whizz up and down on our scooters – these had large wheels, unlike today's models. This didn't always go down well as this space was used for its original purpose as a drying room in which the women of the flats would occasionally still hang up their washing and we would be scooting right through the clothes hung out to dry – so, on these occasions our scooting might be interrupted by cries of 'Boys, boys, ye're dirtyin ma washin!'

Rose Street, despite its city centre location, was a quiet place back then with very little traffic about. I can recall lying in my bed at night, staring up at the ceiling and being able to trace the path of passing headlights outside and how these were far from continuous as they would be nowadays. But the street was busy enough at certain times of the day because it housed three industries. There was Middleton's, which employed several hundred, ranging from printers to clerical staff to packers. Then there was Harrott's across the road, which produced gloves, and they employed about 100. So early of a morning and then in the evening, as the workers came and went, the street was full of the sound of feet – but not cars; workers didn't own such things then.

Most notable of all for me as a boy was Kennerty Dairies. The milk was supplied from their farm out at Culter, but the Rose Street depot acted as the distribution centre and that's where the horses were stabled. One of my most vivid recollections is of waking to the sound of horses' hooves and the rumble of milk carts as the milkmen set off to make their early morning deliveries. Those horses gave me the feeling of living in the country.

Middleton's was later destroyed in a huge fire. It threatened our home and we had to be evacuated and sought shelter across the street at number 42. The factory was left in its ruined state for a period and then finally demolished. New apartments were built on its site and this altered our idyllic existence – the new development took away our garden and turned it into a parking lot while, worst of all, we lost our drying loft playroom to

Bill Cooper's parents at the Shakkin Briggie, 1930s.

The fire which destroyed Middleton's of Bill's Rose Street, 1968.
(IMAGE BY KIND PERMISSION OF ABERDEEN JOURNALS)

accommodate the construction of two new flats.

And later Harrott's factory was also burned down and Kennerty's too disappeared. For me this mix of the residential and the industrial created a rich boyhood pattern, one that I feel a great deal of nostalgia for.

Bill Cooper. b. 1936. Rose Street. Interviewed 2018.

An early pleasure:
Young Cliff Milne tells
Santa what he wants,
at the Co-op grotto.

Me and my
mate
Gordon
would go to
Pittodrie and
look for
some mannie
to lift us
over the
turnstiles.

A standard Saturday

During a typical Saturday me and my mates would go around the doors and ask, 'Ony ald claes, missus?' We would collect as much as we could, tie them up into bundles and take them to a scrappie, who would then weigh them and give us cash by weight. Our trick was to stuff stones into the pockets and make these old clothes as heavy as we could get away with. Often, we would come away with a couple of bob, which in those days was a good amount.

I would always be ready to run messages for my mother – anything to get the odd penny. Doing stuff for her would cover the morning; in the afternoon I would pop round to the local Coca-Cola depot and offer my services to the drivers, helping them with their deliveries. I would jump into the back of their Bedford vans and help to hand out the bottles from the shelves. In this way you might be rewarded with a few pennies and maybe a few bottles of Coke. Our usual practice was to drink one bottle and keep a couple to sell. We would use an old air raid shelter as our den and in there I might be able to sell a bottle or so, or trade them in for marbles, etc. A bottle opener became a regular item in my pockets.

After that me and my mate Gordon would go to Pittodrie and look out for some mannie to lift us over the turnstiles. In those days spectators stood on an open terrace and could drink. So, at the end of each game there would always be rich pickings of discarded bottles to collect.

We would then take the empties down Spring Garden to St Andrews Street, there to a shop which made their own version of Coca-cola. The man there would buy our empties and use them for his products– unlike nowadays, nobody back then seemed to insist on a standard size.

It was now the late afternoon and time for some entertainment, so we would head to George Street for a visit to the Grand Central cinema and a bout of Abbott and Costello or the Three Stooges. We'd have spent some of our cash on sweeties, so we could sit there stuffing our faces in comfort.

After the cinema, it was back to the house for a meal and the usual query, 'Far hiv ye been?' To which I would always say, 'Oh, jist roon aboot'. After supper my father would go off to his club, the Dockers' Club. I'd go to the club and open the door and wait in the doorway. Sooner or later my father would show up and I could badger him for a sub. He would always be in a good mood with the drink inside him and might slip me a bob or so. Sometimes his mates would be feeling generous, so you would always come away with a few shillings.

So that was my standard Saturday – a money-making exercise, but more than that, something of an education in how the world of the street could be made to work for your benefit. I think all these experiences helped me to make my way in the world, despite my disadvantages of small size and a bad stutter.

In a nutshell that is how I got through my boyhood – academically not a success, but able to make my way through hard work and by becoming street wise. Compared to now, my life then might seem tough, even deprived, but at the time I did get a lot of enjoyment, growing up in the East End of Aberdeen. And I was far from being alone in this. My class at Torry Academy consisted of 11-plus failures, but many of them made their way in life. One of them went to Hollywood and became a successful film director, another dealt in antiques, another was a skilled cabinet maker, another a partner in an engineering company, while, as for myself, I ran my own second hand antiquarian book-selling business, exhibiting at book fairs all around the country, as well as being a stained glass specialist. Learning how things work, how to get on with people, how to watch out for opportunities, to be quick on the uptake – all the products of a good street education.

Clifford Milne. b. 1951. West North Street. Interviewed 2018.

He gave me a real lift: The infant Margaret Lakin in her father's hand at the home in Kincorth, 1950/51.

He was a great story-teller

Both my parents would have left school at the standard leaving age. Generally, they were both supportive of the notion that education was important for their children. In their kind of working-class background, academic achievement was highly respected. However, my mother still held the belief that it was more important for boys to achieve since girls would most likely 'just' get married.

My father was a great story-teller. He would make up stories and encourage us to do the same. From a very early age he would tell us fairy stories and play around with the language by, for example, transposing the first letters of names – so that we'd be told the story of 'Little Rude Redding Hide' and he would keep that up for the whole story. Or he'd start off with something like, 'At last the elephant managed to get out of the fridge'; we'd look at him and he would then say, 'But before that…' and then he'd trace his story right the way back to its beginning.

He was very observant of characters that he encountered in his daily work; he'd tell us wonderful stories about these people. He loved his crosswords and would tell us that if he had to choose between his four cryptic crosswords a day or his meals, he'd choose the former. Under his influence I used to write my own stories, from the age of six. I remember one early one was about an old couple who couldn't have children and who, one day, opened their door to find that a baby had been left there on the doorstep in a cardboard box. I made up all kinds of adventures and carried it on right up to the end. The last line went, 'He arrived in a box and went in a box'; always been a bit morbid, you see…

Margaret Lakin. b.1949. Kincorth. Interviewed 2004.

Wee Margaret at a wedding with family members including parents and brother Brian.

The three sisters: Betty on left with Mina and Mary, 1939.

More than 70 years later, Betty with husband Kenneth, taken not long before their deaths in the same week in 2018 – after 65 years of marriage.

What fun we had in that flat!

The house in Ann Street had three rooms. There were five of us children there plus the two parents. They slept in the settee bed. My mother kept the place gleaming; she was my father's queen. I can remember coming in at the door and always noticing how the fireplace was shining bright so that you could see the reflection of it in the linoleum.

What fun we all had in that flat! I can remember sitting on the chest of drawers where the gramophone was and watching my brother John getting ready to go out to the dancing: white shirt, shoes that were gleaming. He was a good looker was John. We'd be sitting there and he would call out; 'A penny at the end of the week if you play my favourite ones.' These were just the songs of the day, the popular songs of the 1930s.

There was always plenty of music in our house. Sometimes of an evening the table would be pushed back and we'd have a musical evening. There might be 20 people in the flat at one time; mother would serve up soup and oatcakes. Father would lift you up onto the table and ask you to sing your party piece. He had a lovely voice himself. My mother just had to touch music; she was full of it.

There would always be visitors coming in; always someone at our table for a meal or gathered in front of the fire for a chat and a laugh. And father would have his budgies. They would be allowed to fly around the room; they would perch up on the picture rail and then dart about. Father had one special favourite, Jimmy. One day he went into the aviary and called out, 'Jimmy,' in his usual way. Then he felt something at his feet; it was Jimmy's body; he had trodden on it. That just about broke his heart.

Elizabeth (Betty) McHardy. b. 1930. Ann Street. Interviewed 2004.

Riding the Hazlehead zebra with sister Pauline.

Pleasures away from home: Riding the Butlins scooter with Dad, Bill, Mum, Lesley, sister Pauline and Dorothy up at the front.

Shopping was an adventure

Going into town was always something of an adventure and the visit to the Co-op Arcade was a thing to look forward to. That's where the uniform and the shoes for school would be purchased and then you could watch the assistant pop the money and the note of sale into a small metal pod which was then whooshed and whisked along some sort of pneumatic track up to the sales office; you'd stand there and wait for the magic moment when the pod would come whizzing back and the assistant would open it and hand over your change and the receipt.

The big thing about the Co-op was the divi; I can still reel off my mother's number: 55567, a wonderfully memorable one.

Dorothy Dunn. b. 1953. Co-op Arcade. Interviewed 2016.

Pleasures of the beach: Dorothy, right, with friend Avril Anderson, 1960.

A happy boyhood:
David Brown strolling along, aged 10.

The real drawback in both our flats was the fact that we had a shared toilet on the landing.

A PROPER UPBRINGING

A tenement flat in the heart of the city

The family home was at 53 Skene Street, right in the centre of the city. From the outside, the buildings there are much the same, being solidly constructed, traditional Aberdeen granite tenements, quite imposing and rather beautiful. Inside, back then, they did lack something in modern facilities, but they've now been refurbished.

There are four floors and to begin with we stayed on the first one, just above the shops at street level. But later we moved up to the second floor, the reason being that we got an extra room and, most important of all, an electricity supply.

As I was an only child we weren't really cramped for space. The real drawback in both our flats was the fact that we had a shared toilet on the landing.

My father was a draper. He'd started off in the Co-op at Loch Street. My mother worked in the cash department and those were the days when someone like my father, on closing a sale, inserted the customer's money into a little steel canister and sent it whirring along a network of pipes to my mother, who would then remove the cash, pop in the change and receipt and send it back. I'm not sure whether they ever used this system for personal communications but, anyway, they started courting and got married.

One of my great memories of that tenement was the stairs. When we had the second floor flat you would have to ascend five flights of stairs. They were arranged in sets: 11, 7, 7, 10 and finally 9. I used to count them off, a necessary thing to do in the winter when it was completely dark; so it was '11-7-7-10-9' and then your door. These stairs had to be cleaned and polished according to a strict rota, week about.

In the depths of winter the water in the toilet would freeze up; we had to keep a small paraffin lamp burning beside it which was just enough to keep things above freezing level. But it could have been worse; like a lot of people as late as into the '60s, my mother's friend, Mrs Summers in Summer Street, had her toilet outside.

I passed the whole of my boyhood in that tenement flat. My father was six years away at war, serving in North Africa. But you can hardly say he was able to return to a land fit for heroes. Their wish was to get a council property which would have its own bathroom and toilet and so the names went on the waiting list. But it wasn't until 1984 when they

A set of photos of David with his parents in the uniform of Aberdeen Grammar school, aged 9.

finally got one, just round the corner, and that was only because by now he had terminal cancer and was finding the stairs too much of a struggle. He died within the year.

For people of that class back then the prospect of acquiring your own home was unthinkable. That would have entailed taking out a mortgage and that meant credit and worry. I know when I got married and took out a mortgage for all of £4,000 my mother was horrified. All that debt hanging over our heads for the next 25 years!

My parents were very much of the old school: no debts, respect, honesty, straight dealing, good manners, and an honest day's work for an honest day's pay. I was brought up accordingly. Whenever we visited my aunt over in Garden City in Torry I would be warned to be on my very best behaviour. My uncle Willie worked for the railways and he and Auntie Evie had been able to travel all over Europe on free passes. They were considered to be slightly higher up the social scale. So the warnings came thick and fast: don't grab the best piece on the plate when it's passed round – take the rich tea biscuit with a polite, 'Thank you' and leave the fancy cakes; only speak when you are spoken to; no shouting or loud behaviour – and always, always, show respect to your elders.

And at home it was dinned into me that I must never run up the stairs or stamp around on the floors, not with our floors covered as they were only in linoleum: to do so might disturb the people in the flat below.

At the back there was a hemmed-in yard and that was where the wash house and the coal cellar stood. Washing was a hard task, one that had to be carried out each week on the day appointed by the rota.

My mother had to go down to the wash house, carrying a syrup tin filled with paraffin, in which she had soaked kindling overnight, and that's what was used to get the fire beneath the boiler going. It had to be lit early in the morning and once the water was hot enough a big scoop would be employed to transfer it into one of the two wooden sinks.

All the women would make an early start; this led to an incident involving our tenement neighbour Mrs Menzies. In those days the police were still regularly patrolling the streets and as part of their beat they would go in and up and down the stairs of tenements looking for anything untoward. Well, this night at three in the morning, they noticed movements on the stairs and so immediately went to apprehend the culprit. But it was only Mrs Menzies, anxious to make an early start to her day's washing.

David Brown. b. 1946. Rosemount Viaduct. Interviewed 2014.

Gloria she will be!

Father and daughter: Bob and babe in arms Gloria.

My daughter's called Gloria – how that name came about is this. Just after her birth I was still puzzling out what she should be called. I was walking down by the harbour when I suddenly saw this trawler. I read its name: 'Gloria' and immediately said to myself, 'That's what I'll call her – Gloria.'

Gloria's comment: so I'm named after a boat – and it wasn't even an ocean-going liner, just a blooming trawler…

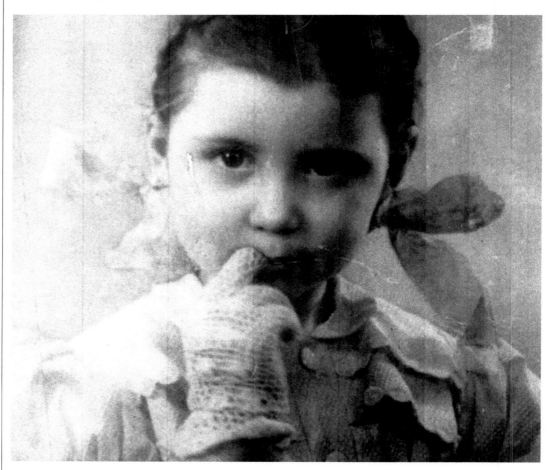

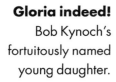

Gloria indeed! Bob Kynoch's fortuitously named young daughter.

Robert (Bob) Kynoch. b. 1927. The harbour. Interviewed 2018.

Standards of decorum

S tandards of decorum were much more prim than would be the norm nowadays. My parents once went to the Tivoli for a variety show. This was quite a daring move as many in our community would have considered the music hall theatre to be a den of iniquity. Sure enough, they returned home sniffing with disapproval. Apparently there had been a comedian on stage who had treated the audience to what they considered a disgusting story involving a drunken husband returning home on a Saturday night, tiptoeing into the bedroom and in his stupor accidently sitting on the mirror. When he woke the next morning it was to discover he'd put Elastoplast all over the mirror- instead of his own backside. My parents considered these references to bottoms absolutely beyond the pale.

Then there was the time when my mother invited a pair of friends over for tea. Each of them had a son in medicine and one of them had landed an important post in Manchester. It was at this point that I heard the voices suddenly descend into a fraught whisper – apparently he had gone there to act as head of the venereal disease clinic. Or there was the day when my mother looked out of the window to see our neighbour, Mrs. Leiper, hanging out the washing – and wearing a pair of slacks! But then she wasn't actually from Torry but Belfast....

Ronald (Ron) Caie. b.1938. Torry. Interviewed 2014.

Ron's mother, Elizabeth Grant, an accomplished young violinist.

Episodes from a well reared youth:
As a member of the 58th Life Boys, 1947. Jim Couper is top right.

A butcher's boy

Being a butcher's family we were never short of meat, but that didn't mean we dined off the fat of the land. Dad would bring home cuts as part of his wages, but these were usually the inferior ones, the best being reserved for the customers. He would go to work in a collar and tie and was very conscious of having to serve the public with all that that entailed in terms of manners and dress.

Home life was never harshly strict, but you knew there were firm standards that you had to follow. My parents led quite simple and blameless lives. Drink was hardly ever indulged in and on the rare occasions, when my father might have joined workmates at McBride's for a convivial pint, my mother maintained that she could tell from the way he opened the gate that he had been drinking. She herself had no more than a small glass of sherry once a year and that was enough to make her tipsy.

My father did, like most men in those days, smoke like a chimney. He would inhale Capstan Full Strength and I would be sent up to the Co-op to get his packets. Johnny

Opening bat for 58th Boys Brigade cricket team: Jim is front row left.

Davidson would serve me and exclaim, 'Yer faither must chaa nails an' spit oot roost wi thon things'. When working over the accounts in the shop, Woodbines would be the order of the day, however, since they were easier to stub out when a customer entered the shop. My mother didn't smoke and it's a habit which, fortunately, I've never taken up, but it contributed to my father's death at the age of 51.

As a pupil at Robert Gordon's College: Form master Sandy Fraser. Jim is middle, back row.

In the First XV Robert Gordon's rugby team: Jim is front row left.

James (Jim) Couper. b. 1935. Woodside Fountain. Interviewed 2014.

The much-cherished daughter: Linda Duncan as babe in arms to proud parents John and Janet.

Linda becomes a parent in her turn: With father and grandfather, 1980.

It wouldn't happen nowadays!

I was an only child. My main memory was how I had to look after myself of a morning. My father wanted to build up a butcher business and needed money to buy in all the necessary equipment, the freezers, the slicing machines and so on. So my father and mother decided to use her skills as a home baker to set up their own business. They got a bank loan and bought a tenement nearby, and used its downstairs to run a home bakery and rented out the upstairs flats.

I was no more than three when they started on this next step and my routine then was to be left in the house by myself, as a bakery has to start up very early in the morning. I would get up completely by myself, use the potty left by the bed and then have my breakfast, which was a bottle of National Health orange juice and a buttery already buttered. I then had to dress myself – I often left the house with the kilt on the wrong way round and my sleeves all over the place, but I would make my way along the road to the bakery shop.

Even back then Great Northern Road was very busy with trams, lorries, cars and horse-drawn vehicles; I would also have two side roads to get across. But none of this fazed me; to me this lonely routine became quite normal and I thought nothing of it. Yet I never left my own children in the house by themselves till they were 14 at the earliest.

Linda Duncan. b. 1951. Great Northern Road, Woodside. Interviewed 2014.

In later life, George Fraser ran a successful grocery store with his brother Atholl for many years in Bank Street.

Ready to serve the public: George is right, accompanied by Atholl, cashier Miss Annie Davidson and Andrew Thom.

She always kept it gleaming

The building at 561 Great Western Road was an ordinary Aberdeen tenement with three storeys and we were up on the top floor. We were lucky: our toilet was on the landing, not out in the back yard as was the case with many others. My parents would sleep in the bed recess in the kitchen. The bedroom held two double beds. The other room was 'the parlour'; this was kept strictly for special occasions and for visitors. This room had a three-piece suite and a display cabinet, which held the 'relics'. The floor was covered by a carpet square which would be turned each year so as to ensure even wear. Fitted carpets were unheard of then.

The stairs had to be polished by the tenants every week. Mother used old-fashioned polish; she would leave it absolutely gleaming. There was no toilet paper in those days. The evening paper would be carefully cut into little squares and hung up on a nail.

Heating was by coal fires. For us on the top this meant lugging up pails each day. The old doctor, Dr Thomas Gibson from Golden Square, would make his house visit and say, 'Mrs Fraser, put those scuttles down at once. That's no job for a lady!' and he would insist on taking up the two pails full of coal, himself. He was one of the old school of doctors. They carried out home visits in those days, night and day; two-and-sixpence a visit.

We always had good meals: homemade soup; always a milk pudding. Mother would make a meat roll and potted head for spreading. Lovely! She'd make beef tea if you were ill, to build up your strength; she would take some meat and grate it down and boil it up to make a drink out of it.

For clothes, we were always well turned out. Mother had a Singer sewing machine, which she operated by a treadle. I would be sent down on the tramcar to Woolworth's to buy a pair of pockets, which she would sew into our trousers. At school the poorer

> I would be sent down on the tramcar to Woolworth's to buy a pair of pockets, which she would sew into our trousers.

The smile was always ready: George Fraser, a later life image.

children would get their shoes inspected by the teacher and if necessary would have them soled and heeled by the Council.

There were plenty of visitors: my mother was one of 11. My Auntie Jessie stayed in Anderson Avenue; I called her 'Yellow Duster' and that was because she would follow you around with her yellow duster, she was so house proud. And if it had been snowing and you came into her hall, she would cry out in agony at the thought of all those marks that might be left on her floor.

Those houses at Mannofield have been maintained in good order even to this day. I recently noticed that the flat across the landing from us at 561 was on the market – for an asking price of £59,000! In our day the rent was 10 shillings a week.

I've got happy memories of my childhood. I can name every tenant in the Mannofield tenement. There was old Mr Stewart, the retired County Council roadman. He would say to my father: 'Geordie, you come down and we'll have a musical evening.' Then he would put on his old gramophone records and we'd listen to all the old Scottish numbers. I can still see the way he would take out his big red handkerchief and wipe the records before he put them on to the turntable. We would listen to Harry Lauder.

Between the wars it was all tramcars and buses. There were also horses. I remember the big Mitchell & Muill's bakery carts, which pulled up the road out to Deeside, all the way to Culter each day. That needed four horses. They would stop at Mannofield and when they opened up the carts you could see the steam rising; the bread was still hot. In those days there were four milk firms which all used horses: Kennerty, the Co-op, the Crown Dairies, the Mastrick Dairy. Everyone would get their milk delivered to the door then.

George Fraser. b. 1919. Great Western Road. Interviewed 2006.

Naturally, we didn't have a car ourselves

My father was foreman mechanic at Brown's Garage in Stanley Street. He got no more than £3 a week even as foreman, so money was always in short supply. That was the normal wage for a skilled tradesman in those days. But we were always well shod, well turned out and had enough food on the table. We had little in the way of luxuries, but I had a very contented childhood.

He was clever with cars at a time when car ownership was in its infancy and cars required a lot of maintenance. Brown's was a family-run garage which held the franchise for Chrysler, so it dealt with some pretty fancy vehicles for well-to-do West End folk. I remember the garage as a wonderfully exciting place. It employed a group of young apprentices and a big job for them was to clean and polish cars. Great care had to be taken so as to make each vehicle absolutely shining and spotless. Special soft cloths would be provided and they came in sanitised bags. However, these cloths were really no more than old bits of lady's apparel – hats, vests, underwear, all nice and soft. I can remember

Helen Hendry's father, George Ritchie, in his World War 1 Flying Corps uniform.

Granny Ritchie with Helen, brother Bob and cousin.

how the apprentices would sometimes dress themselves up in these pieces of lady's clothing and then prance about.

In those days only the rich had cars and they would expect special service. Father was very good at his job and was well appreciated by his West End customers. There were these two old ladies, the Misses Scott, whose father had owned the Devanha Brewery over in Ferryhill, and they had inherited his Daimler. Naturally, they didn't drive themselves, so every Sunday they would ask my father to take them out for a run, usually up Deeside. We all had to go along as well and my brother and I just hated these excursions since we had to sit there quietly, all dressed up and being on our best behaviour. We would take flasks and biscuits and a tartan rug.

Once they invited us into their house for tea and I can remember how splendid their

My brother and I just had to sit there: backs straight, polite behaviour, speak when spoken to.

Helen and father
when he was home on leave from World War 2 ground crew work , 1939.

tea set was: the plates all depicted a scene from Sir Walter Scott's *Ivanhoe*. But my brother and I just had to sit there: backs straight, polite behaviour, speak when spoken to.

Naturally, we didn't have a car ourselves – people just couldn't afford them then. But my father was trusted with all these fancy vehicles and with the garage itself. He held keys for it and would be expected to run immediately to the garage if anything untoward happened. I remember this dark and windy night when the garage doors were blown open. The police came round and father had to go to see that everything was secure. Well, as luck had it, this was just about the one night in her whole life that mother was out – she'd gone to see a play at Carden Place Church. So all father could do was shout at us, 'Look, I've got to go to the garage – but I'll be back as soon as I can.' Well, I was no more than six and here we were, my brother and I, all alone on this dark night with the wind howling around the tenement. And I was an awful daddy's girl so, when he left, I just stood there bawling my head off. This neighbour heard me and she came out onto the landing outside and called out, 'What's the matter, dearie?' 'Oh, the police have come and taken our father away,' I shouted back.

Helen Hendry. b. 1921. Hartington Road. Interviewed 2013.

Just a snap of the fingers

There was discipline. If we went into town as a family, we had to go up to the Auchinyell Bridge to get the bus and as that bus processed along Broomhill Road and more folk got on it, my father would snap his fingers and that was the signal for us to stand up and let the adults get a seat. It was a respect for your elders that was being instilled into us.

Clothes-wise I can smell some of the shops: Isaac Benzies, the Equitable, the Co-opy. But my Mother made all our clothes to save money. She really made a smashing job of them. But I used to hate when I got my older sister's hand-down coats. Shoes were Little Dukes because my Father maintained if your feet were right you were all right. We'd go to this man, Mr Nicol's shed, and we used to love when he put seggs in our shoes because we could slide along Broomhill Road and the sparks would fly. It was years and years before my older sister and I got girls' shoes and that's why we maintain our feet are okay.

We played a lot in the house, putting a cover over the table; it was a fort or a house or a hospital – and you let your imagination go and you made your own fun. But Saturday night was the night we all sat round the fire, listened to Scottish dance music or the 'McFlannels' programme and it was the one time my mother bought sweeties. She'd buy boilings and they were put in a jar and the jar was passed round us as we were listening to these programmes.

Martha Alexander. b. 1937 Charlotte St. Interviewed 2015.

> We used to love when he put seggs in our shoes because we could slide along Broomhill Road and the sparks would fly.

48 years later and still together

When I was older the teenagers would gather at the café run by Ma Brooks just by the railway bridge. My sister didn't really approve of my choice of boyfriend in Jim and once she burst in upon us at the café and ordered me home: 'Don't you realise you're keeping bad company?' Jim was thought of as a real cool dude, snappily dressed and with a hair style to match, just the sort to arouse suspicions in a respectable family. But she couldn't have been more wrong – here we are 48 years later, still together.

We were brought up with solid values. Mum would warn me, 'If ever a boy asks you to go alone with him then you can be sure he's not a nice boy'– and that was about the sum total of my sex education. I wasn't allowed to go up the road arm in arm with a boy – loose behaviour. My skirts were inspected in case they were too short and whenever I stood by the window my father would enquire if I'd remembered to put a petticoat on so as to make sure my legs wouldn't show through in the light. If I was judged to have too much make-up on I would be asked, 'You're not going out like that, surely?'

The pattern was that you worked for a couple of years, you got engaged for another two while you saved up and then you married and that was you settled down for life. And that's exactly what happened to me. When we got married, I was 20, Jim was 22 and we are still here. You were brought up to follow the model of your parents and that meant having a sense of responsibility. Wedding vows were to be taken seriously.

The wedding was at Ruthrieston Church South [now South Holburn] and the reception at Pharaoh's Restaurant at the corner of Rose Street. It was a fine and friendly affair with 100 guests but nothing too elaborate. A far cry from a woman I met recently who was enquiring after a reception at the Raemoir and was being quoted £12,000 for the basic booking. We left the reception early to drive off to our first night – at the Amatola. The plan was to tour around for the honeymoon, but the car broke down the next morning and we landed up back at home, entering with the morning milk. 'Oh no, I thought we'd got rid of you,' was my father's greeting.

Moira Mapley. b. 1950. Holburn Street. Interviewed 2014.

The daffodil girl: Jim and Moira Mapley's daughter on the banks of the Dee, Carol aged three.

The young Jim Mapley with friend Stewart Milne – who later became an Inspector in the City Police.

Jim once more haunting the Duthie Park with pals, Stewart and Jim Currie – who later became a minister.

Summer term at the High School for Girls: But no summer dress for Frances, pictured back centre, in proper uniform.

Frances with brother George and parents – both sporting their home made kilts. Christmas 1950.

A well-ordered upbringing

My father was a hairdresser by trade. As a boy he had a Saturday job as a 'soaper' – that is he had to prepare the customers for their shave. He continued doing this during his summer holidays and then, when he was old enough to leave school, that became his career.

Apparently at his work he was sociable like any good barber, chatting to the customers and putting them at their ease, but at home he sought peace and quiet. He was a rather strict parent and I, as the eldest child and a girl, was the object of his discipline. There was nothing harsh about it, but there was an insistence on good manners and on tidying away the toys before his return home. He was also physically reserved – no cuddles or effusive declarations – but he was simply of his time in this. As he became older he did mellow and when my brother's children arrived he settled into the role of the fond and tolerant grandfather and continued to mellow until his death at 92.

I was never a rebel; I was never the sort of '60s girl who wore outlandish clothes or dyed my hair purple, but my father maintained his strict grip on my behaviour and appearance till I was into my 20s. I had to be in by the time he set down; two minutes past the appointed hour was simply not acceptable. Finally I had to tell him, 'Look, I'm 23 and earning my own living.' His reply: 'My house, my rules.'

Frances as babe in arms with her grandparents and father.

Frances Davidson. b. 1940. Garthdee. Interviewed 2015.

**A very young
Wendy Bradford** on
a visit to grandparents
Watson in Kincorth.

Very much a weekly routine to life

I know when my parents looked back and described my growing up, that they worked hard and would struggle financially, but I was never aware of any of that. If we didn't have something, we accepted that was because we didn't need it. I know that my mum's sister and her husband were very good to my parents. My auntie would make huge pots of soup and share them with my mum; everyone would just help; there was that sort of family camaraderie.

I suppose there was very much a weekly routine to life. On a Sunday you would visit alternate sets of grandparents. I would always go and stay with my Granda and Grandma in Kincorth for one week of the school holidays. My grandma was a great baker; she'd lived at Schivas House where she'd been a housemaid. So that was always a great thing about going to stay with her, getting to do the baking and make shortbread and getting my Granda's piece ready because he was still working, doing shifts in the Police. He had this little medicine bottle that she filled with milk and then we made his piece and wrapped it up in waxed paper from the loaf, and it all got put in this little box and off he went.

And then I'd get to help her do the housework because that, like the washing, took ages with twin tubs and hanging it out, and that round plastic thing that you put on top of the spinner and pulled the lid on. She was very good at making clothes as well and I had my little apron and a little head scarf like my granny. I used to have to go and dust the skirting boards with my finger in a duster – that was my job.

I had happy times at school. We did lots of other things through the week: Red Cross, Brownies, Guides and dancing. I know Mum and Dad didn't have a lot of money but we did loads of things. And then we had church on Sunday and there were so many children who went to that. That was just your traditional life where people did things on certain days. Washing happened on a certain day when it was your turn to use the drying green. And before the lady upstairs passed away, Mum said you weren't allowed to put any washing out on a Sunday – that would have been frowned upon.

Wendy Bradford. b. 1972 Forbesfield Road. Interviewed 2016.

Wendy aged 7 and
ready for the Brownies.

Margaret's father, Charles Gray, still well turned out in his 80s.

Oh, Charlie will see to that

My father was a trained engineer, the sort that could cobble together a car out of spare parts, an engine from one vehicle and the chassis from another. But he was also very much the soldier, even after the war. He was a smart upright figure, always well turned out. You'd see him coming along the street in a blazer, grey flannels, white shirt and tie, and on his feet a pair of white bowling shoes that he'd acquired in a charity shop. People would turn their heads to look at him; he stood out.

He always insisted on keeping our shoes spic and span and gleaming. This meant the soles and the insteps as well as the surface. He was constantly warning us not to scuff our shoes in any way and that included being careful when sitting at table not to rub the instep against the bar. He was a devout Mason and was anxious to ensure that when he went off to the Temple in Crown Street to take part in the ritual and when he had to kneel and expose the underside of his shoes, the world would see that they were just as clean and cared for as the uppers.

On Sundays we would go out for a family walk and the two of us, my brother and I, would have to march along with our heads held high and backs straight, always a pace or two in front of the grown-ups. My brother would be in short trousers and three-quarter socks while I would have on a clean dress. We had to walk properly so as not to scuff our best Sunday shoes.

We were brought up under the general rule of 'Children should be seen and not heard'. Good manners were essential; at the table you wouldn't dream of speaking unless you were spoken to first. At the end of the meal you had to ask permission to leave the table – and you certainly wouldn't be allowed to if there was any scrap of food left on the plate.

My childhood was a very happy one and my memories of both my parents are very warm ones. My mother gave us an excellent and caring home life. She had high standards – she ran the sort of home where the floors were so highly polished that the rugs would skid along the floor – but we always knew that we were her main priority.

And my father, despite all his ways, was a very helpful and sympathetic character. He had his little sayings which might make him seem gruff and stern. If you were to ask him if it was all right for you to do something, as likely as not the answer would come, 'Oh, p- y- b- s' – Please your bloody self!' But you also knew he was really on your side. And if any neighbour's child was going without, then he was quick to offer to take them in the car on one of our family outings. Not for nothing would my mother say to anyone who needed a window fixed or a bike puncture mended, 'Oh, Charlie'll see to that.'

Margaret Mann. b. 1941. Nigg. Interviewed 2015.

Smartness from the very start: Margaret Mann aged 4.

A thrifty pair

We never went too far for our holidays, but then we didn't need to. We had close relatives living up in farming country in Banffshire. There was our granny with a croft near Banff and an auntie and uncle near Cornhill. We loved visiting them both. We thought ourselves absolutely safe during the war because we reckoned the Germans couldn't possibly know where granny lived so they wouldn't be able to drop a bomb on her house – and they never did. This was a small croft which ran to seven acres, enough for a milk cow and a couple of calves.

We enjoyed complete freedom out there; we could run around to our heart's content and also help out with the harvest jobs.

The uncle and aunt – Bill and Jessie – were a very thrifty pair who didn't believe in spending any money whatsoever. Nor did they hold with credit. Their one luxury purchase was a car and this was paid for by cash, not even by cheque. They saved up by putting any spare cash into tin boxes: one each and both kept beneath the bed. They wouldn't divulge how much was in those boxes, not even to each other.

They had very few expenses. They were childless and could more or less live off the land. My uncle was a big beekeeper and managed up to 30 hives. He produced so much honey that he could sell off enough each year to collect what in the end amounted to a small income.

Aunt Jessie had her eggs to sell and that's how she filled up her tin. She never spent anything on clothes and was quite content to go around in what were little better than hand-me-downs. Vans came round with groceries and she could barter some of her eggs in exchange for the necessary foodstuffs.

Eventually each tin box was bulging with notes. Latterly we would remonstrate with them concerning the lack of safety involved, as they never locked their doors. 'What if word got around that you had all this cash lying about the house? Why, someone might come in one night and mug you.' They agreed to 'see to it' and find somewhere. On our next visit we asked them if they had indeed looked out somewhere more secure. 'Oh yes, our boxes are no longer in the house – they're on a shelf in the shed outside.' This was a tumbledown shed which could have blown away any minute in a gale. Not only that, it was where they kept their paraffin, so the whole fortune could have gone up in smoke.

But they never did mend their ways. He died first and then she took a stroke and had to go into care. We had to go to the house and sort out their belongings and we found an old handbag lying at the bottom of a wardrobe which still had notes in it.

Robert Mann. b. 1936. Belmont Road and Banffshire. Interviewed 2015.

> They saved up by putting any spare cash into tin boxes: one each and both kept beneath the bed.

The children's Hospital, Castle Terrace, as it was when the young William Booth attended it in the 1920s.

HEALTH AND WELFARE

Let him run about like a normal boy

I'd get up on the back of this older lad, Danny Yule, and pretend to be riding my horse in search of Red Indians. We decided to have a go at piggy back; he got up on my shoulders and I held my arm behind my back so as to hold him on. We staggered about for a bit, laughing and whooping, but then we stumbled and fell over. I fractured my elbow, so badly that my hand was twisted right round so that my palm now faced outwards. My mother rushed me to the Sick Children's Hospital which was then just nearby in Castle Terrace, down the steps in Virginia Street. I was eight years of age.

We were seen by this young student doctor, a bad-tempered fellow with red hair. Because I had food inside me he couldn't give me any anaesthetic. He told me to remove my shirt, but with my arm all twisted the wrong way that was impossible so he took a pair of scissors and cut it off. Then he commanded my mother, 'Right, you just hold his shoulder tight while I try to turn his arm back round'. I let out a yell of agony; his response was to slap me across the face. He then put some bandages on, shoved my arm in a sling and told us to go.

That was the start of weeks of suffering. I had to report to the hospital each morning where we were seen by a Dr Chalmers. What he did every visit was to put my arm into a sink which he then filled with hot water. Then he would gently massage my hand and put on talcum powder. The idea was to gradually loosen up the arm and then get it back into the proper position. But we never got far; the arm would always stick at the same position and this went on for day after day.

So then he came up with the brilliant suggestion that I should go home and that my mother would hang me down by my arms from a doorway and then suddenly let go. But each time she tried this I automatically dropped to the floor. I couldn't endure that pain of staying put.

The next thing he tried was to give me a whiff of chloroform. I went out like a light. When I came round I found I was all bruised; he had tried to yank my arm down. But this didn't work either; the arm only ever came down so far. Finally the day came when he told us, 'I'm very sorry but we've done all we can. He'll just have to learn to live with it'.

> This young student doctor, a bad-tempered fellow with red hair, commanded my mother, 'You just hold his shoulder tight while I try to turn his arm back round'.

We were slowly walking along the corridor when suddenly we heard these footsteps running after us. It was a nurse: 'Mr Mitchell wants to see you.' Now this Mr Mitchell was a surgeon who had the nickname Cripple Mitchell on account of the fact that he'd had a bad leg and had managed to cure himself of it. We were taken to his room. He took one look at all my bandages and said, 'What's all this nonsense?' He undid them and threw them onto the floor.

As it happened my father had just begun a new job as foreman out at Culter Paper Mill. We explained to Mr Mitchell that we were shortly to be moving out to Culter. His reply was, 'Culter. The very thing. You should let young William go out there into the country and run about like any ordinary boy and climb trees and forget about having a bad arm.'

We settled to life away from the city. I did as I was told. I was only eight and had been brought up to accept what adults told me, so if Mr Mitchell said my arm would get better of its own accord then it would get better. And that's exactly what happened: the arm did come down by itself and within a few weeks everything was right as rain. I've never had any trouble with it since – and that's 85 years ago.

William Booth. b. 1914. Frederick Street. Interviewed 2007.

This baby's dead!

I actually had quite a dramatic entry into the world. Two years previously, my mother had had twins, but they had been born dead. So my parents approached this second pregnancy with some apprehension. Everything appeared to be going well but she became overdue and that created fresh anxiety. Our GP at that time was the local doctor. She was very much of her time in that she assumed as a doctor a position of irrefutable command, seeing no need for bedside niceties.

As my mother was going into labour, she came round to the house, swept in, sounded her out and then pronounced, 'Oh, this baby's dead!' Just like that, no softening of the blow. My father took this very ill and decided to go for a second opinion. He called in another GP. He immediately summoned an ambulance and my mother was rushed into Foresterhill. There she was attended by a young obstetrician, a Dugald Baird, who went on to great eminence in his obstetrics field, so much so that he was later knighted. He safely delivered me. So I can claim that the very first human hand to touch me on my entry into the world was to go on to become a knight of the realm.

Ronald (Ron) Caie. b.1938. Torry. Interviewed 2014.

A dramatic entry into the world: Ron Caie was delivered by a young obstetrician who later rose to such eminence as to earn this portrait for the Aberdeen Medico-Chirurgical Society.
(IMAGE BY KIND PERMISSION OF THE ABERDEEN MED-CHI SOCIETY)

The father: SGM Kynoch, at the Middle East front, 1942.

The mother: The infant Douglas Kynoch (right) with his mother and brother David

Divorce was very uncommon then

It was as a returning soldier in 1945 that I first knew my father. The day he returned to me, this strange man appeared firing off questions at me — what I liked doing, who my friends were, how I was getting on at school. I grew so distressed at this interrogation that I burst into tears and ran off.

I realise now that my father was simply trying to establish a relationship with me; but the position was complicated by the fact that the marriage was really over. My mother was unhappy and felt she had to leave him. One night soon after his return, she came through to where my brother and I were sleeping, stood between our two beds and told us that she was leaving Father that very night. She then asked us what we wanted to do: did we want to go with him or stay with her? Well, of course, there could only be one answer to that. I was six years old, my brother seven.

Divorce was very uncommon back then. It was something I could never bring myself to talk about or even to mention to anyone. Right through school and even at university I kept quiet about my family situation – people simply assumed my father was dead and that my mother was a widow.

More traumatic still was an incident that arose a little later. One day, as we were coming out of Sunnybank School and setting off to walk home, a car drew up and invited us to go for a ride. It was driven by my uncle and my father was with him. Well, a car was quite a rarity then and the prospect of a ride in one was exciting so we got in. The car whisked us off to my uncle's house. It was an abduction!

We were kept there for three weeks and sent to another school. Much later, I was told by my uncle's daughter that I wept more or less continuously during all those three weeks. Finally, my mother went to a lawyer and got the whole thing sorted out and we were returned to her. Access visits were arranged once a fortnight; and these went on for some years in the course of which we met Father's new family; but then, for some reason, they stopped seeing us; and by the time I was 14, Father had disappeared from our lives altogether. As I say, I was happy to let people think he was dead, but I knew he was out there still living and working in Aberdeen. I remember seeing him once, driving by in a car, like some ghostly apparition. I now had a phantom father, and so it remained till I made contact again in adult life.

Douglas Kynoch. b. 1938. Elmbank Terrace. Interviewed 2014.

I had to act as my mother's interpreter

My mother, although quite healthy in every other way, was profoundly deaf as the result of some childhood illness. So I had learned at a very early age sign language. My mother had been at school, at the School for the Deaf in Westburn Road. She lived in Torry as a child and had to travel every day and had a completely different sort of education from the rest of the family; none of them were deaf at all.

It wasn't a bad education: she certainly learned sign language and attempted a form of lip reading. In her generation there was a tendency for the deaf to keep together as a separate community. She married somebody with full hearing. I once took her to visit her sister in Hull – my aunt – and she told me that their mother would not allow any of the brothers or sisters to learn sign language. There was a refusal to recognize by her parents that she was deaf. The father in particular was nasty to her. That nastiness I recollect as a child in people's behaviour towards my mother.

I don't remember learning sign language as a child, I just learnt it. I don't think people realize what a burden it is to a child. Whenever the doctor came and Dad was not there,

Douglas grew up to become a familiar face on TV and was at the forefront of the new Grampian TV in the 1960s.

An intelligent woman: Edith Nicol's mother, Helen Milne, 1951.

it fell on me to do the communication with my mother. That could be quite frustrating. The thing is with deaf people, even if she's not understanding what somebody's saying, she would still smile and nod and hope that that would be the right response, yet I would know from what she was actually telling me that she didn't agree at all with this person and I would say to them. 'No, that's not right, you're misunderstanding what my mother actually thinks' – and they would say, 'But she's smiling and nodding…are you sure you understand? you're just a child…' It was all quite difficult.

The problem which haunted me through my childhood was that the neighbours looked down upon my mother. There was this perception that deaf people were stupid. If you have to ask people to repeat themselves, they can't be bothered and they simply say, 'Oh, it doesn't matter.' And you end up feeling stupid. But my mother was actually extremely intelligent. She was a great one for doing crossword puzzles. She visited the Art Gallery and was keen on the visual arts. She was a very tactile person; if you can't use one of the senses there's the tendency to develop the other ones. But it could be quite difficult when we were visiting museums and she was constantly trying to touch things.

Edith Nicol. b. 1952. Mastrick. Interviewed 2001.

The dentists downstairs

Our flat in George Street was situated above the surgery of the dentists, Gourdie and Gallon. Now, Gourdie had scared the life out of me when I was 10, so much so that I flatly refused to return to any dentist, even though I knew I really needed to. By the time I reached 16 I knew I couldn't put it off any longer. By this time Gourdie had been joined by Ron Gallon, a handsome man who looked like Rock Hudson. Mum told him of my terrors so he came up to our flat to try to persuade me to give him a visit.

I burst into tears and wailings. He began to talk me round: 'Look, I'll give you a little pill and that will calm you down. Then I'll give you a spot of anaesthetic and I'll just start on one tiny filling. You won't feel a thing – I promise.' So that's what I did. I sat there with my eyes closed in absolute terror until I heard him saying, 'And how was that?' 'Are you really finished? I didn't feel a thing!' 'Yes, and I've actually completed three fillings.' From then on Ron Gallon was my hero and all dental fears had been banished.

I had been too fond of sweeties and that had been my problem. My school pal's mother ran a stall in the Green and that did me and my teeth no good at all. I had had this really bad experience at the dentist's when I had a filling drilled into a front tooth with no anaesthetic. Years later a dentist remarked on all the cross nerves I had in that area of my mouth and how painful that childhood drilling must have been. So, after all, it wasn't just my cowardice that was to blame.

Margaret Dundas. b. 1938. George Street. Interviewed 2016.

On the look out for another sweetie? An infant Margaret Dundas out shopping with her mother.

It wasn't only me being abused

During this time, something else happened to me – it's kind of blanked out now, but I don't mind speaking about it. Two members of my family abused me; it was my father through the week and my grandfather at the weekends.

My mother went away for a while and my grandparents took in my two younger sisters – one was four years younger than me, and one was six years younger. I was left to do everything at home – do the garden, do the house, plus still keep my job as well.

I got out on a Sunday morning one time and I'd got some pocket money from one of my uncles and as he was taking me back to the house at night in his car, my mind was working, 'I've had enough. I'm not putting up with this.' I remember going up the road and his car broke down. So I ran to the house and I went in, and packed some things into a brown paper carrier bag; my cardigan had holes in it; my nightie was a bit ragged and I had a pair of old slippers, but I thought, right, that's it.

I had this money in my hand and I thought I could get the bus back to my grandmother's. So I took to my heels in case my father would be coming back to the house. I hid beside a garden where I could see the bus and I thought if I hide here, I can wait until the bus is coming, and then I ran to catch it. I came off so as to change buses and hid again until the bus came and I caught it to my granny's. When I went in, my granny knew straight away. She asked, 'What's happened? There's something happened.' And I said, 'I'm not going back. I can't go back.'

I couldn't bring myself to tell my granny that both of the men were abusing me, I just couldn't. My father phoned that night. "She's got to come back." And my granny said 'No. She is NOT coming back. You've done enough to that lassie – no more!'

Then I had my daughter, and a few years later I had my son, but the husband – well the ex-husband now – turned out to be a waster as well. He wanted to be married at home, but single outside. He and my father were close pals, so it was just drink, drink. In the end it was mental cruelty what he was doing to me. He said he'd put wire at the top of the stairs and I could trip and fall down. So myself and my two children went across to the battered wives' place in Kincorth. I hadn't been battered, but it was mental cruelty. So I was a single parent from the time my son was six months old and my daughter was three years old.

It took my ex-husband six months before he would agree to get out of our house. When we got back to our house it was like freedom. No more watching the clock for when he'd be coming back, wondering what he was going to do. I raised my children. My son is doing very well for himself as a joiner. My daughter stays just at the end of the road. And I've got grandchildren.

It wasn't only me being abused by my father and my grandfather; we were at a family funeral and different cousins were coming and telling me about other uncles. We wondered about my father – my brother and I – because his father bad-used him; I don't mean 'that kind' of abuse, but he just gave him a really hard time. And it's a few uncles, well a few sons on my [maternal] Grandad's side. And these are stories about other

> I couldn't bring myself to tell my granny that both my father and my grandfather were abusing me, I just couldn't.

members of the family that I have just become aware of quite recently. It had never occurred to me it was happening to anybody but me.

I was watching an episode of *Emmerdale* quite a few years ago and it was to do with that – the lassie was getting abused – and I just picked up the phone after I'd watched it as I thought, for some reason, I've finally got to tell my sister. So I phoned her up and said, 'I've something to tell you.' And her next words were, 'I know. It's happened to me.' All that time, I really thought I was the only one, it was just me.

When I'd phoned my sister, I was in my early 50s and that was the first time I had told anybody about that. I hadn't said a word to anybody – not even a friend, or my own family.

You went home from school and you're wondering, 'What's it going to be tonight?' You were just waiting; it's like what you read in stories: the footsteps on the stairs… is he coming in here? We used to hear my mother sometimes and I'd wonder, 'What's he doing to her this time?' It's an awful thing to say, but he was just an animal. She was so hard working and everything – and she didn't deserve that.

I didn't know anybody was being abused like me. At that time, it wasn't in the papers – not like now – or in TV programmes. So I thought it was only me. And you do, you think that you've done something wrong; it's your fault that they're doing this to you. And, not only that, when it was my father through the week, and my granda at the weekend, you think that maybe this is just what happens.

I never told anybody about what was going on at the time and I have never reported it. With hindsight, I wish I had, but I wasn't brave enough. We were literally terrified of my father.

You never knew what was coming in the door. You'd say, 'Is he goin' to be bleezin' drunk the night again? What's he goin' to do?'

Another thing from then that just shows the time my mum had with him; it happened every Friday night and all day Saturday. Just inside our door, there was like an electric cupboard with the meter and all the rest of it. And there was a little runner across it. My mother would really be there but 'she wouldn't be in' – because under the runner there was a stack of payment books and I had always to watch and take out the right one. You'd maybe get four of the men coming on a Friday night for money at different times – they were tick men – from lots of the shops. But my mother had to do that because she wasn't getting the money from him. She had her Co-op divi which would help to give us clothes for school, but she wasn't getting money from him so she just had to take things out on credit.

I've come a long way and I'm really happy with who I am now. And it's good being able to help other people. I volunteered in the special needs nursery for five years. Thinking about the people who've helped me at various difficult times has made me want to give something back

Marion Douglas. b.1948. Bucksburn. Interviewed 2016.

Not for the unmarried

Absolutely no regrets: The 17-year-old Dorothy Dunn with her John at a dinner dance.

Y ou might look back on the Seventies as an era of freedom, but the pubs still closed at 10 and the last bus home was about 11 pm. When I went to the Beach Ballroom I would often go home by myself, getting off the Garthdee bus from which I had to cross the railway line, duck under the fence, then up Deeside Gardens, along to Northcote and all in the dark. I never came to any harm. And now the young folk don't go out till 10.

I first met Robert when I was 14 and we were an item for about six months before breaking up. Although we were both going out with others, we always ended up together. I knew he was the one.

At 16, I went to the family doctor to ask for a prescription for the pill, but he turned me away, pronouncing that he couldn't possibly give out contraception to an unmarried woman; his advice was that we should simply abstain. I then went to the family planning clinic only to be told that I would need to bring a note from my doctor before they could do anything for me.

At 17 I became pregnant. I refused to be anything but positive about the situation; as far as I was concerned a child would be a blessing. When I told Robert he was quite clear: 'You are not having an abortion.'

My response was, 'In that case we'll have to get married.' And so we did – which we wanted to do anyway. My father's ultimatum was an abortion or leave home, so I chose the latter. Neither of my parents came to the wedding, but we were reconciled before my first son was born.

I went to live at my sister's and then later to Robert's mother. Gradually we built up our own home, first in a flat in Tillydrone, then four years later one in Heathryfold. One or two moves later and we are now well settled here in the Bridge of Don, still together after 47 years, and still with no regrets.

Even if Robert hadn't stood by me I would have gone ahead with the birth; I was quite prepared to be a single mother if necessary. So we had Gary when I was 17;

Roy followed two years later and then came Bruce when I was 21. We didn't have much money, but what we did have was our love, our togetherness and a strong determination to make our own way and be good parents.

Dorothy Dunn. b. 1953. Airyhall. Interviewed 2016.

Still happily together 40 years later, taken at their Ruby Wedding celebrations. 2011

It couldn't have worked in my case: Mike Forbes alive and kicking, aged 4.

Sex education was unheard of

Sex education was unheard of. I remember how I would find this black thing hiding at the bottom of my mother's wardrobe; it had a rubber ball attached at its end and I would take it and play with it. I'd fill it with water and swoosh it about. But I never took it outside; I knew my mother would give me an almighty row for that. It wasn't till after her death that I at last discovered what it was all about. My sister and I were clearing out the house when she informed me that the mysterious object had been a douche, used for contraception purposes. Well, it couldn't have been all that infallible – it didn't exactly work in my case.

As we got older we began to experiment a bit. Our researches consisted of taking a few girls into the air raid shelters and kissing and cuddling – but before we could ever get any further my mother would be at the entrance roaring for me to come on out. There seemed to be a network of spies in the Circle: if any of us did anything suspect then sure as anything one mother or another would be at the door reporting the misdeed.

My parents took the *News of the World* each Sunday. I kept coming across two mysterious words in it and they were, 'rape' and 'intercourse'. I just couldn't work out what they could mean, so one day I plucked up the courage to ask my parents. My father immediately jumped out of his chair: 'To the kitchen. At once!' I scuttled off into it, with him following. 'Sit down!' he ordered. 'So you want to know what those two words mean, well…' At this point his courage seemed to fail him and he just stood there humming and hawing. Finally he demanded of me, 'Well, you know how babies are born?' I didn't really, but I felt it best to blurt out a 'Yes', whereupon he turned on his heel with the comment, 'Well, that's what those two words are all about.' And that was the end of my sex lesson. I was 14 at the time and still utterly innocent. I'd glimpsed copies of *Health & Nature* and had come to realise that women had something called breasts, but what they were for I didn't understand.

Michael (Mike) Forbes. b. 1945. Ruthrieston Circle. Interviewed 2014.

We didn't see our son for 10 weeks

In the summer of 1964 a typhoid epidemic broke out in Aberdeen and our eldest son, Craig, was a victim. He was just on two at the time – in fact he celebrated his second birthday in the Sick Children's Hospital – and that made him just about the youngest patient in the ward. He was in for 10 weeks; his birth weight had been a bouncing nine-and-a-half pounds and at the height of his illness that was the weight he returned to.

The epidemic had been spread through the meat counter at Low's supermarket at Holburn Junction. We were living at Windsor Place, so that was our nearest grocery shop. However, usually I went up to Mannofield for my weekly shop, but on this occasion we were entertaining an aunt and uncle and had planned to take them for a Sunday run and picnic up Deeside. It was Friday evening and I was anxious to get something in to make

Isolation ward:
Relatives could only
'visit' their young loved
ones by peering
through windows.
(IMAGE BY KIND
PERMISSION OF
ABERDEEN JOURNALS)

sandwiches, so I popped into Low's. My next door neighbour was in front of me in the queue and she bought some slices of tongue. I took the pressed ham because Craig had only just begun to eat meat and detested anything with any fat on it.

Well, we had our picnic and ate our sandwiches. The next Sunday we decided to take a run up Deeside, but on the morning I noticed that Craig was unwell. He was sitting on my lap in the car and as we were returning I could feel how hot and sweaty he was becoming. However, he was a sufferer with his tonsils so the obvious cause was another bout of tonsillitis.

Then we turned into Windsor Place and to my amazement I saw that there were four of five ambulances parked outside the neighbouring houses – in Victoria Street, in Albert Street, in Thistle Street. I realised that something serious was up. Straight away I was on the phone to our doctor, Dr Lynch. He came round, carried out an examination, saw Craig's throat was red and inflamed and thought that it might be the usual tonsillitis. He prescribed a double dose of penicillin and promised to return the following morning to see how things were progressing.

Oddly enough, Craig did seem to improve during the night and in the morning I was sitting with him, chatting away quite happily as he lay in his cot. Then I looked out of the window and saw my father coming up the path. I opened the window. 'How's the bairn today?', he called out. 'A bit better,' I replied. 'Oh, thank God for that!', he exclaimed. But a couple of minutes later it was Dr Lynch who was coming up my path –

HOW TO STAMP OUT TYPHOID

THIS AFFECTS YOU!!

Wee Alickie of the Green Final lends his voice to this typhoid health advice publicity notice, 1964.

> I would go to see him and stand there till they closed the curtains. We never missed a visit. Come rain, hail or shine we stood at that window.

and next door I could see that their doctor was also striding up to their door. The doctor came in, made a swift examination and then pronounced that he would be summoning an ambulance immediately. 'But I can take him in the car', I offered. 'No, I'm sorry, but he has to go in an ambulance,' I was told with some firmness.

That was the last we saw of Craig without a window between us for 10 whole weeks. He went down the path at the very moment an ambulance was coming to take our neighbour's daughter to the hospital. During all those weeks we were not allowed to go into the ward; all we could do was stand outside the window and peer in. In fact it wasn't till the 10th day that we were informed that as his temperature was at last beginning to subside we could now take a peep at him through the window.

Terry and I hurried up to the hospital; we eagerly looked through the glass, but could see no sign of our Craig. Then suddenly we got a glimpse of this little scrap of a human being standing up in a cot. The only way we could tell it was our Craig was by the mop of curls on his head. Terry broke down and so did I. We knew that Craig must not see us in that state so we returned to the car and drove off in order to take a minute or two to settle ourselves.

After a few minutes we felt sufficiently composed to make a return and Craig's cot was pushed up to the window so we could get a full view of him. He was nothing more than skin and bones. As the days went by and we kept up the visits he did begin to regain weight, but he was still not allowed to move out of his cot. They put a pinafore on him with four tapes attached and these were used to tie him into the cot. Each day at 12 I would go to see him and stand there till they closed the curtains at seven in the evening.

We never missed a visit. Come rain, hail or shine we stood at that window. He regained his strength and soon he would stand there shouting out, 'Parcel! Parcel!' He knew we would be bringing him a present of some kind. As the weeks went by we noticed that the ward was becoming emptier and emptier; the other children were beginning to be discharged, but no sign of Craig joining them. We were told that they were now demanding four clear blood tests as the condition of discharge. The days went past.

We were getting impatient, but they kept telling us the same: 'He's not ready yet. He's got to have four clear blood tests'. As it happened I had an aunt who had a close friend who was working in the lab at the City Hospital, which was handling all of the typhoid tests. She made enquiries on our behalf and came back with the news that Craig Pettitt's tests were indicating 'all clear'.

I went straight up to the Sick Children's and demanded to see the doctor in charge. 'I've come to take my son home.' ''I'm very sorry but he's not ready yet – he has to return four clear tests, you see'. I told him my news from the City Hospital; 'And who gave you the authority to have access to that information?' 'Guess what, I'm his mother and that's all the authority I need.'

So, after 10 long, long weeks, they let him out. He came along the corridor towards us, so weak and so long since he'd been on his feet that a nurse had to hold him up. I had

The 1964 typhoid patient grows up to become a father himself: Son Craig with his own son on the day of his daughter's birth.

his present in my hand, a small toy car. As he staggered towards me I held it out and he took it in his hand. As soon as he felt the flesh of my hand, his tired feeble little legs suddenly seemed to gain a spurt of power and he positively leapt into my arms. He put his arms round me and around Terry and so the three of us finally walked out of the hospital, arms clasped round each other and into our car.

On that day we just didn't want to share him with anyone else, even the rest of the family who we knew would be waiting in the house for the return. So we drove him down to the beach and sat there hugging and cuddling him. We had our son back, but to begin with things were a bit rough. Craig had clearly been disturbed by his ordeal and began to stammer. We consulted the doctor and enquired about therapy. 'No, he doesn't require therapy; he just needs to be at home,' we were told. It was reassurance he needed.

We were always scrupulous about hygiene; I would steep his toys in the bath with Milton in it. We had simply been the unfortunate victims of a contaminated slice or two of pressed ham that had been cut on an infected slicer at the grocer round the corner.

All this is now 50 years ago this summer. Craig himself has no memories of the time he spent 10 whole weeks of his life as a very sick little boy in an isolation ward. And now he's 52 years of age and a father and grandfather in his own right.

Aileen Pettitt. b. 1937. Sick Children's Hospital. Interviewed 2014.

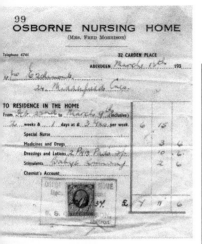

Osborne Nursing Home bill

Well worth the cost: The bill for Marjory Rose's delivery, 1937.

22 years later: Taken at Marjory's graduation, 1959.

Cheap at the price?

I was born in February 1937, at the Osborne Nursing home. I still have the account which my father had to pay- these were the days before the NHS of course. It came to the grand total of £7.11.6 and that included itemised payments for things like 'stimulants', 'baby's laundry' and 'dressings'. Now, my father wasn't a wealthy man by any means; I'm not sure how he would have scraped together the money because at that time, as an ironmonger for James Mutch Ltd, he wouldn't have been earning much more than £3 a week. I know that when he married in 1936 he had to inform his mother that he would no longer be in a position to give her the usual half-a-crown a week. Still, £7.11.6 – I hope he thought I was cheap at the price!

Marjory Rose. b 1937. Osborne Nursing Home. Interviewed 2015.

No scented soap back then

Today, in 2015, my husband Sandy and I, in our comfortable home have two bathrooms. Seventy years ago when I was growing up in my Wallfield Place tenement, in 1944, eight people had to share one toilet on the stair landing – the six of us and the two old spinsters living in the flat on the same floor.

There was no wash-hand basin with scented soap, hygienic wipes or pretty hand towels in that freezing cold cubby hole on the landing. Nor can I ever remember washing my hands at the kitchen sink after using the toilet. Soap was rationed like almost everything else and there was a severe shortage of paper during the war so we never had proper toilet paper. The *Sunday Post* and the *P&J* were also reduced in size during those war years, but once everyone had read them, they would be cut up into neat six-inch squares, hooked on a wire and hung up on the wall. And even that had to be rationed to a few sheets per visit because too much newspaper might block the pipes. Sometimes I was lucky and found a piece with enough of The Broons or Oor Wullie to have a quiet little read.

During the night we all used chamber pots or 'gaesunders' as we called them. In the morning these would be discretely covered with a cloth and carried down to the toilet to be emptied. Then they would be rinsed out in the kitchen sink and put back under the bed.

Elizabeth (Liz) Strachan. b. 1939. Wallfield Place. Interviewed 2014.

DIFFERENT WORLDS

A real treasure trove: A 1940s set of Arthur Mee's *Children's Encyclopedia.*

A radical upbringing

There is this radical theme which runs through my family background, on both sides. I still have the membership cards that belonged to my great-grandfather and which show he was a member of Britain's first Marxist party, the Social Democratic Federation, under the double leadership of William Morris and Henry Hyndman.

I was very conscious of this background when I was growing up. From an early age, I knew my household was 'different'. We took *The Daily Worker* for a start. My parents did inflict some quite restrictive experiences on me. My mother wouldn't let me read books with pictures in them. I was forbidden to read American comics. They seemed to be scared that they would damage my literacy. Nor was I permitted to read anything produced by D.C.Thomson, since this was a non-union firm. So that knocked out the *Dandy* and the *Beano*. I simply went elsewhere to indulge in my forbidden pleasures.

My parents were deeply anti-imperialist. But one thing my mother did allow me to read was Arthur Mee's *Children's Newspaper*. By golly, it was dull! The other formative reading experience for me was the *Children's Encyclopaedia*, again Arthur Mee. This was such an imaginative publication for children, a real treasure trove. My mother, when she started earning, had started buying parts of it as it came out – she was a still-room maid at Watt & Grants. Later, such was her attachment to it, she would continue to buy parts as

Something in it for every child: A typical page spread from the Encyclopedia.

she came upon them in second-hand shops. A wonderful publication. I reckon the *Children's Encyclopaedia* has had a huge and unacknowledged influence on my generation. It was so well conceived for encouraging children to discover knowledge; there's something in it for every mood; you just keep coming upon absorbing stuff in it.

But one thing I couldn't keep quiet about at school was my political sympathies. In Year 3 English, at Robert Gordon's, we had a debate. You got to choose a topic and then make a persuasive speech to the class. I did mine at the time of the Suez crisis in 1956. I was actually stopped by the teacher in mid-speech and not allowed to continue. She found my views to be seditious.

Colin Milton. b.1943. Cairncry Road. Interviewed 2003.

We all spoke the Aberdeen lingo at home

We all spoke the Aberdeen lingo at home and in the playground – that's what I was brought up on. But coming into the school, you changed into English, into polite language. But my language was also mixed in with my country connections. As a young boy, I would go out and stay with my Auntie Annie and Uncle George at Netherley where they lived on their croft. I was always delighted to get away into the country. I felt at home there, more so than back in the town. I enjoyed being with the hens and their one cow that they milked every day and with the sheltie that they kept for work about the place. And Uncle George, being a crofter, used a scythe for cutting the corn and I remember him being there of an evening, sharpening his scythe ready for the next day's work.

I've always held that picture in my mind. A bit idyllic no doubt, but so different from

Peter and sister Nancy at the country croft, 1938.

Uncle Tommy showing off his horse, 'in his ain braw rig-oot'.

The country connection: Uncle Tommy 'taks his axe tae the loaf'.

being stuck in the back-end of the town. It gave me a freedom so that I always wanted to return to it straightaway whenever I got back into the town.

My mother's mother was also staying with them out there. She was probably only in her 60s, but to all of us she was 'auld granny'. Auld Granny was a law unto herself. She had only a few ragged old teeth left and had great difficulty in chewing her food. I used to watch fascinated as she was at her eating. I've actually written a poem about it – it's in Scots, in the Doric, needless to say. That's what they all spoke there, out at Netherley. I've inherited a mixture of the two – if I'm with one group or the other for any length of time, I'll lapse into the appropriate language.

The speech thing is important to me. I find if I've written any poetry the only ones that really work are the Scots ones: conversational, familiar, the intimate, personal ones. They are the ones that link back to the time I was a child; the formative influence of the language that surrounded you in childhood is very strong. That's where my most personal language has come from, that's the place where my most natural feelings are.

The grandparents at their wedding at the croft 'nae far fae Aberdeen'.

Peter Murphy. b. 1932. Esslemont Avenue. Interviewed 2002.

> I wanted to join the Brownies and the Guides, but wasn't allowed: they were seen as quasi-military organisations.

My parents were Communists

My father was originally in the shipyards, but then the General Strike of 1926 came along and there was a big downswing in the yards and so his job came to a sudden end. He worked in the fish market; he was a fish carter who delivered the fish to various establishments about the city.

I remember him telling me that as a boy he had been fee'd to a farm out at Westhill. It was a terrible time for him. The only time he got off was on a Sunday; on the Saturday night, after work, he would scrub up, put on his only good set of clothes and walk all the way into town, right down to the Beach, where his parents stayed. He would then have his Saturday night out, at the dancing or whatever, and stay overnight. On the Sunday all the relatives would come visiting. In the evening he would walk back ready for another week's hard labour. He got very little to eat. He stayed in a bothy where he had to sleep on wooden benches.

My mother was very active, politically. She was continually getting sacked for sticking up for workers' rights. She told me that one of the practices at the time in the mill was to attempt to clean the machine while it was still running. The rule was that it should be turned off, but the employers expected it to be kept running at all times otherwise money would be lost. If the worker lost an arm or got hurt then that was treated as the employee's fault. If you did dare to turn off your machine then you would find your wages docked.

She was a woman of great character: red haired and fiery. Although as a child I took it all as the norm I came to realise that my family was not a typical working class one. We had sets of Dickens and Shakespeare in the house. There was lots of classical music. Our Sundays would be taken up with walking up to the Castlegate to listen to the speakers.

My parents were members of the Communist Party. Father came out after the Hungarian Revolution, but Mother kept her membership right to the end. She would never budge. At that time the Party's committee room was above Mitchell & Muil's near Back Wynd and Mother would spend hours there working for the Party. Quite a number of University lecturers were members, but they kept their identities secret otherwise they would have lost their jobs. They would work behind the scenes on policy.

There's still a bit of communism in me though I don't believe in Stalinism or totalitarian rule, but at that time I thought the cause was right for the sake of social justice. I joined up when I was 16. My parents saw Churchill as a warmonger. When he came to Aberdeen after the war to receive the Freedom of the City all the other kids were out on the street with their Union Jacks and I was kept inside. I remember my mother saying, 'Not for that warmongering man, oh no.'

I wanted to join the Brownies and the Guides, but wasn't allowed: they were seen as quasi-military organisations.

I can remember my parents talking of the Depression and the times when my father would go down to the harbour each morning and stand with all the others at the gate to see who would be picked for work that day. He wouldn't get picked because he refused to hand over a bottle of brandy or some such sweetener. He even came home once and said that he reckoned he would have to give in and hand over the bribe but mother would have none of it: 'Never! We're not going to give in, never!'

Sandra Schwitz. b. 1941. Rosemount. Interviewed 2005.

I was brought up staunchly Socialist

My father was a great Socialist. I was brought up in this staunchly Socialist atmosphere – which had the result that for many years I was a Conservative. I remember all this talk when I was still young, in '45, that you shouldn't vote for Churchill because he was a warmonger.

My mother was very close to the Labour party, but my father would have nothing to do with them. He was always speaking of the 'smiling thieves of Transport House'. He came to the conclusion that at the end of the day the Labour party would always let the working man down, that they would go along with the bosses. And do you know why? It was because they wanted, above everything else, to be respectable.

This meant showing that you were educated. This was one of my grandfather's beliefs:

The descendants of Les Wheeler's Left-leaning father: A May Day march and rally, parading in Union Terrace, 2018.

> For my father, Socialism was a whole way of living. Socialism was not a party so much as a movement, a religious movement. He had a dog that gloried in the name of Bolshie.

you should be able to speak to the bosses as they spoke. Beyond that, you kept fit, you didn't drink, you didn't eat meat. My father was a vegetarian. He had all these books on Swedish exercises – callisthenics. For him Socialism was a whole way of living. Socialism was not a party so much as a movement, a religious movement. He had a dog that gloried in the name of Bolshie.

My father was almost like the village atheist, the one who would criticise the common beliefs of others. He would say, 'I'll tell you what the Labour party is like – they've got nothing and they want to share it with everybody.' He never got over his disillusionment at the time of the General Strike. As a union representative, he had worked hard to persuade his men to come out and they had agreed – on the very day the strike was called off. That tore at his heart. At the end of the day the men had their families to feed, yet they were prepared to make this great sacrifice and they were then betrayed.

He held that all religion was bunkum. He did relent sufficiently to allow us to be baptised, but this had to be in the Unitarian Church which was thought of as a Socialist church. It was the one that the local Labour MP, Hector Hughes, attended and we knew Hector Hughes; he came to the house frequently. My mother had wanted us to be baptised because she was from old farming stock. My father relented but he had his great moment of triumph when the minister ran off with the lady organist, taking the church funds with him. That summed the whole thing up for my father.

Leslie Wheeler. b. 1939. Charlotte Street. Interviewed 2004.

I was conscious of two different worlds

What has made my life somewhat complicated is that from the very start I was conscious of coming from two different worlds. I am the product of a shipboard romance between two entirely different people.

Officially, my father died when I was two and he was in India, a long way from where I was then living in Aberdeen with his widow, my mother. But as I began to find out more about the man and the circumstances of the marriage I became more and more convinced that he didn't really die at that point, but that he simply disappeared.

I'll tell you the story as far as I can gather it. My mother came from a solid Aberdeen family which was distinguished by a high level of craftsmanship and artisan skills. My grandfather on that side was a superb stonemason who did high class work in granite.

In the mid '20s my maternal grandfather was well settled in Aberdeen, working as a prized craftsman in a granite yard. But, years before, his brother had emigrated to New Zealand where he had set up a poultry farm. Word was sent back that this farm was doing so well that it would benefit both of them if my grandfather were to go out to New Zealand and become a partner in the flourishing business.

My grandparents and their two living daughters – my mother, Edith, and her older sister, Jeannie – undertook the two-month journey, but when they got to work on this

The high up parent: Bill Brown's father as the second in command, East Bengal Railways.

The mother's background: Her 'highly skilled' granite worker father here in the centre of a group at Taggart's Yard, Aberdeen.

poultry farm they discovered that all promises of a partnership had faded away and they were there simply to act as unpaid labour. So my grandfather determined to return to Aberdeen. After a couple of years they had saved up the necessary money and set sail for home.

The boat called in at Calcutta whereupon this small, dapper and very self-confident Englishman came on board to join them on their journey back to Britain. He was in his late forties and had recently become a widower. He had four children, who were presently being educated in the south of England.

So when he came across this attractive and, as he thought, innocent and biddable young working class woman from a solid peasant stock back in the North-east of Scotland, he must have been immediately taken with the notion of making her his second wife.

The courtship developed. Each time he came back to England to see his children at their boarding schools he made the rail journey up to Aberdeen to see my mother. After a year or so he proposed and my 25-year old mother became wife to this 49-year old widower. Not only were the ages far apart, they came from completely different worlds. My mother was from the skilled working class while he was a high up administrator in the British Raj, being second in command of the Eastern Bengal Railway.

However, my father kept his Indian life separate: while she was residing in Aberdeen, he would be going back to India to run its railways system. She never did go out to join

Aged 6 and all dressed up for the wedding of his half brother in London, 1936.

him, so when I arrived two years later my mother wrote to tell him, 'We have a son'. His reply was revealing: "Naturally I am very pleased we have progeny – but I can't help feeling it's a pity it isn't a daughter. Boys are so costly to educate'. That was my paternal welcome into the world – and, I have some cause to reckon, the reason he soon cut and ran. After all, my mother had maybe 20 further years of fertility ahead of her so she could easily have given him another seven or eight sons, all of whom would have demanded an expensive upbringing.

The story came back that he had gone down with dysentery on one of his lengthy rail journeys across India and died. There was a photo of a gravestone in Calcutta but it was a strange plain affair with one slab covering the whole thing and the simple inscription, 'David W. Brown' on top. I'm pretty sure there was no body beneath it.

Besides, he must have come to realise that there were huge differences in background and attitude between himself and his young and somewhat callow Aberdeen bride. My mother had worked as dressmaker, in a workshop along with other common young women. He spoke with a pronounced colonial drawl, she in a broad North-east tongue. If she had gone out to live with him in Bengal she would in all probability have become overfamiliar with the coolies and let the side down. There is little doubt that the ladies of the Raj would have looked down on this 'simple' Aberdonian woman and her accent, and would have made disdainful fun of her behind her back.

I was brought up in a working-class household where all the speech was in the dialect of rural Deeside and not of the city. My maternal grandparents, who lived with us, were originally of farming stock, and to them city speech with its equidistant syllables and whining nasal bleat sounded ridiculous.

Yet not even our rural speech was good enough for what my mother had in mind for me. She had married a 'clever man' and made it clear from my earliest years that I must aim to quit my working-class origins. From the age of five I must accompany her on her long daily trek to the city centre where she had found ill-paid employment and must attend no less a school than Robert Gordon's College. There I would learn English, the tongue of the successful. So I learned to read English but not to speak it. In those days all the speaking you did in class was to give one-word answers.

The outcome was that when I was six and accompanied my mother to attend a half-brother's wedding in London, I found I couldn't make myself understood. This was tragic. Here I was, destined for betterment and failing to speak sense in the one place that mattered above all others.

There was only one thing to be done: I would mercilessly tutor myself. Every evening before I went to bed, I would rehearse to my mother the English words I had gleaned that day. It's 'house' not 'hoose', I'd tell her. It's not 'canna' but 'cannot'. It's not 'gaed', it's 'went'.

So much I had learned from my meeting with my father's first family. More was to come. When three years later the eldest of them made a brief stay with us, I asked him to write something in my autograph book and here is what he wrote:

He who knows not, and knows not that he knows not, is a fool. Shun him.
He who knows not and knows that he knows not is a child. Teach him.
He who knows and knows not that he knows is asleep. Wake him.
He who knows and knows that he knows is a wise man. Follow him.

This was real thought and its orderly expression such as I'd never experienced before and a sudden revelation of something I seemed to have longed for without ever knowing I longed for it. I didn't even have to strain to commit these lines to memory; they imprinted themselves there right away – and have never left me. Beauty of one sort had delighted me in the songs of Robert Burns, which my grandfather had made me learn 'to sing to the visitors'. That was beauty in the heart's service, and had kept alive in me a love of Scots that I could easily have lost in my quest for proficiency in English. What my half-brother had shown me was beauty in the service of the mind, of clarity and wisdom. For this my other, my secret endowment had been lying in wait, and had pounced upon it.

Further such pounces were to come. I vividly recall that day our Primary 7 master introduced us to grammar. He lifted a ruler and said, 'This object is called a ruler. The word "ruler" describes this object. The ruler is not a noun; it is the word "ruler" that is the noun. His words had this same beauty of clear thought, something I was beginning to

The Scottish relatives: A 16 year-old Bill (left) on the occasion of the Glasgow cousins' visit 1946. Grandmother is left, grandfather is in skull cap back row, Bill's mother is back row right.

84 years later – Bill photographed at the celebrations of his 90th birthday, May 2019.

feel had a firm connection with that separate English half of me which I was beginning to develop. And yet this clarity was to be found in Scots too. I had begun to explore more of Burns than his lyrics. I had discovered *The Second Epistle to Davie, a Brother Poet*. This not only had the beauty of a metrical music all its own: it contained beautifully expressed snatches of wisdom such as this one, containing as it did the distillation, as I was later to discover, of David Hume's moral philosophy:

> *The hairt aye's*
> *The pairt aye*
> *That makes us richt or wrang.*

And so, when our master bade us be prepared to recite to the class something of our own choosing, this was my choice. His comment was memorable. 'Well, Brown,' he said, 'that was of course extremely impressive. It would have been better, however, if we'd known what on earth you were on about.'

Yes, that was our famous Gordon's College. Its boast was that it turned out 'first generation professionals'. But the price for that would be a profound disdain of common speech and inevitably of the folk who spoke it – one's own parents and all who had gone before them.

What now do I make of those two worlds I seem to have inhabited, my two endowments? Certainly, without the second, the one which gradually disclosed itself through the beauties of mind, I could never have attained even the partial understanding I possess of such matters, or of my halting attempts to express such understanding. But the things that truly matter – a welcoming kindness in our approach to others, the unquestioning response to another's crucial need, the willingness to learn a craft and a devotion to that craft which accepts only the best, all these together with love of beauty, of truth and goodness – those were the things my common craftsfolk gave me, the riches of my first endowment.

Bill Brown. b. 1929. Kincorth. Interviewed 2014.

CHURCH, MOSQUE, FAITH AND BELIEF

Today the Church, like this old photograph, might appear to be somewhat battered and faded. This image reminds us of the time when the Church was seen as the very heart of its communities. It is from the early 1920s and is of the Guildry group, with their winners' shield, attached to the Congregational church, Shiprow- and now converted into the city's Maritime Museum. The author's mother-in-law, Betty Lakin (then Beattie) is left, front row.

On the doorstep: A youthful Andrew (left) with fellow members of the All Saints group. To his left are Derek Masson, George Masson with Patsy O'Brien in front, late 1950s.

In later life Andrew Milne pursued a committed career in the police. Here he is with his shield awarded at the police college at Tullyallan for prowess at table tennis- a sport he honed during those All Saints years.

'Our little All Saints group': Under the dynamic leadership of Father Ron White, the youth put on an annual Christmas show. This is the cast of *Jack and the Beanstal'*. Back row (l–r): Eric Harper, Mike Robertson, Mike O'Brien, Margaret Hay, Patsy O'Brien, George Masson, Audrey Masson, Derek Masson. Middle row: Douglas Lamont, Mrs Vera White, Father Ron White, Mrs Mary Hay, Madge Gillanders. Front row: Evelyn Masson, Liz Hay, Kathleen Lakin, John Hay.

It's part of my heritage

I was brought up to be an active member of the Church. It's part of my heritage. I liked the music, the hymns. But no-one who knows me would describe me as piously religious. I have a belief and a creed; more importantly, I have trust, and sometimes trust is more important than belief.

Going to church was part of my upbringing. It was a social centre, a mini-cultural centre. There were sales of work, there were the dances. But really, All Saints, Hilton, was a unique group of people at a unique time. Ronnie White was the priest in charge. The Church was interwoven into my life; that was a normal experience for my generation. But now it's no longer part of the general social fabric; it's now unfashionable to belong to the Church.

I've always tried to work out things for myself. To say that religion has become part of the fabric of my own life…well, I'd like to be able to claim that, but I can't be sure. Going to table-tennis in the church hall, attending dances there – these were strong inducements. But maybe it was simply a rather cliquish business, our own nice little All Saints club.

I am aware that there has been historically a strong link between the Church and the educational system in Scotland. But if the results of losing that strong Church link are what is becoming more apparent in the society around us, then God help us all. Marx used to say that religion was the opium of the people; and now it's opium that is the opium of the people. Not to mention heroin and the hard drugs lined up with it. What can be coming next?…

Andrew Milne. b. 1943. All Saints, Hilton. Interviewed 2003.

Our whole family were church goers

I was baptised by the Reverend Scudamore Forbes at West St Nicholas Church. I've still got the small New Testament I was presented with. Here it is, with the minister's inscription inside it: 'Helen Jane Ritchie was baptised by me, Scudamore Forbes, at the West Church of St Nicholas, this day, 12th February, 1922'.

My great friend became Muriel Fraser, of 222 Great Western Road. But Muriel was suffering from TB and passed away when she was only 22. She was a lovely young woman, with a complexion of peaches and cream. Frequently when I went round to visit her, she was in bed and I would tell her the news of the day while she lay there. She was a very Christian person and I found her faith an inspiration to me. Her death and the manner of it actually made me an even firmer believer. I was told how once when her mother went up with her tea, Muriel told her, 'Lift me up. I see my Lord waiting for me!'

Our whole family were church goers. On a Friday evening there might be a lantern slide show run by the Temperance Society. My brother would run away and refuse to attend. His theory was that the Temperance people would stop us getting any ginger ale at Christmas. We had our own family pew – Number 3 it was – and for this you paid eight shillings a year. If anyone ever strayed into a reserved pew, oh what a fuss that would cause.

Helen Hendry. b. 1921. West Church of St Nicholas. Interviewed 2013.

Our whole family were churchgoers: An infant Helen with her parents, 1923.

Helen and brother Bob, 1925/26.

Best friend and a lovely young woman: Helen Hendry (left) with Muriel Fraser, who tragically died of TB aged 22.

A place of light and romance: An Edwardian post card of St Machar's overlooking a glistening river Don.

The wonderful end window of St Machar's Cathedral.

Let there be light!

A great boyhood event was to walk all the way into Old Aberdeen and attend the Christmas Eve service at St Machar's Cathedral. The minister there made a great point of proclaiming the Christmas time as a period of welcoming light. I can still hear his voice booming out that 'For far too long churches in Scotland have been places of darkness. So, let there be light!' and then the lights would be switched on and the wonderful end window would be brilliantly illuminated.

Bill Cooper. b. 1936. St Machar's Cathedral. Interviewed 2018.

I was packed off to Sunday School

A lthough the family was only occasional church-goers, I was packed off to Sunday School. I found the whole experience disconcerting. There was a strict separation of the sexes: boys sitting one side, the girls the other. But this distinction also spread into the attitudes of the teachers, who were constantly telling us boys that we were badly behaved and not nearly as nice as the girls were. Yet there I was, doing my very best to act properly and to conform; but no matter how hard I tried, it was no use – I was one of the branded sex and that was that. I resented this and inwardly found myself rejecting the whole Sunday School set up.

The climax came when my aunt, who came from Edinburgh, and who was my

godmother, witnessed me up on a stool, having my sporran adjusted on the kilt I had to wear to the Sunday School and, noticing the look of intense distaste on my face, asked whether it was really a good idea to persist in sending me somewhere I obviously hated. And that was the end of my Sunday School days – and since then I've hardly ever been inside a church.

David Brown. b. 1946. Rosemount Viaduct. Interviewed 2014.

The Cubs had a greater appeal than the Sunday School attached to the church. David Brown, first right, 3rd row, with sixer stripes to the fore, a member of the Beechgrove Church 25th A pack.

He stayed the distance too: As a member of the 17th Aberdeen Grammar School troop, receiving the award of Queen's Scout, 1963.

I would carry out my services and preach sermons in my own Doric and that seemed to help establish a bond and a warmth between us.

The making of a minister

When I was growing up, the kirk had no great importance for me. Like most kids I was packed off to the Sunday School. This happened to be attached to Holburn Central Church, a most dismal place. It was a dark, gloomy building with dark brown panelling and dirty cream walls inside. I hated it.

The first day of Sunday school I got home and was asked by my mother how I had liked it. 'I'm nae gaan back.' One of my grievances was that all the other children had managed to sit there dangling their legs, but mine reached down to the floor and so I could not. My mother had a word with the teacher and the next week I found myself placed on a higher seat and was able to dangle my legs down just like all the rest.

But the Sunday School experience didn't get any better. A few weeks later I was going up the stairs to the tenement flat and met the woman from next door polishing the banisters. 'Well, Joyce, how did you like your Sunday School this week?', she asked me: 'Ah'm nae gaan back.' 'Oh dear, what's the matter?' 'Weel, it's Jesus this an Jesus that and Ah'm fair scunnered o hearin aboot this Jesus.' Mother laughed when she was told: 'Well, I could do something about the height of the seat – but I don't think I'll be able to do much about Jesus.'

It was such a dreary Sunday school. Blessedly, the war intervened. My mother didn't want me out on the long walk down to Holburn Street during any air raid, so I was allowed to leave. From then on, I was a little heathen and on Sundays was able to run free. I remained in that happy state till my 14th year when I was now at the Central school. One of my pals there had a brother called Charlie, who was a prefect. She told me that he was going to be preaching a sermon at the youth club they went to, out at Woodside Congregational Church. 'Oh, you must come along with me – we'll get our death of laughing at Charlie's sermonising.'

Well, three of us went. But Charlie actually acquitted himself very well. I can still remember the theme of his sermon: it was about how God looked over us and watched out for us even when we weren't aware of it. He was like the radar equipment on board a ship, scanning the horizon for dangers. I listened and became impressed. The minister was this super young man who'd been a miner in Shotts. He'd spotted this little group of young girls listening so intently. After the service he made a beeline for us: 'You've been working very hard during the service, I could see that. I think we should go on a ramble.' We went off and ended up playing on the putting green together. At the end, as we were leaving, he called out, 'See you next week.'

I began to go regularly over to Woodside. My mother wasn't best pleased. She had been brought up strict Church of Scotland and to her the Congregational Church was dangerous stuff. But then I fell unwell and the minister, Willy Russell, he was, came to visit. In no time at all he had my mother quite charmed and eating out of his hand. So I could now continue to go to Woodside Congregational Church with her blessing.

The church there was much more than just a place for Sunday worship: the Youth Club was the centre of a whole range of activity. I threw myself into it all. I became a junior elder; I began to help with the services and to preach sermons. The church was now embedded in my life. What helped was that I was part of a group of other like-minded young folk, who were committed. It was all great fun, but, at the same time, quite serious. You'd go to a dance, there'd be some smooching, but you knew it would never go too far. We all thought alike; we all valued the same qualities in life and in each other. We had a common set of beliefs and they were the Christian ones.

So when I found myself all those years later, 12 years into an academic job that had become very dry and confining, it seemed quite natural for me to take my Divinity degree and then to look out for a kirk of my own. My first charge was in Newington, Edinburgh. I was there for seven years before I decided I'd like something a bit more rural.

After a spell in Orkney, I got the combined charge of Alford, Keig and Tullynessle. Seven years further on, in 1987, I shifted to Strathdon, Corgarff, Glenbuchat and Towie. All this was right up my street: I loved the area and I got great support from the people, who were no-nonsense, straight folk. I enjoyed the ethos of the Congregational Church which has always had good following in the North-east – the democratic approach and the close working relationship between congregation and minister has always appealed to people in this part of the world, and it certainly suited me. I would carry out my services and preach sermons in my own Doric and that seemed to help establish a bond and a warmth between us.

But while I was there, I had a huge operation on my pancreas. The surgeon was a brilliant young man and that probably saved me. He carried out an investigative operation to begin with, then sewed me up and hoped for the best. But I got worse and worse and so he ended up by removing the whole organ. That was a very drastic step to take then and I was written off. Basically, I was sewn up again, put in intensive care and left to die as peacefully as possible.

While I was unconscious, I had a near death experience. I dreamed I was walking along this long dark tunnel, on its sandy floor and surrounded by dark high rocks. I was travelling towards a golden light that was shining at the end of it. I had a companion and I said to him, 'Weel, isn't that richt bonny?' 'Oh, aye,' he replied, 'but ye'll be gaan back. Ye've still jobs te dee.' I longed for that light and had no wish to return to my previous existence; I opened my mouth to remonstrate and the next moment I was awake, lying in intensive care, with a feeding tube and on a life support machine. There was a man in the next bed; I looked over to see who it was and all I could see was this gaze of blank astonishment on his face that I had come back from the dead.

I enjoyed my time out on Donside. The people were much more direct and straightforward than had been the case in Edinburgh: no backbiting, no politics or rows. But then my way has always been to muck in and just get in with it. If you do that, then it'll a' gang fine.

Joyce Collie. b. 1929. Woodsde Congregational. Interviewed 2007.

'A most dismal place': Holburn Central Church in the 1930s when a young and reluctant Joyce Collie had to attend its Sunday School.

Tauqeer Malik (centre) with fellow Aberdeen Muslims September 2018 posing to celebrate the granting of a lease for their mosque. (IMAGE BY KIND PERMISSION OF ABERDEEN JOURNALS)

The devout Muslim: Tauqeer Malik with his son Ali Malik in front of the grand Mosque in Medina, Saudi Arabia, 2015.

I am a devout Muslim

Most Pakistanis want nothing to do with the Taliban. One of the saddest results of this is the bad reputation it gives to my native land in the eyes of the West. I find that Scots people have only a sketchy notion of what Pakistan is like and their views tend to be coloured by all the headline violence they read in the media. Yet the Taliban is a product of the West. When the Americans were bent on the defeat of the Russians, who were occupying Afghanistan, they encouraged and gave support to the Taliban – and thereby spawned a force which has now grown beyond their control. Once the Russians had quit Afghanistan, the Taliban regrouped as an anti-West movement, intent on what they claim as prosecuting a pure form of Islam. But their beliefs are a terrible corruption of my religion.

They have utterly distorted the teachings of the Prophet and the Koran. I am a devout Muslim and what I follow is a religion of peace and goodwill. We are taught that to kill one person – of whatever religion or none – is to kill humanity. When we strive to save a life, we do it as an act that will serve our fellow humans. This is our fundamental creed and because of the headline acts of terrorism, our religion and our way of life, tend to be an object of suspicion – a sad outcome that isn't helped by lurid reporting in the Daily Mail and the rest of the right-wing press.

But personally, I can honestly say that the people of Scotland, and especially my Aberdeen, have never given me anything but kindness and support. I owe such a lot to this city. Islam teaches us to help our fellow human and this is the belief that I strive to follow. In this I am simply being a good Muslim; you will find that in charity giving, the Muslim part of the population is at the top. In Aberdeen, especially, we have devoted time and money to helping the homeless.

To be a proper Muslim is to adopt certain disciplines in your daily life. We are supposed to pray five times a day – that is something which for practical reasons I don't always manage to do. But I do read and recite the Koran regularly. For us, the care of our family is paramount: my duty is to feed, shelter, clothe and protect my family, my wife and my four children. I feel this connects me to God, as does the doing of good deeds. Nor will I touch alcohol – though I have sold it as part of my business as a service to the public.

I strongly believe that what spiritual power and strength I possess is a force given to me by Allah. His presence is with me always. Yet our religion isn't well understood among the general population here in the UK. What people brought up in a Christian environment don't often appreciate is the great overlap between our two beliefs. We share the same stories and the same prophets; you will find Moses, Mary, David, John and Jesus revered in the Koran. They are part of our common belief in the same God- and that is something we also share with Judaism too.

Tauqeer Malik. b. 1971. Aberdeen City Council. Interviewed 2018.

Islam covers a broad spectrum

My family belonged to a sect of Islam, called the Ahmadiyya community. This was founded in the late 19th century by a man named Mirza Ghulam Ahmad. The main thrust of his teachings was to restore Islam to its core beliefs of peace and morality; he preached a tolerance of the best of other religions such as Christianity, Buddhism and Hinduism.

This means a separation of state and religion, a regard for the beliefs of others and a rejection of extremist misapplications of Islamic law. I myself have become an agnostic but many of these tenets greatly appeal to me; I certainly believe in tolerance and moderation.

Such an interpretation has appealed to the sort of family we were- educated, secular in outlook, liberal in attitude. But such a digression from hard-line teachings has led to the sect becoming outlawed and its members persecuted. It has been expelled from its original base in Punjab and its adherents have had to spread into other countries. Its present headquarters are actually in London, at the Fazi Mosque in Southfields. The mosque is one of the earliest in Britain, inaugurated in 1926.

I was well educated and brought up as bi-lingual, in both English and Urdu. This I've always regarded as a great boon since it means that I have a living relationship to the great riches of Urdu culture and its literature. My maternal grandfather was a very fine poet and the author of many books.

I was actually born in London when my father was studying organic chemistry at Imperial College. But when I was four, we returned to Pakistan. My upbringing was in Karachi. I was educated and grew up there. One of my most vivid memories is being taken to see my mother's younger brother who was being incarcerated as a student activist by the military dictatorship of Ayub Khan. I was only six at the time and had little understanding of what was going on so, quite innocently, I asked him, 'Uncle, what have

A preacher for peace and tolerance: His holiness, Hazrat Masroor Ahmad, Worldwide Head of the Ahmadiyya Muslim Community.

A faith that prizes togetherness: Members of the Ahmadiyya Community join hands in worship

I have more or less left any faith behind. I am a scientist and must subject any religious beliefs to the test of scientific scepticism.

you done to be behind bars like this?' I have never forgotten his reply, 'Son, sometimes to gain your freedom you have to stand behind bars!'

My own political awakening peaked in medical school where I ran foul of the regime, which, at that time, was headed by one of the country's line of dictators, Zia-ul-Haq. I was a student leader in Karachi and we were holding demonstrations in favour of a non-repressive rule. We marched and planned to burn an effigy of ul-Haq, but the police arrested us and we were charged with sedition. Fortunately for us, Pakistan is an hierarchical society and if, like me, you had good contacts among the elite, than you could expect to be treated leniently. So I was only behind bars for a few days.

I was a student during the heady days of the 1970s and early '80s. I became very active in the National Students' Federation and developed firm socialist leanings. My own beliefs moved away from any unquestioning adherence to Islamic teachings and towards an anti-imperialist, socialist and secular philosophy.

Pakistan has become less and less tolerant and more and more a fundamentalist Muslim state. To the outside world the country I was brought up in has descended into something like Europe in the Middle Ages when people were persecuted for their heretical beliefs and burnt at the stake. But it's really a minority which is calling the tune there; many in the Pakistani middle classes and professional people are actually tolerant, well-educated and politically aware. The tragedy of Pakistan is that it is being held to ransom by a fanatical and superstitious minority.

All this has confirmed me in my agnostic ways. My brother has remained quite religious, but I have more or less left any faith behind. Not only have I seen what an intolerant following of religion can do, I am a scientist and must subject any religious beliefs to the test of scientific scepticism. The result is that I have come to see much of religion as a collection of fairy tales, useful as a crutch to comfort believers when confronting their mortality, but no more than that. If you ask me what are my comforts, I would tell you: music, books, the hills, golf.

Izhar Khan. b. 1960. Karachi and Ferryhill. Interviewed 2016.

Vanity! Vanity! sayeth the preacher

Religion had a potent hold over a fishing community like Torry until after the war. The Brethren were in command of many homes and their edicts were repressive in the extreme. Music was frowned upon; an organ had been donated to their hall and one zealous member got hold of an axe and smashed it to pieces.

They met in a tin hut on the banks of the Dee – the 'Tin Tabernacle'. My great aunt Lizzie attended. She was an upright, austere figure, her silver hair tied up in a bun, always dressed in black and to be found sitting by the fire with her bible in her hand. No radio and no newspapers were permitted to pollute the moral atmosphere of the house by allowing the wicked ways of the outside world to infiltrate.

Her two daughters defected to Willie Still's church in Union Street and that was regarded as black treachery. They were forbidden colourful clothes or even the merest hint of lipstick. My aunt would shake her head and pronounce, 'Jezebel! Painted Jezebel!' upon their heads. Another of her frequent judgements was the pronouncement, 'Vanity! Vanity! sayeth the preacher'.

Her funeral took place in her house with the Brethren faithful descending on it like a cloud of black crows. The preacher entered and gave the address in a whining nasal accent: 'It was in the year of our Lord 1895 that our dear departed sister, while walking down Victoria Road, met her saviour'. This was the moment of revelation when she gave herself up to God – but I had visions of her proceeding down Victoria Road and Christ coming towards her, along the pavement swinging his lantern, for all the world like the Holman Hunt painting, *The Light of the World.* I had to stifle my own giggles at the thought.

Ronald (Ron) Caie. b. 1938. Victoria Road, Torry. Interviewed 2014.

But not to his face

The church was important to us. We'd all go each Sunday, dressed in our finery and on our most impeccable behaviour. The minister would call in regularly. This could be quite amusing. Granny Bird came to stay with us towards the end of her life and when the minister called in, she would sit there, smiling and nodding, but mother knew at the end of the visit she would have to rush him out the door in case he heard the inevitable snort of, 'Silly bugger!'

Wilma Gillanders. b. 1944. Victoria Road, Torry. Interviewed 2006.

No radio and no newspapers were permitted to pollute the moral atmosphere of the house by allowing the wicked ways of the outside world to infiltrate.

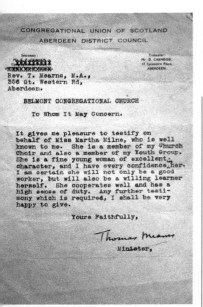

CONGREGATIONAL UNION OF SCOTLAND
ABERDEEN DISTRICT COUNCIL

Rev. T. Mearns, M.A.,
356 Gt. Western Rd,
Aberdeen.

BELMONT CONGREGATIONAL CHURCH

To Whom It May Concern.

It gives me pleasure to testify on behalf of Miss Martha Milne, who is well known to me. She is a member of my Church Choir and also a member of my Youth Group. She is a fine young woman of excellent character, and I have every confidence her. I am certain she will not only be a good worker, but will also be a willing learner herself. She cooperates well and has a high sense of duty. Any further testimony which is required, I shall be very happy to give.

Yours Faithfully,

Thomas Mearns
Minister,

To whom it may concern: testimonial provided by the Reverend Thomas Mearns, for a young Martha Alexander, in the 1950s, at a time when the church still played a formative role in many young persons' lives.

A studio photograph of Martha aged 20 around the same period.

The church was a place for worship and for social activity. Martha (2nd right, front row) with daughters Fiona and Carole to her right, among a happy group at the North and East Church of St Nicholas Choir's annual dinner dance, Pharaoh's Restaurant 1972.

The church was the hub

We were very involved in the church – because it was the only place to go to. At the church we had Sunday School. I remember we got a postcard and that postcard had all the books of the Bible written on it and we had to learn so much every week: 'Genesis, Exodus, Leviticus, Numbers, Deuteronomy, Joshua, Judges, Ruth…' I wonder now what good it did us.

The Brownies, the Guides, the Life Boys and the Boys' Brigade were just choc-a-bloc. The Church was the hub and I think – I'm not highly religious – but a lot of what's stopped folk going to church, well, I blame schools for having Sunday football for the kids for folk'll take their kids to football rather than take them to a church to get some inspiration.

There isn't anywhere now that you could say is the hub of the community, but the Church definitely was back then.

Martha Alexander. b. 1937 Charlotte Street; interviewed 2015.

The church took over some of the boys

Now there was a family stayed in Nelson Street and they'd six children and they only had two chairs. Mother and Father got a chair to sit for their dinner and the six kids stood round the table. He was unemployed. She used to go out in a morning and went round all the vegetable shops and got yesterday's vegetables cheap. And there was a big pot of broth made every day and the kids stood round the table; Father and Mother had a plate, but the pot of soup was put in the middle of the table and the kids ate out of that. Yet, when they grew up, two of them went into nursing and I think the church took over some of the boys and I know there were two ministers (among them) and they all did very well, but the church took them over.

That really was the only hope you had – if somebody helped you.

Gladys Morrice. b. 1920 King Street; interviewed 2016.

The Four Pillars of the Kirk

In 1940 I joined the Life Boys at Ferryhill South Church. Within a few weeks the minister, the Reverend Merricks Arnott, invited me to become a Door Boy. Three other lads were recruited and so our team of four Ferryhill South Church Door Boys was formed.

Our duties meant that we were to be at our posts 30 minutes before every service. We had to open the doors as the congregation arrived, bid them a 'Good Morning' and take any hats, coats and umbrellas which needed hanging up. We also had to ensure the doors were kept closed so as to keep the draughts out. Since this was a constant battle, we became known as the 'Kirk Draughtsmen'.

During the service itself we took up seats in the gallery and then during the singing of the final hymn we left to open the main doors and then to take up position at our own door. Following the Benediction, we opened the curtains, taking as our cue the start of the organ voluntary, and hooked back our doors.

The routine for the evening services was the same except that after the congregation had departed, we had to go up and down each pew and turn up the cushions so that they wouldn't gather dust between services. We collected up any lost property; returning this to their owners wasn't usually a problem since we quickly got to know where all the members of the congregation sat.

On Communion Sundays we had to gather all the glasses in large basins, remove the stainless-steel holders and fold all the white pew cloths and the communion table cloth ready for laundering for the next communion.

All these duties soon became routine though the job did require considerable commitment. We had to make ourselves present for every service. But we did get paid. We were on the Stipendiary staff of the church and our wages of £2 per annum were entered into the annual accounts. We frequently got tips at Christmas and after the Communion service. And Mrs Wilson, the caretaker, would give us bags of bread pieces to take home for our mothers to make into bread puddings – and this while bread was rationed during the war.

We did all this for some four or five years and earned the title of 'Pillars of the Kirk'. This title notwithstanding, we did get up to a few naughty exploits. We used to taste the wine left over when cleaning up after Communion – and didn't find it at all nice. We found, quite by chance, that when we put on the switch for the deaf aids to a setting, we

A pillar of the Kirk: Door Boy and BB member Bob Cooper, Ferryhill South Church, 1940s.

Bob celebrates his 80th birthday.

Before he left Grampian TV: Douglas with GTV colleague, June Imray.

Since those days, Douglas has become a noted author of local lore. Here he is with his *The Minister's Cat*

could tune it into the radio. Now this was long before the days of transistor radios so, while waiting our turn for the BB table tennis on a Saturday afternoon, we could sneak into the church and listen in to the football on the deaf aids.

The Cowdray Club next door to the church retained a key for the hall and we discovered that, as pillars of the Kirk, we would never be challenged when we asked for the use of the key. We played a lot of badminton on wet holidays and nobody ever found us out. Being a Door Boy is something I will always remember. It taught me the meaning of commitment and of service. This has stood me in good stead throughout my life.

Robert (Bob) Cooper. b. 1931. Ferryhill South Church. Interviewed 2014.

I felt that God wanted me to move on

After six years with Grampian TV, I left to join the BBC. The television news programme 'Reporting Scotland' was about to start up and they wanted someone to present that, as well as making occasional regional contributions to the new Nationwide programme from London.

While I was doing this demanding work on television, I'm afraid my anxiety neurosis took a serious turn for the worse, so I tried to find spiritual help. I'd always believed in God and had been a churchgoer for most of my life, but I was really only a nominal Christian. All that changed because of my illness. I made a commitment to Christ in my early thirties and through contact with the charismatic renewal movement, which had just got going in Scotland, I had a wonderful deliverance from chronic anxiety and was never troubled by it again.

Within a year from that day, I had left my job in television. I was beginning to feel that God wanted me to move on to pastures new and I arranged to go into a Christian retreat in Ireland for a while to decide.

The outcome was I gave up my top job in television to work with a Christian radio station operating from Glasgow. This was only a short-term posting, as it turned out; and after a year, I returned to the BBC as a freelance radio broadcaster. This gave me the time to work on a Christian autobiography (which is still in progress).

Over this long period, the Church in general has been in a steady state of decline. The rise of secularism and of atheism grieves me greatly, while the Church of Scotland has fallen away from Biblical truth to such an extent that I can't belong to it any more. The one thing that keeps me going is my belief that all this will change. I believe that God is going to intervene in human affairs. Then everything will be transfigured, you will see.

Douglas Kynoch. b 1938. The BBC. Interviewed 2014.

Since his TV days, Douglas Kynoch has written a number of books in both Doric and English., including *Here's tae us. A Personal view of Scottish History* and *A Doric Dictionary*.

We are great believers in spiritualism

My father was drowned in Aberdeen harbour. My mum and dad had separated. He got a job as a night watchman on the fishing trawlers. It was round February and he'd gone to the Comrades Club at the bottom of Market Street to have a game of darts, and then he'd headed back to the boat. The boat departed the next day and my father was reported missing and the Police were informed. They came to the house and questioned my mother. He had just disappeared.

We are great believers in spiritualism, our family, and five weeks later my mother was at church and my father 'came through' the medium and spoke. The medium said, 'I've got a man here with a bouquet of flowers in his hands and he's giving it to me to give to you.' And she went on, 'He can't get breath. I feel he's choking.' My mother knew this was my father and asked, 'What happened to you?' He'd slipped on the icy deck and fallen into the harbour. He said, 'I'll be up and you'll see me in five days.' Sure enough, exactly five days later his body was found. It had been stuck underneath the pontoon in the harbour; it had had to be moved, and my father's body floated to the top. When he was found, he had a set of darts in his pocket and he had two or three coins – I've still got one of the pennies at home – and a pound note.

Kathleen Porter. b. 1928 Albion Street. Interviewed 2016.

> The medium said, 'I've got a man here with a bouquet of flowers in his hands.

So I joined the Moonies in Frankfurt

As a young man, I went across to Frankfurt and got a job teaching English as a foreign language. One evening after work, I was stopped by an American who was telling me about his church – the Unification Church. I thought, I'm not interested; I've got my own church at home. But I was invited to go along that evening to a meeting and I thought, here I am, two days in Germany, why not?

I went along; they were very friendly, and their ideas were not in any way alien to me; I was brought up more or less in the church, so I thought, right, that's great. So, I went along again the next evening and heard a bit more about what they were saying and, after that, I'd a bit of a pause and went back to work. But then I met him again in the street and he said 'Why not come on a weekend course in the Taunus Mountains just outside Frankfurt?' And I thought 'Why not?'

So off I went to the weekend course – and it was the Moonies. I'd never heard of them, but I was interested in what they were saying; they were very personable, young people like me – so I had great comradeship with them. And being in a foreign country, it was very good to have people to speak to, many of whom could speak good English as well. Anyway, I ended up joining them. I was based in Frankfurt, and I was on the street pretty quickly as a missionary, trying to get people to come along to our meetings and ultimately to join 'the family' as they were known. And that was it for about a year.

Living conditions were fundamental; you slept in sleeping bags on the floor. Your diet

The man he was briefly a missionary for: The head of the Moonies, Sung Myung Moon, and his wife upon their thrones.

Allan Paterson was far from alone in his adherence: The Moonies were especially strong in Korea, where, in the 1980s, mass wedding ceremonies became a popular recruiting tool.

An American, Will, began to say, 'You must waken up here. Haven't you been brainwashed with some of the ideas you're trying to forward to me?'

was very simple food. You were kept busy almost 24/7 either studying, evangelising or, in my case when I got the opportunity to go to Berlin about a month later, I was the person in charge of going out and earning a living for the family group.

In Berlin there were about six of us and I worked to support the rest and evangelised after work. I'd several jobs there – a cleaner in the British Army Hotel and then a job labouring for the British Army at Spandau. We had meetings every three months in our head office in the Taunus Mountains.

However, I was beginning to feel a bit uneasy about some of the doctrines; Sun Myung Moon as the Messiah – I began to question that. The beginning of the end of my time with the Moonies began with another American, Will, who began to say, 'You must waken up here. Haven't you been brainwashed with some of the ideas you're trying to forward to me?' And he put that seed in my mind and I thought, hold on – I want some time away. So with great difficulty, I managed to break away from the Moonies; you can imagine the pressure I came under. Fortunately, I had a job, so I could say, 'Right, look, I'll make my own way'. And Will, this American guy, said, 'I'm going away to Paris for three months, please come and stay in my accommodation – the rent is paid – until you get yourself straight and decide what you want to do'.

Allan Paterson. b. 1951. The Moonies, Germany. Interviewed 2015.

Christian Democracy at school

We had a headmaster, Sir James Robertson, who was extraordinarily eloquent, so fluent in the way he spoke. People used to stand up for him even after he'd retired. J.J. Robertson was, of course, a celebrated national figure, but we were not really aware of that then. But we were certainly aware of him as this sort of God-like figure: we didn't see a lot of him in the everyday sense, but he was there on the stage at

Assembly and we'd see him at the centre of things. I remember him tearing a strip off us when, as a class, we'd been particularly difficult to a music teacher. We were gathered together and Robertson came in and gave us this very stern lecture; he had us all quivering in our seats. He had that power, that presence.

I know he wrote the 1947 Report for the Government on Secondary Education and that in it he used the term 'Christian Democracy' as the touchstone. There was certainly a strong emphasis on Christianity at the school then. I think he actually had a degree in Divinity and, in a way, he was more like a minister than a headmaster. He came over, in the way he spoke especially, as someone in the pulpit. 'Christian democracy' – when I think about it, it's quite true.

Peter Murphy. b. 1932. Aberdeen Grammar School. Interviewed 2002.

A God-like figure:
James J. Robertson , Rector of Aberdeen Grammar School, with his staff. Centre front row and the sole figure in academic robes, 1950.

Attendance at Assembly was compulsory

A berdeen Grammar School would certainly have thought of itself as a Christian institution. The assumption was that all the boys came from families that adhered to the Christian faith. I remember a traumatic experience as a boy when, in the Primary department, Miss Stewart asked us all which church we went to.

Now, my family didn't actually go to church, largely because my father was something of a scoffing atheist. I was horrified that I was going to be the only boy in the class without a church to offer- so when it came to my turn, I said, 'Oh, Beechgrove, Miss'. To

I spent the several weeks in mortal terror that she would talk to Mr Pirie about me and that my horrid secret would be shamefully uncovered.

which Miss Stewart replied, 'Oh, so you have Mr Pirie as your minister, then'. That brought home to me that I had lied and that I had offended against the Holy Ghost. I spent the next several weeks in mortal terror that she would talk to Mr Pirie about me as this up-and-coming young member of his congregation and that my horrid secret would be shamefully uncovered. Apparently, that didn't actually happen – my sins never did find me out, though theologically they still could, I suppose.

But that incident shows you the kind of pressure we were all under to think of ourselves as practising Christians. At school we certainly got our dose of the Bible and of religious instruction. It really was instruction – I don't think there was ever any hint that the Bible could be questioned in any way. Attendance at Assembly with its prayers was also compulsory. It was a strictly mono-ethnic community: one of my tasks as prefect was to patrol the hall to catch late-comers and absentees. Then they would be turned over to the Deputy Rector for suitable treatment. And there was this boy called Cohen whom I caught one day coming in late. I told him, 'Look, I'm going to have to hand you over as being too late for Assembly,' to which he replied, 'Oh, but I don't have to attend. I'm Jewish'. I'd never met anyone who had told me that before – or realised that such people still existed outside the Old Testament. Apart from that, I can't recall anyone at the Grammar then who was from any other ethnic or religious background.

Duncan Rice. b. 1942. Aberdeen Grammar School. Interviewed 2003.

A Catholic education

I'm not a practising Catholic now but like a lot of us, when it comes to my last gasp I will probably look to be buried in a Catholic cemetery. It's part of my culture; it's what I am. Our Catholicism was never up front; we didn't go to mass on a Sunday but being Catholic defined us. We all had our first communions; we were all of us confirmed in the faith.

But my Catholic upbringing has certainly left its mark on my moral outlook. The first word that comes to mind for most Catholics is 'guilt' – and I'm no different in that respect. You will be found out; you've got a guardian angel; you'll have to account for yourself at the Day of Judgement. But looking back, I don't want any of this to sound like the kind of sadistic and oppressive experience you hear stories about nowadays – it wasn't like that for me at all. But it was strict in a religious and a moral sense. The notion of 'punishment' was ever-present. I don't mean physical punishment, but the idea of punishment itself, of having to give an account of yourself before some higher authority. I do believe that that feeling is a permanent part of my being.

It's as the Jesuits say, 'Give me the child till seven and I will give you the adult'. And although I'm no longer a religious person I do still have a great affection for the faith. I like nothing more than the smell of a newly blown-out candle or of incense; they conjure up so many memories for me. My Catholic schooling shaped me – and I've no regrets about that.

A series of beautiful granite buildings: A 1960s shot of the rear of the Convent of the Sacred Heart School, also showing its splendid tennis courts, at the period when Lynette Mitchell was a pupil.

I went to St Peter's in Nelson Street; I remember the school fondly. I passed the 11-plus there. I was offered a scholarship to go to the Convent of the Sacred Heart, the fee-paying secondary school for Catholic girls, which was situated at Queen's Cross.

On Fridays you had to wear white gloves at the end of the school day because that's when the judgements were handed out. At the Convent there was no physical punishment but, all through the week, there were 'spies' on the watch who would be silently noting down your behaviour. The last thing on Friday was this gathering in the school hall. Your record of behaviour for the week had been noted down in a book and a report prepared in the form of the 'note'. You then had to walk forward and collect and read it. The gradings went from 'excellent – very good – good – indifferent, to 'no note'. You were being judged publicly and it could be a humiliating experience. I once got 'no note' because I had been observed climbing a tree. I don't think many 'excellents' were ever awarded. You then had to hand in your note as you left the hall and the Mother Superior would be standing there; there was never any suggestion of anything physical – she had called you and that was enough.

What was different about the Convent was the real family atmosphere of the place. We were all bound together; we all shared the same experiences, the uniform, the notes. We had great pride in our school. I suppose the building had a lot to do with that, too. The Convent was made up of a series of beautiful granite buildings in Queen's Road, which housed beautiful corridors and religious statues, with nuns moving through them.

All of us were subject to the institution's discipline. The nuns had to get permission to leave the premises – to vote or to see the doctor. But it did seem as if they had their ways of finding out about things. I met my future husband when I was 14 and started going around with him. He was a Protestant – though I don't think he was actually aware of this categorisation then. Anyway, my mother received a telephone call and was asked whether she was aware that her eldest daughter was to be seen going around with a boy who was 'not of the true faith'. It seemed as if the Convent had its network of spies: I'd given my boyfriend the school scarf to wear as a love token and that was that.

I wasn't aware of any Catholic bias in the curriculum. I would describe it as a traditional, solid academic syllabus. Actually, you felt that academic success was not the

The gradings went from 'excellent – very good – good – indifferent, to 'no note'. It could be a humiliating experience. I once got 'no note' because I had been observed climbing a tree.

top priority at the school so much as the whole person and the attempt to make you a better person. Good manners, consideration for others, behaving well – after all, we were Catholics and each of us had her own crown in heaven. Some might be more bejewelled than others, according to our deeds on earth. I will still say to my husband after a little kindness I might have performed, 'That's another jewel on my crown.'

The school closed down as a secondary in 1970/71 and now there is no secondary Catholic school in Aberdeen. I actually think that's a good thing; I don't think you should divide people up on religious grounds. But then we're fortunate in Aberdeen in that the city, unlike others in Scotland, has never had a great sectarian issue. I remember once going to a party in Edinburgh and this guy coming in and saying out loud, 'Right, which side are the Fenians sitting on?' That could never happen up here.

Lynette Mitchell. b. 1950. Convent of the Sacred Heart. Interviewed 2004.

Our minister became a father – at over 50

Religion played an important role in my family. The church was just across the road and that's where I went to the Girls' Brigade and the Junior Choir, where we rehearsed shows and performed on the stage at Powis School. My mother was a member of the Guild and my father was an elder at West St Clements at Footdee. My granny and my aunts were mission folk, a commitment which guided their entire lives. They'd go over to Footdee for their services; in the centre of that community there stood what was known as the 'Schoolie', a building just like a small church with a bell at its centre and everybody in Footdee seemed to go to it. My uncle was a lay preacher there. Living over in Powis Place I was a bit of an outsider, but my aunts attended faithfully. These were untrained lay people who would stand up as the spirit moved them and offer their public testimonies of faith before the whole congregation.

My aunts lived for their mission and their faith. They were very strong on adopting an evangelical approach to spreading the Word; they also collected money for the less fortunate, especially the children out in Africa – whom they, in those pre-PC days, termed 'darkies'. They had a collection box set aside for this purpose. In this they saw themselves as following in the footsteps of Mary Slessor; you could say that my aunts adopted her as their shining example. They were great story tellers and would amuse me with their tales, which usually had some moral point to them – parables really.

But then the church was an important part of most people's lives. I went to the Sunday school at the Powis church. I never found this an imposition; the services were quite lively and child-friendly with plenty of rousing chorus singing.

Our minister was a Mr Skakle . He was a bachelor, brought up by four of his father's sisters, since the death of his mother in childbirth. I must admit we all considered him to be a confirmed bachelor, who needed to be looked after by the older generation of women in his life. The aunts put him through his education and his theological studies

A church-going family: Granda and Granny Smith with Jess, May, Eleanor and a young Pat at the door of the Powis Terrace home.

A well-liked minister: The Reverend Skakle, front, in the Powis Church nativity, 1953. A young Pat Brown (Smith) is the Wise Man bearing frankincense to his right.

Everybody in Fittie seemed to go to it: 'The Schoolie' still standing in the heart of the old fishing community.

A slightly older Pat in her Sunday best, in a city graveyard.

and he remained ever loyal to them. We children would play little tricks on him like taking up his hat and tossing it around during Sunday school classes – but he took it all in good humour.

But, one by one, the aunts died off and, to everyone's astonishment, at the age of 47 Mr Skakle took a wife – and in those days, unlike now, 47 was regarded as late to marry. Not only that, she bore him a daughter and so our minister became a father. The congregation was delighted for him and his wife.

He was very nice man, who often turned up at the house for a cup of tea and a chat. But, oh dear, his sermons were, perhaps, not aimed at our teenage minds, being somewhat too academic and serious for us. But all in all, he was a well-liked minister.

Pat Brown. b. 1940. Split the Wind. Interviewed 2015.

An important focal point

We lived in Northfield and at that time it was all quite new and full of people who were keen to take advantage of their improved surroundings, having moved there from the crowded centre.

The church acted as an important focal point. I joined the Youth Fellowship and made many good friends there. The minister was Ross Flockhart, a man who had a great influence on my development. I used to babysit his four children and came across his large library of books. 'Feel free,' he would say pointing to the shelves – and I did. When I reached 14, he handed me a large Russian novel with the words, 'You must read this. And we will discuss it.' It was Boris Pasternak's *Dr Zhivago*. I did as he told me and I knew I was entering a world of big characters and important events. That book has stayed with me ever since.

I graduated to Sunday School teaching, but still was an enthusiastic member of the Fellowship. We met in a wooden hut. We were encouraged to debate the issues of the day and the ways in which the Christian message could be applied to everyday living. One of the many speakers Ross Flockhart brought along was George MacLeod, the founder of the Iona community. He gave a provocative address; his words stirred us up into thinking for ourselves. It was such a privilege to have access to folks like him at a formative time in our lives.

Ross Flockhart was a short and chubby man with a cheery face. He had an excellent way with young people and was always anxious to see us develop as independently enquiring young men and women. He would push you into discussion and a reconsideration of views; his intention was to broaden the mind. He confirmed for me the message of my own family, that the world for the young was full of possibilities and that 'you could do it' if you really went for it.

Margaret (Meg) Forbes. b. 1944. Northfield Youth fellowship. Interviewed 2015.

> The minister was Ross Flockhart. I used to babysit his four children and came across his large library of books. 'Feel free,' he would say pointing to the shelves – and I did.

Holiday in a tramcar

I was a member of the Boys' Brigade at Melville Church at the bottom of Rose Street. One summer my brother and I had the great adventure of spending a week at the Tramcar Camp. My aunts were very involved in the YWCA and they went regularly to this Tramcar Camp and once invited the two of us along with our mother, to join them there.

The 'camp;' was an old Aberdeen tramcar which had been transported out on a trailer to its resting place in a field at Drumoak, just below the Park Bridge, which in those days was still a toll bridge, run by an old woman who lived in her cottage there.

We camped out in the tramcar itself and this had been neatly converted into accommodation. You'd enter in at the door to find a dining and sitting area downstairs, then upstairs was a partitioned dormitory, which held five beds and had a dressing room at the end. The toilet was situated in the woods nearby and water had to be fetched from a

The Tram Car Camp

**Enjoying their
week in the tram
car:** Bill and older
brother Gordon with
their mother, right, and
one of the YWCA
aunts, at the door of
their tram car.

**My aunts'
allegiance:** A 1933
YWCA keepsake.

pump behind the toll house and taken in buckets to the tramcar.

It was a memorable week out there in the countryside and by the Dee. Scouts had their camp in the next field and the YWCA ladies would invite Scout officers over for supper – to the great excitement of both parties. The tramcar is long gone now and no doubt in these days of foreign holiday, a week camping out in it would be regarded as hopelessly primitive, but for us, and for whole generations of young Aberdeen women, it gave them their only real taste of exotic adventure. That tramcar in its field in Drumoak was Majorca and Florida for them – and no doubt just as enjoyable.

Bill Cooper. b. 1936. Drumoak. Interviewed 2018.

Encounters with the supernatural

At the start of my work in Aberdeen I had to stay in digs. My mother got the post of housekeeper to John Smith at number 1 Queen's Cross. I went to see her and Mr Smith suggested that as he had plenty of spare rooms why not take one of them and move in? So that's what I did and so I took up residence in a room in the staff quarters. This was in a small space underneath the stairs, but the rest of the house was a large luxurious building. It had originally been constructed for George Washington Wilson, the famous 19th century photographer. It hadn't changed much since that time.

A haunted house?
Number 1 Queens
Cross, as it is today
– a branch of the
Clydesdale Bank.

**Memories of its
earlier days:** The
plaque commemorating the time when
the distinguished
photographer,
Washington Wilson,
lived there.

For me, a young 17 year-old girl, it was like living in some time warp.

Number 1 Queen's Cross was where I had my first encounter with a ghost. I was 17 and had been to the Aberdeen Motor Club dance at the Northern Hotel. I had taken a taxi there but met up with a friend of my brother's who offered to give me a lift home. He did this and then drove off.

I was about to turn left to go to the side door when I suddenly saw this woman in a long dress. I assumed that, like me, she had been to a dance. I called out to her, 'Can I help you?' She ignored me. I repeated the question but still no flicker of a response. She went up to the front door and appeared to be about to pull the doorbell which would set off the bells in the servants' quarters. This was two in the morning so I was nervous that she would awaken the whole household. I started to run towards her, calling once more, 'May I help you?', but all she did was turn at the top of the stairs and look out towards the drive in the direction of Queen's Road. She then gave a wave and had the most beatific look of joy on her face as she did so. That done, she turned on her heel and walked straight through the front door as if it was opened for her.

This was no fleeting glimpse but a full encounter; all the details were quite clear to me – the costume suit tapered at the waist which she was wearing and which I recognised as belonging, not to my era but to the 19th century, the lingering wave down the driveway, the look of radiant happiness on her face.

The next morning at breakfast in the servants' quarters I remarked, 'I think I saw a ghost last night.' Later that evening, there was a knock at my door and there stood the maid. 'I wanted to tell you that I've also seen that ghost.' She then went on to relate how she had once been taking a tray up the stairs from the kitchen when, about a third of the way up, she encountered a fine lady coming down. As a servant she naturally backed down to allow the lady to pass. But there was no sign of recognition on her face, only this look of great joy. The lady reached the bottom and then passed straight through the door into the wine cellar, a door which was always kept locked. She also told me that, when she had been interviewed by Mr Smith for the job, he had asked her, 'Are you scared of ghosts?' Apparently, the previous maid had packed her bags and walked out, claiming she had been frightened off by a ghost.

Later I worked out who the ghost must be. I was looking through a book of old Aberdeen photographs when I saw a picture of the house and also one of the young ladies who had been living there when it was first built. It was George Washington Wilson's daughter and, there she was, staring back at me from the page.

I don't actually believe in ghosts. To me once you are dead you are dead and that's it. But my conclusion is that moments of extreme emotion can leave behind some sort of force field of energy and that is what I was encountering on those occasions. My awareness was enhanced by the fact that I too was experiencing a similar emotion to the apparent visitations from the past. It was like a hologram in a time warp that you can enter and then you see the incident years later.

Of course, only some of us have this type of experience. I must have a heightened sensitivity to that sort of energy. On the other hand, unlike most people, I am completely insensitive to music, being tone deaf. Well, you can't have everything, can you?

Linda Muller. b. 1945. Queen's Road. Interviewed 2015.

Brian – not a good name

Another important part of my boyhood was the Boys Brigade. We were a church-going family and each Sunday attended the Congregational Church of Albion & St Pauls, which stood opposite the war memorial at Cowdray Hall. All that is now left of that building is the tall brick spire, the rest having been torn down to make way for yet another glass and concrete office block. But back then each Sunday I would put on my kilt and accompany my parents and sister and brother to morning worship. They were members of the choir.

I was into the Life Boys at eight, and then four years later became a fully-fledged member of the Boys Brigade. The BB was then at the height if its popularity; indeed, I believe that, in proportion to its population, membership in Aberdeen outdid every other city in the UK, apart from Belfast.

I loved it all. For one thing the emphasis on physical activity every Friday

I loved it all: A young Mike Davidson receives his award for perfect attendance as a faithful Life Boy, 1950/51. The presentation was in the Rurthrieston South Church Hall and was made by Mrs Howie, the wife of the minister, the Reverend David Howie.

evening gave me the opportunity to release the pent-up energies of the week. For another I took to the discipline and the structure of the organisation and that included all the marching and drilling too. The values of the Brigade also appealed to me since they chimed in so well with those of my upbringing at home. I was firmly brought up to be polite and to respect others. In fact, old fashioned though it might be, I will still stand up if a lady enters the room and open the door for them and give up my seat on public transport.

Each Sunday was dominated by the church in one form or other. You might start off with a BB Bible class, and then attend morning service, then a Youth Fellowship meeting. I never resented any of this – besides, what else was there to do on a Sunday in 1950s Aberdeen? The Sabbath was still kept, with closed shops and cinemas and empty streets. At home, playing outside on the Sabbath was strictly forbidden and certainly no games of cards inside either. For entertainment you had to make do with the afternoon family walk, all kitted out in our best clothes.

I was born at home. Afterwards our minister, the Reverend Hughes, came to visit and to enquire after the new born's likely name. 'Oh, we were thinking of calling him Brian,' my mother told him. 'Oh, no, Brian – that's not a good name. I think we'll call him Mitchell. I can baptise him here and now with that name.' A glass bowl was filled with tap water and he baptised me with my name – 'Mitchell'. And the minister's own name? The Reverend Mitchell Hughes.

Mitchell (Mike) Davidson. b. 1940. Congregational Church of Albion & St Paul's. Interviewed 2016.

The rich social activity it offered us: A Rutherford Church Halloween party 1949. An 18 year-old Campbell Murray goes for an apple, far right. The Reverend Samuel Ballantyne keeps watchful guard.

It was so different in my young day

My boyhood centred very much on the church – not just as a place of worship, but for the rich social activity it offered. This was Rutherford Church, situated at the top of Loanhead Place. Its minister in the '30s and much of the '40s was the Reverend G. Gordon Cameron, 'a quiet, saintly man'. He was succeeded by the Reverend Samuel Ballantine, a most imposing character, who stood at six feet three and walked everywhere. The congregation was a large one, approaching 3,000 on the roll and several hundred would attend on a Sunday.

For the youth of the district in the late '40s and early '50s there seemed be something on most days of the week. For me, Tuesday meant Drama, Wednesday Badminton, Friday

the Boys Brigade, Saturday Scottish Country dancing. On Sunday there was the Boys Brigade Bible Class, 'Pew boy' duties, followed by Sunday School as a teacher and, in the evening, Pew Boy duties for the service, then, later in the evening, Youth Fellowship.

I had the honour of being a Pew Boy for 10 years from the age of 14 till I graduated from the University at 24. The Pew Boys were selected mainly from the Boys Brigade and there was a team of four. Our main duty involved greeting members of the congregation by opening the doors for them and giving them a polite welcome. We were also responsible for working with the beadle to keep the church clean. This entailed sweeping, dusting and polishing, especially the brass umbrella hoops on their stand.

Twenty years on: The old boys of the 2nd Aberdeen Boys Brigade Company celebrate their 75th anniversary, 1972. Campbell is first left front row.

The young sergeant, Campbell leads the left flank, at the Battalion's camp at Crathes, 1949.

The Rutherford Church Youth fellowship, 1951: Campbell is 2nd male left back row. The Reverend Samuel Ballantyne dominates the front row.

All this might seem rather tying but we regarded it as a privileged position, since we had been entrusted to act as the public face of the church. Besides, we did get paid – 28 shillings a quarter, no less. And there were some laughs too. You got to look out for the regulars. There was one old boy who unfailingly came each Sunday, accompanied by his two sisters. He was a smoker and you'd see him puffing away at his pipe till the very last moment, whereupon he would pop the pipe into his pocket. One Sunday he did this too hastily, with the result that we were treated to the spectacle of him sailing into the church with a spiral of smoke curling up from the inside of his coat.

This was the era when the church still commanded a widespread following. I've still kept up my allegiance but sadly I now appear to be in a minority. Rutherford, once so large and so powerful a presence in the community, is now no more. Falling numbers and problems with the upkeep of the buildings meant that in the 1990s, a union with Rosemount Church in Caroline Place took place. The discovery of dry and wet rot in the Rosemount buildings made it necessary to return to the Rutherford buildings. So the congregations were shuttled backwards and forwards between the two buildings with the consequence that people began to drift away. At a later stage, with the retiral of the Reverend David Graham, the Presbytery of Aberdeen and the Church of Scotland decided that the congregation should be dissolved because of low numbers and the age profile of the congregation being too old. This despite the fact that the Church was actually financially solvent.

The tragedy of the Church is that it appears to have lost the youth of the country. It was so different in my young day. I couldn't wait to get into the Lifeboys, which I did at age seven, two years earlier than the normal entering age. Then, on to the Boys Brigade at 11. In 1951, while only 19 and still a student, I was appointed Captain of the company – the 2nd Aberdeen Company. At that point we had a complement of 54 boys. I was the youngest captain in the Aberdeen Battalion and possibly the youngest in Scotland and only the fourth captain of the company since it was formed in 1887.

Campbell Murray. b. 1931. Rutherford Church. interviewed 2016.

What would Jesus do?

I qualified as a teacher of Religious Education and, in 1976, I was appointed to Northfield Academy. When people heard of my subject, they often looked pityingly at me and remark, 'Teaching RE these days – that must be tough.' But I can honestly say that I enjoyed every minute of those years.

So much depends upon how you present your subject and on your ability to show respect for your pupils. This has to be a two-way process: my attitude was always, 'If you

A life-long commitment: A youthful Alistair McRobb, back first right, faces the morning at his Boys Brigade camp, Fettercairn, 1963.

> My attitude is quite simple and it is this: 'What would Jesus do?' Forget all the additions of theology; just ask yourself that one central question, 'What, in this situation, would Jesus do?'

want me to respect you then you have to grant me and my subject respect too'. Once that bond was established, I could be confident that I could offer them something worthwhile. I had a story to tell. I mean look at how much meaning is packed into those short parables in the Gospels. Stories like the Good Samaritan and the Prodigal Son are direct and simple, but they open up all sorts of thoughts about how we should conduct our lives with one another.

My own faith is a lifelong one. I have always felt at home in the Church, and that it has given me the opportunity to join with others in the pilgrimage we are all making through this earthly life. I would describe myself as a liberal, as someone who refuses to get stuck in dogma. It is so easy to pick up a bit of scripture and use that to browbeat people, to run from one reference to another to prove a point. My attitude is quite simple and it is this: 'What would Jesus do?' Forget all the additions of theology; just ask yourself that one central question, 'What, in this situation, would Jesus do?'

I realise that church attendances are falling all the time, but I believe that people still carry around within themselves a belief that there is a spiritual dimension to life and that they have a hunger for its fulfilment, one which in this secular age is not being met. The answer is not to try to cram people into a building one day a week, but to go to the essence of the matter. The reason that, despite all the findings of science and the distractions of our materialistic times, religion has endured is because it has the power to pierce through to the hearts and minds of human beings.

A number of factors have conspired to undermine the common faith of the people. Since the Thatcherism of the '80s, and all that emphasis on economic growth as the sole measure of social progress, we have become more and more involved in mere acquisition, in physical comforts, and have neglected the thirst of the soul. Then there is the abuse of religion by a whole range of bigoted hard-liners who have only given weight to the argument that religion can be a dangerous, repressive force.

It's difficult not to look around at all the rush and all the urban decay amidst the personal acquisition and not feel that ours has become a broken city. The prosperity of Aberdeen with the oil industry which has grown up since my childhood has, perhaps, aggravated the spiritual neglect here to a greater extent than elsewhere. We have put private wealth above social care.

Do people really feel more secure and at ease with each other as a result? People seem lost and have ceased to interact with each other in the way that I could enjoy in my boyhood in Northfield. I left school 53 years ago when the churches were thriving and stood at the heart of their communities. I can't accept that in that short time they have become no more than empty shells.

I think back to the 1950s and the days when cities would run a Kirk Week each year. I have a friend who has vivid memories of one that was held in Aberdeen and of the day when the Archbishop of Canterbury, Michael Ramsey, gave a keynote address in the Music Hall. The place was packed and with people mainly in their 40s. They all stood up to sing the *Old One Hundredth* and the power and sincerity that came from all those throats was such as to overwhelm the Archbishop, quite visibly. I think too of the giant figures who filled the pulpits in those days and of the inspiring messages they handed their congregations Sunday after Sunday. I think of John Archie Robertson at Mounthooly and the way in which he could take up a story from that week's newspapers and blow life into it through the conviction of his preaching.

You have to ask where has all that energy gone? I think it is still there waiting to be released again, that man cannot live by bread alone and that each passing day in modern Aberdeen only goes to prove that point.

Alistair McRobb. b. 1946. Northfield. Interviewed 2015.

SOME NOTABLE LIVES – 1

At the side of one of Aberdeen's greatest sons, Denis Law – and his wife, Di – with Lord Provost Crockett on the balcony of the Town House on the occasion of his being granted the Freedom of the City, November 2017.
[BY KIND PERMISSION OF NORMAN ADAMS – ABERDEEN CITY COUNCIL.]

Definitely classy:
Buff Hardie, Steve Robertson and, at the piano, George Donald.

'Aberdeen' to me meant Hilton and Woodside, which was regarded as a sort of sub-Hilton, though it did have a number of terrific chip shops.

Scotland the What?
Couthy but classy

When I was around three or four we moved from 217 Hilton Drive to 90 Hilton Road, which was a step up in the council house hierarchy. This was a well-positioned house, standing just at the corner of the Road and the Drive and directly across from Hilton Primary School which is where I went when I was five. I was very happy there and as it was a step across the road from us, my parents were spared the trouble of taking out the family 4x4 to embark upon the school run each morning.

It was a marvellous environment to grow up in. You had freedom to go off and play in the Stewart Park, along with all the other young lads in the district. The park had two large strips of grass, one of which – the 'Big Greenie' – was reserved for Grade cricket. Woodside played there for many years. When they came to practise we would hang around and watch and be ready to chase after any stray ball. We felt it was a privilege to be allowed to pick up a real cricket ball and return it to a real player. And then on the other strip we could pay our own games: football and cricket.

Life was quite local: 'Aberdeen' to me meant Hilton and Woodside, which was regarded as a sort of sub-Hilton, though it did have a number of terrific chip shops. In the summer time especially, we would walk down there and purchase a bag of chips to round off our evening at the Stewart Park. A lot of families would send out their kids to the chipper to buy in the family tea, but my mother tended to see that as a bit beneath us and I don't recall ever having a fish supper as our evening meal.

Apart from our own area, there would be rides on the bus down to Union Street and the city centre. On Sundays there might be an outing to Hazlehead Park, which meant two journeys: the bus down to town, then the number four tram up through the West End, culminating in the last half mile along the rattly track to the park itself. It was a trip that would take us past these wonderful granite houses along Queen's Road. We could only gaze and dream; every time we passed a particular one, my father would cry out: 'That's mine!' This was going to be the house he would purchase for us all when he won Strang's Pools.

In fact, buying any sort of house was just a dream: we lived in council property all through my childhood. My parents never did own a house or a car – in fact, they never owned very much at all, apart from the furniture and the clothes they stood up in. By our standards theirs was a hand to mouth existence, but in those days that was quite normal. The family economy was geared to the weekly wage which was, however, broken into by quarterly events. Every three months there would have to be the journey into Broad Street to the council offices to pay the rent, but the expenditure was offset to some extent by that other great regular money event, the paying out of the Co-op divi. This was a crucial element in the family budget: if ever you were going to get that new pair of shoes it could only be at divi time.

Our social and economic status was very much the norm for the time and the area. Almost everyone was in a similar position. In any case, we lived in a decent enough

council house. It contained a big bedroom, a little one, a small kitchenette, a sitting room and a bathroom. With only the four of us I could never feel I was missing out on accommodation.

As a child I was fearfully asthmatic and this apparently would cause my mother much distress; the spectacle of me heaving for breath would send her frantic. I still carry a puffer around with me, just in case, but it's been under control since those early childhood days. The family doctor in those days was a splendid man called Harry Mackay and I would have to be conveyed to his surgery every Tuesday evening, in Clifton Road, for a painful injection in my backside. This job of taking me was entrusted to my elder sister, Ella, and apparently I would go off quite happily with her, but then struggle and protest as we approached the surgery and it dawned on me what this evening walk was all about – I must have been a slow child! I would attempt to run past the house and have to be dragged in, where Mrs Mackay would be waiting with a bar of chocolate for me. This just about balanced out the ordeal of the injection, but it was a pretty tense equation for me.

My memories of my childhood are, asthma apart, very happy ones. There was sport and there was the wireless. My earliest taste for comedy comes from evenings round the wireless listening in to 'ITMA' and 'Bandwagon', with Arthur Askey and Richard Murdoch. 'Dick Barton Special Agent' at 6.45 each night was compulsory of course – I can still sound out that signature tune, 'the Devil's Gallop'. Then there was 'The

How they started. Buff as member of the Aberdeen Review Group, 1967. From left — George Donald, Quentin Cramb, Buff, Margaret Hardie, Steve Robertson, George Reid, Rose McBain, Douglas Kynoch, Anne Brand.

The Scotland the What? trio outside the scene of some of their greatest triumphs, His Majesty's Theatre where they played night after night to packed houses all through the 1980s.

On one glorious occasion we went down to see the relatives at Montrose and when I ran up to see who was driving the train at the station I found that it was my Uncle Jim.

McFlannels', a sort of Glasgow 'Archers', in which the characters were named after various materials – the McCottons, the more up market McSilks and so on.

The great treat was always the cinema. We would go down to the Astoria at Kittybrewster, which was a very smart and later addition to the Donald empire. The admission was fourpence for the front stalls, ninepence for the back. My parents would always take the ninepence option – three bob for the four of us and a not inconsiderable outlay.

Each Friday my mother and her sister – Auntie Nell – would go to the Gaumont (known at that time as The Picture House) down town and once I got to Robert Gordon's College, I might be invited to join them after school. This would mean high tea at the West End café which was run by Mitchell & Muil's. There you would get haddock and chips accompanied by a toast rack with room on it for six whole slices, followed by a cake. My mother and aunt would usually take just the one cake and carefully slice it in two, but if I was there and had some exam success to celebrate, I would be treated to a whole one to myself. Then at six p.m., on to the pictures. This timing was never changed even though it meant you would arrive right in the middle of the main feature. You'd watch it from that point, catching up with the story as you went. Then came the 'little' picture followed by trailers and the Gaumont British News – complete with cockerel and fanfare, 'telling the truth to the free people of the world'. The way the cockerel weather vane would end up displaying its letters as 'NEWS' I always found most impressive. So, you'd see the big films of the day in two separated half chunks, and back to front. Auntie Nell had an uncanny ability to spot the beginning of the scene where you had started watching the film three hours before and at that point would start getting her things together to make a prompt exit.

Among my relatives, she was a figure that loomed over my childhood. Her husband, my Uncle Jim, was an engine driver. My father worked for the LNER and this entitled him to 12 free passes for the family per year. We tended to use the tickets for a trip down to Edinburgh and a day at the zoo. But on one glorious occasion we went down to see the relatives at Montrose and when I ran up to see who was driving the train at the station I found that it was my Uncle Jim. When we pulled into Aberdeen I was able to go up to the cab and be let onto the footplate – a great memory.

My mother and Auntie Nell would visit each other on a Tuesday, turn and turn about. When the visit was to our own house in Hilton there would be some great flights of conversation to listen into. The house overlooked the bus stop where the staff of the school would gather after four o'clock to catch the number 18 back into the centre. The pair of them would sit there concocting the most amazing romantically speculative tales about the members of Hilton School staff waiting there – liaisons between male and female teachers and so on. One of the bus stop regulars was this mannish caricature of a PE instructress who would stand there in her tweeds and heavy brogues, the unwitting object of my mother's and my aunt's observations, including Aunt Nell's withering comment, 'Look at her – never a stocking on her and it's January!'

As for the theatre, I can only remember once being there as a child. This was 1938 when my sister took me to see the Student Show, which that year was entitled 'Beating Time'.

My father never did come to see me perform, either on the stage or at cricket. I can't be sure why this was so. One thing to bear in mind is that he was an old man by the time I was doing these things: he was 47 when I was born and my mother was 40. They'd got married in 1915, Ella was born in 1923 and I came along another eight years after that – so you could say they were regular in their habits. My mother did come to see me in the Student Show but father never. Nor at sport, yet he'd been a good cricketer himself and had played for Brechin. Maybe the root cause was a certain amount of fear: maybe he was too nervous that I would fail.

What you might call my cultural background was the Stewart Park, Mannofield and Pittodrie, rather than His Majesty's Theatre. But then none of us in Scotland the What? comes from a performing background. We no longer put on regular shows, but the other week we went down to St Andrews to do a one-off performance for our old friend Jimmy Spankie. He subjected us to a sort of Desert Island Discs, with our favourite performance items taking the place of the eight records. As we looked back over the journeys we had made to reach this point it emerged that each of the three of us was something of a rebel against his background. None of us had been given any parental encouragement in that direction; indeed, in George Donald's case there was the positive discouragement of being told, 'Git awa fae that piano an tak in the sticks fer yer mither!' He tells the story that when his mother took him to see Cornel Wilde playing the part of Chopin in the biopic and the scene came where the dark red drops of blood from his TB fall onto the white keys, George's mother turned to him and urgently whispered, 'See, George, that's what you get for playing the piano.'

The women behind the success: Left to right – Anne Logan (married to producer James Logan), Eva Robertson, Isabelle Donald, Margaret Hardie.

One of my choices was from the time when D'Oyly Carte came to Aberdeen to put on Gilbert & Sullivan. I wanted to go and see it – by now I was in my 20s – and I can remember my father saying to me, 'Fit div ye wint tae ging an' see that for – it's jist a lot o' folk singin!' An accurate if somewhat superficial summing up of the whole business, I suppose.

Although I'd always followed comedy on the radio I had no vision of myself as a performer in it. However, when I got to university I did take an interest in the Student Show simply as a 'good thing' to be involved in. By this time I had become friendly with a guy called Eddie Fraser who'd been Dux at Aberdeen Grammar School and was taking Classics along with me. As it happened, he was the show administrator. I had let my first year go by without attempting any active interest and when the second year came I still had no intention of getting involved. At the start of the Easter holidays, I went down to the Union to meet up with Eddie for a cup of coffee. While we were there this chap, George Sinclair, came over to our table and started to talk with Eddie on Student Show business. At that time George was the leading power behind the scenes. He later became Head at Powis Academy. Anyway, they were talking away about the Show, with me politely sipping my coffee, when George suddenly turned to me and barked out, 'You in the Student show? No? Well, come to the rehearsals for the Men's Chorus tonight. It's good fun.'

Noo far wid Auchterturra be?' Buff in the heart of deepest Aberdeenshire.

That little meeting changed my life. I went along and did, indeed, find it good fun. There were a dozen of us in that chorus; our role was to sing along as backing and to do a few elementary dance steps. I enjoyed it: quite apart from the chance to meet a few girls, the Student Show was a most ecumenical event to which the whole spread of the student body contributed. I could meet people like Medics and Engineers that I would normally never have been aware of.

I was also given one small part. This was of the Torry cyclist who cycled out to the country where he encountered a farmer. I had this line, 'Hiv ye ony eggs, mister?', to which he replied, 'Git awa oot o my neeps ye toons dirt!'- to which I replied, 'We're nae touchin yer neeps, mister. Div ye hiv ony eggs?' On the first night of the show I dug up an authentic Aberdeen accent from somewhere that must have been imprinted deep in my semi-consciousness and it proved to be something of a showstopper. Well, the sound of that laughter came at me from the audience as a drug; I just wanted more and more of it.

For my third year, 1952, Eddie Fraser was again administrator and I was keen to be involved. I found myself invited to a meeting as early as October, 'for those interested in that year's Show'. Exactly what it was to be about was not clearly explained, but when I turned up I found myself one of a small group who would be expected to write the script. I set to and supplied quite a lot of material, writing in parts with myself in mind, of course. Later in the year, Eddie Fraser was asked to supply a few lines about me for Gaudie, which was running a column of thumbnail sketches of various student notables. This is what he told the Gaudie readers: 'For this year's performance Buff Hardie wrote a number of parts with himself in mind but, fortunately, competent casting saved the Show!'

So that's where it all really started. To me, the natural thing to do was to use local characters and local accents. I can't say I was really trying to develop anything of substance; my main aim was to work in as many funny lines as I could and I found the local settings and voices useful. In my final year, with the Honours exams looming, I couldn't take a stage part, but I did supply material. That was the year when I had seen D'Oyly Carte at HMT and had taken something of a shine to Gilbert & Sullivan. This was also Reg Barret-Ayres's first year of involvement with the show and we got together on a sketch called 'Impatience'. It was a kind of cross between 'South Pacific' and the 'Mikado', with American soldiers and Japanese maidens. Reg was a wonderfully gifted musician and my role was to supply the lyrics. I found the discipline of hammering out lyrics in an Aberdeen accent was not so unlike the exercises in composing Latin verse that was a feature of my Classics course. I enjoyed the mental exercise and found the challenge of sticking to tight structures and regular metre an excellent writing discipline.

During the show itself, I would slip in and stand at the back to see how things were going. Towards the end of the week, Jimmy Donald, the theatre's owner, came up to me. He must have spotted me hovering about; I honestly thought he was about to accost me for not having a proper ticket, but instead he came up to me and made the comment, 'A very good Show, this year.' I was just in the middle of, 'Oh thank you, Mr Donald!', when he continued, 'Yes, a very good Show. It ends at ten to ten, in good time for the folk to catch the Stonehaven bus.' So that, and not any superbly witty lyrics to be heard on stage, was his measure of quality.

When I graduated I won a scholarship to Sidney Sussex, Cambridge, where I read Law for a couple of years. When I got back to Aberdeen I felt it was about time that I got into a job that would bring in some money. My parents were never well off and here I was, having spent eight years since leaving school, six at study and two in the army. I also felt that it had to be somewhere in the area as my parents were ageing and my sister by now had emigrated to Canada.

I joined the Health Service. I know it sounds a bit po-faced, but I wanted a career where I could feel I was putting something back into the Commonweal. All this study had left me with no great practical skills – being steeped in Latin didn't exactly qualify me to fly an aeroplane or operate on anyone, so I embarked on my career as an administrator in the National Health Service, for which I had a genuine and idealistic admiration.

Handing on the torch: to the next generation. Buff with his son, John Hardie, of the highly successful *Flying Pigs*.

I know it sounds a bit po-faced, but I wanted a career where I could feel I was putting something back into the Commonweal.

Steve turned
to me and
said, 'Look,
do you fancy
getting
something
together for
this year's
Edinburgh
Festival
Fringe?'

There, I was inspired by two people above all others. First there was May Baird, the wife of the great Sir Dugald Baird and a considerable figure in her own right. She was Chair of the North Eastern Regional Hospital Board for more than 20 years. After my first meeting, she came up to me and said, 'I'm so glad to meet you, Mr Hardie. You have the kind of talent the Health Service is looking for'. After that my admiration for her judgement and decisiveness knew no bounds. Actually, she was a real giant; it was she who should have been Britain's first woman Prime Minister. She had all of Thatcher's qualities, plus charm and a sense of humour.

The other inspirer was Denys Beddard who was the Hospital Board's Chief Administrative Medical Officer in the early '60s. He had come up from England and had something of the looks and charisma of John F. Kennedy. He later went to Northern Ireland as Chief Medical Officer just as the Troubles were about to break out. I remember Lady Baird remarking, 'With Dr Beddard there it'll be all right. He'll soon sort them all out'. But the situation proved to be beyond even his powers – and Lady Baird had made one of her very rare misjudgements.

That was the day job. After graduating I became part of a small group, mostly of ex-Student Show types, called the *Aberdeen Revue Group*. That's where I met my wife, Margaret. Our producer was a super guy called James Logan and he had spotted this superb comic talent among a later crop of Student Show performers and invited her to join our Revue Group. I know I could be accused of bias, but I really do think that Margaret has been to the female members of the show what Steve Robertson and George Reid have been for the men – simply the best ever. I'm not sure how we actually became romantically entwined: she and I would be there among the others for coffee after the rehearsals and it just seemed to happen.

We also had Derek Brechin, who was a terrific singer and the best Frank Sinatra impersonator you could ever wish to see – better than the original in fact! The Revue Group flourished for nearly 10 years, then we decided that January 1967 at the Arts Centre should be our last ever show, after which we should go our separate ways and get on with our careers. It proved to be a very happy experience – it must have been because nine months later our first child, Katharine, was born.

That's the way it was going to be: work and family life, but then two or three years later Steve and I were invited to write that year's Student Show, *Running Riot*. We enjoyed being back at it again and at the end of show party at Hazlehead, Steve and I found ourselves popping outside for a pee. As we were lining it up, Steve turned to me and said, 'Look, do you fancy getting something together for this year's Edinburgh Festival Fringe?' By this time Steve was an Aberdeen solicitor and he had developed an Edinburgh contact who would look out a venue for us. In those days the Fringe was still a smallish intimate thing and not the monster it has now become, so I felt that it would be worth a go.

His contact did indeed find a venue for us, a small church hall, and we put together a late night hour-long revue, which we decided to call Scotland the What? Our rubric went, 'Three men; two chairs; one piano – and the promise that you won't leave without laughing'. We were very lucky in what happened next. There was this highly perceptive guy, Neville Garden, who later became a prominent radio man but was then acting as Festival critic for the *Daily Express*. The night he came to do us, he had just emerged from four hours of Wagner at the Usher Hall and was ready to laugh at anything – which he did.

When the crit appeared in the *Express* it proclaimed that he had just seen 'the funniest show in the whole Festival'. We also got a positive review in the *Scotsman* and from that point the show just took off. We'd been prepared to regard our visit to the Festival as a venture and were quite expecting to lose money, but found ourselves emerging with a bit

of a profit. So we decided to get up another show and go down the following year. Jimmy Donald junior, now in charge of HMT, saw both the shows and after the second one approached us with the offer: 'Put both the shows together, turn it into a two-hour show and I'll give you the theatre for a couple of nights. I'll bear the cost of the advertising; any profit we'll split down the middle'. Well, you don't get an offer like that too often in show business so, once more, we decided to give it a go.

On the two nights, a Friday and a Saturday, the Aberdeen folk came flocking in, to such effect that it was decided to put

Receiving their MBEs, 1995.

on a third show, which had to be on the Sunday. This was just about unprecedented for HMT – after all, Sunday meant time-and-a-half in pay to the staff. But there was still enough profit to make the show a success, enough for Jimmy Donald to tell us, 'Put on another show and I'll give you a week.' We were still busy at our day jobs, so it took us two years to get the material together. In the meantime, on the odd weekend, we were taking the show round venues like the Adam Smith in Kirkcaldy and the Macrobert at Stirling. And as the years passed, by dint of synchronising some of our holidays we were able to accept selected invitations to appear at some of Scotland's major theatres.

Something which had begun life as a hobby was now showing signs of developing into a possible second career. Time passed. The others were keener to make the break and go full-time than Margaret and I were. Our children were at a certain stage and I had a decent job with a good pension at the end of it.

In the end, we decided to take the plunge. I was prompted to some extent by the events of the Winter of Discontent which was marked by strikes and industrial action all through the public services. Grampian's health service, where the unions were very active, suffered more than anywhere else in Scotland and I became somewhat jaundiced. I began

We had to be utterly disciplined: if we found a new sketch was not bringing in the laughs then we would jettison it.

to feel it was time to move on. We were also advised by Jimmy Donald, who told us that, if we could keep up the flow of original material, he reckoned we could look to get another good six to eight years out of it all. I was now 53 and that would take me up to more or less retirement age. In the event we went on for another 12, ending in 1995.

I do realise how fortunate I have been in the way that things have turned out. I enjoyed a satisfying career in public service and just when I was beginning to feel the strain there I was able to convert what had been a hobby into what I did for a living for the final 12 years of my working life. And I was able to do this with people I've always liked and enjoyed being with. To this day we remain good friends. I've been in show business, but never really felt myself to be in danger of being swallowed up by it. Indeed most of the people I have met there have been very agreeable; I suppose one of our saving graces was that we have never been perceived to be a threat to anyone; we've always been responsible for our own material, which has never trespassed on to anyone else's territory. I've also felt our performance standards have risen. I've been very fortunate to have worked with two such richly gifted performers. Look at George: has there ever been anyone else who had his facility for singing sophisticated and complicated lyrics at the piano, accompanied only by himself? Flanders & Swann have been an influence on us and I admired them greatly, but there were two of them doing what George does by himself.

We've been fortunate too that the Aberdeen audiences have taken us to themselves and have decided to give us such a warm reception at HMT. But we've taken care to prepare carefully and not to overstretch our material. The nature of our show stayed incremental so that we could simply slot items in and out. We kept to the two-year cycle, too. We put on a new show for Aberdeen each alternate year and in the interim we could take the show on the road, to Edinburgh, Glasgow, Inverness, Stirling, Kirkcaldy. During the time on the road we could try out new material and find out whether it worked or not. We had to be utterly disciplined in this: however much time or love we had lavished on a new sketch, if we found it wasn't bringing in the laughs then we would jettison it. In this way by the time we returned to HMT we had our new show ready, tried and tested on the road.

Is the North-east a particularly rich area for comedy? Well, humour of our type, rooted as it is in a strong and distinctive locality, is part of a pattern you can find all over. I think we've managed to strike the balance between what is local and what is universal – which can, of course, be much the same thing, by which I mean a universal theme exemplified locally. One critic called us 'Couthy but classy' and I like that. That was always James Logan's dictum to us: 'Keep it classy!' The decision to wear dinner jackets came about much by chance but it has contributed to the balance of our style. It was when we first appeared at the Fringe and had to decide what to wear. The fashion then on the Fringe was baggy jumpers, but we didn't see ours as a baggy jumper act. As it happened, for our professional jobs, we had all acquired dinner jackets so we decided to go for that.

I can't see that the North-east will ever run dry as a well for humour. So much of what you can extract from the area is universal, anyway: people and types exhibiting human nature in a recognisable setting. We once put on a cabaret for a conference of psychologists at the University who came from all over. I did my Councillor Swick bit and afterwards this guy came up to me and said, in a Lancashire voice: "I know that Swick – only back home he goes under the name of Councillor Entwhistlle from Oldham.'

But actually, I don't like to analyse too much in case it disturbs the whole thing…

Buff Hardie. b. 1931. *Scotland the What?*. Interviewed 2006.

Sadly, Buff's three Scotland the What? partners, Steve Robertson, George Donald and producer James Logan, are no longer alive, but their performances can still be enjoyed through a number of books, discs and videos.

Problems? What problems?

I was born in Rosyth, in 1922. My father was a doctor there. He'd been a medical missionary in Iceland. At that time he'd just returned from there and was very short of cash and with four sons to support. Then he died suddenly at the age of 45. This left my mother with her four sons and no income of any kind. Some of my childhood was spent in what I now realise was poverty. But I didn't know this at the time. We lived in a council house and somehow my mother managed to look after us all.

You could say I am the product of a one-parent family. My older brother, Stanley, who later became Professor of Education at Glasgow, acted as a substitute father to me. He's 10 years older. So I grew up without any of the feeling of deprivation that is commonly attached to the image of the one-parent household.

Our lifestyle, moreover, was very similar to what my peers at school appeared to be experiencing. So, I wasn't really aware of 'going without'. In the '30s, in any case, so many people were in that position, in that period of Depression, when there was so much unemployment.

I got my one shilling a week pocket money and that seemed to be sufficient. It didn't occur to me that there could be any other way of growing up. Nor did the school make me feel any sense of deprivation either. Its ethos, its curriculum and the attitude of its teachers were such as to leave me quite content with the world I was living in. The school never made me feel that anything about the outside world should be changed. It was simply assumed we would all just follow our parents into the kind of position they held. That is a large disappointment to me in the education system as I experienced it in the '30s – it was a training in contentment, in acceptance.

In some ways, however, I was a bit different because I was going to go on to the university. My father's background and the example of Stanley pointed me in that direction. But I could only go there if I won sufficient bursaries to pay the way. I did that.

Professor John Nisbet, 1922–2012.

> I did get third place in the entrance bursary competition at Edinburgh University. At that time I seriously thought of trying my luck as a golf professional.

My school was Dunfermline High, a six-year Secondary school, but only four of us in my year went on to university. The bursaries were generous in enabling us to get through the university without having to draw upon the family resources too heavily. And this was at a time when the expenses of university were quite modest: the fees came to no more than £25 a year of which the Carnegie Trust would meet £15. We all either lived in digs or travelled in each day.

It was only when I reached 19 that I began to be aware of the wide range of social differences that existed and that I could start to challenge the role and the status that God had apparently given me. The notion that education could work in entirely the contrary way, that it could be the means of opening up new opportunities, didn't appear to be widespread then. The assumption was that the educational system was there to train you for your position in the social structure as it then was.

Many of the aspects of the 1930s system seemed to be designed with that end in view: the selection by examination at 11/12; the division of schools into 'Junior' and 'Senior' Secondarys could, at bottom, be regarded as ways of reinforcing the received class differences, of supporting things as they were and must continue to be. Not till I got to university did I realise that education could be the means of challenging rather than of reinforcing these things.

Secondary school was so boring. It all came down to a matter of memorising passages of notes and from material in books with which to pass exams, culminating in the Highers. We would spend period after period working away at old exam papers. I shouldn't grumble as I did get third place in the entrance bursary competition at Edinburgh University. But at that time I seriously thought of giving the whole thing up, of trying my luck as a golf professional. It was Stanley who, in 1940, persuaded me to give university a chance. I went to Edinburgh with the intention of giving it one term only, in order to see what it was like.

After two months or so I realised that the university was the place where I would be content to spend the rest of my working life. It was so completely different from the secondary school: it appeared to contain none of the social conditioning and the repressive teaching I had been accustomed to.

It seems dreadful to me now that the school system should have been so limiting and so lacking in stimulus or innovation. This is perhaps one of the reasons why, after my war service, I decided I would go into teaching myself and try to change things. I quickly came to realise that from the position of the classroom teacher it would be impossible to achieve any such ambition, that I was trapped within the system. So I went on to take a postgraduate degree in Education. I did well at it. When I came out with that degree in 1949 I now felt I had the necessary background and position with which to change the world and reform its educational system!

It all seems quite arrogant now, but then young people tend to be arrogant. And in 1949 everything seemed to be opening up. There was so much to be done after the war; there was no shortage of jobs and of prospects. When I graduated I had four good jobs

on offer before me, one of which was as an Assistant Lecturer at Aberdeen University. This was the poorest paid of the four, but it was the one I decided on.

My plan was to take a Ph.D. in three years and thus to arrive at a position from which I could really reform the system. So I came here to Aberdeen University in 1949. After I'd been there scarcely a month I realised that this was the life I was content to lead for good. I didn't want power, money or position; what I really was happy to do was to lead an academic life. I settled for the life and have now been here for some 54 years! I've never had any particular wish to move. Yet I had not forgotten my desire as a young man starting out to win the power and the position to change a system which I had found to be so inadequate and limiting. I think that one of the reasons I've stayed on in the university has been the realisation that as an academic I could have more influence.

In the '50s and the '60s, the academic side of education – what we would now call 'educational research'– was regarded with contempt by most people involved in education and there was little funding for it. Today, educational research is an integral part of the decision making process; there's a recognition that planning and evaluation are both essential and that they require the disciplines of research.

This success dates back to the '60s when a series of important educational reports began to appear – Newsom, Robbins, Plowden – all of which carried their investigations with which to back up their recommendations. In the '70s, research became regarded as essential. I now found that I was in a position of some power and influence. I held several important posts – I was chairman of the Educational Research Board and of several of the curriculum committees in the Scottish Office.

I accepted that a position carries with it certain moral imperatives. My parents were members of the Brethren and I was raised according to a very strict Christian upbringing. The moral side of things has always been present for me.

John at Upperton, the last occupied cottage in a clachan, Glenbuchat 2002. For many years John maintained a holiday cottage in the area and took a great interest in its history and sociology.

Schoolboy

Why the '60s should be such a turning point in social thinking can be answered in half a dozen ways. There is change and then there is the reaction against that change. In the '80s Thatcherism represented a massive reaction against what had been happening in the '60s, against what we saw as the age of liberation and they, as the decline in standards.

But whatever the reaction, later the influence of the '60s could never be completely put aside. In Aberdeen we began to look at the wastage of talent that was created by the early leaving from their school education of a whole generation of capable people. When I look back on my career, the thing I am most proud of is the introduction of the Access courses which enabled those who had left school at 14/15 and without academic qualifications to take courses that would offer them the opportunity to enter the university. Through the Access scheme a whole range of people, who beforehand would have been denied any chance of Higher Education, were able to take degrees and often very good ones.

I think that things now are a lot better than they ever were. You hear complaints by politicians that standards have dropped – this is complete nonsense. Standards in every respect are far higher than they were in my own childhood. Hardly any of my contemporaries went to university – only 2% of the age group did so, whereas now the figure is 50% who go on into Higher Education. No matter how much you may protest that 'higher education ' no longer means the same, the fact remains that

School teacher

nowadays more and more people are able to reach levels which formerly would have been the preserve of a tiny elite minority.

I also think that the general standards of literacy and numeracy have risen. I think there have been great improvements in educational levels and in opportunity, just as there have been in living standards over the last half century.

I get annoyed when people complain that standards have fallen. I know that whenever we were at a dinner party or some other social gathering and someone, in recognition of my position, would say, 'What do you think can be done about the problems in education?', I would reply, 'What problems? Things are so much better nowadays in education – what problems?' But then my wife would kick me under the table; I then got into the habit of simply smiling and saying, 'So, that's what you think, is it? How interesting.'

At his professorial desk

John Nisbet, b. 1922. University of Aberdeen. Interviewed 2003.

From Big Hoose to Toon Hoose

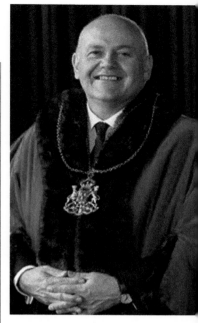

Barney Crockett,
Lord Provost

I was James Crockett originally, but I had the nickname Barney from Primary School and it's carried right through. I was born in Aberdeen in 1953 at Foresterhill. I grew up in what was at that time, Aberdeen's biggest tenement at 27 Miller Street in the harbour area, known at the time as the 'Big Hoose'. It was a giant, ancient warren of a building which was hundreds of years old.

It was a very crowded area at the corner of Baltic Street, an area at that time that was known as Fittie; now folk speaking about Fittie mean what we used to call Aul' Fittie, a tiny subsection of Fittie. Fittie then had thousands of people and now there's virtually nobody living there as the huge warren of tenements in and around Commerce Street, Clarence Street, Church Street, Baltic Street, Cotton Street have all gone.

I first went to York Street Nursery, at the age of two. We had a very progressive City Council at that time and there was a full-day nursery provided for the poorest parts of the city, including Fittie. I think it probably had originally been done for the workforce to make sure that the women could get to work during World War 2.

It was a terrific experience. There were two rooms, each of which had about 100 children under the care of a very small handful of staff. It was very drilled by modern standards; we had a compulsory hour's sleep every day. They used to take out 200 camp beds and have 200 children sleeping – no doubt based on health theories at the time. It was quite a luxurious situation for the kind of children I'm speaking about and with lots of quite expensive toys too.

The Big Hoose belonged to the company that my father worked for – SAI Chemical Works – so everybody in the building had some link to SAI [Scottish Agricultural Industries]. Most of Baltic Street also belonged to SAI, so the members of the workforce were living a few metres from their work. Our back green faced onto the Chemical Works and you had this incredible industrial atmosphere; it was opposite the mountains of coal for the Gas Works, which was next door.

I went very briefly to St. Clement Street School before it closed and then went to Hanover Street which was, at that time, quite certainly the most deprived school in Aberdeen. Back then, Aberdeen was a very different place. Nearly everybody attending Hanover Street lived in what would be seen nowadays as primitive conditions in very crowded tenements with outside toilets. Within the area also was Aberdeen's worst housing at Castlehill Barracks which was a world of its own.

People nowadays can hardly conceive what it was like. We were compulsorily washed every week. We were marched to the 'Aberdeen Corporation Sprays' and we were scrubbed. The Spray Baths were just next to the school and people used to go at night; they would pay to go and have a shower. It had fairly primitive, gigantic shower heads; you would be completely immersed in boiling hot water in the shower.

We had weekly roll calls because we did have homeless children, so we'd all to stand up and say our addresses. We had three children like that; one would have given her address as the night shelter in Constitution Street and two would say 'No fixed abode'.

I grew up in what was at that time, Aberdeen's biggest tenement at 27 Miller Street in the harbour area, known at the time as the 'Big Hoose'.

A young Lord Provost Crockett: An apprehensive young Barney eying up the family pet

Seated at his first committee table, aged 18 months

Toddling through his Big Hoose, aged 2

We were made very aware that the Head Teacher was a strict disciplinarian in the Scottish mould, but he was very caring in trying to encourage attainment from kids who would have been from very rough environments. He used to take aside the most potentially able kids and give them special lessons.

By modern standards, the playground was rough and ready; you wouldn't be allowed to have playgrounds that were so violent these days. People now have a rosy view – I think the level of violence was very high, but it wasn't seen as an unacceptable thing.

I moved from there, as did thousands of others, to the peripheral housing estates and in my case it was to North Balnagask Road, Torry; new flats and big excitement when I was 10 years old. I went to Victoria Road Primary School in an area which was much less deprived than Hanover Street.

The content of my schooling was also very drilled. There were about 33 children in the class at Hanover Street. There was a lot of deprivation and outside the school it would be quite rough with a lot of violence. In the classroom there was a lot of rote learning of tables. We used to do bills, a very antediluvian way of working out folks' messages. We had the *Radiant Readers* reading books.

We had no sports of any kind at Hanover Street. There was no playing field nearby and we just had gym exercises. Victoria Road was different; we had a gym and we did eventually get a little bit of football. I played in the Victoria Road football team; they had a school kit but, comically, it was absolutely ancient, with huge baggy trousers and washed out woollen football shirts.

At Hanover Street, nearly all the kids were from severely disadvantaged backgrounds whereas at Victoria Road School there was a mixture. There were kids from the traditional, well-known trawling owner family names who had grander houses on Victoria Road. The tie of living in a flat that belonged to my father's work probably had been a disincentive to moving. It was very convenient and the rent was notional. My father wasn't overwhelmingly enthusiastic to move because he had a very dense social network there; he lived among the folk he worked with and then met in the bars. There used to be a gigantic Victorian bar called the Eastern Star where the roundabout is now for the Beach Boulevard and that was a big attraction.

Probably too, there was a division between the men and the women as well. The women would aspire to the council housing and the men would be keener to live amongst the folk they worked and socialised with. The women were maybe more aspirational for the children as well.

On moving to Torry, I remember a feeling of apprehension as it was new. I was aware of feeling that the council houses seemed so grand to me and I thought the people used to them would be so superior to me that I would stand out like a sore thumb; and folk now will fail to understand that Torry was seen to be infinitely superior, in terms of social grandeur, to the area we'd left. The houses we moved to were brand new and everybody around was new.

I remember, for example, playing football for Victoria Road against Hanover Street and

being reminded that the Hanover Street kids were notably poorer than the Victoria Road ones. One of the friends I'd had in Hanover Street remembered me when we played football and we got chatting. He would have been fairly typical of the poorest 20% of the kids at Hanover Street who were reliant on charity. He had tackety boots of the kind you used to get from what's the ancestor of VSA [Voluntary Services Aberdeen] on the Castlegate; there used to be a place on the Castlegate that gave out boots and wellingtons and gym shoes to poor kids. The boots had two holes in them so everybody would know they were parish boots. The wellingtons were brown so everybody would know you'd got handout wellies.

But there was definitely no limit to the expectations in either Hanover Street or Victoria Road Schools; there was an enthusiasm for helping people to get on. The clouding issue in Victoria Road was the turbulence of staff because it was a difficult environment for the teachers. The Head there was the archetypal Scottish Primary head teacher from the Isles, a disciplinarian but very keen to help.

I was there for a couple of years and then it was the era of the 11-plus, which I failed initially, and was originally awarded an intermediate place to do a certificate course at Torry Secondary School, as it then was. But Aberdeen had an appeals system which was mainly used to get kids from poorer areas into the Senior Secondary school at Aberdeen Academy. From memory, only one child out of the class passed first time round to go to Senior Secondary, but another four of us got through on appeal to go to Aberdeen

Aberdeen City Council, 2012: Barney is front row next to, then, Lord Provost George Adam.

In 1970s flares at the wedding of fellow Torry loon David Kennedy, here with friends Alan Dawson and Dennis Mitchell.

Graduation Day 1975 with father Jim.

Academy. It was very much for the kids from the big housing estates and remaining tenements of Aberdeen. It was seen as a slightly lower status Senior Secondary school compared to the Grammar School and the Girls' High School.

I was just beginning to become aware at that stage that my going to the Academy was a big source of pride for my parents. That was particularly the case later when you decided whether to leave school or stay on. My father made it clear that while I could go to SAI to work and I would have a privileged potential there, he wanted me to continue at school and he took enormous pride, as a labourer, that his son was going to do better than he had.

There were some teachers who believed that Aberdeen Academy was a social experiment gone wrong, that it was ridiculous to take kids from the poorer areas that could 'never amount to anything'. I'm not saying that was the dominant view, but it was there. The Maths teacher did actually say on day one, 'Don't tell me which of you is from Torry. Give me two weeks and I'll tell you'. He implied he would know by our bad behaviour and all round slovenliness and ignorance.

On the other hand, we had totally inspirational teachers. There was a teacher called Mr Dalziel who had helped to develop radar – a brilliant man who was driven by being an evangelical Christian. I do remember that, like many people at that time, I was in S4 and anti-establishment with great long hair, but I loved his teaching and did really well when the exams came.

So I stayed on after fourth year. I did reasonably well and got university entry – again a huge matter of pride to my father. I went to Aberdeen University to study History. As regards my aspirations at the time, I think it's a classic Scottish thing, perhaps, but from very early on the model of success to me was to be a teacher. You thought that was the optimal way to please your parents and also to contribute to giving people the opportunities you had had. Teachers were the professional role model you had been exposed to over the years and that is maybe particularly underscored in the case of Aberdeen Academy pupils.

Teacher training was interesting; there was huge turmoil because it was the era of gigantic cuts in teacher recruitment, so there was very little chance of a job at the end of it. When I left teaching college there was nobody getting a job so I went and did various things and it is really comical how I got into teaching. I was working offshore as a dishwasher and all sorts of things. One time, when I came back onshore – because I'd done teaching practice there at Summerhill Academy (which was also in a state of turmoil) asked if I would do some supply teaching.

So I was working offshore for two weeks, then doing some work in Summerhill Academy for two weeks. I didn't think to say that, as a protest, I hadn't registered with the GTC [General Teaching Council]. I mean if they refused to give me a job then I refused to pay the 40 quid, or whatever. So this became a crisis; they couldn't pay someone because when it came to payment they asked 'What's your GTC number?' and I said 'I haven't got one'.

With Lead Curator
Shona Elliot at the
Aberdeen Art Gallery
Hub, examining a work
by the celebrated
Aberdeen artist,
Alberto Morrocco.
[BY KIND PERMISSION OF
NORMAN ADAMS –
ABERDEEN CITY COUNCIL.]

Anyway, I went along, just before going offshore as a steward, in my steward's uniform, to kick up a row about not getting my pay and the Assistant Director of Education said he had to leave because he was due to be interviewing for teacher posts. I asked 'What do you mean, you're interviewing for teacher posts?' We were in Woodhill House and it was in Summerhill Academy he was due to be interviewing. So he said, 'If you turn up to the interview, you'll be interviewed.' So next thing, I'm running up the Lang Stracht in my steward's uniform and I get there just in time to be interviewed as a teacher.

I got offered a job in Speyside High School. This was a newish school that was being set up with a lot of young teachers. I taught History mainly, with a bit of Modern Studies. I had a great time there but, again, because of the nature of the era, there were very few promoted posts. After four years, I saw a job in Shetland. I applied and went to Mid-Yell Junior High School. One of the things I was interested in at that time was how communities worked with schools; most people thought it was crazy to go to a remote island but, for me, virtually no place in the world worked better than Yell at that particular time.

I was there for four years and then I applied for a head teaching post in Orkney. I became Head Teacher in North Walls Junior Secondary School in Hoy; similar-ish, but not quite the same because the social side in Orkney is very different. It was mainly incomers, people who didn't come from Orkney, and it was a very, very deprived school. A lot of people had come because there was cheap property. I got on very well there too.

Then I moved from there to be Head Teacher of Farr High School in Sutherland.

I remember a progressive guy at a meeting of head teachers asking me what I was going on to do. This chap said 'Racial equality... in Grampian? Won't that be like being the snake catcher of Ireland?'

That was again very remote and again a very high attaining area.

I left teaching to come back to Aberdeen – and that was the end of my teaching career after 14 years. I moved to become the Director of Grampian Racial Equality Council. I had a particular interest in racial equality and, in particular, in migration and I thought that there was going to be a huge change coming in Aberdeen, and that it would be interesting to be involved in that. But I was out by a decade or so. I remember a very progressive guy at a meeting of head teachers in Highland asking me what I was going on to do. This chap said 'Racial equality... in Grampian? Won't that be like being the snake catcher of Ireland?'

Racial Equality was in the voluntary sector, but it was linked to the local authorities. It was mainly funded by the Home Office. During the time I was at Grampian Racial Equality Council, one of several great things about that job was that you got a bit of involvement in everything.

You got a lot of access to different cultures. I used to train police officers across the Highlands and lots of similar things. I was also involved in a lot of voluntary sector things including Langstane Housing, housing the homeless. There was a one-day-a-week post came up as Housing Ombudsman for Scotland, so I got that post for a while, covering the voluntary sector housing associations for the whole of Scotland.

When I was ombudsman, I couldn't be involved in politics. But afterwards I could and there was a by-election came up in Aberdeen – a very controversial one – and Labour had some difficulty in thinking who the best candidate would be and I said I would be willing to do it. So I was the sacrificial lamb. But after that, I kept going and fell into the Council at a later stage. If I'd known what it was like, I'd have said 'That doesn't suit me'. Having been on Grampian Racial Equality Council, I was very much trying to smooth things over and promote good relations and being non-confrontational. So if I'd known how the Council is really, I'd have thought that I'd never fit in there – but, strangely enough, I have.

Many things are better – but you can see why folk are sometimes ambivalent. A lot of this is based on not realising what things were really like. I do a lot on Facebook on nostalgia and local history and people say we should never have knocked this or that building down, or whatever. And while it may have some truth, at the time nobody thought that you wanted to keep those buildings because conditions were such that nobody would dream of living there nowadays. For example, I had a very wealthy businessman come up to me when I'd been doing a talk on the history of the cinemas and had mentioned the Grandie [Grand Central]. He had lived near there and he said, 'My parents couldn't get a council house and as my father was a plumber, he put in a sink in the cellar. So I was largely brought up in a cellar, totally underground with no window and just a sink. And that's how we lived'.

So yes, it has all changed and in an amazingly short time when you look back. I remember the day the Queen Mother opened the Beach Boulevard. That was a big event and we all thought the modern world has come. We didn't even get out of the classroom, although she was just outside the window, but lots of other kids had been marched out from their primary schools to wave flags. The *Evening Express* had an old photograph of them a wee while back and there are these kids waving a Union Jack outside a shop at the corner of East North Street and Wales Street and the wall of the shop is painted with an advertisement for 'The Best South African Wines'. I roared with laughter at the thought of most modern people seeing that, who may think they never knew that wines were popular in Aberdeen in the late 1950s, but this was absolutely deadly rot-gut fortified wines for down-and-outs that would kill you. But people looking at it now would think, 'A wine shop? That's very good for Aberdeen,' and wouldn't know it was just round the corner from the Model Lodging House.

Barney Crockett. b. 1953. Fittie, Torry and Town Council. Interviewed 2016.

Barney Crockett was formerly Leader of Aberdeen City Council and in 2017 became the City's Lord Provost.

A complete transformation

I was born in Blackburn, West Lothian, a small mining village. I was the youngest of three kids. My father was a miner and my mother a nurse. Mine was a very poor, deprived upbringing. There were no carpets on the floor and, often enough, lunch was a jam piece – no butter, just the jam; and dinner could be simply two jam pieces. My father was an alcoholic and quite abusive. That sort of harsh behaviour among the men of Blackburn was not untypical. The dangers, hardness and sheer filth of life down the mines led to this physical brutality as it did to the need to escape through the drink. He wasn't an evil man, rather a victim of his circumstances.

My father was a tyrant and as a boy I became a poor, timid creature, totally lacking in confidence and distrustful of adults. Anyone in authority over me freaked me out.

I left school at 15 and it was assumed that, like most lads in Blackburn at that time, I was destined for the pit. But I had seen what it had done to my father – the dangers, the hardships, the dirt. So no, not for me!

I enrolled at Bathgate Technical College into an engineering course, took a particular interest in electronics, passed and landed a job at Ferranti's. I started as a lowly craft apprentice – and loved it. I did well and ended up with the prize as the Apprentice of the Year.

So there I was, at 17, embarking on a worthwhile career and growing in confidence. Unfortunately, along with the electronics, I was also learning something else: how to drink. The seeds had been laid when I was 10 and sitting on my grandfather's knee. He was drinking from a bottle of beer. 'Do you want a drop?' I ended up taking a whole bottle and was promptly ill, passing out and peeing myself. Everyone appeared to treat this as a huge joke; I had become inducted into the local culture of alcohol.

After my year of initial training I had a bit of money in my pocket and could embark

Howard at his place of work: Aberdeen Harbour, 2013.

SEAFARERS' PORT INFORMATION LEAFLET

ABERDEEN WELCOMES ALL SEAFARERS

ABERDEEN SEAFARERS' CENTRE

184-192 Market Street, Aberdeen, AB11 5PQ
Tel: 01224 590 036
(answering machine outside opening hours)
www.aseafarer.com

SHIP WELFARE VISITING ORGANISATIONS

	Aberdeen Seafarers' Centre Port Chaplain	07754 141 076
	Apostleship of the Sea Port Chaplain	07757 042 722
	The Mission to Seafarers Port Chaplain	07581 625 941
	Fishermen's Mission	01224 584 651
	Norwegian Seamen's Church Port Chaplain	01224 211 933 07768 472 134
NAUTILUS	Nautilus International	0151 639 8454
RMT	RMT	020 7387 4771
ITF	ITF	020 7403 2733

A welcome berth: information leaflet for the Aberdeen Seafarers' Centre where Howard Drysdale is the Port Chaplain.

on a regular habit of drinking. Each Saturday I would go to the pub and get as drunk as a skunk. But all this meant that I felt myself to have become a real man – in Blackburn terms. There I was, into the girls, drinking hard, good at my work at Ferranti's, with a bit of cash in my pocket. The guys who used to give me grief now treated me with respect. I had arrived. I was fast entering into a life of debauchery.

The Church was playing no part in my life at all. The only time I had ever attended was for the Christmas and Easter services at the school. I would sit there, looking for ways of diverting myself, usually by chewing up bits of paper and flicking them at the turned backs in front of me. There was one committed Christian at the school, but he was a real weirdo: specs, bad complexion and a weedy voice. He simply confirmed my suspicion that Christianity was for oddballs, not for real men like myself.

But the feeling was growing that something was wrong with my life. When I became 20, I decided to leave Ferranti's and join the Navy. Because I was 18 I was allowed go to the NAAFI and get drink. At that time the Navy was very much drink orientated: it gave out daily rations of beer. But there was this very important difference: the Navy was also religion orientated. We were required to attend religious education classes and to go to Sunday worship. Then it would be a question of full uniform, on parade and marching off to church.

My progress towards the Church was a lengthy and rocky one. There was no Damascus moment of blinding revelation, rather a gradual inching my way to the goal of an openly committed Christian life and service. In the Navy I first of all went to church because I had to. I didn't find the experience an inspiring one – the padre who took it was an old man, covered up in robes, glasses perched on his face and possessed of a dull, monotonous voice.

But the Religious Education classes proved to be something different, full of the sort of questioning and discussion I was ready for. 'Why are we here?'; 'What is the meaning of life?' Then the proffered Bible: 'It's all in here. Read it and then you'll find out what life is all about.'

I decided I really had to find out more about this Bible business; I opened the book and read through the first chapter which is, of course, Genesis. I was quickly disillusioned: I mean, men living to 900 years of age, a garden with an apple tree, a tower built right up to the sky – this Bible is simply a load of fairy tales!

But then the Fleet Chief, Arthur Lockwood, approached me. He told me he was running a Bible study group; would I like to come along? He would pick me up at the main gate and take me there personally.

We started, not with Genesis, but the gospel of St John. I read through it in preparation and still thought much of it was far-fetched nonsense, but then I thought of my big chief coming for me personally and so off I went.

The meeting was held in his house; there were 12 of us present. He began with, 'Howard could you read the opening six verses for us?' I did this without much thought as to their significance, but to my amazement Arthur spoke for an hour on the meaning of

these six short verses. I found what he had to say fascinating; I hadn't realised that the Bible was so packed with meaning.

The message was beginning to strike home; I wanted to know more; I continued to attend the Fellowship meetings. I then discovered the Sailors' Rest, in Portsmouth, an organisation that had been first set up in the 1800s by a wealthy spinster lady who had seen sailors come ashore and drink all their money away and squander it on prostitutes. I began to spend my Saturday evenings there – really, because I knew that Wrens would also be present. I was still at it.

Then came a day when I returned to the camp, a bit drunk but still intending to go to the church the next day, as part of my quest to find out more about this Christianity. As I was getting ready, a mate made a remark: 'Don't you think you're being a hypocrite? I mean what were you doing last night, among the drink and the women?' What do you think Jesus feels about all that?' The question stopped me in my tracks.

However, the following Saturday found me once more at the Sailors' Rest, but, to my surprise, no one seemed to be there. Instead, there was only the Missioner, who informed me that they were all away at a concert, which was to be held at the Pentecostal Church in Portsmouth. Perhaps we should join them? So I went along, looking forward to some sort of pop concert, but when I arrived I found 1,000 people there and no drums or amplifiers.

A huge choir came on the stage, 100 strong. They sang of the virgin birth, of the prophecies of Jesus's coming, of death, the resurrection – of all the basics of the faith which by now I was used to hearing. But this time the words and the music and the message seemed to pierce right into my very soul. I sat there, thinking, 'I am a sinner. I have offended God in so many ways!' I turned to the Missioner and asked, 'What do I have to do to become a true Christian?' At the end we prayed together and, there and then, I gave my life up to God.

It was a complete transformation. Up till then I had become interested in Christianity, but I had continued to be a self-centred, evil sod, getting drunk and chasing skirts. I continued to drink for a while, but now in moderation; eventually I stopped altogether and became teetotal, as I still am to this day. I became a clean living, considerate young man, one who wanted to follow Christ in thought, word and deed. I also became a much

Howard shares good cheer with some of the many foreign seafarers who dock at Aberdeen each year.

A job which leads to meeting some interesting people. Howard with former Deputy Prime Minister John Prescott, 2015.

Port Chaplain I might be, but I was still a human being with a sense of humour and a no holier than thou mentality.

happier person. Although I had been chasing what is commonly thought of as a good time I realised that I had become more and more dissatisfied, that there was an emptiness burning away at my soul, something which I had been attempting to cover up by embracing the good-time life.

I decided I had to leave the Navy and train for the ministry. It was while I was training I met my future wife. Anne walked into church one Sunday and I immediately knew this was the one I was going to marry. It took me weeks to find out all about her, to start to walk her home, to offer her a platonic friendship. A year later we were married and on our way to raising four children.

After my training, I settled down to life as a Baptist minister. But nothing was smooth sailing. We had a son who was diagnosed with a potentially terminal illness. He did pull through and eventually made a good recovery, but we had to nurse him along for years.

Then my wife suffered a haemorrhage and lay in a coma for three months, leaving me with four children to look after as best I could.

In 2000 I applied to become a chaplain in the Royal Navy. I had been missing the company of seafaring folk and relished the opportunity of seeing the world. For me it was a dream job and with my experience I assumed I would walk into it. My application was successful; I was given the starting date of May 2001. But then came the bombshell: the Joint Ministerial Board sent in my psychological profile, recommending that I be turned down as 'not being in keeping with a naval way of life'.

But God's plan was at work. While I was returning from London, my wife got a phone call asking that I meet a representative from the Board at a service station near Hamilton – he was driving down to Southampton from Glasgow; he had some important news for me. Apparently, someone on the Ministerial Board had been in touch with a strong recommendation that I was an asset to the Church and would be just the man for any vacancy they had for me.

And that's how I came to be in Aberdeen, Chaplain to the Seafarers' Centre. My remit was an open one: to tend to the welfare of seafarers in the port of Aberdeen. I started in 2001. I found there was plenty to do. Usually the port of Aberdeen has 20 to 30 ships at berth at any one time. I had little idea as to how to make a start on my job. The first vessel I went onto was a Norwegian one. I went up on to the bridge and attempted to greet the man I took to be the captain. 'Hello', I said as brightly as I could muster. 'Ja,' came the response. 'Yes, I am the Port Chaplain.' 'Ja.' 'I bring you greetings from the British International Seafarers.' 'Ja.' Searching desperately for some way of making a wee bit of progress, I came up with, 'I have a minibus and I can take you and the crew round Aberdeen to show you all the sights'. At this the captain brightened up, 'Good – you can take us to the prostitutes.' 'But I'm the Port Chaplain!' 'The Port Chaplain? Only joking!'

How true that was I wouldn't know – but what I did know was that this Norwegian ship had given me a story to use on my next visit elsewhere and a way of breaking the ice. It was the kind of anecdote which I could use to demonstrate that, Port Chaplain I might be, but I was still a human being with a sense of humour and a no holier than thou mentality. I realised that as seafarers will spend nine months of the year on board, their ship is their home and that nobody has the right to intrude upon it to tell them how they should behave. I make it a rule never to preach on ship; I will wait for any questions and then respond to them and, if they don't come, then I will accept that and confine myself to issues of general wellbeing.

My job is, essentially, to be there for them. This can take a whole range of demands. I'll give you an example. I was on board a vessel, manned by Filipinos, just before it was due to sail. I bade them all farewell and was just going down the gangway when I was stopped by a shout. 'Please, I need to send some money to my wife – can you help?' A crew member came dashing after me. I was handed an envelope; I assured him that I would arrange a wire transfer. Later, when I opened the envelope, I found it contained 3,000 dollars in ready cash – and this from someone I would most likely never meet again. He trusted me.

I can say that this has always worked both ways: my seafarers trust me and, in return, I have never been let down by any of them. I run the centre here in Market Street as a refuge, a place where seafarers of all nationalities and creeds can come and know they will be welcomed and will be safe. Ninety per cent are non-British; in any one year the port of Aberdeen can expect to entertain 100,000 seafarers from 100 various nations. And it's not just oil-related either: Aberdeen handles large cargoes of wood, salt, fuel and wheat on a regular basis. There are 80,000 ship movements a year.

We don't go in for any organised fundraising; we rely upon spontaneous donations to keep going. We get no Government grant. My philosophy is that God will supply our needs. The business community will frequently answer the call to assist us. Just yesterday I was at a business lunch when this business man turned to me: 'I've known you for 12 years and in all that time you've never asked for anything and I've never given you anything. I think it's about time I did'. My response was, 'The only donation I want from you is a personal encounter with Jesus'. 'What do you mean by that?' 'Come into the Centre and we'll have a chat.' He did and he brought a cheque with him. But for me, the discussion we had was the more important aspect of our meeting.

We operate the Centre as an openly ecumenical one and will never attempt to proselytise. The priority is welfare, pure and simple. But I make no apology for being a self-declared evangelical Christian who believes that all men and all women need to know God through Jesus Christ, that He is the truth and the light and that nobody comes to the Father except through him. But I will always respect others' rights to believe how and to what extent they can. After all, my God is a God of mercy and of grace, not of punishment and of judgement. That's what brought me to God: if I had simply been told I was a miserable sinner when I was seeking my own way to God then I would never have found Him.

Howard Drysdale. b. 1955. Aberdeen Seafarers' Centre. Interviewed 2014.

A Christmas away from home: Howard and two volunteer helpers wrapping up Christmas gifts for seafarers forced to spend that time of the year many sea miles from their own homes.

IN TIME OF WAR: THE HOME FRONT AND BEYOND

Aberdeen Land Army women on parade: Bill Cooper's (see elsewhere in book) aunt, Annie Nell Cooper, is 3rd left.

> There was fear: even now if I hear a siren, I feel the twist in my stomach.

BOMBS OVER ABERDEEN

(IMAGE BY KIND PERMISSION OF ABERDEEN JOURNALS)

The camaraderie of the shelters: A group of neighbours settle down for another night of air raids. Tullos, 1941.

Ten Green Bottles and all that

There were the Anderson shelters, and the shelters at the school: smelly, concrete buildings out in the playground. You had your little case which contained a change of clothing and two malt tablets upon which we were supposed to survive for the 14 days it might take for them to find and dig us out. We would have to grab this case and go off to the shelters for what seemed like night after night.

There was a lot of community spirit, during the war. There was one Anderson shelter to each block, so it meant six families sharing it, including eight children. We got through the night by singing community songs; there was a lot of *Ten Green Bottles*.

There was some fear: even now if I hear a siren, I feel the twist in my stomach. The knowledge that there was someone up there, looking down on us all, and intent on killing us. We did a lot of tourist-style visiting of bombsites the day after. I can still recall the mixture of awe and excitement at seeing well-known buildings reduced to mere rubble. I was taken to see the damage at Split the Wind and can recall gawping at the devastation there, the day after it had been hit.

Charles Barron. b. 1936. Union Grove. Interviewed 2005.

Charles Barron all wrapped up for another night in the shelters.

The shelter was dank and smelly

I started school at Broomhill; what I particularly recall about my time there were the air raids. The instruction was that when the siren sounded you were to go to the shelter in the playground. I hated it; the shelter was so dank and became very smelly. For the toilet we had to use a bucket and this could become horribly foul as some of the children had diarrhoea with the nervousness of the bombs and the machine guns going off all around us.

The young Anne Russell (first left front) does her bit for the war effort by collecting for the Red Cross.

Every city school had to prepare for the worst: Here a 1940 class of Ashley Road School pupils line-up, gas masks at their side.

Anne Russell ready for Empire Day, 1951.

Ron Caie Fighting off those German bombers single handed.

We were given rubbers to chew on during the raids and this was to stop our teeth chattering and us biting our tongues. One little girl couldn't stand being in the shelter and having to use the communal bucket. The thought of squatting on it and pulling down her pants was more than she could bear, even though the boys were expressly forbidden to look. So, one time she simply ran out during the raid to get to the toilet. The headmaster and the janitor went after her. Just then a plane began to strafe the school, so the Head flung his body over Dora and then the jannie threw his over the pair of them.

Anne Russell. b. 1932. Broomhill School. Interviewed 2015.

German planes overhead

To me, growing up under the conditions of war, the noise of bombs and enemy aircraft became a way of life. I got to be able to distinguish between the sounds made by German aircraft and those of the RAF – the Germans sounded much nastier! The warnings would go off, the Bofor guns would shoot off, 'duff-duff-duff' at the harbour and then you'd hear this menacing 'yak-yak-yak' as the enemy came nearer and nearer. We ducked for safety into our shelter, which was a cubby hole beneath the stairs.

You could hear the bombs whistling overhead, coming so near that you could swear they had hit the house next door. There would be a rattle, a shake and a thump running through the house. But it was Menzies Road that was blown half away, and the blast had knocked out hundreds of windows.

After the war was over, shortages and rationing were still very much in place, Mr Wood, the grocer in Torry, informed my mother as a great favour, 'We're getting in a supply of bananas next week – but don't tell anyone!' I overheard and for the next few days was in a fit of anticipation as to what this ultimate food sensation would taste like. The day came: my mother went to Mr Wood's, received her three bananas discreetly wrapped up in a brown paper bag and brought the prize home. She took one out, sliced it up, put it in a bowl with milk and sugar sprinkled on top and handed it to me. Well, the banana was still very green and what was meant to be a wondrous bowl of delight tasted simply horrible. An early lesson in the futility of human wishes.

The great day had been in May 1945 when Churchill was able to tell the nation that the war was won. I grabbed my grandfather's Union Jack, ran outside and dashed up and down Victoria Road, announcing to all and sundry that victory had been declared. The fact that everyone was also in on the news didn't deter me; I saw myself as the bearer of glad tidings to the whole of Torry.

Ronald (Ron) Caie. b. 1938. Victoria Road, Torry. Interviewed 2014.

Ron Caie's mother, Elizabeth Grant and cousin collecting 'for homes for wounded soldiers' in 1915.

The bombs brought the roof down

The war came when I was 10 and my brother 12. Each evening before going to bed we would set the table for breakfast – sugar bowl, jug of milk, cups and saucers with cups turned upside down, all set out on the table. But this night the bombing was very near and the roof was brought down. We had to leave the flat for six

Damage in Great Northern Road after the raid of July 1941. (IMAGE BY KIND PERMISSION OF ABERDEEN JOURNALS)

Rescuers dig for survivors after German bombs destroy McBride's Bar, Loch Street, February 1941. (IMAGE BY KIND PERMISSION OF ABERDEEN JOURNALS)

weeks before the damage was put right. In the room where my granda and brother slept there was a beautiful black mantelpiece, a really gorgeous thing it was, the showpiece for the whole home.

Well, we got to the shelters all right and passed the night there. But when we got back the next morning all you could see was the mantelpiece lying at an angle with a gaping space beneath it. You could peer through it all the way down into Hutcheon Street four floors below.

Whenever the sirens sounded Mum would get us all up. I used to go over to the window and take a look out; you could see the planes and the searchlights. 'Oh, it'll just be a waste of time; I'm going back to my bed.' But then the bombs started landing. One hit the Broadford Works just across the road; then the meat market behind us was hit. So, Mum got us all up and made sure we put on our coats above our pyjamas. For us the shelters were at the bottom, across George Street and into the basements there – 'the sunks' we called them. We had to cross the street to get into them and I saw a sight which has never left me. There was this man crawling along George Street, crying out,

'Help me! Help me!' He stayed at the corner of Catherine Street and his house had taken a direct hit. His wife and family were all killed outright. The street was covered in glass and rubble and here he was just crawling through it all.

It's true that the bombing did pull people together, but there was a fair amount of looting too. Mum used to help out a lady who ran a shop in Holburn Street and in return she would be given little treats to take home with her – a tin of salmon, a small bag of sugar, a tin of fruit, that sort of thing; real gold in those days of rationing. While we were out of the house, a gang up from Glasgow had moved in to carry out the repairs. When we finally got back into our home, all her precious hoard of goodies had quite disappeared.

We never really had any doubts that victory would come in due course. I never heard any talk of a possible defeat. Churchill helped to keep us all going; he was the man who pulled us all through.

Margaret Leiper. b. 1929. George Street. Interviewed 2014.

> His wife and family were all killed. George Street was covered in glass and here he was crawling through it all.

Mourners line the streets to pay last respects to some of the 98 people killed during the raid of April 1943. (IMAGE BY KIND PERMISSION OF ABERDEEN JOURNALS)

Nearly 100 were killed that night

The biggest raids came in April 1943. I was at a Boys' Brigade display in the Music Hall. We were half way through our performance when the Adjutant announced: 'Right! Go home! The performance is over.' That was it; he never actually told us an air raid was on – whether to avoid a panic I don't know.

But it meant that there I was, a young lad of no more than 12 years of age, left to find my own way home with German planes overhead and dropping bombs. I made my way

I had reached Charlotte Street when there came this sudden roaring noise and the flares of tracer bullets seemingly all around me.

through the darkness and had reached Charlotte Street when there came this sudden roaring noise and the flares of tracer bullets seemingly all around me. I took to my heels and ran for dear life; I was nearing the top of the street when a hand came out of a door and the command of 'Come here, laddie!' I was dragged in off the street and pushed down into a basement to shelter there till the raid had passed.

Afterwards I had to walk home through broken glass. When I finally arrived home, I discovered that all the windows had been blown in. Bits of bomb casing had smashed through into the house and were embedded in the plasterwork. My mother had taken my brother and placed him in a crib by the side of her bed – shards of glass had been scattered all over the bedding. Another part of bomb casing had driven its way into the granite facing of the house. A slater later tried to fill it in, but you can still see the marks on the wall to this day.

That was the biggest raid on Aberdeen; nearly 100 were killed that night. The German planes would fly over from Norway and they used the Dee and the Don as markers.

Douglas Mitchell. b. 1930. George Street. Interviewed 2014.

How the local press reported the incident.

A sight which always preyed on my mind

I've thought about this over and over ever since and I always find it horrendous. Here we were, at the Grammar school, going to assembly, to the morning prayers and hearing all the golden names being read out to us of the latest fallen. These were still kids, 18-year-old boys who'd left school the year before. It was a great thing then to become a fighter pilot; these were the great warrior heroes for the young – and yet the death rate was absolutely hellish. It was a matter of bright young lads leaving school and then queuing up to die.

I actually saw a corpse of one of the fallen. It's a sight that has always preyed on my mind. We lived in Anderson Drive and a German plane came down into the ice-rink there. The pilot tried to jump out but was killed; his body was left lying there until the ARP wardens came to take it away. But a strange thing happened; while we were standing around looking at this smouldering wreck, with its body beside it, a grey limousine suddenly came racing down the Drive and drew up; a uniformed figure got out, stood to attention above the corpse and then saluted it, before getting back into the car and racing off again. All this honour stuff, saluting his gallant enemy. *Pro patria mori* – I've never gone for all that. I could see and smell that body.

William (Bill) Ord. b. 1929. Anderson Drive. Interviewed 2003.

Four German airmen killed in the Anderson Drive incident were interred in the Old Cemetery at Dyce.

All of a sudden, we saw an aeroplane

Kathleen Porter (right) at the outbreak of the war, with sister Elsa and her 'other' Grandma, who lived in Bedford Road.

In time my Grandma had moved to Ruthrieston Circle from Albion Street; that was during the war. On one occasion while visiting my Granny, the sirens had gone off 'Woo-oo-oo-oo-oo', warning people the Germans were coming. It was terrifying when you heard the sound of the sirens. We could hear this droning noise: 'Brrrrrrrrr' and then, all of a sudden, we could see an aeroplane coming over the houses and heading towards Anderson Drive. Granny lived upstairs and at the end of the lobby was a bunker – where they kept the coal. We were all on top of the bunker looking out the window at the aeroplane shouting, ' Look at the plane!' I looked up and this plane was so close, it could have landed on the roof. You could see the pilot, his head half out of the cockpit and he had on a helmet. We watched it going over the top of the houses and disappearing – then crash!

We all walked from Ruthrieston Circle to Anderson Drive to see where the plane had crashed on the ice rink. The reason I'm remembering this is that the ice rink was like a big shed – but you couldn't see the aeroplane because the shed hid it. It had crashed just behind it. In front of the ice rink were drills where they grew tatties. There was a bird, like a little wren, sitting shivering in the drills and we picked it up and it died in our hands – it had been the shock of the crash, I think.

Kathleen Porter (née Hay). b. 1932 Albion Street. Interviewed 2016.

The dogs that barked

Too young to fight in the war: but the Army caught up with Bob Kynoch soon after – on National Service 1945.

When the war came, we were living in the harbour area. There were plenty of raids there because the Germans could quickly fly across the North Sea from their bases in Norway and look for shipping and industrial targets in Aberdeen. A neighbour had a couple of Airedale dogs which would break out into barking and howling even before the sirens went off – they seemed to have some sort of sixth sense that danger was approaching. Then we would make for the shelters, which were situated by the bonded warehouses full of highly inflammable whisky, by the bridge on Marischal Street. Dad would carry my brother, me and my younger sister, and Mum had my baby sister in her arms. Granny refused to join us: at the very first raid she had been hurrying off to the shelters in the dark, ran into a lamppost and emerged with a pair of black eyes. That was enough to put her off the whole shelter business.

In the shelters we did our best to keep spirits up; there were sing songs and someone would always be looking out and giving a running commentary – 'Torry's fair gettin it the night!' Of course, it was all rather scary, but you did get used to it.

I remember the German plane that came down by the old ice rink in Anderson Drive. An army truck came along to pick up the bodies which were simply flung in the back with a tarpaulin to cover them. My uncle, who was working at Dyce airport, hitched a lift and was told to sit at the back – 'the front's a bit full' – completely unaware of the

A recent picture with his first grandson, Marshall.

enemy bodies just beside him, all hidden under tarpaulin .

I had no doubt we would win the war, however grim the bombing became. Why? Because we had Churchill; I reckon it was his leadership which won the war for us; we all used to crowd round the wireless set to listen to his speeches and they inspired us. I reckon he was the man who put the fear into Hitler.

But my father decided that the harbour area was getting too dangerous for his young family and so we moved out to a place on the outskirts of the city – Danestone Circle – which to us was more or less in the country. And what happened? A bomb fell on Middlefield School just across the way from us. Miss Spicer, one of the teachers, had been fire watching and she lost a leg. The blast pushed our window frames in a good two inches and there was glass and debris everywhere.

Look at this photo frame here: 'This frame was made by H. Kynoch out of pieces of wood after the German raid on Middlefield School 1943'. People picked over the debris, looking for souvenirs I suppose, and this is what my father found.

There were bombs on to Sunnyside Road. My father went over to see what he could do to help and came across this woman who was hanging out of the window with her two children – all killed. All the father-in-law could do was to take them down and lay them out in the garden. The husband had been away with the Army – he had played for the Dons – Cummings was his name, I think.

Robert (Bob) Kynoch, b. 1927. Danestone. Interviewed 2018.

WAR SERVICE AT HOME

No-one messed with Mr Andrew Lewis

It was a hard school. Recently a group of us got together at the Maritime Museum and looked back on the old days at John Lewis. There were these old guys who were there during the war and one of them had a wonderful story to tell us. Because of wartime security the harbour was closed off; there was barbed wire running all round it and guards on duty. The young lad in the office – a Harry McLennan, then only 15 – was told to go down to the harbour to get some measurements. He tried to go through the gate and got arrested.

He told them, 'But I work for John Lewis.' 'Is that right, laddie? Well, we'll see about that.' 'Let me just phone my boss there'. 'We'll do any phoning.'

Well, the phone call came into the office that one of the John Lewis employees had been arrested. The message was taken through to Mr Andrew Lewis himself and he was not the manager for nothing. He opened up this drawer and pulled out a gun, complete with holster, strapped it on and cried out, 'Come with me!' They jumped into the car and sped down to the harbour. He went straight up to the guards and demanded, 'What have you done with my man?' They went into the guard block and dragged him out, at which point Mr Lewis drew his gun, brandished it in the air and shouted out, 'That's my man! He's coming straight back with me.' They then got into the car and drove straight back to John Lewis's. No one, but no one, messed around with Mr Andrew Lewis.

Ronald (Ron) Fiddes. b. 1939. John Lewis Shipyard. Interviewed 2006.

We were all sworn to secrecy

Come the war I was called up and went into the Royal Signals. Because of my training in radio, I was placed in a special communications unit and sent down to Bletchley. Everything was top secret and I never did find out exactly what was going on, even though I knew it was all to do with code breaking. My job was to help maintain the wireless sets and to work the Morse code.

I took the King's Pass where I was required to swear on my life to obey His Majesty

> He drew his gun, brandished it in the air and shouted out, 'That's my man! He's coming straight back with me.'

Bill Dalgarno: An Army photograph.

Bill Dalgarno at Bletchley Park, working his way through another set of '500 groupers'.

For many years Bill acted as Chief Technician to Aberdeen College of Education. Here he is, left, on his retirement being congratulated by his Head of Department, Bob Cooper.

and to serve my country and never to disclose the true nature of my work. Our letters were all heavily censored. We stayed in billets and would be driven in and out.

My task was to send out messages in Morse code – what these consisted of I never knew. All I got handed to me would be lists and lists of figures. You'd have to work your way through '500 groupers', that is 500 groups of five figures each. My hands would become very tired, so I had to develop the knack of using my left hand so as to give the right one a rest.

Discipline was very strict. My supervisor was a bit of a hot head and he would stand over you with a revolver to make sure you were keeping to regulations and only following the exact figures on the paper in front of you. There was always the temptation to use a code of our own to tap into the latest deals on the black market.

William (Bill) Dalgarno. b. 1925. Bletchley Park. Interviewed 2014.

The great Aberdeen spy scare

As a young constable in the early days of the war I got involved in what became 'Aberdeen's spy scare'. It was 1940 and I was alone on the beat on a night shift. It was the blackout and everything was pitch dark. I was coming down the incline at the Spital, trying the shop doors, when this figure suddenly loomed up in front of me. 'Oh, bobby, there's a spy making signals from an upstairs window in the convent!' So, he took me to his top floor flat in St Peter's Street. From it you could look out onto the convent and, sure enough, I could see what appeared to be a series of Morse code flashes.

'I'm sure someone's signalling to a German submarine out at sea,' he told me. A sergeant came and arrived while the flashing was still going on. He turned to me, 'Constable, there's no need for you to stay here. Please proceed with your night shift –

Could this have been a nest of spies? A recent shot of a disarmingly peaceful looking Convent of St Margaret, in the Spital.

but I must warn you not to say anything about this incident.'

The next day when I reported for duty, I asked him what had happened. His answer was a brief, 'Oh Smith, don't you concern yourself with any of that. The matter has been taken care of – that's all you need to know.' And as far as I was concerned that was that. Whether the spy was taken away to the Tower of London to be shot as a traitor or whether the whole thing had an innocent explanation, I couldn't tell you. And nor can anyone else; to this day the tale of the spy in the convent must remain an untold mystery.

That story shows how nerves were on edge during those difficult days. Aberdeen got its share of bombardment and on a full moon night you'd come across groups of people out on the streets anxiously peering up into the sky on the lookout for any enemy planes that might be taking advantage of the extra light. 'Bombers' moon' they called it.

Douglas Smith. b. 1919. The Spital. Interviewed 2015.

A life well lived: Doug Smith in his 90s and still wondering whether or not he had reported an actual German spy.

I particularly liked the riveting work

During the war I went down to Birmingham to work on aircraft assembly at Vickers Armstrong. We were making Lancaster bombers. My friend got called up and was posted down there; even though I was no more than 17 I decided to join her.

I was still in the dark as to what I would be letting myself in for. I had to go into digs and my landlady ran a place I can only describe as basic. It was so cold you had to put the syrup onto hot water to make it run onto your toast.

Then I had an accident at the work; the guard slipped while I was boring holes and my finger got slashed. So, I ended up in hospital, feeling generally run down and with this bad wound to my finger. But I refused to feel sorry for myself even though I was three months in the hospital.

When I got out I resumed my work. I did make friends in Birmingham. The city itself was very industrial – hardly the bonniest spot on earth. But the folk themselves were friendly. In the factory I met all sorts and we all got along. We'd all go to the pub and have a sing-song. These were the great war numbers like 'Roll out the barrel' and 'We'll meet again, don't know where, don't know when'.

At the factory I proved to be adept at the work. I particularly liked the riveting work. We wore nothing in the way of protective gear. Some of the work was repetitive and boring – like having to work the big press hour after hour. But I was conscious that everything we did was for the war effort and that did spur you on.

An Aberdeen woman. b.1924. Vickers Armstrong. Interviewed 2011.

He too died serving the war effort

My father tragically died early, when I was only five, in an accident. This was during the war when he had declared himself to be a conscientious objector, went before a tribunal and was enlisted into an occupation which aided the war effort. For him, this meant driving loads of timber that was being felled up Deeside by the British Timber Corps. He was on the side road downhill to the main Crathie road, driving a tractor with a trailer load of timber to the sawmill, when the brakes failed. This had happened once before, but then he had managed to jump free in time. This time he was not so fortunate. He had time to shout out to the others, 'Jump! Jump off!' but he got trapped in the tractor and was hit by the heavy timbers and his whole body was crushed. Death was instantaneous.

Conscientious objectors were not highly thought of usually and came in for a lot of opprobrium as war dodgers. Usually, when one of them died, the press announced it under the lines of, 'Conshie killed'. But my father was so well thought of that nobody publicly raised his status and the P&J simply said, 'Aberdeen Man Killed'. The simple stone on his grave read, 'ERECTED BY HIS FELLOW WORK MATES, CRATHIE' and many attended his funeral, showing their high regard for him.

The death hit my mother hard. I can remember the day of the accident and the loud, strong knock on the door and the police asking to be let in. Then the sound of adult voices, followed by my mother dashing back into the flat and grabbing a towel which she wrapped round her face and sobbed and sobbed into. The police were very worried about her mental state, but they did manage to extract from her the addresses of her husband's sisters and brother and they came to the rescue.

I must, however, emphasise that little of my father's beliefs or actions meant then very much to me, not at such a young age. I did not know of his beliefs nor could I have understood them even if I had been told of them. My real memories of that time are of my mother's great distress at the news. I was told that I kept asking when my father was going to come home. I grew into the knowledge that I was a boy without a father and that was because he had died in an horrific accident at Crathie.

William (Bill) Cooper. b. 1936. Rose Street. Interviewed 2018.

The father he scarcely knew: Bill Cooper and father.

Cartoon of the First World War: Fortunately attitudes had become more enlightened by the time Bill Cooper's father became a conscientious objector.

THE DOMESTIC FRONT

My mother was a wartime clippie

My mother became a clippie in the First World War. She told us of the time when the bus was taking wounded soldiers up to Woodend Hospital (the Old Mill Hospital as it used to be called) and this butcher's boy got on, carrying his basket of sausages for delivery at the hospital. Well, for sheer devilment the boy opened the back door of the bus and trailed the links of sausages behind the vehicle, whereupon the soldiers burst into the song, 'There's a long long trail a-winding'.

Helen Hendry. b. 1921. Aberdeen Trams. Interviewed 2013.

Helen Hendry's mother in action as a World War 1 clippie on the military hospital run.

Liz as a babe in arms, with her grandparents, 1940.

That great rationing delicacy: a tin of 'Emergency' spam.

Liz Strachan's parents, taken in 1961, shortly before her father's death.

There was rationing for my first 15 years

By 1940 there was a severe shortage of food because most of Britain's foodstuffs came from other countries in ships and the Germans were waging U-boat war against them. So, to ensure that food was distributed fairly, everyone was given a ration book allowing each person to have a certain amount of a particular food – one ounce of cheese, two ounces of butter, eight of sugar and so on.

Coupons were required for beef and mutton; other cuts also became rationed: tongue, heart, liver and head and some utterly nauseating stuff called jellied tripe which my older brother, Gordon, took great delight in telling mother was the inside of a cow's stomach. Sometimes the butcher was unable to supply his registered customers with even these vomitus bits. The best cuts, of course, were going to the Forces.

Grandad often came home with a rabbit. He used to lay the furry dead thing, with its stomach split open and gutted, onto the kitchen table. Then Grandma would skin it and take out any extra nasty bits that Grandad had missed and rinse what was left under the cold tap. My stomach would revolt when it was boiled and brought, all greasy and grey, to the table.

Chickens were for egg production, but when an old hen got past laying eggs, the butcher would sell it for eating. They were scraggy old birds that had to be boiled for hours to make them tender. One hen would feed the six of us, with the left-over bits laid aside for Dad's lunchtime sandwiches. On the second day the bones were boiled again for a soup, which looked like stagnant pond water.

The shops always had vegetables, but they were the ordinary ones like potatoes, carrots, turnip, onions, leeks and cabbage. Posh vegetables such as peppers, mangetout, asparagus, sweetcorn were unheard of.

Fish wasn't rationed, but it was expensive and not always available as fishermen were at risk of enemy attack. Our upstairs neighbour was a fisherman and often gave Mum a large chunk of cod, which she boiled as usual. But it was full of bones and she served it with the skin.

I was always hungry. I didn't really need to be, but so much of the food was horrible. I was a dedicated vegetarian at the age of four. And behind Mum's back, Grandad and Grandma would give me most of their sweetie ration.

Grandad and Dad heeded the Dig for Victory campaign and grew carrots, rhubarb and potatoes in a dug-up section of the washing green. For a good crop they needed manure and this was generously provided by the Co-op milk horse, a creature of habit, who most days deposited a steaming heap somewhere in our Wallfield Place. This was shared out among all the tenants.

Grandma was a carrot freak and used them in all sorts of ways. She invented carrot lollipops. A raw carrot on a stick was tasty and nutritious. She added carrots to jam to eke it out and I reckon she invented the original carrot cake. But this was a far cry from the delicious confection we enjoy today. This was made from dried eggs, dried milk, saccharine, margarine and grated carrots and baked in a temperamental black oven stove

whose temperature couldn't be regulated.

Although the war ended in 1945, rationing for most things continued for some time. Long queues formed outside the Co-op in Rosemount Place to buy the first bananas that reappeared in Aberdeen in 1948.

Bread rationing stopped in 1948, sugar and sweets only in 1953 and meat and everything else not till 1954. So there was rationing for the first 15 years of my life.

Elizabeth (Liz) Strachan. b. 1939. Wallfield Place. Interviewed 2014.

Liz Strachan has written her own autobiography: *Snippets of a Happy Life,* published 2014.

A generation of Aberdeen children grew up knowing nothing but rationing. Here Third year boys at Torry Junior Secondary School help with the issue of ration books in 1941.

THE SPANISH CIVIL WAR

Bob Cooney
on service in Spain,
1938.

In his prime he had been viewed as a fine orator, someone who would clamber up onto the Wallace Statue and draw an audience.

He retained his faith in socialism to the end

Bob Cooney, my uncle, became one of the leading lights in the International Brigade which went out from this country to fight for the socialist cause in the Spanish Civil War. Bob rose to be a Brigade Commissar which meant that he was in charge of his men's welfare and had to motivate them and lead them into battle.

Bob came from a large, poor but ambitious family. His father was a cooper and something of a swimmer and athlete, but he died suddenly of pneumonia. This left his widow, Jane, who was only 37 and had seven children to bring up. She had to find rooms and take any odd cleaning job she could. But she was determined to ensure her brood would get on; she ruled them with a rod of iron, not to mention regular bashings with the back of a hair brush.

Bob had to leave school at 14; he was apprenticed to a pawnbroker – more first-hand evidence of desperate poverty. He began to take an interest in socialism and to attend the open-air debates at the Castlegate. He was convinced that only a workers' revolution would change the system; mere argument could never do it. So, he joined the Communist party. Bob became a speaker right from his teens.

The Depression years added to his conviction that direct action, not mere debate, had to be followed. In 1930 he packed in his pawnbroking job and devoted himself to full time political agitation.

It was idealism that drove him on. He went out to Spain in 1937 with no military experience at all, went to Tarragona and received no more than five weeks basic training, which consisted of little more than learning the parts of a gun and how to dig yourself in for trench warfare. He was given an ill-fitting uniform, sturdy boots, a Soviet rifle and a food bowl. He turned down the opportunity of officer's training, insisting that he wasn't in Spain to pin stripes on his uniform.

He was soon in the thick of the action, but in the end the superior air power of Franco's forces and the massive fire power they could command pinned the Republicans back. Bob fought bravely, rallied the troops, was captured, then escaped. Conditions became harsh and the food supply broke down so that a ration of half a slice of bread became the norm.

Bob was one of 2,400 Brigade volunteers from Britain, of whom more than 50 lost their lives and 1,000 were wounded. Nineteen came from Aberdeen and five of them were killed. The defeat was inevitable considering the vastly superior resources of the Fascists, who were aided by Germany and Italy. But it took three years to come about and at the final parade of the brigade in Barcelona they were told, 'You can go proudly. We shall not forget you.'

On his return to Aberdeen Bob was so emaciated and so covered in sores that that his mother wept to see him.

Although the Fascists won, Bob never considered that their victory was anything more than a temporary one. He saw the battle of Ebro as the opening shots of the Second World War, that 1945 brought about a delayed victory and a vindication of those early actions. He argued that the Spanish campaign with all its atrocities was responsible for opening the eyes of the public to the true nature of fascism.

He was a smallish man but packed with a restless energy. He worked in the building trade, but after the war he found himself blacklisted in Aberdeen and was forced to seek employment in Birmingham.

When he retired, he returned to Aberdeen but life became tough for him. He had played a leading part in the housing campaigns after the war years and led squats at the Torry Battery and the old Tillydrone POW camp. You could say that these actions stirred the city into its massive house building drive, one which saw 1,000 homes per year being put up.

But his marriage was effectively over and in the end he more or less had to live on the streets. He finally found accommodation in the Nelson Street area, but it was of the lowliest kind. His end was very sad; he had to go into Kingseat, his mind taken over by all the ideas and songs and stories which were constantly buzzing through his head. He found sleep or any kind of repose difficult. But he always kept his sense of humour and retained his faith in socialism right to the very end.

Really, he came to be seen in Aberdeen as something of a colourful eccentric, a doughty warrior who had fought the good fight but whose day was now done. In his prime he had been viewed as a fine orator, someone who would clamber up onto the Wallace Statue and draw an audience to heckle, to listen and to laugh at the torrent of words. He had cut his teeth like many of his generation on the 'Stance' at the Castlegate where people would gather to engage in debate about religion and about politics. The place had a natural appeal in those days of crowded tenement and workplace living; it was an open area where fresh air and room to move around in could be enjoyed alongside the rich entertainment offered by a range of speakers, among whom Bob was an undoubted star.

Aberdeen volunteers in Spain: Bob Cooney (centre) with Archie Dewar and Bob Simpson.

Neil Cooney. b. 1943. Catalonia. Interviewed 2015.

THE POST-WAR ARMY

> Our pay as new recruits was no more than 18 shillings a week and out of this you had to pay all your NAAFI bills. And out of this pay I still managed to send home 10 bob to my mother.

I wouldn't have missed National Service

When I was called up, I had never been further than Stonehaven in my life. But now I had to report to a place called Blandford, which apparently was in some county or other called Dorset. I took the overnight train down to King's Cross, a 12-hour journey. When I got off the train, I had no idea where I was. For all I knew it could have been situated in the Middle East.

I spotted a pair of Military Policemen, so I approached them: 'Look, I'm off to my National Service and I've got to get to Blandford but I haven't a clue how to get there.' They told me I would have to cross over to Paddington and take a train from there. They took me to the tube and away I went.

I was nervous and felt a bit lost. But I soon settled in. Once you got to the camp and were measured for your uniform and looked around, you realised that you were one of a whole group of new recruits, all in the same boat as yourself. I soon made pals; I had no difficulty in making friends with people from all over the country.

Our pay as new recruits was no more than 18 shillings a week and out of this you had to pay all your NAAFI bills – for a cup of tea and biscuit when the wagons came round in the morning and then for any dinner at the NAAFI – sausage and beans, egg and bacon, that sort of cuisine. You went there as much for the atmosphere and the companionship as the food – to listen to the piano, a game of darts. And out of this pay I still managed to send home 10 bob to my mother.

The first six weeks were basic training: marching, map reading, PT and so on. You were also introduced to Army discipline, which was tough and designed to break us in. We had this sergeant who was constantly reminding us: 'You might have broken your mother's heart – but you'll never break mine!'

Each morning you would have to make your bed up strictly to order. You had to fold the blankets in a certain order, pillow squarely on top, kit out for inspection. You were also inspected daily to see whether you had shaved properly – and any stray hair left on, it would be met with, 'Get that off at once!'

Any misdemeanour entailed a charge and I got it more than once. The punishment might be extra cook fatigues, peeling the tatties and doing the washing up, or extra

weekend guard duties.

One time a pair of us were sitting on our beds and this Corporal entered. He was a 21-year regular and had a dim view of National Service men. Stand up!' he ordered. We assumed he was joking and were slow in obeying. 'Right, outside and run up and down the road till I tell you to stop'. It was pouring with rain and he kept us at it for 20 minutes.

At that moment I hated the Army but, on the whole, I loved my two years and wouldn't have missed my National Service for the world. That sort of unreasonable discipline simply made us feel a greater sense of solidarity with each other. When it came to the day of our demob and the realisation we would now be scattered back all over the country and never see each other again, there were tears.

Harry Black b. 1930. Blandford Barracks. Interviewed 2016.

Aberdonians celebrate VE Day: This news photo might have become faded over the post-war years but the joy is unmistakable as they make their way down a beflagged Marischal Street to see the ships in the harbour.

Ken Raitt's first National Service placement, in Shropshire, 1958. He is second left, middle row.

My mother thought I'd run off!

So, the time came for National Service and I went off on the 28th May 1958 when I was called up. Now, I was a young loon and an only loon and my mother was very concerned about me going away into the big, bad world by myself. When I did my initial eight weeks' training we got to phone once a week.

After the trade training, and passing all the exams there, I was told I was going to Portsmouth. So, I phoned home and said I wouldn't see them until Christmas. Well, this was a tragedy they thought – my being sent to Portsmouth.

We were all packed ready to go when I was called to the Warrant Officer's office to be told 'Change of posting for you. You're going to RAF Kinloss for pipe band duties.' I was quite happy with that and so next I was on the train up to Aberdeen. I arrived in Aberdeen at about three o'clock in the morning.

Now, I hadn't told anybody I was coming and I went right home to 323 Holburn Street and knocked at the door. My mother came to the door and said, 'What have you done? You've run off from the RAF?' She was going to get the Police because I'd run off as I couldn't stick it. Oh, michty what a state! But we eventually got her calmed down with a cup of tea. I think I had to leave at eight o'clock that morning to get the train from Aberdeen to get up to Kinloss. But that's a day I'll never forget – the state my mother got in when she thought I'd run off from the Forces at four o'clock in the morning.

Kenneth (Ken) Raitt. b. 1939. RAF Kinloss. Interviewed 2016.

In as a boy, out as a man

A wee tale about a neighbour's son in Kincorth. When he was called up, he was just one of many young men who mucked about, sometimes annoying neighbours and so on. All of a sudden, he wasn't there. Six weeks later, having undergone an intense period of square bashing, he returned home on leave. He was a different man. Wearing the uniform of the British Army, walking up the street, head held high, all the men and, especially the women, greeted him with respect. He wanted nothing to do with the lads he had kicked about with just six weeks earlier. He had graduated from being a carefree young loon to being a responsible disciplined man.

At that time doing your National Service was seen as a duty and photos of men in uniform were displayed in most homes. Many men were married in the uniform of their regiment.

I asked him one day how did it feel to be in the British Army. He replied, 'I'm not in the British Army; I'm in the Gordons!'

Alexander (Sandy) Gallacher. b. 1941. The Gordons. Interviewed 2015.

> Wearing the uniform of the British Army, walking up the street men and, especially, women greeted him with respect.

EDUCATION

Aberdeen Grammar School staff, 1968 in the final two years before it began to turn into a Comprehensive, renamed – briefly – Rubislaw Academy. A youthful David Northcroft is to be spotted second row slightly to left of centre, while Arthur McCombie – 'Mr Grammar School – is front row, third right.

> One of the older pupils, a fisherman's son, went back to school when he'd left and took this teacher over his knee and skelped his arse.

HAPPIEST DAYS OF YOUR LIFE?

There was a lot of the strap at school

There was a lot of the strap at the school, my God, yes! At the secondary school you got quite a few whacks. I remember one teacher, a woman, and she'd treat her strap with something, so it could stand on end and it was rock hard. She had no mercy, it really hurt.

There were some characters in those days. There was a teacher who was a hard nut, a real hard case. One of the pupils, an older pupil than me, a fisherman's son who lived in Crown Street, and who was over six feet at that time. Well, you know how sometimes when people leave school, they go back to school to thank the teachers? He went back to school when he'd left and took this teacher over his knee and skelped his arse. He said, 'That was for all the beltings you gave me'. Of course, the teacher was too embarrassed to do anything about it, so he never said a word.

Jim Butler. b. 1923. Ruthrieston School. Interviewed 2015.

They tied my left hand behind my back

My mother was anxious to get me into school as early as possible, so when I was no more than four-and-a-half, she managed to enroll me in the school that was attached to St Margaret's Church in the Gallowgate. There I was taught by nuns and they gave me a hard time of it. My main problem was that I am naturally left handed and we had to write with a dip pen, using ink wells that were placed on the right, and this meant I had to stretch across with my dripping pen. As you can imagine, I would leave a trail of ink blots across the desk. So I was made to learn to write with my right hand — the nuns would tie my left hand behind my back to ensure that this would be the case.

I was at that school for six months before it was closed and we were all transferred to Causewayend School. This was a definite improvement — except that I ran into another difficulty: I found the spelling tough going. I later learned that I have a form of dyslexia.

Because of all these issues, I'm sure, I developed a stutter. One evening when we were all at home, there was a knock at the door and there stood the Headmaster. He had come round to our house to suggest I see a speech therapist. This was a real surprise for my mother as till then my stutter had only been apparent at school.

Clifford Milne. b. 1951. St Margaret's Episcopal School. Interviewed 2018.

'Parish boots! Parish boots!'

Most of the kids were clad from the Castlegate. Now the Castlegate was what, further south, they call a flea market – all baskets of clothes and that sort of thing. And some of the women were very good at sewing; they would buy things and wash them and iron them and then alter them. And the kids got their school clothes that way. Times were hard.

Now, when I worked later on, the works manager told me he was one of a big family and they were poor; they were brought up in Torry- and he got Parish boots. And the Parish boots had an eyelet in them to let the pawnbroker know that these were Parish boots and you couldn't pawn them.

But the trouble was, the other kids recognised them and they used to shout, 'Parish boots! Parish boots!' So, he says he took them off every morning and hid them in a hedge somewhere and went to school bare footed and came home and put them on on the way home at night. His mother didn't know that he wouldn't wear them to school

A source of cheap clothing for Aberdeen school children: the Castlegate in the 1910s, a decade before Gladys Morrice went to her school.

I can
remember
the boys in
the short
trousers and
when they
were wet,
they'd smell.

for the kids shouting at him.

Now, the teacher must have accepted him and his bare feet. I can't remember anyone in my class in King Street in bare feet. But I can remember the boys in the short trousers and when they were wet, they'd smell, and their knees were all sore and everything. And the boys in my class must have hated me because the teacher used to make me come out every day and they'd to put their hands on their desks and I had to look at them to see if they were clean. Now, that wasn't fair to make a child do that, and the other kids must have detested me. I never said any of the hands were dirty even though they were; some of them weren't half washed.

Gladys Morrice. b. 1920 King Street. Interviewed 2016.

Sunnybank had some bad memories

Sunnybank had some bad memories for me. There were some very poor kids at that school, kids who came from what we would now call disadvantaged homes. They would be belted in class for getting their sums and their spellings wrong, day after day, and I would sit there feeling heart-sorry for them. 'How can they be expected to get that right?' I would think to myself as the strap came down on them. I realised that with the houses they came from they didn't have a chance – but that made no difference to the way they were strapped.

'I started school at Skene Square': Betty McHardy aged 6 at Skene Square. She is in the 3rd row, 2nd right.

There was one girl in our class who had a sister that had a bairn to her own father. Then I remember once going down to the old jute works at the bottom of the hill, which was used to house the really poor folk. I took a look in; you could see that a whole family had to live in one small section with only an old torn curtain to separate them off from the others. One of the kids in our class had to live there.

It made me so angry, watching these poor skinny loons lining up every day for their beltings. They'd come back to their seats blowing on their hands and whispering, 'It's nae se bad the day, ye ken'. Every day that happened; I can see those faces yet. Some people just shouldn't have been teachers. Kids today certainly could do with more discipline, but not like that, not like that.

Elizabeth (Betty) McHardy. b. 1930. Sunnybank School. Interviewed 2004.

PRIMARY SCHOOL DAYS

The wrong Cliff

Moving to Torry meant a new school: Victoria Road School. I remember my first day at Assembly and the Headmaster standing there in front of everybody, telling them that he was welcoming a new boy into the school and that everyone had to be nice to him and that he was called Clifford.

Well, I went home as usual for my midday dinner. As I was still eating, there was a knock at the door and there stood half a dozen young girls asking if they could accompany Clifford back to the school. They asked me if my name really was 'Cliff'– and that explained their friendliness – all because of Cliff Richard who was a megastar, especially among the young females back then.

So, I got quite a lot of nice attention – until it all gradually petered out. However, I was able to make my mark on the football field and at running, and that helped to get me accepted. And I would go in early each morning and sit with the Jannie in his warm boiler room and then help him with the handling of the morning free milk, which we all received back then.

Clifford Milne. b. 1951. Victoria Road School. Interviewed 2018.

> There was a knock at the door and there stood half a dozen young girls asking if they could accompany Clifford back to the school.

I felt at home at Kittybrewster

I adored my teachers, two in particular. One of them I had in the Infants and she was old so I could think of her as a kind of grandmother. This was Miss Cordiner. She actually retired while I was with her. On her very last day everything went by the board; lessons were usually quite rigid and structured but on this last day she cleaned out her cupboard in front of us all.

I can still see her laughing and crying as she came upon her various school possessions. She made presents out of what she found there; I think all of us had something to take home with us.

Then we had Mr McLeod in Primary 6 and 7. Such a character! He was an old fashioned teacher. I remember Mr McLeod's ritual of sitting on the sill with his legs up

A well established city school:
Kittybrewster began life in 1899, as the cover to its Centenary Book shows.

The future schoolgirl rebel!
Margaret Lakin with brother Brian, a year before she commenced her academic career.
(See p 185)

on the radiator. He had this daily ritual: he'd hitch up his trousers, take out this crisp white handkerchief – beautifully ironed always – and then he'd use it to wipe his moustache.

Every Friday he would give us this arithmetic and spelling test. He'd mark our books, get us to vacate our seats, emptying all our things from the desks, and then go to the back of the room. Then he'd call out the names and the marks and throw the jotters at us, name by name.

The boys were called by their surnames, the girls either by their first one or by a

'Miss'. You'd be then re-seated in different desks according to the order of your marks.

In those days the teacher was the centre of everything in the classroom. The predominant image is of us all sitting at our desks in rows– a sea of desks surrounding you. It was a very academic school but caring with it. I responded to that combination. I'd go home and make up my own sums and write my own stories.

I found Kittybrewster a place I felt completely at home in. It was a big old building but I liked it. I can still see the high ceilings and their high set windows. But I always refused to use the outside toilets. My mother used to tell the story of how each evening as I came home she would have to watch out for me, keep the front door open and the door to the toilet, so I could run straight in, ripping off my bag and my coat and sprint straight up to my relief. But there was nothing intimidating for me at that school.

Margaret Lakin. b. 1949. Kittybrewster School. Interviewed 2014.

The Dem had a uniform

A t age five I went to the Demonstration School, in John Street. The school had a uniform: maroon blazers and berets, grey skirts and trousers. This was purchased at the Co-op Arcade in Loch Street or at Isaac Benzies. We also wore sensible brown lacing shoes in the winter and Clark's sandals in the summer.

Despite its title, the 'Dem' functioned as a traditional primary school of the time. There was great emphasis on the Three Rs, on grammar and spelling and the multiplication tables. We also had to learn up facts about dates and capitals for History and Geography. There were friezes on the walls, which were changed according to the seasons of the year. There was a considerable emphasis on homework – usually spellings

The Kittybrewster staff in 1953, a year before Margaret Lakin started there. Her Miss Cordiner is 2nd row, 2nd right. The Headmaster is Mr Sutherland.

In uniform: Kareen on a visit to London for which her mother insisted she sport her Dem School blazer.

Her first year at the Dem: Kareen Edwards is 3rd from right, front row. Her great friend, Dorothy Dunn (Hodgkiss) is seated beside her and the teacher is Miss Glassie.

or sums. Long before the internet we would visit the public library to research the 'find-out' topic.

I have happy memories of my primary school, enjoying classwork, music, French lessons, netball, being in the Brownies and playing with friends.

One of the things I definitely didn't enjoy about school in those days was all the corporal punishment. I absolutely hated watching people getting the strap, and every week there would be at least one person strapped. I found it quite sadistic.

But things were different then. My old piano teacher, Miss Brown, would cane me over the knuckles if I got notes wrong or, as she judged, I hadn't practised enough. My mother sent me there for lessons. Although I love music, I don't have much aptitude for piano playing, so the canings were quite frequent. Those Wednesday evenings were terrifying times for me as I knew I was likely to be caned at Miss Brown's. Although my mother was not a violent parent her attitude was that I should have practised harder. That's the way it was in those days!

Kareen Edwards. b. 1953. The Demonstration School. Interviewed 2005.

The kids were so appreciative of little

I went into Ian Sharp's [the Headmaster's] office to meet with him and he said 'You know, Mrs Alexander, the children that come to this school never see their mothers in dresses or skirts; they're always in trousers. I would prefer my staff to wear skirts.' And that's all he needed to say; it was the standard to live by. My back garden borders

Middleton Park School and I see the young teachers going in now: trainers and jeans. And I think if they want respect, they need to gain respect and their first way to win respect is dress. And I'll be absolutely honest – my teaching time in Sunnybank was the best time I ever had because the kids were so appreciative of little. If you put out new crayons or pencils, 'oooh', the excitement that got up. I remember there was one little girl, she wore a jumper three days the right way and two turned back to front because the other side was dirty. They were happy kids.

The pupil became a teacher: Martha with her own class – Middleton Park School 1991.

Martha Alexander. b. 1937. Sunnybank School. Interviewed 2015.

A brush with fame: The young Martha Alexander, a pupil at Broomhill in 1947, is instructed in PE by Archie Baird, teacher and the inside left in Aberdeen's Cup winning team of that year.

'I used to love Charities Week'. A student in pursuit of another penny for his collecting tin, 1968. (IMAGE BY KIND PERMISSION OF ABERDEEN JOURNALS)

I used to love visits from the students

Another thing I used to love about school was when the students came when it was Students' Charities Week. They were just wild. They used to come running into the class, shaking their collection cans; we were told which day they were coming so we could bring our ha'pennies. I remember them running into the classroom and making a lot of noise and jumping up onto the desks and just getting to be wild. I thought 'Wow! I want to do that when I'm older'; I thought it must be great being a student. I don't know if the students still go around the schools – probably not; they would probably have to sign PVG [Protecting Vulnerable Groups] forms or something.

Dianne Morrison. b. 1967. Rosemount. Interviewed 2015.

A good place if you were one of the elite

What I now see, and with a sense of shame, is that while Primary school was a pretty good place to be in if you were among the elite – and I was one of them – for the baddies it must have been a place of horror. This was made worse by the belting that went on and the being shouted at. Teachers then seemed to believe they had to assume a stern, unbending persona.

As a 'goodie' you got certain privileges. You might be appointed ink monitor. Each desk had a little hole with an inkwell in it and they had to be filled each week, by the monitor. There was also the opportunity to act as the milk monitor. Each morning, the jannie would bring in a crate of milk and place it by the radiator so it would get warmed up. The bottles had cardboard tops and the monitor had to pop straws through them. A great honour.

Goodies like me didn't feel any compassion for the less fortunate. However, we didn't go in for derision either, just ignored their predicament, or took it as part of the nature of things. After all, it was football, rather than academic work, which we used as the measure of esteem and some of these dummies, being big and strong, could do well enough in that field.

You walked to school, played in the playground for a bit, then the whistle would blow, and you had to line up and be marched into your classroom. The day would begin with some kind of religious observance, a Bible story perhaps. Then straight into the serious stuff: sums, spelling, passages that the teacher would read out and then make you answer questions on. These you would take out to her desk and get them ticked, or not. There were demonstrations of how to do sums, but mostly we just sat there, working through rows of examples from the textbook. You had to learn up lists of things, of spellings and, in Geography, of products, of main cities, of rivers and capes. And this from a book called *Chambers No. Lumber Geography*. You'd have to read a chapter, learn it up and answer questions on it the next day.

Much of our time was spent absorbing information. Actually, I quite liked that. Boys,

The rather inaptly titled *No Lumber Geography* text book , 1944 edition, that Douglas Young encountered at Broomhill in the 1950s.

especially, I think, go through a period when they enjoy just learning up facts. When I was 11, I could have told you all the capitals in the world, the longest rivers, the highest mountains. The most precious book I ever got was one my brother bought for me for Christmas when I was about 11 and this was *Pears' Cyclopaedia*. It had everything in it, all the facts and wonders of the world. I would pore over its pages for hours and commit its marvels to my memory.

Douglas Young. b. 1940. Broomhill Primary School. Interviewed 2004.

I have much to thank them for

The first few weeks of school, at Mile End, didn't go well for me. The teacher tried to dissuade me from holding the slate pencil in my left hand by rapping me over the knuckles until they were bruised. Left-handedness, she told my mother, when she went to the school to complain, was the behaviour of a wilful child. Mum was a match for any teacher and gave Miss Brown such a tongue lashing that it was heard all over the school and I was never punished again.

But after that bad start I loved school. Teaching methods in the Forties were so different from what they are today. I hate to think how many of my brain cells are clogged up with all the things we had to learn by heart.

Every morning we clasped our hands together, bowed our heads and muttered the *Lord's Prayer*: 'Our father who chats in heaven, Harold be his name'. As there was a nice boy in the class called Harold, I was quite happy that God had the same name. We had to get off the Ten Commandments by heart; what exactly was 'adultery' and what was a 'graven image'? And none of our neighbours in our crowded tenement block owned an ass or an ox for me to covet.

Day after day we chanted out the times tables and the lengths, the weights and areas and the currency. We chanted difficult spelling words – dee, eye, eh, double are, ho, ee, ah, spells DIARRHOEA!

We had to learn by heart long passages from the *Golden Treasury,* beautiful poetry which, although it might not have meant much to me as a child, has brought comfort and joy to me in later life.

Anyone over 30 looks old to a child so unfortunately, I remember all my primary teachers as grim-faced old maids who didn't seem to like children. But these ladies, under the most difficult circumstances, gave me an education second to none and paved the way for my later success at Secondary and then at University. I have much to thank them for.

Elizabeth (Liz) Strachan. b. 1939. Mile End School. Interviewed 2014.

Long Measure			
12 inches make	...	...	... I foot (ft.)
3 feet	... ...	...	... I yard (yd.)
5¼ yards	... ...	...	... I rod, pole or perch
4 rods or 22 yards		...	... I chain
40 rods or 10 chains or 220 yards		...	I furlong
8 furlongs or 1,760 yards		...	... I mile

Land or Square Measure		
144 square inches or 12″ x 12″ make		I square foot
9 square feet or 3′ x 3′	...	... I square yard
30¼ square yards...		... I square pole
40 square rods, poles or perches	...	I rood
4 roods or 10 square chains	...	I acre
160 sq. rods or 4,840 sq. yards	...	I acre
640 acres	... ...	... I square mile

Weights			
16 drams (dr.) make	...	...	... I ounce (oz.)
16 ounces	... ...	...	... I pound (lb.)
14 pounds	... ...	...	... I stone (st.)
28 pounds	... ...	...	... I quarter (qr.)
4 quarters or 112 lbs.	...	...	I hundred-weight (cwt.)
20 hundred-weight or 2,240 lbs.		...	I ton (t.)

'Every day we had to chant out our times tables and lengths and weights'... This page from a contemporary text book shows the sort of arithmetic Liz Strachan and her generation of Primary pupils had to cope with.

The labourer's son:
Peter Murphy and
father 1932.

SECONDARY SCHOOL DAYS

I was conscious of being a labourer's son

Living as I did in a tenement in the 1930s, I got used to the fact that my parents were relatively poor. It made me aware of having to compete when it came to schooling. But Mile End Primary School was situated in the West End and it proved to be effective in getting me keen to do well in the 11-plus exam. Robert Gordon's was touted as the best secondary school but instead, I got the next best thing- a 'free place' at Aberdeen Grammar School.

Before I passed the Qually exam and gained a place there, I have a vivid memory of me and my friends shouting at Grammar schoolboys passing us on their way to school: 'Awa Grammar Turdies!' As kids we used to regard the Grammar boys as being a cut above us. Although we wouldn't have used the term, we were 'working class' kids and they would have been certain that that is what we were.

I was conscious of being a labourer's son, from a grubby two-roomed tenement just across the street from the school. I remember being extremely upset at the thought that some of my better off compatriots might see me, out of school in the early evening, delivering newspapers. Oh my God, what would they think of me to be doing such a thing? I had to deliver papers because we needed the money. I had to make a contribution to the household finances, even though it wasn't very much.

The values of the Grammar School were broadly academic ones. But there were quite a few teachers there who also gave me insight into life's great possibilities as well. That's why I would call the Grammar then a liberating institution. I don't know whether it intended to be like that as an institution, but the individuals within it made it that way for me. The school could accommodate pupils in terms of their individuality and that was a very important feature of the Grammar as I saw it then. We weren't dragged into some kind of academic maelstrom; we were given the opportunity to look at things in different ways

Looking back, I'm quite proud to have been a Grammar School boy. The school did have something about it. It had for instance, a formidable Rector in Sir James Robertson, a prominent advocate for moving towards a more comprehensive approach to education in Scotland. It was good for me to go there; it did a lot for me. It was a question of self-

Peter, aged 10, with sister Nancy, 1942.

discipline, I suppose. The school helped me in some degree to accept myself, to recognise that I had achieved something. I think that it was a combination of factors – the ethos of the school generally, and a certain number of individual teachers who had an impact upon me.

Above all, it gave me the necessary preparation for going on to Higher Education – and even winning an unexpected bursary to Aberdeen University, one which led me eventually to becoming a teacher – including a spell back at the Grammar in the English department – and an advocate for the freeing up of the education system for all our children.

Peter Murphy. b. 1932. Aberdeen Grammar School. Interviewed 2002.

> The school helped me to recognise that I had achieved something.

I took to it from the start

I took to the school from the start. I was aware of being poorer than most, despite my bursary. I had to be very careful about not ripping my blazer or losing a football boot, either of which would have been a disaster for my family. I was conscious of having to turn up for the new school year in the same old blazer I had worn the year before, whereas the rest seemed to be sporting new ones.

'The school worked hard to make sure you were proud of being a Gordonian'. An iconic picture of the entrance to this 'proud' school.

> One Maths teacher would prefer to belt bottoms rather than hands. If a boy was wearing a kilt, then he would lift it up at the back to get at the site of punishment.

The education I received at Gordon's was very conventionally academic, very book driven. But I thrived on all that and felt completely at home. It was all very clear-cut; you knew what you had to do and that if you did it you would be praised.

The teachers at Gordon's varied wildly in character and quality. They were free to act as individuals, even to the point of eccentricity. Some were cruel and if they had acted like that nowadays would be behind bars.

One Maths teacher, who still wore pin-stripe suits and high buttoned collars, would prefer to belt bottoms rather than hands. If a boy was wearing a kilt, then he would lift it up at the back to get at the site of punishment. None of this then struck us as dubious– an innocent world! We just accepted it all, even the terrible screams you could catch down the corridor.

The school worked really hard at making sure you became proud of being a Gordonian. At Assembly the latest sports victories would be announced and pupils, past or present, who had made a mark, would be detailed. There was Athole Still, the swimmer, for example, and a number of boys who had made the Scottish Schools rugby side. There was a great insistence on the correct dress. Sporting prowess was held in great esteem. It underlay the House and the Prefect system. I never became a prefect, despite my academic record, because of my complete sporting failure.

Generally, you were being trained to enter one of the professions or to occupy a significant position in the business world. Most of my contemporaries seemed to be destined for the Law or for Medicine; there was also teaching, but that seemed to be at the bottom of the professional pile. We were always being reminded of what we should be aiming at, that this coming exam would mark us out as a future lawyer or surgeon. I can't recall any boy in the Fifth Year who didn't have his sights on University and one of the professions.

Charles Barron. b. 1936. Robert Gordon's College. Interviewed 2005.

A good solid school

Ruthrieston was a good solid school. I've got fond memories of it. The school was doing its best for us. We wore a new school uniform: a black blazer with a gold badge and a tie to match. And we were all given a good grounding.

The era I was brought up in was completely teacher-centred in its teaching. I've no regrets about that. So, not getting to a Senior Secondary school hasn't scarred me in any way. In fact, going to university in my late twenties was a good thing. With some experience of life behind me, I got so much more out of it all.

We had no sense of being the poor relations of those who were at a Senior Secondary school. We had a well-equipped school, which gave us a sound training. We also had sports, up at Harlaw. Our PE teacher was Miss Imper, who wore a powder blue blazer, which had something to do with her being an Oxbridge blue. It was a matter of 'Jolly hockey sticks, girls!' We'd go up there all through the winter; the ground would be frozen, but we had to be there in our shorts. Our shins would be blue with the cold and sore with the blows of the game. All very character forming! Then we had swimming at the Uptown Baths or at the pool at Middle School. So, there was no sense of going without.

Sandra Schwitz. b. 1941. Ruthrieston Junior Secondary. Interviewed 2005.

A bit of a teenage rebel

I was very rebellious at secondary and made sure that my parents never saw a report card. We used to have to address our own envelopes at the school, so I always knew when they were about to be posted off. I would then go down to the General Post Office in Crown Street and pay my sixpence to institute a special search. I'd tell them that my parents were awaiting an important cheque. Then I'd sign the report card for my mother to show the school that it had been duly received and read; to this day I can still produce a passable copy of my mother's signature. I just didn't want my parents to be reading what was being said about my bad behaviour at school. The terms used were 'distracting', 'disruptive', 'inattentive', 'chatters constantly' – and so on.

My mother thought it poetic justice that I later became a teacher myself – indeed a Head Teacher too – because I had evidently made life hell for my own teachers at school. There was quite a group of us at the High School who were rebellious like that. I've often tried to work out why I was like that then, because basically I'm an achiever and I certainly had the ability to do the work.

These were the '60s. It was the days of the mini-skirt and so we would roll up our school skirts; you'd wear a belt to disguise what you were doing. Then they started to carry out inspections; they would ask you to raise your jumpers to find out the real height of your skirt and whether you were using a belt. If they discovered that you were, then you had to take off the belt and unroll your skirt. We would be challenging the school all the time.

Everything was very authoritarian and very prim. They laid so much emphasis on being lady-like and demure – and none of these things was I. Another flash-point was the school beret. I resented the fact that so much time was taken up with this issue. I remember Miss Macnab [Headmistress] once took up a whole Assembly on demonstrating the importance not only of wearing the beret, but also exactly how it should be worn. She gave us a series of bad examples: she described one unseemly version as the 'seaweed on the rocks' style – and this was the one I favoured. This was where you would pin the beret right at the back and back-comb your hair over it, virtually obscuring the beret – hence the name 'seaweed on the rocks'.

Margaret Lakin. b. 1949. High School for Girls. Interviewed 2004.

High School for Girls.

WE SUPPLY CORRECT SCHOOL WE AS OFFICIALLY APPROVED.

BLAZERS, GYM TUNICS BLOUSES, TIES.

BLAZERS, exactly to sketch, selected by School Authorities,
16/9 to 25/-

GYM TUNICS, 22 to 39 inch, in three qualit
11/6 to 26/6

BLOUSES, square neck or with collar, All one price, 9/11

SCHOOL TIES, . . 3/11

Enquiries will be appreciated.

ESSLEMONT & MACINTOSH, LTD.
UNION STREET. ABERDEEN.

What Margaret should have been wearing: An advertisement for the 'correct' High School wear 1950s.

A High School reunion, 2003: Lindy is to be glimpsed 2nd row from the top, 2nd right.

All those riches await her: Lindy Cheyne at the start of her High School career.

The High offered such riches

I never regretted the High. It offered so much, such riches. The quality of the teachers was outstanding; back then in the '50s the school could boast a staff which in any later period would simply not have been available. These were women who had come through the war, were unmarried and who devoted their whole lives to the school and to their subjects. These were mature women who were passionate about their work and about seeing that their pupils made the best of themselves. When you were in their classrooms you were always aware that behind the immediate subject in hand there lay a breadth of knowledge. That, I believe, is the secret of good teaching – the ability of the teacher to inspire a sense of confidence in their expertise and to convey a spirit of commitment to what they were doing.

Right from the start, I had this sense of privilege in being a High School girl. There would be Miss Rose, our Headmistress, making her presence felt each morning. First thing as you entered the building you would see her standing at the stairs, ready to shake your hand and to use your own name. The routine would be, 'Good morning, Rosalind,' to which you would reply, 'Good morning, Miss Rose'.

The school motto was 'By Learning and Courtesy' and I now feel that it is the final one of that pair which is missing from education today. But we certainly knew all about it. Ours was a school without any litter, one in which you would never have dreamt of cheeking your teachers and in which you knew your place. To misbehave would be to invite the sky to fall in, but this was no cause for resentment; we knew the framework of discipline was there to ensure we would follow the right path, that we were cherished as future citizens.

Rosalind (Lindy) Cheyne. b. 1943. High School for Girls. Interviewed 2016.

'Mr Grammar School' retires

An RGC Lower School line up: Arthur is top row, 3rd from right.

Aberdeen Grammar School had in the past been a great Imperial school. Its pupils tended to go on to serve the Empire as civil servants, as soldiers, as doctors and so on.

But you know, there was always this quite ambivalent attitude towards the school in the town. The School Board minutes are full of complaints about the conduct and standards achieved by the pupils. I remember once reading out some extracts which listed the current complaints, about smoking, and swearing and truancy, and getting the

'Mr Grammar School' actually attended the other place for his own education. Founders' Day at Robert Gordons College, 1946 and Arthur McCombie is to be seen as a leading Prefect, just behind Rector Collier.

Arthur developed into a fine sportsman while at the school. Here he is opening the bowling in the 1947 County Cup Final at Mannofield.

response, 'Oh, I know – isn't it terrible what pupils are like nowadays,' – and telling them, 'Nowadays? This is from the Minutes of 1892!'

By the time I arrived there, however, the school had developed a heritage that you felt was worth trying to live up to. I remember all the rows about the changing of the name when the school became 'Rubislaw Academy'. I used to maintain that it was what came out of the door that mattered, not the name that was engraved above it. Over time, I became very interested in the history of the school and have now collected a lot of information about it. I remember that when I retired and got my presentation, the photo appeared in the P&J under the heading 'Mr Grammar School Retires'. I found that very flattering.

Personally, I had no real regrets about what happened. Once the policy is made then you just have to get on with it; that's life. As for those who moan about 'decline', well I would argue that things are different, not necessarily worse. So much depends on what you are trying to achieve, on what your objectives are. We now live in a different world entirely. When you step outside the situation then everything that has happened might appear to be quite disturbing, but when you are in the middle of it you just get on with it, and from that point of view things seem much less dramatic.

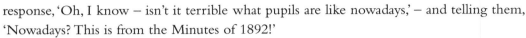 **Arthur McCombie.** b. 1928. Aberdeen Grammar School. Interviewed 2005.

Arthur L McCombie is the joint author, with Brian R. W. Lockhart, of Bon Record: A History of Aberdeen Grammar School, *Birlinn Books, Edinburgh 2012.*

Books offered me companionship

The future academic star: Henry combing the beach at Macduff, with sister and friend, 1951.

Above everything else, I read, and I read. I devoured anything I could find in print, especially reference books. We had a small shelf of volumes in the flat, but they contained two sets of encyclopaedias and I would go through them from cover to cover, eagerly taking in the hard facts as the capitals of the world, its longest rivers, its highest mountains and the world's biggest countries in order of size.

To imbibe such phenomena gave me a sense of being in control of life. Another motive was to fill the days of a somewhat solitary existence. Books offered me a constant companionship. I was the first of my family to get into Senior Secondary education and then on to university. My parents were anxious to give me all the opportunities that they had missed out on and made many sacrifices to support me. It was only a three-room flat, but space was cleared to give me my own room and study area.

Fortunately, I had gained a Foundation scholarship to Robert Gordon's College otherwise studying there would have been impossible. As it was, my parents willingly gave up luxuries such as holidays and a TV set and such household goods as a fridge.

All this was typical of the times and my background. Before the '60s those going to university were a tiny minority: society required only a handful of graduates to fill the

Henry at his first academic conference, Paris, 1964. He is the one in a bow tie.

posts of lawyer, doctor, teacher or minister, while the rest of the able young were expected to go into apprenticeships to generate the work of what was still a predominantly manufacturing economy.

So, I was determined to make a success of my educational opportunities; I was terrified of failure because that would have meant letting my parents down. That, and a determination to beat all the Primary Duxes in my class drove me on.

But life at Robert Gordon's College was far from easy. I never had any problem in coping with the academic side of things but, nevertheless, each day for those first three years I would go off to school in fear and trembling. In those days the College had a staff which ruled by fear, backed up by the belt. Thrashings were a common feature virtually every day; boys were belted for anything and that meant not only disciplinary matters. Boys were thrashed for not doing well enough academically, regardless of ability or mitigating circumstances.

One or two of those teachers could only be described as sadists. There was a Maths teacher who was universally hated on account of his brutality. I reckon such brutes destroyed more than they made. I was academically keen and something of a swot so I managed to avoid the worst, but there were some who were psychologically destroyed by that regime.

Now the school is utterly unrecognisable, and very much for the better. But looking back, I feel my progress there rested for a while on a knife edge. If, for example, I had had the wrong Maths teacher I would have been so oppressed by thoughts of his brutality that I could have gone under. But I got through it all and by Year 4 began to enjoy the school. That was when the staff started to treat us as individuals and not just as young savages who had to be beaten into shape.

Henry Ellington. b. 1941. Robert Gordon's College. Interviewed 2016.

Professor Henry Ellington went on to enjoy a distinguished career, mostly at RGIT and Robert Gordon University, firstly in his academic field of Physics and then as a pioneer of the application of gaming and simulation in both teaching and in industrial projects. He has also written the official history *The Robert Gordon University: a History.*

Further honours came his way: Henry poses with his DLitt degree from Robert Gordon University, 1996.

Defying his Headmaster's prediction: Denied a Senior Secondary education, Jim Wyness nevertheless went on to become a History graduate, school teacher and then to act as Aberdeen's Lord Provost in the 1990s.

A man of learning: Jim at home amidst his beloved books, 2003.

Teachers were like gods

My sister went to the Central School from Broomhill. I was set to follow her, but it didn't happen, although I know I was bright enough. I was in hospital for spells as a child with stomach trouble and that held me back. I remember telling the Headmaster that I wanted to go the Central and he shoved my head into one of the flip-up lid desks, held it down and thumped the lid up and down on it, shouting out, 'You are not going to go to the Central School, you stupid boy! You are not going to go to the Central School! Now tell me what you are not going to do.' 'Not go to the Central School, sir'. I can only assume that he didn't want pupils from his school to go after something he didn't think they could manage. But teachers could be brutal then and were allowed to make these judgements. They were like gods; you didn't challenge them or question their word.

James (Jim) Wyness. b. 1933. Broomhill Primary School. Interviewed 2005.

Jim Wyness began working life as an electrician at John Lewis shipyard; later he confounded his headmaster's judgement by studying as a mature student at university and became a History teacher. A long-standing member of the Labour party, he also served as a councillor and completed a term as Lord Provost to the city.

MEMORABLE TEACHERS – AND PUPILS

That's my Michael they're shouting about!

When Michael Gove was one of her pupils.

What he went on to become: Michael Gove in his Lord Chancellor's robes.

I was teaching at Kittybrewster when a young Michael Gove was a pupil there. He had a tough time of it did Michael, largely because he was that bit different. He looked like a young Mr Pickwick with his spectacles always stuck in some book or other. He was something of a soft target for the bullies and more than once he had to endure having his head stuck down the toilet. He had no aptitude for physical activity and never learned how to do somersaults effectively. But, of course, intellectually he was in a class of his own.

I'm very proud of what he has gone on to achieve in his political career. I can see the photographs of him all dressed up in his Lord Chancellor robes and think back to those days when he was a chubby bespectacled, physically awkward little primary school boy. Years later I was down in London when he was Minister for Education and witnessed these placard-wielding demonstrators marching past, chanting out, 'Down with Gove!' I stood there thinking, 'Oh no, that's my Michael they're shouting about!'

Eileen Pike. b. 1940. Kittybrewster School. Interviewed 2015.

The good friend:
Ex Grammar School pupil, Robin Cook in his Foreign Secretary days.

Robin Cook – a good friend

One of the few bright spots during my time at Aberdeen Grammar School was my friendship with Robin Cook, who later went on to be an outstanding MP, Foreign Secretary and leading light in the Labour party. Like me, he was small and red haired; we both entered the Kindergarten on the same day and naturally gravitated towards each other. His father was a Science master, who had been a high-flying researcher in munitions during the war, but who had given up that career in despair at the effects of the firebombing of Dresden and then turned to doing something for the younger generation by becoming a teacher.

Partly because of Robin's enthusiasm I went along to the Literary and Debating Society with him. I enjoyed the cut and thrust of debate and relished all the banter though I never actually could bring myself to get up on my feet and make a contribution. Robin, however, was keen to make his mark and proved to be a lively and telling speaker. I can claim that I was present when, as a small S1 pupil, he made his very first speech in public.

After he left school and entered Parliament, we rarely saw each other, though we did keep in touch. I know he developed a reputation as a somewhat waspish Commons performer, one who could lay about him to the point where opponents would fear his tongue, but I always found him very pleasant and easy-going. A good friend.

David Brown. b. 1946. Aberdeen Grammar School. Interviewed 2014.

Jock Robertson – a colossal Head Teacher

That formidable Headmaster: Jock Robertson, front row centre left, with his Central School Prefects, 1953.

I was a pupil at the Central from 1942-47. Our Head was Jock Robertson, while the Aberdeen Grammar School had James Robertson. Both had a great reputation, but we were proud of our own Robertson. To us he was a great novelty act, an eccentric character who was famous for his direct observations and his pessimism. He could be relied upon to lower any occasion with some sort of doom and gloom remark. When I was awarded the top bursary, he was naturally pleased that one of his pupils had got one over Aberdeen Grammar School and the High, but he marked the event by telling me, 'Well, you've got the highest bursary. I suppose you've done quite well, but, to be honest, I don't think the standard could have been very high this year. '

He was a tall man with a long lugubrious face and small piggy eyes. His own subject was Maths but really, he couldn't teach for toffee. When we had him in the Sixth, he reduced us all to complete confusion with his attempts to explain the intricacies of advanced geometry to us. But he was a colossal character and one we cherished for his memorable pronouncements. Mostly he couldn't open his mouth without letting some pronouncement of doom issue forth from it.

Joyce Collie. b. 1929. The Central. Interviewed 2007.

She was utterly dedicated to our progress

Keith Taylor as one of the Primary 6 class at Skene Square School – he is the one in the lumber jacket.

L iving in Summer Street, I went to the nearest Primary school, which was Skene Street. The school served me well. I had the great good fortune to have as my teacher Miss Helen Smith, who took us in the final crucial year leading up to the 11-plus. She was very ambitious for her pupils and was prepared to drive them on with extra coaching and good strong teaching. I can remember her taking some of us for extra work after school hours, coaching us in topics such as sequences that were liable to come up in the 11-plus.

I wasn't the only one to be helped by her through the 11-plus in my year. Three of us landed up in the top class at Robert Gordon's College, and then went on to the University. This was some achievement for a school such as Skene Street. I believe she had as a friend and rival, a teacher at Mile End, which was a school with a very different

> His own subject was Maths but really, he couldn't teach for toffee.

Two years later and with the 11 plus triumphantly negotiated, in his First year class at Robert Gordon's College. Keith is back row, 4th left.

catchment area, and she would vie with her to see how many pupils they could get through the exam.

She was a formidable character, one who would make clear her views, and her priorities. I did well at football and got into our very successful school team. I remember sitting in her class one afternoon waiting for the call to join the rest of the team to go to an afternoon cup replay at Pittodrie, as a reward for all our success. When the door opened, and my name was called out, her attitude was, 'Keith, are you going to that match at Pittodrie?' When I assured her I was, her comment was, 'Well, don't blame me if you don't do as well as you ought to in your exams.'

Miss Smith was, I should guess, in her late 30s. I am very grateful for her advice and efforts on behalf of my classmates and myself. She was utterly dedicated to our progress. However, the people I owe most to in life would always be my parents, who, by their encouragement and sacrifice, ensured that my brother and I would benefit from opportunities sadly, like so many of their generation, never available to themselves.

Keith Taylor. b. 1938. Skene Street Primary School. Interviewed 2006.

You knew never to cross Goofy

The teacher I really remember at Middle School was Miss Grace Gordon, nicknamed 'Goofy'. She was a tall, unbending figure in her 50s and very tough and very fair with it. She was a great help and encouragement to me.

She had this bookcase which contained all sorts of titles, including lots of wildlife and

The Middle school, Gallowgate – since demolished, but as it was when Kenny was a pupil there in the 1940s.
(IMAGE BY KIND PERMISSION OF ABERDEEN JOURNALS)

sports books, both of which had a great appeal for me. If all had gone well on a Friday afternoon, she would invite you to look through her books and take out a volume to read over the weekend. 'Mind that you wash your hands before handling my books!', she would warn us.

She did have a big strap, and, by God, she could use it! But I never got it from her. You see, I was a keen and well-behaved pupil and was anxious to keep on the right side of her – not just to avoid punishment, but to make sure I'd be able to get at those books of hers. She could be extremely abrasive and fierce. You knew never to cross Goofy; in her classroom we kept absolute silence.

But at the end she did get annoyed with me. When I was 14, I decided I would be leaving school even though I was doing well. She came up to me, 'They tell me you intend to leave. How very stupid of you; if you stay on, I can guarantee you'll make a success of it'. But at home cash was tight and I was keen to get a wage and put a penny or two into my mother's purse. So, leave I did.

Kenny Courage. b. 1932. The Middle School. Interviewed 2014.

MIDDLE JUNIOR SECONDARY SCHOOL											
Pupil's Name: Kenneth G. Courage Date of Birth: 19 . 4 . 32 Age at Entry: 12											
SESSION	1945 -194			1945 -1946 .			194 -194 .			194 -194 .		
TERM	1st.	2nd.	3rd.	1st.	2nd.	3rd.	1st.	2nd.	3rd.	1st.	2nd.	3rd.
CLASS REFERENCE	1B₁		1B₁	1A₁	11B₁	11B₁						
SUBJECT												
English (200)	93		130	134	134	138						
History (50)	37		44	34	43	44						
Geography (50)	39		40	39	34	43						
Mathematics (150)	117		130	145	145	125						
Science (100)	72		80	90	86	65						
Art (50)	27		36	27	37	35						
Technical Subjects (150)	86		89	90	90	91						
Summary Per Cent	62.8		73.2	74.5	75.9	72.1						
Music	59		59	71	78	70						
Physical Training	72		72	76	78	76						
Scripture Knowledge	60		64	60	84	76						
No. in Class	35		34	29	27	21						
Place in Class	5teg	4	4	1st.	1st.	2nd						
No. of Times Absent	7		–	3	2	–						
Signature of Parent or Guardian	1											
	2 M. Courage.			M. Courage								
	3 M. Courage.			W. Courage								

Progress: Very good. Conduct: Very good.

Date of Leaving: 28/ 6/ 46.

ALFRED A. EDDIE, M.A.,
Head Teacher.

Leaving school at only 14 – despite his 'good progress'. Kenny Courage's last ever report card from his Middle School.

A tale of two hair styles: Setting out for the High – an intent 13 year-old Edith Nicol.

Four years later: Now a Senior pupil, Edith sports both the school uniform and a Jimi Hendrix coiffeur.

It was all thanks to Mr McGregor

I was picked out to pass the 11-Plus. I had a great sense of wanting to get out of the working-class, even at that age. I had an aunt – her teachers wanted her to go on to become a teacher, but my grandparents wouldn't hear of it. They couldn't afford it. They had a large family – nine children. So, she had to go out to work. I remember the story of how she sobbed her eyes out at the bottom of the tenement they stayed in. I remember being told that she shouted up from the bottom of the stairs for all the neighbours to hear, 'You're just a bunch of skinflints!'

Another aunt was very keen, when she knew I was clever, that my experience of education should be different from her generation's. They had all left at 14, I think. She encouraged me a lot. 'You're clever – you could be a teacher. I'll buy you the suit.' She had this perception that a teacher had to wear a suit, a nice jacket and skirt. She made me realize that education was a means to better myself.

You're not going to believe this next bit. I did pass the 11-Plus. My parents then had to fill in a form as to where they wanted me to go to Secondary School. I was desperate to go to the High School. I believed the High School was the top of the tree. I'd read all these boarding school books about girls and that's the kind of life I imagined myself leading.

My parents put me down for Summerhill. They said they couldn't afford the High School – the uniform and all the rest of it. I went to see the Headmaster, Mr McGregor about it. I was devastated – I knew that Summerhill meant leaving at 15 and getting a job. My mum – this is true – my mum wanted me to work at Woolworth's, behind the counter. This was because the girl across the road worked there and my mother felt it was a really nice job. Between us – Mr McGregor and I – we concocted a bit of a story. My parents were informed that because I was so clever it was compulsory for me to go to the High School and that I couldn't possibly be permitted to enter Summerhill.

My mother for years later spoke about the fact that I was so clever that I had to go to the High School And I remain proud of my working class background.

Edith Nicol. b. 1952. Muirfield Primary School. Interviewed 2001.

We won't hear a word against Miss Rose

Firmly in control:
Miss Rose with her
Sixth year girls, 1956.

My final two years at the High School coincided with the last years of the reign of Miss Rose. She was quite a personage was Miss Rose. She would sweep down the corridor in her robes like royalty, while we underlings were required to shrink back against the walls and proffer her a curtsey. She never even acknowledged our presence. A stern, slim and very upright character, she could strike fear into the staff, let alone the pupils. She was the living embodiment of the school motto, 'By Learning and Courtesy'.

But although she didn't appear to notice us, she must have done. There was one day I had been chasing around with the boys in Westburn Park; Bob Selbie was after me right up to my door. I threw my bike down and rushed in, only to slip on the highly polished floor that my mother always kept. My blazer got caught up in the doorknob and it ripped. It was brand new and such an expensive item couldn't be replaced just like that.

Fortunately, my mother was a trained dressmaker and she was able to make a neat seam along the tear. The following day I went to school in my neatly repaired blazer, but the very next day a letter arrived at home complaining that I had attended school in a non-uniform blazer. Miss Rose must have spotted the fault – and yet she hadn't spoken to me about it, or indeed on any other occasion during my school days up to that point.

I retain a great deal of loyalty to the High. I have been President of the F.P. Club and now of the Memorabilia group. It's noticeable that those of us who actually experienced her regime, almost automatically assume that we were the true 'High School' girls. Talking of those days, the 'Prime of Miss Jean Brodie' comes to mind – 'la crème de la crème' and all that. We were encouraged to become young ladies. Most of us won't hear a word against Miss Rose. To do so would be regarded as an act of betrayal.

Aileen Pettitt. b. 1937. High School for Girls. Interviewed 2014.

Smartly attired:
High School girl Aileen
Pettitt at the start of her
school career.

THE TEACHERS' VIEWPOINT

Walker Road pupil in Miss Cook's Primary 4 class. Margaret Donald is the one with the ribbon in her hair.

I got enormous satisfaction out of it all

I went to Walker Road School. I was one of those children who simply loved the school. I liked counting and I loved reading. Friends from those days tell me that their main memory of me is walking up Menzies Road with my head in a book.

The teaching was very formal at school: plenty of teacher instruction, of pointing at the blackboard, and plenty of repetitive sums and writing practice. I think that's what started me off on the whole idea of becoming a teacher myself; I loved the order and regularity of it all, the way everything had to follow a timetable and fit into place.

When I graduated, I went for my interview for a post with the City and, to my great

joy, found there was a vacancy at Walker Road and that the Headmaster was happy to have me. So, I went back to my old school, but now as a teacher.

I loved my teaching. Each morning I would run up the brae from my home in Craig Place to Walker Road so as to get to another day's teaching. I began with the Infants. I got enormous satisfaction out of taking children who couldn't read, write or count and

Margaret with her second-ever class – the Walker Road Infants of 1951.

Walker Road teacher, 1968. Margaret is first left front row. At the right end of her row sits Miss Shaw who taught Margaret when she was a pupil at the school.

then at the end of two years helping them to master all of that. But there would always be some in the class who found it more difficult, so I got into the way of setting the rest some work to do while I could go and sit with the stragglers and give them individual attention. So, when what was called in those days the 'Adjustment Class' – usually with 8 to 12 pupils in it – was set up, I was happy to take it on. For me this was a wonderful experience.

I had my own little room where I could make up my own work sheets and organise the learning materials just as I wanted and then spend time with those who were experiencing learning difficulties. I could create a really intimate family atmosphere. My great joy was to teach children to read, to write and to spell – the basics – but without which nothing else is possible. It was so satisfying to take children to whom these tasks were a mystery and then a couple of years later return them to their mainstream classes, confident and able.

Margaret Donald. b. 1929. Walker Road School. Interviewed 2014.

Deprivation in oil rich Aberdeen

Setting the right tone: The entrance to Westerton School.

You know there's an impression that because Aberdeen is a relatively affluent oil rich society that there is no real deprivation in the city but, believe me, that is not the case. Westerton was right in the middle of an area of poverty and need. But the parents were most supportive and backed all our efforts to lift the morale and the status of the school. I just had to tell them of my plans and they were unhesitating in their support.

I was keen that pupils shouldn't miss out on the sort of outings and activities which any West End school could take for granted. I persuaded the parents to bank a pound a week with the school, which could then finance a skiing trip to Glenshee. A request for £100 outright would have been impossible, but our little savings scheme did the trick. I toured the charity shops for the ski clothes so as to make the whole venture affordable.

The Glenshee skiing trip became an annual fixture. I also introduced cross-country running and organised a team to compete at the schools' meet at Kirkcaldy. Cross-country only required a pair of trainers, not the expensive equipment that other sports did. We were up against a host of private schools and didn't win any medals. But no matter; it was a happy outing and we had fish and chips on the way home.

We introduced a uniform policy, nothing elaborate, just a sweat shirt designed by Marks & Spencer. When the H.M. Inspector came, he was impressed at the spectacle of 300 children all in uniform, seated before him at Assembly. I ran a prefect system and each Friday afternoon invited the prefects to have tea with me and the Depute Head, Mrs English, to discuss any points of common interest.

Our aim was to bring the school, the parents and the pupils all together and encourage them to feel that they were sharing a common purpose in making their school a success

'We made sure that they didn't miss out': A Westerton group on a ski trip to Glenshee.

for each and every body in it. So, we set out a contract for all parties to read and to sign, which set out what was to be expected of them. My whole intention, and that of my staff, was to build upon the work of my predecessor by lifting the aspirations of the school and to impress upon both pupils and parents that although they might live in a poor area of town, they could have the same experiences and ambitions as any West End child.

I finally retired in 2002. I can look back on a lifetime's work during which I can honestly claim that I never experienced a day when I was reluctant to get up and go to my job.

Dorothy Bothwell. b. 1937. Westerton Primary School. Interviewed 2016.

When I first went to Northfield, I loved it

When I first went to Northfield, I loved it. Those were the days before the Parents' Charter came in, so we always had enough bright and willing pupils to make up a couple of classes of Higher English. We had our troublemakers, of course, but discipline was easier. The school had an excellent social spirit among the staff. There would be golf outings, discos, parties. The school was very much part of the community too. The Northfield Fair each year was a massive event, which would raise thousands. Most parents had a high opinion of the school and what it was doing for their children.

'In the cause of the Scots Language': Les Wheeler enthuses his audience at a North-east writing workshop, Mayfest 2018.

Towards the end, I became what I can only call complacent. I had no interest in moving. I would find myself saying something and then thinking to myself, 'But that's exactly what I was saying this time last year, and the year before that'. I'd be repeating the same old jokes and doing the same interpretation exercises. Then Jim Merrilees came along as my Head of Department. I started off going to our feeder Primary schools on a Tuesday afternoon for Scots language stuff – storytelling and poetry – and he gave me his full backing. He encouraged me in my attempts to branch out into the Scots.

Nowadays I'm in the schools more than ever. I've been in 50 this year alone. I do storytelling, singing, poetry. I'm tremendously impressed by the kids. I've never had the slightest problem. Sometimes a teacher will apologise in advance and warn me that this is a 'difficult' group, but I have no bother.

In some ways the cause of Scots language is more potent than ever – and in some ways not at all. As an everyday language I haven't much hope for it. Local talk is now no longer embedded in the daily lives of the young the same as it has been for the previous generations. Everything has become standardised. Much of our Doric depended on a horse-age technology that is now dead.

Leslie Wheeler. b. 1938. Northfield Academy . Interviewed 2004.

My ambition was always to be a teacher

From whenever I could remember, my ambition was to become a teacher. My primary school was Ashley Road, a traditional establishment, both in appearance and ethos. It was all rote learning, with the daily chanting out of the tables and a great emphasis on spelling. I responded to all of that. At home I had my own blackboard and easel and would line up my dollies and teddies to give them lessons. I think I was quite hard on them.

At the very start of her High school career. Elizabeth McCombie as a Primary 1 pupil.

My Secondary School was the High School for Girls. I was so proud to be a High School girl. There I was, going off down the street, all dressed up in the full High School rigout: three-quarter socks in black, a stout pair of shoes, gym tunic with a square neck, a square-necked blouse, a hat and, best of all, the blazer with the badge sewn onto it. I was as proud as punch.

During all this time, my ambition to become a teacher never left me. I duly got my degree at Aberdeen University and completed my year at the College of Education.

Eventually I became Head at Rosewood Infant School; later we amalgamated with another Kincorth school, Kirkhill, and as the Head there was about to retire, I got that position. And that's where I saw out my career.

During all that time in the Primary and Infant sector I saw many changes. The Kincorth schools gave me a completely different social environment to the one I had been brought up in at Ashley Road Primary School in the 1940s. Most of the parents were supportive, but there was a pocket of them which seemed to resent the school and

And at the end. Last day at school and Elizabeth, bottom row, first left, is one of a leavers' group who encounters a sweep and persuades him to pose for this 'lucky' photograph.

its efforts to impose a disciplinary framework on their children. It got to the stage that when the phone rang you could never be sure what you would be hearing at the other end, whether it would be yet another volley of insults and complaints about some imagined injustice that had been allegedly imposed upon their dear Jimmy or Annie. Sometimes the abuse contained obscene language. There was this older girl who had gone up to Kincorth Academy and who, if I had given her little brother into trouble, would spend her lunch break coming down to our playground in order to shout abuse at me. Years later I happened to bump into her at the airport and she made a point of coming up to me and being as nice as anything.

But, as I said, that was the exception. Most parents made the effort to be understanding of the complexities of trying to run a large urban school.

As for all the changes that were visited upon the curriculum, well I think they are best summed up by answering the question 'Better?' with the word 'Different'. In many ways the shift to a more pupil-centred personal approach was for the better, but there were losses too. The insistence that all rote learning had to be abandoned in favour of a 'knowledge by personal investigation' approach was overdone. It could lead to a surreptitious teaching of the tables once the Inspectorate's back was turned. A lot of lip service had to be paid to the new methods for the sake of career advancement. What happened is that most teachers worked out their ways of compromising between the old and the new – not necessarily a bad thing either.

I was happy with my career and I was happy to retire from it. It was very satisfying while it lasted, but I can't say that I miss it.

Elizabeth McCombie. b. 1934. Kirkhill Primary School. Interviewed 2016.

> As for all the changes that were visited upon the curriculum, well I think they are best summed up by answering the question 'Better?' with the word 'Different'.

> If I'm in the corridor and I spot a bit of litter I will bend down and pick it up. You've got to show that you are part of what everyone has to do for their school, that you're not a remote figure in an office.

You must work at it every single day

I try to bring a model of achievement to my work here as head teacher. It's something you must work at, every day. If I'm in the corridor and I spot a bit of litter I will bend down and pick it up. You've got to show that you are part of what everyone has to do for their school, that you're not a remote figure in an office.

I don't really have much truck with that school of thought which tells us that we mustn't impose these values on working-class kids. The example I was given at my home is the one that I would hold out for all classes: 'If you say you are going to do something, then make sure you do it to the very best of your ability'. That's what I call really caring for the working-class kid. Caring doesn't mean simply being nice all the time; it's not being permissive.

What I try to communicate to all pupils is, 'You are important. Your progress is important. If you are failing on some commitment, then you are failing yourself; you're not fulfilling your potential. You are better than that. My job is not to be nice to you, not to stand back and smile at you as you fail, but to celebrate your success. You can do it!'

Standards are important and so is attention to detail. Deportment, dress, behaviour, are all part of it. I tell the pupils here that school uniform is important, that the school is not a fashion parade. If we had free dress here, then the 30% who take free school dinners would be made to feel like second class citizens. School is their real opportunity to get on to the ladder of success and if they are being made to feel inferior then they can't do that. When you show up for a day at school then you have to show that you are up for it, that you are not here to be casual.

I've always enjoyed good support from the parents. It's taken time to build up. When I became Head, I started doing something I don't think any other large school in Scotland does and that is to make a point of meeting each pupil with their parents individually. We hold a 15-minute interview. We go over what the school expects from each of its pupils. We agree that behaviour is important, that homework is important. We agree that discipline is important, that without it learning is impossible. In this way I'll hold 240 such individual meetings each session.

In my day, the patterns in society were more rigid; things are more open now. But it can still be the case that if you are working-class then the expectations will be lower, and sometimes pupils are quite content not to rise above them. But if you communicate to people that they are thick then the response will be, 'Right I'm thick and I'm badly behaved. OK, I'll show you just how thick I am and just how badly I can behave!' That then becomes their achievement.

But I always say, 'No, wait, you can do this.' What we want is a can-do mentality. What we are saying is, 'Show how strong you are. And working together we can do it — you, us, your parents, we can do it together'.

Lenny Taylor b. 1945. St Machar Academy. Interviewed 2005.

SOME UNIVERSITY EXPERIENCES

He was a great practical joker. He kept a collection of guns and used a Luger to demonstrate basic principles of physics.

A wonderful lecturer

University was a wonderful time in the early '60s. Aberdeen University was still a small, intimate and friendly place and the quality of its teaching was excellent. I was privileged to study under the great R.V. Jones – not only a wonderful lecturer, but an outstanding character in British scientific life. He is the man who, during his intelligence work at the Air Ministry in the Second World War, probably came second to Alan Turing in the contribution he made to the Allied victory. He came to Aberdeen thanks to his wartime friendship with Winston Churchill. Churchill came up to Aberdeen in 1945 to receive the Freedom of the City and on learning that the Chair of Natural Philosophy was vacant insisted that 'The job must be given to that young man!'

Another notable feature was his fathering two amazingly beautiful daughters in Susan and in Rosie, one of whom actually became Miss Universe.

He was a brilliant lecturer. He was a great practical joker, a talent which had been invaluable in devising methods for the defeat of Nazi Germany, and this helped him to think up ways of imparting knowledge in the most startling fashion. He kept a collection of guns and used a Luger to demonstrate basic principles of physics. He put up a screen and on its other side he had a pair of tumblers. One was filled with water and the other stayed empty. He would then fire off a bullet at each; the empty one would shatter into pieces while the full one simply disappeared. This showed us the force of pressure. No Health and Safety considerations; R.V. Jones was a law unto himself!

Henry Ellington. b. 1941. Aberdeen University. Interviewed 2016.

Professor R.V. and Mrs Jones pose for this domestic shot in the year of his retirement from his position in the Chair of Natural Philosophy.

The school prize-winner: A 16 year-old Alfred Alexander, Inverurie Academy, 1935.

Same hat but 70 years apart: As a bright young man in 1938 and as a sprightly nonagenarian, 2008.

The oldest student in Britain

I'm the oldest undergraduate in Britain, you know. I was 90 in February! My own studies at Aberdeen University stretch back to 1937. Then, in 1992, I returned to take an Honours degree in Geography; I graduated with that in 1996 and then went on to take a BSc in Ecology. Currently I'm studying for another MA, in Sociology, so that will make three degrees in total. Keep the mind active, that's what I say, keep studying, keep learning new things and you'll never get past it.

I was born in Rhynie, in 1918. My father was the Headmaster of the school there. I must admit that I was disappointed in my father: he was a man without very much in the way of go. He could have gone further in his life, but just seemed content to idle along, out in his country schools.

At school, my first idea was to become a doctor, but in those days the school had a policy of only putting its top 10% forward for the Highers, so as to keep up its success rate. I ended up as a butcher, after the war. It was my grandfather's business, Rueben Laing, the well-known Aberdeen firm.

I retired from the butchery business at age 65; then I saw a job advertised at Baker Tools at their Bridge of Don branch. I applied, was interviewed, got the job and was there till I was 80. Then after that finished, I remember walking past Marischal College with a friend. 'Look, that's the place I did my Diploma in, back in 1937', I told him. 'I think I'll go back and do something else at the university.' So that's exactly what I did. I had my interview and was accepted. I met one of the interviewing panel later and he

said, 'We didn't interview you – you interviewed us!'

And, when I graduated, the student newspaper, *Gaudie*, carried a message from me to new students, 'A welcome letter from Alfie Alexander to new students at King's: "As you may know I am in my 90th year and some 70 of those have been spent in and out of the University".

From that you can conclude that you are never too old to learn, that you can learn something new every day. By keeping your brain active you will never become Alzheimerised. My philosophy is: act young, mix with the young and you'll never feel old. Good luck, God bless, have a happy time at the University'.

My belief is that knowledge is power. The younger students invigorate me. I can't think of anything worse than sitting around doing nothing just because you've reached a certain age on the calendar. Learning is my hobby, one I've no intention of stopping. Believe me, I'll be around for a long time yet!

Alfred Alexander. b. 1918. Aberdeen University. Interviewed 2008.

Alfie with the tankard that his fellow students presented him with to celebrate his 90th birthday.
(IMAGE BY KIND PERMISSION OF ABERDEEN JOURNALS)

I vowed that nobody would ever speak to me like that again

I went to university, first of all, to study Medicine. I passed through into my third year without difficulty. But that's when the problems struck. This was the year of our pre-clinical at Foresterhill. But our consultant there was in the terminal stages of cancer. He had lost all sense of time and would come in at two a.m. to do ward rounds, getting his staff out of bed and disrupting the routine of the ward. When we came in to be taught, the staff and the patients were exhausted.

After three weeks of this my fellow students and I decided that action simply had to be taken so, as Class Representative, I went to the Dean of Faculty. Being young and naïve I stuck my neck out. I explained the situation and he let me talk for 10 minutes. He then drew himself up to his full 5 feet 3 inches: 'Dr X is a much better clinician than you will ever be. If you persist in your complaints, I will ensure that you will never graduate from this university and if, perchance, I am not there when you sit your final examinations, I will certainly make sure that you never get a post.'

No doubt, this being 1969, there was a deal of sexism involved in all this. I was a female in a course where three-quarters of its students were male, but he was also a notorious bully, one who behaved like this to all his staff. Anyway, there I was, just 19 and shaking with fury. I had been brought up to respect the medical profession and also to have faith in the justice of their systems. There and then, I vowed that nobody, but nobody, would ever speak to me, or to any student, in such a manner again.

This was at the end of September. At the Christmas exams I passed everything except Pharmacology – this consultant's subject. I saw the writing on the wall and realised I would have to prepare myself to make other plans for my future. When the same thing happened at the summer exams, I approached Jo Grimond, who was the Rector. He advised me to go through the SRC [Students' Representative Council]. But by now I wasn't sure I actually wanted to join a profession where people like that could wield power. So, I decided that what I would do would be to get outside his little system and fight people like him from the outside, to get at the very roots of the system.

So, I switched courses, took Music as an Arts subject and added in my Medical passes so as to make up a Science degree. Jo Grimond had been sympathetic and told me that if ever I needed a job, he would get me one. After graduation, he got me a job with the Rowntree Trust, and into a project which aimed to bring the arts and creative activity

A position of some power – as Lady President of the Students' Association, Aberdeen University, 1970/71.

Another successful Charities Campaign – Jenny surrounded by the spoils, 1971.

'I began to have some influence': Receiving the Mastership of the University, 2011.

The University still some years away. Jenny receives her first ever kiss, from the fortunate Malcolm Strachan, 1952.

into grass roots communities. This suited me down to the ground. But I have always kept my finger on the pulse of the University and in the 1990s I got onto its Business Committee and began to have some influence.

I acted as I did because I've always been brought up to believe that you owe it to others to pursue causes, to refuse to exist only in your own wee bubble and, when a matter of social justice raises its head, to go out and do something about it. I accept that this will make me a scary wifie, a pushy lady in some eyes.

So maybe that act of injustice by that Dean of Faculty has turned out to be a positive influence over the rest of my life. As Jo Grimond said at the time, 'Jenny, all this has been very painful for you — but I think you'll find it has given you the spur you needed and that you will now go on to be the kind of person who takes up causes and makes things happen'.

With a friend and supporter. Jenny chats to Rector Jo Grimond with future husband Murdoch, 1970.

Jenny Shirreffs. b. 1949. Aberdeen University. Interviewed 2014.

A LADDER OF OPPORTUNITY

I owe a lot to Jean Coutts

One of the
other
children
came up to
me and said,
'Let's go
and see
Miss Coutts.
You get
a sweetie
from her!'

One of my teachers at Broomhill was Miss Rennie. I guess we all have some angel figure among our early teachers and she was mine: a wonderful lady who gave me enormous encouragement. With her, it suddenly became a clever thing to draw well. When I was still at Primary school, I had to spend a lot of my time on my own. I contracted polio and was a long time in the hospital. This was during the big outbreak of '33 at the time when the iron lung had just been invented.

But this did mean me missing a lot of early schooling. I think that is why I became innumerate. I just couldn't understand Arithmetic at all. Its language was a mystery to me. At the Qualifying exam my failure with numbers meant that I could not expect to pass into Senior Secondary and must instead go to a Junior Secondary.

For me, the vital figure was Jean Coutts. One day I was out playing in the street at Ruthrieston; one of the other children came up to me and said, 'Let's go and see Miss Coutts. You get a sweetie from her!' Jean Coutts was an accountant, a spinster – and an active socialist. But I'd no idea of any of this at the time; I just followed the rest. When I got there, she asked me all about myself and what I wanted to be when I grew up. When I told her it was an artist she was very interested.

One thing led to another and I became a frequent visitor. I owe a great deal to that lady. She opened all kinds of doors for me. She was a very active member of the Education Committee; 'The Battling Baillie' she was called: a wonderful lady, one who was very much devoted to the ideals of socialism, 1930s and '40s style: an exemplary woman with a house full of working-class kids that she was anxious to help, in whatever way she could.

She was promoting a scheme whereby kids from that background, and with some talent or other, could be given the chance to get on. That's how I came to get my opportunity to get into the Grammar School, despite the failure at the Qualifying exam. Others followed my example. I might have been something of a guinea pig, but within a few years there was a whole stream of us moving on.

She did all kinds of things for me. She thought I needed extra art support, so she arranged for me to meet an art student called Colin Cameron who had his own studio.

Here I was, a kid of 12 from a council house in Aberdeen and I was getting the access to a real artist's studio. And she would invite various people to meet me: I began to get used to a wider sphere of interests. I would listen to classical music on the radio, to the Proms. That's where I first heard Sibelius's *Violin Concerto* and opera.

William (Bill) Ord. b. 1929. Ruthrieston Circle. Interviewed 2003.

They all turn right but I had to turn left

I had been attending King Street School but then, in 1941, I won a bursary to go to Robert Gordon's College. Going there didn't mean all that much to me at the time but I was aware of the rapture with which my mother received the news. Her son's first step on the road to security! All I remember is the sense of isolation which going to this city centre establishment from my home in Urquhart Street meant. Going home, all the other boys would automatically turn to the right up towards the West End while I was alone in going to the left.

I was aware of poverty. In my first year I was invited to play for the cricket team, but that meant purchasing a set of cream flannels and I just knew the family budget wouldn't run to that, so I had to decline. My sister Aileen was six years younger and successful academically. However, the main burden of family aspiration fell on me, the elder and the son. Although the point was never made too explicitly, there was this underlying attitude, common among working class families of the day, that there would be little point in investing too heavily in a female who was bound to be getting married sooner or later. But Aileen held out and did indeed go to university. She took a good Psychology degree and trained as a teacher.

I can't say that I was ever made to feel socially separate, however, either by the staff or the fellow pupils. In fact, we were all made to feel in the same boat by the method of teaching that was employed. There seemed to be a universal approach based upon exam success, on swotting up and on being made to feel you were stupid and could only succeed by dint of obedient, hard work. Fortunately, I had this knack of writing good essays and of passing exams.

So, although I did well at Robert Gordon's College and passed on to University, I left that school feeling I was simply being lucky and that I must indeed be stupid. University meant Aberdeen – the whole Sixth Year at Robert Gordon's College simply moved on into the local university. Nobody thought of going anywhere else; it was the natural progression.

At university I took the only three subjects I imagined I was any good at – English, History and French. But then, greatly daring, in my second year I also put myself down for Psychology – and, with the inimitable Rex Knight holding court, immediately fell in love with the subject. He had this great gift of being able to simplify the most complex ideas through lucid explanation and entertaining illustrations. However, for safety's sake I

On the brink of University. Ralph Dutch as a senior schoolboy, 1946.

With wife Mary, another East-end high flier graduate, on their wedding anniversary, 1984.

'A rare horticultural success': Smelling the roses in his Fountainhall Road garden.

did complete an English degree, got a First and gold medals and an offer to go to Oxford. But by now I was fixated on Psychology, so decided to stay on at Aberdeen and do an M.Ed. for the next two years.

The education I received was a solid enough grounding, I suppose, but for me it had never been more than a line of targets to overtake. The notion that education could be a personal fulfilment, an experience to be enjoyed for its own sake, had never really occurred to me.

But I became aware of the need to get beyond the stifling Scottish traditions in education whereby 'order', 'discipline', academic success', the 'lad o'pairts' are the watchwords, the approach which could be summed up as 'Teach the best and to hell with the rest!' I could never forget what my own Robert Gordon's College experiences had imposed upon me, that sense of inferiority which could only be redeemed by dint of slavish academic exam success and not by bringing out my own character or interests.

But I'm most grateful for all that has happened to me over my lifetime. First must be the sheer, unwavering determination of my parents to support me and to drive me through school and then university. Of course, their attitude towards what an education should be was limited to a functional concept, whereby you stuck at it in order to get yourself out of poverty and into secure employment with a tidy pension at the end of it.

But in that, they were of their time and, despite those limitations, we have a lot to be grateful to them for. With little opportunity themselves to enjoy the fruits of a full education, they were prepared to make the necessary sacrifice that would ensure we didn't miss out. With that as our background and with the expanding social opportunities of the '50s, '60s and '70s to support us, I think we were a charmed generation.

Ralph Dutch. b.1929. Robert Gordon's College. Interviewed 2014.

And with daughter Susie at her BSc graduation, 1985.

Not bad for a loon from Tillydrone

The Tillydrone childhood: Bill Gordon with sister Val, 1943, who also went on to a successful academic career and is presently on the academic staff of a North Carolina university.

The next year they opened a new school at Tillydrone and I had to be enrolled into it. It was a rough area and there were some dangerously tough guys around. The way to get on the side of people like that is to make them laugh, so I developed a reputation for that. Then I moved on to Powis for my secondary education. I enjoyed the sport there but, generally, it was really a question of putting in time till I could leave.

I qualified as an engineer – the very worst one in the whole world! I went through some hair-raising spells at sea before I decided to quit, to get married and to look for a nice onshore job somewhere.

I was on the Broo for six months then fell into a succession of jobs – the Gas Board, the Electricity Board, chauffeuring, being a porter in Marks & Spencer's, selling and delivering sweets. Then my sister's husband, Colin Hall, who was a medical student at the university, told me he'd been reading about this Special Recruitment Scheme for teachers in the paper and reckoned I could go for it. I was very dubious – I hadn't got any academic qualifications at all. He urged me on: 'You can do it, Bill; you can do it!' If it hadn't been for the fact that he was at university himself, I wouldn't have believed it. But here was this university student, telling me I was good enough, despite the fact that he knew I was a Powis kid with not one Higher to his name.

I found myself turning up at this private tutor, Geddes Irvine, at his home in Carden Place. There were nine of us and he would teach us in his living room. He would come in, looking just like Sherlock Holmes. He would tell us, 'My favourite Shakespeare quotation is "casting pearls before swine" – that has some application to the present situation, wouldn't you agree?'

Then I went to the College of Commerce, which had just started up. There, I picked up the requisite Highers and got into the university. To begin with I was completely scared. I looked around me at all those younger students who had obviously been to their Senior Secondary schools. I felt I hadn't even got the basics.

But by Christmas time I was getting the hang of it. I got into second year English and had decided I could go for Honours. Once I was safely in the third year, I realised that I wasn't actually surrounded by lots of geniuses and that I could hold my own. When I had lived in Tillydrone I had often passed by King's on the bus and looked down on all the students going by with their books in their hands or spread out on the grass, studying and chatting happily to one another. I had thought of them as really special, clever people; I could never imagine myself as one of them. I had had this crippling inferiority complex – but now when I looked around me, I could reckon that only half a dozen of them were any better than me and that I was as good as the rest.

I qualified as an English teacher. I found it difficult to get a job to begin with. All the others seemed to be going off to posts in the new towns but, as a married man with family, that was difficult for me. I was interviewed for a job at the Grammar School along with Stan Watson – he got the post. However, shortly afterwards I was at home one night and there was a knock at the door. It was Alex Tait [the Head of Department]. He told

The lad from Tillydrone made it: Bill with the Honours English degree he earned at the age of 30, 1969.

me that at the interview I had actually been his choice and that there was a job vacant after all. I was now in my 30s, I'd been round the world, I had two children; I was worldly wise, but on that first day at the Grammar School I was terrified. I went there with butterflies in my stomach. Here I was, a teacher at the Aberdeen Grammar School, a boy from Tillydrone who had gone to Powis.

Then I moved on to promoted posts at Hilton, followed by Summerhill.

The 11-plus was a system designed by middle-class educationists for middle-class kids, for those who were more confident, more easily articulate; those who came from a background where passing on to a senior Secondary School was built into their expectations. The really bright ones might get through, but below them there were plenty who were just as able to get on as the middle-class kids who did, but who never got the chance, or who simply turned their back on it as not their scene. There was a lot of social determinism at work in that.

I suppose I've got on. I remember doing a spell in the History department at Robert Gordon's; everybody was so friendly and appreciative. They invited me back to do some invigilation. The exam was held in the President's Room and I remember sitting there watching the candidates writing away at their tables, there in their uniforms, and I thought, 'Not bad for a loon from Tillydrone!'

Bill Gordon. b. 1939. Tillydrone and Powis. Interviewed 2007.

There was a tremendous waste of talent because of the poverty

My mother didn't let me stay on at school. I wanted to stay on and the teachers wanted me to, but my mother wanted me out to work. She was very house proud. So, I had to wait – I was married and had children before I went back to college and did a course. And I always resented it, that I wasn't allowed to stay on at school, because there were kids not so bright as me and they were allowed to. However, that was the way of it. There was a laddie stayed in Park Street and he was a brilliant boy. The Headmaster kept going down to the parents and said 'Please let us keep him. This boy can go far!' But no, they wouldn't do it, they needed the money. He finished up in the fish market at what they called 'lumping' fish. There was a tremendous waste of talent at that time because of the poverty.

Gladys Morrice. b. 1920. Frederick Street School. Interviewed 2016.

No sign of nerves here! Allan Paterson in his 11-plus class at King Street School, 1963. He is back row 4th from right.

I was so nervous, I couldn't hold a pencil

The whole thing was built up – that this was going to decide your life from now on, pass or fail. So, when it came to the actual exam, I remember, I was so nervous, I couldn't hold my pencil. I calmed down and thought to myself, this is so easy I must be doing something wrong – and I started to change things. And I then got the second paper and I thought I was doing okay in this but again I was intimidated by the specially printed material we were given and I thought, well crikey, this is really important, isn't it? And I almost gave up.

I always remember when the results came out; the Monday after when we went to the classroom, the teacher did an incredible thing. She asked all those people who passed the Eleven Plus to stand. Well, a large majority passed – we were an excellent class – but all the rest of us were left sitting. I wasn't too downhearted because Mum and Dad said, 'Well, you really tried. Work hard at your school you're going to go to.'

As a child, school was not really a particularly stimulating place for me. I got through it because Mum and Dad said it was important and I was, anyway, a compliant individual at school. But none of the teachers actually saw the methods really as being important. It was predominantly rote learning. But there was no understanding put into the methodology so, in a sense, I was never actually taught how to learn, ever, in my school life, not at all.

I was only taught how to learn when I became a student teacher and, at that time in Primary education, the sector I went into, that was moving forward very quickly. The Plowden Report was '67; there were subsequent reports. New Mathematics had come in and the person in charge, John Page, [Head of Maths at Aberdeen College of Education] was instrumental in taking the New Maths forward locally. I got from him that if you break things down to a fundamental level and gradually build up, if you facilitate understanding in a gradual, developmental way, most pupils will progress well. I never really had that opportunity at all because all the tests that were given were simply testing what you remember.

Allan Paterson. b. 1951. King Street School. Interviewed 2015.

There's a
distinction
between
being
schooled and
being
educated and
in Scotland
there's been
a strong
tradition in
being
schooled.

THE SCOTTISH SYSTEM

The Scottish educational tradition

A Scottish education tradition? I suppose, yes, it does have a particular history; it has characteristics set in the Calvinist tradition – the three Rs is a very clear Scottish tradition. It is one that has stood us in good stead, has given people the discipline for learning, for managing their lives. It is not a very enlightened tradition, but it is one which has given people the basis on which to build their lives and their outlook. But it has not taken you further than that, not taken you into areas beyond those basics. It hasn't introduced you to the broader things in life, the things that would enable you to achieve enlightenment, to exercise the imagination, to gain a sense of vision.

There's a distinction between being schooled and being educated and in Scotland there's been a strong tradition in being schooled. We can certainly use what it has given us as a basis on which to build, but we do need to go beyond that, to go into all those other areas of life which can help us to grow as individuals.

Peter Murphy. b. 1932. Aberdeen Grammar School. Interviewed 2002.

Children are children wherever they be

D uring my teaching career I've taught in Croydon, in Oxford and in north London. Currently, I'm Head Teacher of a school in north London, in a very affluent area. It's obviously a very different world from the one I started out in as a pupil at Kittybrewster.

When I started teaching in Oxford, most of the families were employed in the car manufacturing business – Cowley Car Works. They earned good money and most children wanted to follow in Dad's footsteps so were not motivated to achieve academically. In contrast, here in London, especially in my current post in a wealthy area, parents can be hugely ambitious to get their children into a 'good' school, but often their choice is driven by the status of that particular school rather than what it could offer specifically to their child. The competitive nature of applying to maybe up to 10 different schools causes a great deal of stress.

But, you know, I really do think that children are children wherever they may be. This applies to a multi-cultural school in north London in the 21st century as much as it did to my Kittybrewster in the '50s. But the parents have changed. The systems have been different, too. One thing I can tell you to illustrate that point. When I was teaching in Enfield there were two Heads at other schools there who had also been Scottish-educated. When the National Curriculum was first being mooted down south, they were often asked what had made the Scottish system better than the English one – that mythology was widely held. It was felt that Scotland had always had a set curriculum to cover all its schools, unlike England where things had been very diffuse and variable.

These Heads would tell them that if you went into any school in Scotland you would know exactly what to expect, that they would be all following the same set syllabus. And that meant that there could be no such thing as a 'bad' Scottish school – but nor could there be an outstanding one either. This chimed in with the fears that what the National Curriculum would lead to would be a prescriptive and dull uniformity – the same level of entitlement for each and every pupil, but the same level of teaching and experience, too. I knew what they meant. In Scotland I'd found that what you had done was to teach to the syllabus as given rather than teach the child. That has happened in England now and I have to make a deliberate effort to encourage my staff to not be afraid to strike off on their own tangent occasionally.

I would say that the Scottish system as I experienced it was more democratic. As I was growing up, I encountered a number of peers who came from a more well-off background because of their father's business – fish company owners or whatever. Yet they didn't necessarily have the status that the family of the doctor or the teacher had – money didn't guarantee the esteem that education did. I was raised in a working class household where education was held to be important, where it was regarded as important to attain academic qualifications. Throughout my career I've been aware of this as a contrast.

Here, in London, I find myself the Head of a high-achieving school – but it is not one where parents are driven by academic ambition. What drives them are material outcomes, more and more. To them going to a 'good' school is a status symbol rather than the means of helping their child to achieve academic goals.

Margaret Lakin. b. 1949. Enfield, London. Interviewed 2004.

Margaret Lakin's official Head Teacher photograph, Hadley Wood School, Enfield.

The Scottish system's better

Alex: At Skene Square, I remember on my very first day being sat down in the front row and being given a teddy bear – we all got one. This was at five. Later I remember the arithmetic – I was always good at figures. The teacher would draw this circle on the board and then put numbers all around it. She would keep a pile of pennies on top of the board and hand them out as prizes for so many correct answers; I

On one of the Booth family's regular sight-seeing trips round the country, 1950s.

always got one. But when I went up to the next class – at eight – the teacher there was an absolute tyrant. She had a limp and her hair hung down. She was cruel to the children. There were slates all around the room and she would write hundreds of sums onto them in columns; we each had our own slate and had to do the sums on them. I was always able to do them.

A lot of kids got thrashed at the school and often for petty things like faulty work. Yet not all the teachers were like that; many of them were very fair. Generally, however, they were very strict. At 12 I took the Control exams. At Skene Square I was the Dux; I got 10/6d [52.5p] worth of books as my prize. I got high marks and was able to go into the Central School and into the top stream there.

Beryl: I was at school in Yorkshire. My education wasn't as good as Alex's. I grew up in a pit village, about 16 miles from Barnsley.

In our area, it seemed to me that no child from our village, no matter how bright they were, ever got to High School. You were just stuck with the local school. No one got to go to a school like the Central that Alex went to. I was three years at my Secondary School and left at 14. Any education that I've acquired beyond the basics has just been what I've managed to gather together as I've gone through life.

I think the Scottish system is better. No matter how poor you might be, in Scotland, if you had the ability, you got the chance to go on. Down in Yorkshire, that was impossible for us; no matter if you had passed all the exams, there was still no place for you. You didn't get any of the help that was available here – no bursaries, no help with money for the uniform or to buy books.

Alex: The English standard just wasn't up to ours!

They always ensured the next generations enjoyed every opportunity. Here Alex Booth, with wife Beryl in attendance, serenades his granddaughter Kerry and great grand-children, Jamie and Kyle.

Alex and Beryl Booth. b. 1921 and 1919. Skene Square and Rawmarsh Elementary. Interviewed 2004.

It's very sad the way things have gone

At five, at Sunnybank, I was happy; at six, at Skene Square I was not. The two schools were so different. I was quite shell-shocked; the contrast was so great. You had to line up silently in the playground before you were ever allowed into the school and then a teacher would play out a march while you had to file in, military

fashion. You daren't step out of line for a moment. In the classrooms you were allowed no free movement. Elbows on the desk were forbidden; you weren't permitted to cross your legs.

The school was so impersonal and prescriptive. The typical day in those days at an Aberdeen school was to start off with a Bible story; then there would be mental arithmetic followed by sums, on your slate – how I hated those soury sponges you had to keep to wipe the work off! Then there would be some reading. By the afternoon you would be granted, for a bit of relief, something like singing. But the songs we got at the age of seven were totally unsuitable and incomprehensible: I mean, 'Drink to me only', 'Where the bee sucks' and ' Away with melancholy'. There would also be 'story-writing' – but with no stories! You'd have to go over this set picture of a scene such as 'Winter-time' or 'Autumn Fields', sentence by sentence: 'What is the colour of the sky?'; 'What can you say about the leaves on the trees?'

I went to Miss W's class when I was coming up for nine: absolute silence. She belted, and she belted hard. This was for any mistake in your work, not just for misbehaviour. I was all right as I was good at the work, but I did start to have nightmares because I was always frightened that I couldn't keep it up and would sooner or later get the belt. We lived under this atmosphere of constant fear. Quite a number of the female teachers of that time were like her: bitter, ageing women, unmarried and without any personal experience of children.

We had homework each night. Here, in this inner-city school, children of eight were being asked to use a nib pen and ink at home. We would be given a card with some Victorian proverb written out on it, which we had to reproduce in proper copper-plate style, there on another card, which was made out in double lines so that you knew exactly where the 'ts' and the 'ps' should begin and end.

She speaks from a position of authority: Beryl Mackenzie, centre left, as Deputy Head Teacher, alongside Head Janet Hosie, Portlethen Primary School, 1990.

> Even as late as the 1970s in Northfield, when I was a teacher at Westerton, you'd find children coming to school in the depths of winter with their one cotton dress on.

Duncan (later Sir Duncan) Rice by King's College quadrangle, 2005.

For at least half of the children then going to Skene Square, the culture of the school must have been completely alien. Even as late as the '70s in Northfield, when I was a teacher at Westerton, you'd find children coming to school in the depths of winter with their one cotton dress on. This is what I mean when I say that 'education' can be such an artificial affair. The school assumes that its world of organisation and routines is the norm and that these children will have the social skills and the understanding to operate within it from the very start.

I don't think matters have necessarily improved since then. We should have been allowed to develop things as they were then evolving during my later career, but now there's so much political interference. Paperwork and computerisation have replaced common sense and individual judgement. In the old days a good teacher was a professional, one who had learned from experience and was able to keep all she needed to know about her work and the children in her head. If you'd asked her about so-and-so, she would have been able to tell you about every aspect of the child; it would have all added up to a real human portrait.

But now such information is distributed out onto a series of checklists. Teaching's no longer child-centred; it's government-centred, report-centred. There's no freedom or room for personal judgement. You can't improvise by deciding to let them draw a monster for fun, or take them out to the park to enjoy its sights in the sunshine. Teachers are made into robots; it's all very sad, the way things have gone.

Beryl Mackenzie. b. 1946. Skene Square. Interviewed 2004.

The drive was to get you into professions

The whole drive was to go into the professions. I do have a hypothesis that in the 1950s the Grammar School and other establishments of its type were still about training for full-scale Empire. At them you were, in effect, being socialised and given the intellectual training to take up a post as a civil servant either at home or abroad – this at a time when, really, there was no longer an empire to serve in.

So much of the iconography of the books we were given was that of Empire, so much of the modelling in the books that we read as children was based upon the Imperial ideal. Events such as Rorke's Drift and the siege of Khartoum were presented as exemplars of the great Imperial struggle, of the heroic battles necessary to secure the mission of Empire.

It was, in some respects, a rather dysfunctional education, increasingly unmatched to the world we would actually be going into in the '60s – although it is true that even then many of the boys would be looking to go off into the far corners of the colonies. You must remember that it was then still the intention of many Aberdonians to go out as, say, tea-planters or as civil servants, and although, in the event, very few would actually have done so, there was still this inherited assumption that they would carry on a family tradition in doing so. A lot of the parents of the Grammar schoolboys had served their time in India, in Burma, Ceylon, in Malaya, at tea or rubber plantations, and so on. Many others were retired colonial civil servants.

If you were to make an analysis of the hymns we sang, many of them would be revealed as being about Empire, about the sun that never sets and the mission beyond our shores. We duly developed a youthful enthusiasm for an Empire which had succeeded in colouring so much of the map red. And Everest and the Coronation of 1953 produced a hugely positive charge in that direction.

It started in Primary. The teachers there were dedicated to that ideal: one, Mrs Angus, had lost her husband at the Battle of Britain; there was Miss Stewart who would habitually refer to 'Indians' and 'natives' in terms which made the assumption that these were the inferior races quite clear to us.

The texts we used in class and were expected to read in our own time reflected these timeless island ideals. The books in the library contained the standard classics of the time – Henty, *The Empire Youth Annual, Chatterbox* – that sort of thing. And of course, there was R.M. Ballantyne and *The Coral Island* with its instillation of the Empire ethic.

Duncan Rice. Born 1942. Aberdeen Grammar School. Interviewed 2003

Sir Duncan Rice went on to enjoy a distinguished career as an historian, serving in universities on both sides of the Atlantic. He returned to Aberdeen to take up the post of Principal of the University of Aberdeen in 1996. He was knighted for services to Higher Education in 2009.

At the top of his profession: Sir Duncan Rice as Principal of the University of Aberdeen.

It was all very sad

In 1973 I went to Summerhill as Deputy Head, working with R. F. MacKenzie. He held what others saw as very distinctive views on Scottish education and the need to open it up to a more human, personally expressive approach, especially where so-called disadvantaged pupils were concerned. His appointment was an adventurous one, as he brought with him a reputation as an experimenter and as something of a romantic rebel against the narrow constraints of the traditional academic Scottish educational regime. He came to Summerhill following a controversial headship at Braehead in Fife and as the author of such books as *Escape from the Classroom,* a title which declares his belief that education should be a total experience and not simply some sort of rigid incarceration within the walls of a strictly exam-orientated regime.

I came to Summerhill as an enthusiastic admirer of his ideas. My Guidance position would enable me to help to fulfil his ideals of creating a true community in which all, teachers and young people alike, would value each other as human beings rather than as ciphers in an impersonal system. I wasn't disappointed in the quality of the man I was now working with.

As one pupil later summed it up, 'You know the Headie really listens to what you have to say. He doesn't just wait till you've finished like most adults, and then simply tell you

At peace once more: R.F. Mackenzie in retirement at his Cults home, 1986.

R. F. MacKenzie at his Summerhill Academy, 1968.

what he was wanting to say all along'. He really did believe that the child is as important as the staff and that the Head is no more central to the welfare of the school than the pupils whom he is there to serve.

My younger son met him once. Afterwards he remarked, 'He's kind of odd, that man'. 'Why do you say that?' 'Well, most teachers will ask you what you do, what you're going to do after school, what sport you play, and so on. But you know they are only going through the motions with their set questions. But this man really wants to know about you; he's genuinely interested in you'.

But in many quarters all this was seen as a positively dangerous unorthodoxy. He was an idealist and as such stirred strong feelings in others – some came to love him, but others found that the degree to which he upset their certainties was simply too much to handle. This included members of his own staff who became more and more split into anti and pro factions. Eventually something like war broke out; the authorities became alarmed, the press began to weave their stories and rumours of chaos and a state of anarchic licence began to take hold in the city.

The upshot was that RF was suspended; then some of the pupils hatched a strike plan in order to get their Headie back. Bill Henry, the Senior Depute Director of Education, was appointed to act as interim Head, but because he was due to sail off on an educational cruise I had to fill the breach.

I was confronted by a state of complete disruption; I phoned Jim Clark [Director of Education] and received the reply, 'Oh, I'm sure you'll manage the situation beautifully'. Some of the staff were for trying to put the strike down by forcible means – 'turn the hoses on them' – but I advised a softly softly approach and gradually the atmosphere of confrontation died down.

It was all very sad. If we could have carried out our ideas with smaller units so as to

RF, 3rd left, at an educational conference, Stirling University, 1974. On his right is John Graham, Rector Anderson's High , Lerwick, to his left David Robertson, Director of education, Dundee. Jo Grimond is also in the party.

break up the necessarily institutional setting of a large comprehensive school where conformity is seen as the necessary prerequisite for establishing order, then we might have had a better chance. The problem was that R.F. MacKenzie was going against the whole ethos of the prevailing educational system. That was a world that believed in certainty, in there definitely being a right way and a wrong way. The whole of the social fabric functions on a basis of conformity; in religion, in politics, in sport, individuals are welded tighter into a loyalty to the tribe and any attempt to open matters up to questioning and to deviant thinking is seen as dangerous. But he was an instinctive guy, one who preferred to hold to a fluid responsiveness to the changing situation around him, and people found that both disconcerting and challenging.

Elizabeth Garrett. b. 1930. Summerhill Academy. Interviewed 2015.

For more information on R.F. Mackenzie's life and career, see *The Life of R.F.MacKenzie: a Prophet without Honour.* Peter Murphy, Edinburgh, 1998.

An education afloat

My first promoted post as a teacher of Technical subjects had been at Kemnay Academy. This was a brand-new school and we quickly discovered that Inverurie Academy had creamed off all the best pupils and left us with the less academic ones. So, we had to develop new approaches.

> The tall ships approach is much more flexible and open. It takes the teenage druggies and the bolshie 20 year-olds, gives them trust and responsibility.

Many of the kids came from an agricultural background, so when I investigated what might be relevant to their interests they suggested a garden. In Scotland there was no such course as 'Horticulture' so we made up a CSE course and had it assessed through the Newcastle Board. Ours was very much a hands-on approach. One day Alex Sibbald, the Head, tipped me off that there was an old greenhouse going begging in Inverurie, so we took the minibus, dismantled it, brought it back to Kemnay and reassembled it.

The next problem was water. We dug down into the grounds and soon found our spades were hitting damp. A few feet further on and it was definitely water. We inserted a 56-gallon drum and began to store it. But then came the problem of how to keep our plants watered during the holidays; this was resolved by constructing an automatic watering system, using a windmill and pump.

This was my kind of education! For me the involvement and enterprise shown by these so-called non-academic pupils demonstrated that a problem-solving, collaborative approach works. It confirmed for me that our own ways were too exam driven and narrowed down into a set course rather than what we ought to be doing, which was daring to move out into something more flexible and experiential. But I was fighting against an approach which seems to run through the whole of the UK education system. Look at the status of engineers in this country compared to what it is in, say, Germany and you get the point.

So, eventually I decided to draw upon my experiences in teaching to venture out into something excitingly new. At the age of 51 I decided I would go off to sea. I joined up as a trainee on a Norwegian tall ship and what I encountered there was a real educational experience. Now, in Britain our treatment of new naval recruits is very much based on the rigidly disciplined, militaristic ethos of the Royal Navy. The tall ships approach is much more flexible and open. For one thing it is prepared to take on all ages, from 16 right up to 80 and from all walks of life. It takes the teenage druggies and the bolshie 20 year-olds, gives them trust and responsibility, involves them in demanding, real-life challenges out on the open sea and then watches them mature into a fresh concept of themselves, of their capabilities as part of a team where everyone has to pull together as a matter of life and death.

A lasting memory is of a 17-year old from Aberdeen up on deck whom I asked, 'Are you enjoying it all? Yes, well let me take a picture of you and we can send it back to your folks.' It so happened that his mother was a secretary at Harlaw and so I was able to discuss the photo with her later. She had burst out crying on first seeing it. And when I asked why, her reply was simply, 'Do you know, that's the only picture I have of my son with a smile on his face'.

I had to pay my own way to begin with, but when they saw how I was getting on with the young people on board I was offered the job of looking after the non-professional crew members. I was now a 'sergeant' and had two bars on my shirt, the only non-Norwegian to have this rank.

Some 27 different nationalities sailed with us during my time and English had to be

Mid Atlantic, west of the Azores. The *SS Statsraad Lehrun Kuhl.,* 2012.

used as the common language. We took all ages too. Many of the crew members were female. No distinctions were made; it was a thoroughly democratic ethos.

On one occasion we were in the Straits of Dover sailing along at our usual 15 knots when a big wind began to blow up. Now, the English Channel is like a big dual carriageway, full of busy vessels going to and fro. A big depression was forecast so we hurried on, anxious to get into the North Sea. We started out with full sail – 27 of them – but as the force of the wind rose to gale force 10, we frantically took them in and had to rely on our diesel backup engines. At one point, we were actually being blown backwards. I've encountered waves 200 metres apart and ones that send you down 140 metres until you think you can't possibly rise again and that the ship must certainly broach, cowp over. Then it can be like a ride on the biggest, most frightening roller coaster in the world. All highly character forming!

What the tall ship experience offers you is a total education in taking responsibility and in team work. You have to perform the whole round of tasks from being on the helm to lookout duties, to washing things down, to manning the sails and cleaning the toilets. What those fresh on board quickly come to realise is that everyone's lives depend upon vigilance and on selfless discipline. If the weather blows up dirty, then you might find yourself at the helm, struggling to keep on course and to hold on to the wheel. That's when life becomes very real. It's a situation where you are constantly testing yourself and building on your achievements.

For me it was some of the most adventurous and personally satisfying times of my life. My routine was one month on and one month off, back home in Aberdeen. I only gave it up in 2004 after an old skiing injury flared up to such an extent that I had to have my leg reconstructed, with the result that I could no longer pass the medicals.

John Corall. b. 1946. *SS Statsraad Lehmkuhl.* Interviewed 2016.

SOME NOTABLE LIVES – 2

In full flow: A spell-binding public speaker, James Scotland was always at home behind the lectern.

Theatrical folk are such fun to work with

I lived my early life in Fittie. Although the family moved to Stockethill when I was 12, and I have lived in 14 homes altogether, in Fittie I am still known, not as Edi Swan, but as 'Jock Baxter's Jeannie Anne's youngest'. My mother came from a line of Fittie fisher folk. Her father had been a skipper. She had sisters and there's a photo of them as young ladies all dressed up to the nines. They look absolutely stunning in their hats and their summery dresses.

After I left the Central I enrolled at the Art School. We sported beards and strolled around with berets on our heads, for the entire world as if we were Left Bank artists come to brighten up the lives of Aberdeen. After our classes were over for the day, we would saunter through the town, misbehaving in an attention-seeking fashion. It was small stuff really – a bit of shouting and over-loud laughter, the pretence that we had wooden legs and limped along – all designed to let people know we were different from the normal run of 1950s Aberdonians.

Edi was appointed to be the HMT's first ever Technical Director, 1979–93.

We would all flash around town in our tapered trousers, no doubt a bit above ourselves. In those days the Art School was tiny and we could consider ourselves as sort of arty elite. I was happy to play the part of the sophisticated Bohemian even though, in truth, I was a pretty innocent young Aberdonian.

But at the age of 21, and still a student, I got married. It was the best thing I could have done; I am convinced that without my marriage I would never have got through Art School. I now had a sense of much needed responsibility. This was increased by the birth of our first child just nine months later – a honeymoon baby. So I buckled down, passed everything and qualified as an Art teacher.

My other great love has been the theatre. This started when I was still at Central School. At the end of my fifth year there, the school put on a production of *Jonah And The Whale*. My Art teacher – the marvellous Alexander Burns – asked me to give him a hand in painting the scenery. 'Mix that paint with that powder over there – and fast!' I immediately got caught up in the excitement and bustle of it all. Then another teacher – Mansfield Leslie, a History teacher – invited me to give a hand at the switchboard. He showed me the works, how to pull the levers and so on. More excitement. But the final drama for me, back stage, was the moment when the actor playing God, Sandy Armstrong, the Head Boy, had to address Jonah. To take on the voice of God he had to stick his head in a drum and boom out 'Jonah! Jonah!' A magical and electrifying moment, and to me

the exact one when I became hooked on the theatre.

Inevitably these two loves – art and the theatre – soon came together. In my second year at Art School, Michael Gill, who was painting the scenery for the Students' Show that year, asked me to help him. Next year, the Stage Manager, George Sinclair, asked me to do the same. So I was now through the door of His Majesty's Theatre and involved in the whole world of the stage.

Sheila and I celebrated our 60th anniversary this year and that's how long my theatrical career has been too. Along with the annual Student Show I got involved as scenic artist for the Whatmore Players, who used to come up and do a 12-week summer season. Ani Jasper used to be in charge backstage, assisted by Jean Anderson. The practice was to load the scenic set onto a paint frame at the back of the theatre, then wind it up into position so we could paint it. One day Jean forgot to put the brake on, with the result that her arm got smashed by the handle whirling round. Ani Jasper needed a replacement assistant and quick, so she phoned the Art School for help. The Director was Ian Fleming and in his younger day he had worked on sets at the Citizens Theatre in Glasgow so he was sympathetic to Ani's plight. He suggested me, but there were still six weeks to go before the end of the term. 'Away you go,' he told me. 'You'll learn 10 times more there than we have left to offer you.'

And that's how I became a regular for the Whatmore Players and was with them for several seasons. It was Ani who really taught me. She was a top class professional who'd worked in London's West End and produced sets of such artistry that the Aberdeen audiences were stunned by them. It was she who taught me how to paint wallpaper to such a precision that people would enquire as to where we had acquired such lovely patterns and we had to tell them they had been painted on.

It was also Ani who was responsible for me becoming 'Edi' rather than the more

One of Ani Jasper's inspirational stage sets. This was for the Whatmore Players production of *Anastasia, 1957.*

normal 'Eddie'. She decided to put my name in the programme but misspelt it as Edi Swan and that is the version I have used ever since.

The big moment for us would be when the house lights went down and the audience were all in their seats waiting for the curtain to rise. That was when our set would be revealed and had the whole of the stage to itself in all its glory. Once the performance got under way, the set would simply melt into the background, but for that brief moment there it stood, ready to be taken in by the audience, telling them that the opening was to be set in the 1930s, in a well-to-do home, and so on. Sometimes the set would do its work so well that it would elicit a round of applause – and that was our reward.

It was a non-stop operation and I loved it. Since those early days I've been involved in theatrical design all over Aberdeen. I've designed for the Lyric, for the Musical Society, for the Opera Company, for Phoenix. Anyone with an idea for a show would automatically come to me. My system would be to chat with them first, then go way and prepare a model for the set, usually from balsa wood or cardboard and then go back for an in-depth discussion, and further modifications.

All this while, I was also pursuing my teaching career. On the whole, I enjoyed it, but I did make one big error and that was to chase promotion. I landed the post of Assistant Head teacher at Ellon Academy; the problem was that being in administration took me out of the classroom and, after my daily contact with the kids, I found that so boring.

Ani Jasper fronts a different sort of setting – taken on a visit to Venice.

One Friday evening I was at HMT and having a drink with the stage manager at the end of the show. He mentioned, 'I'm retiring soon.' I blurted out, 'But you've got a great job – why, I'd do it myself!' Jimmy Donald, who ran HMT, overheard my comment. On the following Sunday the phone rang; it was Jimmy. 'Are you serious?' He then went on to explain that the theatre was facing a testing time as there would have to be a complete refurbishment so as to comply with new Health & Safety regulations. He was looking to appoint what would be HMT's first ever Technical Director to oversee the project.

We agreed on a salary. I then received a letter from James Michie informing me I was on the short leet for the Depute Head Teacher's post at Bankhead Academy, but my mind was made up; I was going to quit teaching and move full time into my first and greatest love, the theatre.

So in 1979 I became His Majesty's Theatre's first Technical Director and served in that post till retirement in 1993 – and loved every minute of it. This is partly due to the fact that it's been such an honour to work in a wonderful place. Aberdeen is so fortunate in its HMT and the Tivoli, in possessing not one but two Frank Matcham theatres. In his time that man was recognised as just about the world's leading theatre architect and that

shows in every detail of our own HMT. The theatre works so well at a functional level, yet has such a gorgeous interior.

But what has really made my career in it so special, has been the people I've worked with. I loved the great variety shows that came to the city for a season each year – the Andy Stewart Show, the Fol-de-Rols with Leslie Crowther and Peter Felgate; marvellous entertainers, wonderful days. TV has now killed that sort of variety show off but back in the '50s, '60s, even the '70s, a weekly trip to the theatre was the ordinary person's big night out.

One of the most memorable performers over the years has been Chic Murray. I remember the time he went through a rehearsal with the BBC Northern Orchestra. The members hadn't encountered him before and his act just about slayed them. They couldn't play for falling about with laughter. Another time it was Billy Dainty and his funny walks, and again the orchestra was rolling about.

Theatrical folk can be such fun to work with. Back stage there's all sorts of goings on that the audience never catches a glimpse of. You might think Scottish Ballet would be a totally earnest bunch but you should see the capering behind the scenes. You also realise the hard work they all put in. When the girl dancers take off their socks, it's to reveal a pair of feet which are a red misshapen mess. The male dancers come off wringing with sweat. These guys are fitter and, every day, they put in a greater physical effort than any footballer does over his once a week 90 minutes.

Graduation Day at the Art School, 1957: Edi is 7th left back row, and to his immediate right are Sandy Cheyne and Ian Mackenzie Smith, who went on to become President of the Royal Scottish Academy.

That gorgeous interior: His Majesty's Theatre designed by the great Frank Matcham.

Jock Morgan's speciality was to play a violin under his leg and sing 'I'm a poor little lamb who's lost his way', getting the audience to join in the 'baa baa' bits.

The bigger stars were nearly always fine people. I remember when Roy Kinnear and Charlton Heston came up to appear in *A Man for all Seasons*. After the run was over, Charlton Heston held a party. Jimmy Donald was thrown into a bit of a bother by the thought that this meant we would have to present him with something. I came up with the idea that I would do a caricature of him in a full Highland dress - Heston was very proud of his Scottish ancestry – and I appended the message, 'A Prince among men'. In return he had a photograph taken of the two of us together and wrote on it 'To Eddy'. Under the circumstances I felt I could overlook the misspelling of my name!

Another memorable time for me was when Max Bygraves did his one-man show. He proved to be a lovely, warm character and great fun. After the final appearance I was bidding him 'Good night' when he said, 'In a hurry? No, well come on and have a chat'. We sat together for a whole hour with him telling me all about his life.

And then there was Andy Stewart. He was great; a genuinely likeable man. He put an incredible amount of energy into everything he did. And, unlike most comedians, he was really funny offstage as well as on. Backstage he was forever pulling my leg about something or other.

In this he was the opposite to another gifted Scots performer, Rikki Fulton, who was always fretting about his performance and constantly seeking reassurance: 'Was it all right? Do you really think it went OK?'

Over the years, what characters! Variety shows were a staple entertainment in those days and a performer could keep going year after year by touring round the country with the same old act. An example was Jock Morgan, the self-proclaimed 'finest comedian ever to come oot o Kemnay'. His speciality was to play a violin under his leg and sing 'I'm a poor little lamb who's lost his way', getting the audience to join in the 'baa baa' bits. He was a real veteran, one who had worked out his own routine and was always going to stick to it come what may. In Aberdeen his whole notion was to get through his rehearsal as fast as possible so he could scarper off to the pub. He would come in and plonk his music down by the footlights, completely ignoring anyone whose music might be there already. If Peter Morrison had got there first and insisted on his right to take first place, Jock would stand in the wings and play his music off-key so as to torment him.

He went round Scotland with this one act for over 25 years, never needing to change it, since by the time he turned up in any one place it would be a whole 12 months since his previous appearance. But then came the year that Andy Stewart decided that he would run his shows from Wednesday to Wednesday so as to give his audience – in those days made up of summer holiday makers – the incentive to see his show twice . This meant new material, so he went up to Jock and told him he would have to vary his act. 'Aye, Andy – if that's how you want it.'

Well, when the second round of the show came on, all that Jock did was to go on the stage and run through exactly the same act. When Andy protested, he had his answer, 'But you wanted something different and that's what I gave you.' 'How come? It was exactly the same old programme!' 'No, it wasn't – last week I came on from the left hand

As funny off the stage as on: One of Edi's favourite HMT stars, Andy Stewart.

side; this week it was from the right!'

Aberdeen has a great theatrical history. Exploring the history of His Majesty's Theatre in preparations for its Centenary in 2006, evidence came to light of the city's long association with the world of theatre. Over the years there have been almost 20 theatres operating within the city. They ranged from large showpiece venues – The Theatre Royal, Her Majesty's Opera House (later named the Tivoli), The Palace Theatre and His Majesty's Theatre alongside smaller venues such as The Pavilion, The Alhambra, The Arts Centre and the Lemon Tree. There have been even smaller venues, many of which were little more than flea pits – the Penny Rattler in Albion Street often incurred the wrath of the local magistrates!

Aberdeen has always been a great supporter of the theatrical arts. It has been a great honour to be a small part of that story.

Edi Swan. b. 1935. His Majesty's Theatre. Interviewed 2016.

In 2006 Edi Swan published his 'official centenary history' of His Majesty's Theatre: *One Hundred Years of Glorious Damnation*.

From school reject to university degree: Stanley Robertson receives an Aberdeen University Honorary Master's degree, 2009. He is pictured alongside Professor Tim Ingold.

Stanley receives the congratulations of his family. Left to right: granddaughter Samantha, son Robert, daughter Gabrielle, wife Johnann, and daughter Nicole.

The Traveller's Tale

I am a story-teller, descended from a line of travelling folk. But what I do belongs to everybody; everyone has the power to tune into this other medium. The old story-tellers might have been illiterate – but they were literate about lots of other things.

My father was a corporal in the Gordon Highlanders. I belong to a family of Robertsons who all had the nickname 'sodgers' because my father and his brothers served in both the World Wars. They were wonderful pipers; big strong men, piping men, champion men and athletes.

Mother was a gentle woman. She was a McDonald and classed as an outsider. She was a religious woman. I was brought up with a deep sense of religion and of civic pride. I was always told, 'think of others'.

As for their education – my father never had education of any kind. He could read and write his name. None of my grandparents could read or write. But they had great wisdom. They taught you sets of rules and you lived that way. One teaching the travellers held to was, 'Share a' and share sma'. It didn't matter how much or how little you had, you were to share it. Communally, they lived better than any communist could ever do. They cared for each other.

They were great people to grow up among. We were getting our English, our History, our Geography, our Literature, Current Affairs all through the medium of story-telling. I didn't become a story-teller or a keeper of the lore by accident. I was chosen to it; anointed I was.

That was when I was a wee laddie about seven, on the Old Road of Lumphanan. I was with my great auntie Margaret – she was a wonderful story-teller and singer. One day she said to me, 'Wee laddie, fit's that lyin o'er there?' and I said, 'It's the skull of a dead animal'. 'Describe it, to me'. And I said, 'Well, it's grey and mottled, it's being reclaimed by Mother Nature; it's sinking back into the sphagnum moss; it's covered with wee green and yellow and orange lichens; it's probably become beastie infested'. She says, 'Noo, gae into it's right eye o' the skull an tell me fit ye see'. So I went in and when I did, I saw caverns and canyons, mountains and streams, volcanoes, rivers. I saw birds and every manner of flowers, every manner of persons. I saw the whole world in that eye.

She said, 'Wee laddie, the mantle o' the story-teller will fall upon ye'. She told me that there's two times. There's the life's time, the time of doing things physically. And then there's the dream time. I was only with that dead animal's skull for five seconds. And I've been into that other world many times. It's something I can do at will. When I was five years old I could travel astrophysically; I used to get these out-of-body experiences.

When I got to puberty it was a very difficult time for me. I wasn't just going through the normal adolescence, but at the same time I was going into extra-terrestrial worlds. I thought it was madness, but it wasn't, it was my form of training. I was living in two worlds. I still do. There's the world that surrounds us and this is what is called 'the real world' – but there's a far better world if you can but know it. I've always been able to escape into it; it's with me all the time.

So all these things I write, they're on the spur of the moment, as it comes to me. I'm always writing these silly wee things – *The Good Fairy* – that kind of thing, about the time on the Old Fairy Road with the coming of the spring and being at the old rowan tree, the elm and the oak, where all the last fairies gather, hidden beneath the spring well. Hidden because nobody believes in them any more, they just believe in computers, in this new magic of today. But the fairies see this wee lassie and they see if they can convert her back into the world of the fairies – just silly wee things like that, that's what I write.

The gift never fails me. I've every faith in it. Folk ask me, 'How do you remember these great long stories? But they are part of me. It's like having prompters inside you, prompters from the other side. These are the folk who have passed over. The veil between us and them is so thin. And if ever I forget anything, they just come to give it to me. If I was singing a Jeannie ballad, my auntie Jean just comes to me and I sing it. I can hear her, I can feel her, I can smell her. Her voice tunes into my vocal chords.

It's not just recall, it's a possession; it's something that comes into you. I suppose I'm in tune with all my folk. What I believe is there's a veil; beyond the veil live our folk, the folk who have passed on. Talent never dies, love never dies – they just inhabit a different sphere.

I did get educated. My people knew the value of Burns, of Shakespeare, of Wordsworth, that these were men who had love. They might not be able to read a word, but they knew about such men, that they were witnesses too. Lots of books – and I've read thousands – have moved me. *The Pilgrim's Progress* – I worshiped that book and the hymn too, 'Who would true valour see…' I ken thousands of hymns as well. I've aye been brought up religious.

Aberdeenshire has some beautiful holy places. You can walk there and sense the holiness. I find Lumphanan a special soul-sair place. But I was born into the poorest street of Aberdeen: Sandilands Drive. Once the war was over and father had come back, we found that the neighbours hated us. It was because they had all just come through the war and they needed someone to blame for it all. So the Travellers were picked out for hatred. The neighbours were so coorse that they signed a petition to have us put out of our house. My mother was a very religious lady: she never drank, she never swore and my father was a clean-living man. They never caused any trouble to anyone. Yet now they were doing this to us. Something very deep in human nature was at work through all this.

When I went to Sunnybank School I had a terrible time of it. The thing that got me was the institutional smell of the school. And there were all these children in the one room. I'd never really mixed with scaldy children before and I didn't understand what to

A shot of Stanley in characteristic pose.

Maintaining the family tradition of piping.

The story teller in full flow.

do. I got this slate: 'A is for apple; B is for ball…' straight away from this old wifie, 'C is for cat; D is for dog'. There was no waiting – straightaway there was this wifie bawling it out at us. 'Scaldy' children? That's our word for non-travellers' children. I was the only non-scaldy child there.

I used to get battered all the way home. So I learned to make my own way home – through this passageway, by the Gibbery Wallie. I had to walk through the burn, the water up to my knees. And they wouldn't let me sit beside the other bairns. I got to sit in the corner and had to wear the dunce's cap – a cone of paper with a staple through it, stuck on my head. I didn't get a chance at reading. All the bairns got their books and all I got was this silly wee brown book: 'Sing mother sing. Can mother sing?' And at home, there was my mother reading these wonderful books to us. I was living in two different worlds – and still do. The authorities failed the Travellers' children.

Then we shifted into a really poor area of the town and I went to Hanover Street School. What a super school it was! Every bairn was a poor, snottery-nosed bairn who didn't have ony claes. And there were dozens of Travellers' children there too: McPhees and Stewarts and all that. So we all played together and it was fine.

We had a kindly teacher. But there was a bad brute of a man there too, especially to the Travellers' bairns. He would beat them. But I was only in that school for a year before we tried our Control. I'd never been taught my numbers properly, but I was a good writer. The Control was to test you for passing into Secondary Education. All the Travellers' children were put into Shuttle Lane. This was the annex in East North Street and it was where the dummy bairns, the backward ones were sent.

Eventually I did manage to get into Frederick Street School. It was the lowest class in the school – all Travellers' bairns, again. I didn't progress – we weren't expected to.

I will say there was an angel of a teacher at that school, name of Mrs Margaret McCulloch. She cared for her children. She would bring in a packet of soup for the cold days; she would take the milk we got and make cocoa for us; she would take us on trips. Every Friday we had to write a story and she would perform my story; I'd write plays – 'Slippery Sam' and all that. Now, if I'd had a teacher like that at Sunnybank, I'd have come on in leaps and bounds. But I grew up with such an inferiority complex. I was made to feel stupid.

I left school at 15. I did try to get a job with the Corporation, but I wasn't wanted there. So I entered the fish trade and spent my whole working life in it. Then I got this position at the University's Elphinstone Institute as a Research Fellow. And now I go into primary schools all the time, a treasured visitor. I marvel at all the changes. Take my sister at Shuttle Lane: she was the most beautiful artist you could ever see. And her report said, 'This girl has no common-sense'. They put no value on the Travellers' children then. They are valued now.

I love the English language. As a Traveller I can understand other things, the Wordsworthian faith. For me the influence of natural things is very powerful. My mother would say to me, 'What is the burnie saying to you, Stanley? What does the gorse

sing to you? What does the wind bring to you? What is Mother Nature saying to you, Stanley?' So I was learning from the start in the world of Pantheism. That's why I love Wordsworth.

Shakespeare had this amazing powerful knowledge. What beautiful wording that man had! But my teachers never encouraged me to bring these things into the class. I think they were under caution not to encourage the Travellers' children. Shakespeare, Burns, Wordsworth… and Thomas Hardy and Robert Louis Stevenson. This is what these great writers have done for me – more than any school.

Stanley Robertson. b. 1940. Lumphanan and Shoe Lane. Interviewed 2004.

Shoe Lane during the 1930s when Stanley spent much of his boyhood there.

They met in Grimsby: Ron and Peggy Finnie at the beginning of a fruitful partnership.

Sheffield weds Aberdeen, March 1959.

From a Sheffield back street to a leading Aberdeen jewellery firm

I was born in 1939. My early life was spent in first Sheffield then Grimsby. I have one sister who is older than me. I can't say my childhood was a very happy one. We lived in a tiny detached house with an outside toilet and where you had to boil up the water on a coal fire. To prepare a bath was a mammoth operation, which because of the effort required to get enough hot water to fill the zinc bath, meant that the whole family had to share the same water. I used to have to wait till my father had had his turn; I hated having to get into his dirty water. This was our regular Friday night routine.

My father was almost illiterate and left my mother to take care of all the writing. He was a motor mechanic and then a bus driver. He was a drinker and a devoted smoker. Quite often I would be left there on the pavement waiting for him to emerge from yet another session in the pub. My mother was a lovely woman, the one who kept the household going. She possessed a sweet and long-suffering nature. However, she suffered from running varicose ulcers on her legs. This meant I had to do a lot of the shopping, often having to negotiate tick at the Co-op.

There was little money in the house; my clothes were all hand-me-downs from my sister. The real problem was the controlling nature of my father. He wouldn't allow my mother to go out to work and, as for us, it was a case of having to keep out of his way and not do anything to disturb him. He would fall asleep in his chair and if you as much as merely brushed against him, he would immediately come to and explode. The strap was kept ready for use on the shelf.

Not surprisingly, I grew up a sickly, nervous child. My sister was reckoned to be the clever one and she passed the 11-plus to go to Abbeydale Grammar School; I was constantly tormented by teachers' comparisons to her: 'Why can't you be more like your sister? She was so clever.'

We got little in the way of presents- an orange, a small wooden cart, a silver three-penny bit, a lace hanky from an aunt; these had to serve as my childhood treasures. There were no books in my childhood. My father did buy a set of encyclopedias, but I was only allowed to touch them if I put on white gloves first- the books were for show rather than for learning.

I failed the 11-plus. My mother hated the idea that I would have to go to the local Secondary Modern establishment. So, she managed to scrape together enough to send me to a private place where I could learn secretarial skills. Even there I felt self-conscious. I had to suffer the embarrassment of going along in darned clothes and an old grey woollen jumper.

So, there was little love in my childhood, but it was an upbringing that taught me a lot about life and about people. You could sum it up as character forming.

My life began to change when my sister landed a teaching post in Grimsby. At the age of 14 I followed her to the town, attending the college to pursue my love of art. We had to stay in digs which were hardly salubrious – hairs in the food and a dog called Inky.

And the result: Peggy as a young and very busy mother, in Union Street, 1968.

But after home life in Sheffield it was a great relief. Things also began to look up when I was 15 and my mother moved to Grimsby along with my father, who got a post as an AA man.

To earn cash, I worked in a fish and chip shop – the pay wasn't good, but I could keep the tips. This gave me enough to be able to go off to Cleethorpes with a friend and to buy Woodbines and Babycham. That's where I met my destiny. We'd go to the weekend dances in the Winter Gardens and that's where the RAF lads went too. One of them was this young lad down from Aberdeen, called Ron Finnie, down doing his National Service. We started courting; I was only 16, but I knew this was the man for me.

Ron was a trained watchmaker who had, like me, failed his 11-plus and had gone to Powis School. He had had a hard childhood, with his mother dying when he was no more than a young child and a father who couldn't cope. He had to be farmed out to a children's home in the Spital – but he never speaks about it. He refuses to regard all that as relevant to what he has since managed to achieve.

It was a small wedding – 13 guests, homemade sandwiches. Our honeymoon was two nights in the Lake District; for my going-away I borrowed my sister's coat. I was very innocent.

To me, Scotland was a strange land; the train journey up seemed to take hours. It was a real struggle to begin with. I had to get a job to bring in any money I could, so I got one as a dental nurse. We stayed in a rented flat at 50 Union Grove. This was in a tenement and I had to take my share of cleaning the stairs and, to make sure I didn't let the side down, I had to leave everything gleaming and sweet smelling.

Our plan was to wait four years before starting any family – but within five months I found myself pregnant. This meant we had to quit the flat as the landlord wouldn't accept a pregnant tenant. All our worldly goods had been packed up into a tea chest back in

The business expands: Folk singer and entertainer Joe Gordon opens the George Street store, 1963.

He started as a watch repairer in a single room in St Nicolas Street. Ron bends to his work.

The 2009 award of the MBE for services to charity – a list which includes Alzheimer's, St Machar Academy, Anchor Unit, a range of music charities and a host of other causes. Ron and Peggy pose with the medal after its presentation by Prince Charles in 2011.

Grimsby, but it was late in coming up, so to begin with we had to sleep under coats. Part of our possessions was a fine set of cutlery. Ron was now renting a shop in George Street and we packed up the cutlery into nice boxes and sold it. So we sold our wedding presents!

There I was, a young mother, living in strange city with hardly a penny to my name. But Ron gradually built up his business with watch repairs; beginning from a single room in St Nicholas Street he started professional life with just 150 pounds and his tools. I would go to the shop, waiting outside for him as he worked and worked. Once a policeman enquired as to what I was doing – obviously he thought this young woman was lurking around plying a different sort of trade!

Ron worked from this little single room for three years, basically acting as a repairer of clocks and watches, but also beginning to sell straps, and a few time pieces. He built up things to the extent that we were able to move on to larger premises, a shop at 193 George Street, and take on a member of staff. Here we sold costume jewellery, beads and rolled gold jewellery. I taught myself to string pearls.

We had a strong work ethic, a firm adherence to the moral principles of honesty and reliability. Gradually we expanded into selling watch straps, pearls, diamond rings – investing all proceeds back into the business.

In the 1970s we moved into our current premises, which has grown to be 229-233 George Street. This was a much larger site with plenty of potential but, to start with, it was no more than a single ground floor room full of rotten joists. It was a small affair with a tiny office at the back and a repair desk. Then we moved the office upstairs and had two storeys. Over the following years, as the adjacent properties came on the market, we were able to buy them up and so expand into the extensive corner site you see today.

So those beginnings back in 1957 had been modest to say the least. Gradually we extended our stock and our circle of contacts. Everything was devoted to the business. I would get up at six in the morning, buzz around doing the housework, hanging out the nappies on the line, then off to the shop with the pram, to help with whatever I could. I strung pearls; I worked at costume jewellery. We made a point of never depending on borrowing money and of always paying our bills promptly. Anything we sold would be reinvested.

Home was still a modest affair. After we were forced out of Union Grove we got a flat in Grosvenor Place – no carpets on the stairs. We took Ron's furniture out of storage only to discover that the mice had been at the seats, but we put a rug on the floor, painted up a chest as a nappy drawer, ran up our own curtains. Meals were basic – mince and tatties featured a lot. The housework done, the day was spent at the shop, with the baby in the pram at the back.

The shop prospered. We both of us always set great store by offering people an honest, trustworthy service and one delivered with a warm personal touch. Perhaps because of my tough upbringing I had developed a self-sufficient attitude, never seeking to deceive and always telling folk straight – and jewellery is a trade which is rife with

Peggy among her amazing collection of Teddy bears.

deception and attempting to pass off shoddy goods as the genuine article. We have never chased large profit margins, aiming always to be the sort of family firm which would never rip people off, but would offer good advice and sound value.

We went to trade fairs, we moved into diamond rings, bought empty mounts and set our own distinctive gemstones in them, building up a versatile range of goods from the affordable to the more exclusive. Our aim has been to keep on regenerating and moving ahead. Now we are firmly into the computer age and maintain a thriving e-commerce service. From that modest beginning of a handful of watch straps and alarm clocks we now have stock of over 20,000 items to suit all ages.

Another of our secrets has been our staff. It is vital to maintain an attractive working environment. The result has been a long-serving loyal staff – one of our members has been with us for over 50 years. For recruitment I have sought out those who I know from their background will be prepared to roll up their sleeves and learn their trade from the ground floor up. I reckon I can spot such people through a few encounters. For example, at the bank I went to I was impressed by a young, well-presented cashier. One day I invited him to join us with a view to becoming a manager. Another was taken from my hairdresser's – I knew that anyone working in a hair salon must start off doing all the menial tasks, such as sweeping up the hairs and cleaning out the sinks and would therefore be a willing worker for us.

Now we employ a staff of nearly 50. Our own family has graduated into the business – from sons and daughters through to grandchildren. All this has enhanced Finnies

The cover for the booklet produced in 2017 to celebrate 60 years of continuing service by Finnies.

character as a caring, hands-on business, blessed with the human touch.

I have extended this approach into the wider community. As we have managed to make our way in business and began to attain comfort in our lives, I've also been concerned to involve myself in the community – whether charity, fundraising or organizations. We have never forgotten our origins – that's why, for example, we make a point of sponsoring activities at St Machar Academy, Ron's old school – named in those days, Powis. I have thrown myself into activities; I have built up a reputation: 'Ask Peggy – Peggy will do it!'

In 2009 I was awarded an MBE in recognition of my charity work. The company has supported over 50 charities – Alzheimer's, Police charities, Friends of Anchor at Foresterhill, music, including the Youth International Youth Festival and the Inchgarth Community Centre among them. I have worked hard at this, but I have also received much in return, not just because of the satisfaction of helping people, but because my work has enabled me to meet such a wide range of people and to become part of the very fabric of Aberdeen life.

I hope I can claim that this Yorkshire girl has been good for Aberdeen – there's no doubt that Aberdeen has been good, both for her, and to her. So, I have never for a minute regretted the evening when I met my young RAF Aberdonian at the dancing in Cleethorpes more than 60 years ago.

Peggy Finnie. b. 1939. Sheffield, Grimsby and Aberdeen. Interviewed 2018

Jimmy's Last Hurrah

One of the most vivid characters on the Aberdeen scene in 1960s, '70s and '80s was James Scotland, known famously as both the Principal of Aberdeen College of Education and as a colourful presence on the city's theatrical scene. Sadly, he died before any biographical interview was possible – but a copy of his farewell graduation speech is available, one that demonstrates the range and humanity of the man. It is reproduced here as a slice of an Aberdeen Life well worth the remembering.

But first, a biographical note:

When, in June 1983, James Scotland made his final Graduation Day speech, he was able to draw upon a richness of experience that stretched well beyond his 22 years as Principal of Aberdeen College of Education.

Born in 1917, in an upstairs tenement in the East End of Glasgow, he had grown up to achieve an academic success which entitled him to be thought of as the authentic urban lad o'pairts. Following an education in his local Dennistoun schools, he then proceeded

After the speech was over: James Scotland makes his final Graduation presentations.

The official opening of the brand new College of Education, Hilton, 1968. James proudly accompanies Princess Alexandria.

to take three First Class Honours degrees at Glasgow University, interspersed by a Bachelor of Law. After war service in Italy, he embarked upon a notable career in Scottish education, one that quickly propelled him into the post of Head of the Education department at Jordanhill and then, in 1961, onwards to the Principalship at Aberdeen and his entry into the wider cultural life of the North-east.

This was the position that enabled him to play a full part – and usually in a leadership role – in many of the bodies being then set up to spearhead an era of extensive reform and development, such as the General Teaching Council and the Consultative Committee on the Curriculum. He also maintained a strongly personal commitment to the Police Advisory Council and the Church of Scotland Education Committee. He was, moreover, a regular author and broadcaster: in 1969 he brought out a definitive two-volume *History of Scottish Education*.

This was the official citizen. Throughout it all, he was also sustaining a parallel career as a man of the theatre. Using the punning pen-name, Ken(neth) Little, he was a stage and radio comedian and a prolific script-writer for such as Stanley Baxter, Andy Stewart, Una McLean and Jimmy Logan. He penned six of the celebrated Glasgow Citizens' Christmas pantomimes in the 1950s and during the same decade he was responsible for

The whole world before him: A pre-war holiday shot, 1938.

Not a moment to be wasted: Always thirsty for knowledge, James was in the habit of taking a book wherever he had to go. Here he is, an Army colonel, striding through the streets of Perugia, Italy, 1945.

some 200 radio comedy shows, of which *17 Sauchie Street* was the best known.

Even this was not the sum of the man, for he sought to involve himself in a whole range of cultural and social activity. He pursued all ball games avidly and sustained a life-long passion for cricket as well as an enthusiasm for Queen's Park F.C. and for Jordanhill Rugby Football Club. He was also a private poet and author of some half dozen historical novels, a collector of stamps and of esoteric cigar bands, a war-time expert on chemical weaponry, an incorrigible bibliophile, international traveller and an irrepressible Glaswegian who spoke in its accents all his days, yet who became a fondly adoptive man of the North-east. Throughout his adult life he was an active member, and latterly Elder, of the Church of Scotland.

Increasingly, towards the end of his career, the graduation speeches became infused with the memories and experiences culled from a life-long devotion to the cause of Scottish education and of social betterment. When he came to step up to the lectern for the final time, in 1983, he was making a speech which may be considered both a farewell and a characteristic slice of life as witnessed and lived by its author.

But sadly, he was peering into a retirement that was never to come. Within two months of its utterance, and preparing for a last Monday morning of tidying up his office, Jams Scotland was struck down by a fatal cardiac arrest.

The words that were delivered on that midsummer day, act as memorial to a College Principalship which was vividly enacted and to a life that was fully lived.

The 1983 Graduation Address

This is an important day in your lives, and such days deserve to be treated with ceremony. Some of you when you are old, well into the 21st century, will remember this day, as I remember my own graduation day 45 years ago. It ought to be an occasion worthy of recall.

What is so important about it? Well, for one thing it marks nothing less than an epoch in your lives. You will never stop learning, of course, until the day you die – about your job, about people, about the difficult business of living – but this really is the last day of your formal education. Today you cross the floor, move around the desk, go from Us to Them.

And you could hardly start your career at a more exciting time. You will be joining what has been for well over a century an impossible dream – an all-graduate profession. The whole Secondary curriculum and its examinations are being revolutionized. And I don't have to tell you what problems you will face with those people not much younger than yourselves, the 16- to 18- year olds.

An exciting time, yes, but a minefield too, strewn with difficulties and dangers. The society we live in is deeply perplexed. In the last couple of decades there has been a colossal redistribution of the world's goods, both nationally and internationally, and a sunburst of labour-saving technology. The effect has been not only increased unemployment but the collapse of the work ethic, on which our education system depends. So you will be faced with a formidable paradox when you start your teaching. You and I know that there has never been a time when our society needed education more, but hordes of your pupils and their parents, utterly disenchanted, will believe there never was a time

when they needed it less.

You will also come up against young people as they are, not as they ought to be. Unfortunately some of the decisions in education are taken by those who think they already are what they ought to be. You, and not those decision makers, will have to cope with them, and some of you will have a hard row to hoe.

Is it worth the struggle, then? Year by year in these addresses I have said goodbye to thousands of your predecessors and many of my own old friends. Now the time has arrived for me to bid you all farewell. I have spent over 36 years in the business of Scottish education, as a teacher, as a lecturer, as Principal of this college. If I have anything helpful to say to you, then this must surely be the time. The temptation is to echo the centenarian once interviewed on Radio Scotland.: 'Aye, man, I've seen a wheen o' changes and I've been against every dampt one o' them!' It is tempting, but it wouldn't be true. I've seen changes in which I take delight – a place in the sun, for example, for the aesthetic subjects: when you think of all the joy people have in music and art and drama, it is no more than they deserve. Then there has been a beginning to a breaking down of religious barriers which here in Scotland have troubled us for centuries. A chance too for teachers to play a real part in running their schools and their profession. Here in Scotland we have set up the very first General Teaching Council in the world, and it is a matter of enduring pride to me that for three years I was its Chairman.

His other career:
James as Peter Quince in a Haddow House production of *A Midsummer Night's Dream*, 1980.

The award of a CBE: With wife Jean and son Alistair, 1982.

Alas, there have also been changes in which I take no pleasure. The long struggle to smooth the path of the less gifted has combined with the huge increase in labour-saving devices, I am afraid, to reduce the value of effort. As teachers, in Scotland, moreover, we always seem to preoccupy ourselves with means rather than ends, and I have seen no change in that phenomenon. Let me plead with you – do not allow the waves of day-to-day detail to close over your head. Don't just concentrate on doing things better in the classroom: try to think about why you are doing them. But the saddest thing of all that I see is that education has shrunk into a smaller, less respected place in our community. The politicians still spend a lot of money on it, but there are increasing signs that they grudge it, and so do the voters.

So – there is the educational world I am leaving and you are entering. Fortunately you will find many compensations for its vexations, as I have. You will meet congenial colleagues, men and women with the same view of life as you have, who laugh and are serious about the same things. You will also have your spirit refreshed and rejuvenated by the young folk you meet, wave after waves of them – children whose remarks I have often quoted, like the eight-year old who was asked how the Israelites got across the Red Sea and who answered 'Fine'; the 14-year old whom I asked to identify Archbishop Makarios and responded darkly, 'A man we were asked about in this test'; the sturdy individualist in Primary 5 who, when the visiting Inspector said, 'Have you had to work out all these examples of the same sum?' replied, 'Aye – hellish intit?'; and the immortal 10-year-old whose nativity play contained the following passage of improvised dialogue:

Joseph: I hear that Herod's going to kill all the boy babies.

Mary: 'Tsk, if it's not one thing, then it's another. What'll we do?

Joseph: What about fleeing?

Mary: Good idea. Where to?

Joseph: Shall we give Egypt a go?

Mary: Ok. You get the donkey and I'll get Jesus.'

Many of you will have heard me tell these stories before, but it's an old man's privilege, and, anyway, they are worth the retelling. Every August you will meet youth again and, if you let it, a little of it will flow quietly into your soul and make your teaching days all the happier.

In conclusion, then, as this ceremony, which is a significant one for me as for you, nears its end, what do I wish for you on your eventful journey? I hope you will live to see the day when Scottish education concerns itself with long-term aims as well as the short – with the abiding realities of existence, for we neglect them at our peril. I hope you will see education take its rightful place, universally recognised, in our nation's programme, with the resources to stay there and with nobody shouting for more than their fair share. I hope that by then, teachers will have reached a level of professionalism when the only claim to status is silent, uncomplaining, expert and devoted service. And I hope the climate will be one of co-operation, not incessant dreary confrontation, in a time *when no public group suspects the motives of any other, nor has any need to.*

On this journey to this Utopia, even if you never arrive there, I wish you as much good fortune as I have had in the pupils, students and colleagues you meet along the way. In this connection, then, I wish to draw to your attention a newspaper advertisement which was quoted on the radio the other morning:

Lost — black and white mongrel dog, lame in left forepaw, bald patches on coat, blind in left eye, most of right ear missing. Answers to the name of 'Lucky'.

In short, I wish you all luck, and when you can't enjoy it, the sense of humour to manage without it.

James Scotland. b. 1917. Aberdeen College of Education

"When I was young I honestly thought that the world was Aberdeen.
– Marion Douglas. b. 1948. Bucksburn. Interviewed 2016.

INCOMERS
AND EX PATS

Italy into Aberdeen: A 1925 photo of the leading Italian businessmen – mostly in the catering trade – who by then had become such an integral part of the North east's commercial life. Bob Meconi's granda, Amadeo, is 4th left back row.

ABERDONIANS ABROAD

Aberdeen origins:
Margaret's parents at a wedding, 1950s.

Back home:
Margaret (in red coat) with her North-east family. Nephew Mat Northcroft and brother-in-law David Northcroft at the back, sister-in-law Kathleen Northcroft with great-nieces Erin, Rachael and Abby, alongside their mother, Elaine, 2017.

I still think of Aberdeen as home

I've lived practically all my adult life in the south of England. I still think of Aberdeen as home, of coming up here as 'going home' – but then I have to correct myself, since I know it's no longer really true. I'm not really 'Aberdeen' any more, but I can still get all defensive and protective if I hear the place being criticised. It's like family: you can criticise it as much as you like, but if any outsider does, then you close ranks and defend your own identity. I still boast about Aberdeen, but I know the place no longer has any pull for me. But I did feel it's a good place to have been brought up in. And I can see that those who've stayed on here have had happy and successful lives, too.

One value that I do think accurately typifies the North-east of Scotland – Scotland generally, I think – is 'hard work'. There's this belief that you have to put in the effort to get the reward and that if you do it will come. I haven't found that to be so prevalent in the south of England – maybe I've mixed with the wrong people! But I am aware of a certain chauvinism, of parochialism even. Some of my family will still criticise me for 'betraying' my roots and becoming anglicised. I don't understand or share that interpretation. I am what I am and I do acknowledge that my background is part of that. Although the circumstances of my life have led me elsewhere, I still get a warm feeling whenever I think of Aberdeen.

Margaret Lakin. b. 1949. Enfield, London. Interviewed 2004.

The Londoner: Margaret hurries along by Trafalgar Square, 2019.

An Indian infancy

I was born in New Delhi, January, 1942. The reason I was born in India is that my father (Ned) was then an officer in the (British) Indian Army and had lived in India for the past 25 years. My mum (Alice), also from Aberdeen, joined my father in 1939 after the outbreak of the war having just given birth to my elder brother (Edward) in Aberdeen. She decided to make the hazardous journey after receiving an urgent telegram from my father informing her that if she didn't come immediately it would be too late as the war effort had become paramount. Fortunately for me she didn't hesitate, albeit the journey by train to London was interrupted by bombing by the Luftwaffe. Her flight from London to Bombay (which was filled with senior army officers) included five overnight stays – one of which was in Cairo – and must have been daunting for a young mother carrying a small baby.

The Indian boyhood: Ian in the garden of their New Delhi home, with parents and older brother Edward, 1946.

I was five years old when we returned to the UK and for us that meant Aberdeen.

I returned to New Delhi for the first time a few years back – almost 60 years to the day – and all the memories came flooding back. Up till the age of five, I knew nothing but India. My brother and I were looked after by my own ayah and because she spoke little English and talked all the time in Hindi it was natural for me to pick up her language and over time become fluent in it. I can even remember my parents asking me to translate for them on the odd occasion.

The return visit: Hosted by General Sharma at the old home at 35 Aurangzeb Road.

Still well kept: A picture of the New Delhi home today.

What one has got to realise is that out in British India the parents were busy with their own affairs: as PA to General Auchenleck, my father had demanding wartime duties with the threat of invasion by Japan – especially after the fall of Singapore, Malaysia and Burma and my mother had to see to all the social duties that went on among the network of British Army and Civil Service families there. It was an almost Victorian situation in some ways, in which the children were expected to keep out of the grown ups' way and to be looked after by the servants. I felt no sense of deprivation at all as my ayah devoted herself to me utterly and we developed a very close bond.

My ayah was in her 30s, about the same age as my mother. She was one of the servants who looked after us all; her husband was the cook. They and their families lived in the servants' quarters, which were situated in the grounds of our house. When I revisited the old place I found everything much as I remembered it except that it was now in the hands of the Indian Army and there were now armed guards at the front gate due to the odd outbreak of violence between the Muslims and the Hindus.

We were given a great welcome, almost to the point of embarrassment. When they learned I was actually born in India, they were ready to claim me as a brother. There was certainly no animosity or feeling that I had been one of the occupying colonial power, and they cited such benefits as the English language, the rule of law, railways and education. Indeed they spoke warmly of the British and were proud that they had adopted the old ways. It is worth remembering that British India, with a population of about 500 million, was run by 3,000 civil servants and approximately 60,000 British soldiers and if there hadn't been a general acceptance of us by the native population then this just wouldn't have been possible.

Although there had been a fair amount of segregation, my parents had always taken care to speak of the Indian population with great respect; the servants were dealt with politely and their beliefs and customs respected. When we were living there I had felt no threat whatsoever. I was utterly secure and free in my own little world.

But with the coming of independence in 1947 the British had to leave. My father began to talk about us going 'home' – to me a very strange and unnecessary notion: surely I was already at home, here in India with my beloved ayah and friends? All the talk of Scotland and of a place called Aberdeen meant very little. I remember how my father would draw a tramcar for me and tell me we were going to a land where such a marvel was the regular way of getting about. That was exciting, and when I asked what would happen to my ayah he assured me she would be coming too – though not at once.

Then I can remember sailing home on the Empress of Scotland – filled with returning British troops – the throwing of hats into the Red Sea – a ritual to show that we were now finished with India and were going home. And I can remember howling for my ayah. We disembarked at Southampton and took the train up to Aberdeen. We ended up staying at the family home, 'Roslyn' in Stoneywood with my aunts Sally and Jean who also owned a lovely wee shop in their grounds. After a few months my parents bought a house in Cults and there I resumed a very happy childhood.

Just about the only disappointment of my trip back to India was that I discovered that my ayah had passed away shortly beforehand.

Ian Lakin. b. 1942. New Delhi and Cults. Interviewed 2009.

Go out east young man!

I was born in Ceylon, August 1941. I was later to spend my working life in nine countries in the East. In those pre Sri Lanka days, Ceylon was part of the British Empire and my father was with the then Eastern Bank. He went all over the Far East in his postings; it so happened that he was in Ceylon when I arrived.

After 1945 we were shipped back to Britain. My father owned a house in Cults, which he had inherited, and that's where we stayed.

Look, I'm 100% Scottish but I'm also 110% British. Rule Britannia! I think Britain without Scotland would be a bloody disaster. Think of what we've brought to the Imperial table – culture, the Enlightenment, science, great minds, medicine, engineering, education, grit and determination.

Certainly overseas I came across more Scots than English. Maybe this was to escape home conditions and seek a better life; maybe it was from a sense of adventure, an expression of the enterprising spirit you everywhere find – or at least used to find – in the streets and the hills of dear old Scotia. We were abroad, far from home and pleased to be part of the great British project overseas, but we were always keen to remind ourselves of where we had come from.

Being away from Scotland has engendered a heightened sense of what my homeland means to me. I always blew the trumpet for the old country at the Jakarta Highland Games, especially for our North-east part of it. I would wear my kilt and also at all the other Scottish-themed gatherings such as our St Andrew's Ball and Burns' Night celebrations.

A touch of Aberdeen in Sydney, Australia. A suitably attired Rod Ramsay takes a pause before daughter Kirsteen's wedding.

Doing it properly:
Rod with a pair of drummers from the Royal New South Wales Regiment at Jakarta, 1980s.

My years in Jakarta confirmed my feelings. There was a small but very lively Scottish contingent and we certainly made our presence felt there. The English had their Morris Dancing and their balls, but how could that compete with the bagpipes, the swirl of the kilt and Strip the Willow? We would fly in a band from Australia for our ball and they gave the assembly the works. The Indonesians loved it – how could they resist the spectacle of guys in kilts, leaping about the main ballroom of the Intercontinental Hotel?

I was one of the organisers. We brought in performers and musicians from all over the world. But Jakarta was just one of a number of postings I entered into during my lengthy and adventurous career. When I left Aberdeen University I applied to a number of companies in London which offered opportunities out East. I got a job in Calcutta with Shaw Wallace. I sailed out and duly turned up at the office there. 'What exactly do you want?' they asked. When I explained myself to them they hummed and hawed and then pronounced, 'Take the day off and come back tomorrow.' When I did so, the next question was, 'Do you know anything about ships?' 'Well, I came out on one and I do know that a ship has a blunt end and a sharp one'. 'That's good enough for us,' came the prompt response. 'We're appointing you to the Shipping Department with immediate effect'.

So I embarked on my career in shipping. Two years on, I was with Gray Mackenzie and they sent me to Abu Dhabi to oversee the handling of tankers there – booking the berths, administering the landings, seeing that there was pilotage available and such like highly vital operations.

My posting was at the end of a pipe line under the scorching desert air. We had to generate our own electricity and for three months it broke down. So no fridge, no lights, no air conditioning – it was hell, I can tell you. I used to wallow in my bath, reading Ian Fleming.

After six months of this, I decided I'd had enough. I'd talked about my disaffection with various sea captains and they had recommended that I approach an Edinburgh company called Ben Line.

I wrote off, got an interview and was offered a post. I was posted to Hong Kong for five-and-a-half years and this is where I met my wife, a lovely German girl called Hilke, who was teaching English there.

We hitched up together, spent my leave following an extensive tour of North Africa, the Middle East and the eastern Mediterranean before returning to Hong Kong. While we were there a typhoon struck. Hong Kong suffered a direct hit; our 17th floor flat was swaying about while the two of us huddled together under the bed. The whole place was wrecked – cars smashed against walls, 86 drowned on the ferry.

Then I got promotion to the manager's position in Jakarta. The place appealed to me because Indonesia was just about the last outpost of traditional shipping. Everywhere else had gone over to containerisation – so much faster and more efficient – but as the ports along the Indonesian coastline had draughts which were too shallow to accommodate the larger container ships, the good old ways still prevailed. You see, pre-container shipping is

Back to his roots: Rod among the 'dear old haunts' once more on one of his several return visits to the North east.

a much more human, a slower and less mechanised affair, and I relished the colour and the mingling of people involved in this, the world's largest archipelago.

I had 113 of a staff working for me. Hilke and I built up a lovely home there; I mixed easily with the locals and made many good friends among them.

And now in retirement we live in Australia. But I can look back on what to me has been an adventurous and exciting life. Today, on my visit back home, I will go up Deeside, have a spot of lunch at the Banchory Lodge Hotel and do some fishing in the Dee: all my dear old haunts, the places and the memories that I could revisit via that marvellous man and poet, Charles Murray. He was my great refuge on many a night out East; I would fish out my *Hamewith* and be transported back to the foot of Bennachie.

So, I do know that I made the right decision to follow my father's advice and 'Go out East!' all those years ago. The North-east has given me a solidly rooted start in life – but I suspect that if I had had to live here permanently I would have become fidgety and bored within weeks.

I accept the Empire can never come back, but I'm grateful I caught its final days. And when you consider the role that lads from the North-east of Scotland have played in the great Imperial adventure and the extent to which they have contributed the qualities of steadiness and downright common sense, then we can be doubly proud to have played our part. I know I am.

Roderick (Rod) Ramsay. b. 1941. Cults, Jakarta and Australia.

Rod Ramsay has been awarded both an MBE and an OBE. He reports that on both investitures he enjoyed 'a pleasant exchange with Her Majesty'.

Everything seemed shabby in comparison

In 1949, when I was 12 the family emigrated to Rhodesia. This was just after the war and plenty of others were going off to seek a new life in those days. One of my dad's friends had already gone out and he wrote back, 'Come out here – there's a good life waiting for you.' He helped Dad get a job as an accountant with a firm called Pest Control that specialised in spraying crops and flushing out colonies of snakes or wasps from the house.

We sailed out on the Edinburgh Castle; it took three weeks. I had no idea of what we were going to but I do remember being heart-broken at having to leave our grandparents behind. I can still see Granda standing alone on the platform as our train drew away to

Irene Bryce: Despite the initial misgivings, Irene Bryce did settle back into Aberdeen life and played a leading role in its promotion as Assistant Editor of *The Leopard*. Among the 1975 magazine's production team, she is seated right with, indeed, a leopard on her lap. The back row right features Diane Morgan, Editor, and Lindy Cheyne who, in her turn, a quarter of a century later, was to became its editor.

Southampton. He was watching his family going off thousands of miles to a strange land.

My grandparents are why I came back, to go to their Golden Wedding. Then I met Ian and simply stayed on. But out in Rhodesia we did have a good life. Although we hadn't much money we were able to buy our own plot of land and build a house. This was in the suburbs of Salisbury. We had a lovely outdoor life there. You could go swimming in the pools. There weren't pubs like they have here, but the hotels had clubs attached to them where you could go and dine and drink and dance. There was plenty of tennis too.

I came back to Aberdeen in '62. At that time Rhodesia was a very rich country. It's true that the African servants weren't well paid, but they did have their uniforms, accommodation and keep provided. On the farms they would have free hospital care and schools also. Now it is a ruined country where it's difficult even to get the essentials of life such as bread and milk. It's a real tragedy that everything has collapsed.

I still felt Scottish while I was over there. There was a strong Scottish element out there. There was a Caledonian society and I was in the choir. They kept social events like St Andrew's night and Burns night. But I can't say I actually missed Scotland; we were enjoying a lovely outdoor life.

When I returned it was with no idea of making it permanent. I intended to spend a year and then go back. In fact I felt homesick for Rhodesia for quite some time. It was really only Ian that kept me here.

What struck me on my return was how old fashioned and shabby everything seemed to be. In Salisbury there were big modern skyscrapers and modern electrical conveniences, but here people were still using gas cookers. The shops had no elevators or escalators. The people too seemed very stuck in their ways. Socially life was very limited too. If you wanted to go out at night it would have to be somewhere like the Douglas where the procedure was to line up with all the other women on one side of the hall and wait for some revolting creature of a man to approach you from the other side to condescend to ask you for a dance. Back in Rhodesia the custom was to escort you to parties. Everything seemed so drab and grey after the sunshine of Africa.

Irene Bryce. b. 1936. Ferryhill and Rhodesia. Interviewed 2006.

> What struck me on my return was how old fashioned and shabby everything seemed to be.

Oh for a walk along the prom back home

I married in 1943 and my husband went out to Africa in '45. My husband was a building inspector and my son was born in Africa. I loved it – and we didn't come home until '60. We were in Luanshya and it was lovely. We came home when we saw things in Northern Rhodesia were changing; it's called Zambia now.

I was secretary of the Caledonian Society in Luanshya. At Hogmanay, at two o' clock

The Tea gardens in Luanshya, Zambia, once known as the 'Garden Town of the Copper belt', where Gladys Morrice once lived.

A group of kilted ex-pats at a Caledonian evening in Luanshya around 1950. Gladys's father, Philip Kerr, is on the left.

Gladys around 1947 with daughter Diane and her two Rhodesian Ridgebacks.

on New Year's morning – midnight our [UK] time – Bill, my brother-in-law, was a piper and so was one of the policemen. We had a big car and, at two o'clock after we'd hugged one another and shed a few tears for those at home, Bill and this bobby would go in the front and Arthur, my husband, would get into this big car and have them in the headlights as they piped their way round Luanshya with him behind them. And everybody would be out, cheering and carrying on. The Caledonian Society was a big society... dancing, heuching and carrying on.

When I went out to Northern Rhodesia first, in '46, I was so homesick you wouldn't believe it. Three years later I came home for a holiday and took everything with me; I wasn't going back. I came off the train at Aberdeen Station and I looked around me. I'll be honest; I could have crossed the railway line and got onto that train going back. Everybody looked so glum; it was a dark, dull day; everybody's faces were long. I thought, 'Dear God, what have I given up? All that sunshine and that lovely big house; what have I given up?'

Aberdeen was still home, really – but I didn't want to come to Aberdeen. I thought it was too far north; it was too cold. I wanted to go further south into England where it'd be warmer. But Arthur always said 'A Wordie's horse aye heids for hame.' And while we were abroad, when it was really sometimes terribly hot – we were only 14 degrees from the Equator, you see – he used to say, 'Oh for a walk along the Prom and a breath of cold air'. He was never on the blasted Prom when we came home!

Gladys Morrice. b.1920. Luanshya, Zambia. Interviewed 2016.

Travel really does broaden the mind

I have this travel lust and after four happy years as a Chartered Engineer in the Roads Department, we decided to leave this comfort zone and see something of the outside world. Sandra and I took ourselves off for a year's VSO work, out to a leper colony in Nigeria. Sandra could use her medical training as a doctor and I became a lecturer in Surveying at Benin University.

Leprosy was still regarded as a stigma and its victims were consigned to outpost colonies, so we felt we were doing useful work. But there's a sad background to this; we arrived not long after the civil war, when Biafra attempted to break away, and our colony had been on the frontline of the fighting. All lepers suffer from the same symptoms and have the same needs but, in the war, the internecine struggle outside was replicated within the colony and the Biafrans had been singled out and clubbed to death by the rest.

But we also took away positive messages. I developed a high regard for the capacity of the average African to withstand hardship and to maintain a sense of life and humour under conditions which would be unthinkable to us in the West. We lived in fairly basic conditions – just three hours of electricity a day, when the generators came on, and water only every other day. Fresh meat was unknown since any meat came at the end of a long trek overland from the north and was pretty tough stuff when it finally arrived. Fresh milk was also unknown and each day you would have to haggle for vegetables at the local market. But all this was good for us; it taught us to value the really important things in life – he need to maintain a strong spirit and a capacity to laugh at yourself.

I've been happy to come back to my home city of Aberdeen. I really have discovered that travel broadens the mind, but that it also gives you an appreciation of what you've already got. I love living here in Ferryhill. To me it's a community within the city, a place which supports plenty of local activities and where a nice mix of people can come together as friends and collaborators. And Aberdeen itself is a fine place to live in: it's big enough to contain all the amenities you would look for in a city – both cultural and social – but not so large that you can't be out into the countryside within minutes.

Ross Barrett-Ayres. b. 1947. Nigeria and Ferryhill. Interviewed 2015.

Heading back 'home': The voyage out of Africa, 1960, on board the SS *Pendennis Castle*. Gladys Morrice is on the left next to her parents and husband Arthur. Her sister, Nancy and brother-in-law, Bill, Gordon, are in the centre foreground and her daughter, Diane, is on the right.

<blockquote>
We never thought about where people came from, they were just who they were.
</blockquote>

THE NEW ABERDONIANS

The changing scene

Aberdeen has changed a lot; it's more cosmopolitan than when I was growing up. At my school even an English voice wasn't often heard.

Jim Duffus. b. 1954. Union Grove. Interviewed 2016.

There wasn't a huge mix of people coming and going in Aberdeen when I began school, but it started from that time on. Now, in my children's classrooms, they're from all over the world whereas then, most people were from a few streets away. We gradually had a few people in class whose families had moved in with the oil industry, who were English. And then I had a lovely friend, Ruth, whose mum came from Ghana to work as a nurse. We never thought about where people came from, they were just who they were.

Wendy Bradford. b. 1972. Forbesfield Road. Interviewed 2016.

I found a lot of anti-English feeling

I grew up in a Yorkshire pit village, about 16 miles from Barnsley. We met first at Skegness. My mother, sister and I had gone there to celebrate her birthday. We were strolling along the prom when we came across a notice: 'Dance this evening'. Up to then, I'd only been to local church hall dances but, it being my birthday, I decided to venture to this one.

And there was Alex, singing with the band. He was in the Royal Navy and was stationed at Skegness at the holiday camp, which had been commandeered from Butlin's.

We were immediately attracted to each other; Alex will tell you that as soon as he clapped eyes on me, he said to himself, 'I'm going to marry you!' We passed the whole night dancing together. He complimented me on being such a good dancer; that was music to my ears because I'd never been much of a dancer, but somehow found I could dance with him.

Yorkshire meets Aberdeen: Beryl and Alexander Booth met at a dance in Skegness and carried on dancing into their long married life.

When I first came to Aberdeen I got a job at Cornhill Hospital. I found the local dialect very difficult. It was the days of rationing and at the hospital we had to share out the cheese and the jam and the eggs. I always seemed to get the worst share. And my porridge was always the one that had the lumps in it. Now, how was it that the Englishwoman was the one that always landed with the worst of it? The charge nurse was a lovely woman and she was good to me, but the others seemed to have this thing about 'the English'. Even Alex will talk about being brought up to hate the English.

Yes, I found a lot of anti-English feeling in Aberdeen in the early days. But I think it's been a wonderful place to live. Alex and I have been married for 62 years. We've got a good family. Our two daughters both became teachers. I've lived in Aberdeen for over 70 years. But you would only get the one answer if you were to ask me and Alex about Aberdeen — we both love it.

Three generations later: Beryl and Alex in their Garthdee home, with great grandson Jamie.

Beryl Booth. b. 1919. Yorkshire and Inchgarth. Interviewed 2004.

Those 62 years went on to become over 77 before Alec passed away in 2019 — but Beryl lives on, a new centenarian.

My early memories are country ones

My early memories are country ones. Dad was grieve at Tolquhon of Tarves and I went to school at Udny Green and then at Tarves. We landed up in the town like this: my father had to be brought home from the fields by the farmer. At harvest time, if the conditions were fair, you'd work round the clock, under the moon if necessary. This was in the evening; my father had been working all the day since very early and now he was being brought home ill. The doctor was sent for; he arrived and said that he had double pneumonia. An ambulance was sent for and away Dad went. It was traumatic. As a child, I stood there with the feeling that I was never going to see my dad again. The farmer was crying. I went to the towel that was hanging behind the door and just buried my face in it.

Dad was now in hospital, in the town, very ill — touch and go. There was no penicillin, but there was this new drug, serum. It saved his life. This was September 1933. I was nine. He was in Woodend Hospital, Ward 8. We had to go in and out by bus to visit him. This went on and on. Of course, we'd been living in a tied house and it was obvious we would have to get out. Jim Currie, Dad's old pal as a youth, now lived in Aberdeen and was visiting Dad in hospital. They had four rooms in their house at Kintore Place. It was arranged that we would come and stay there till we could get a house of our own in town.

So we were now ensconced in Aberdeen. I went to school at Skene Square. It was all a bit of a culture shock. I was now walking through streets, playing in streets. I had to learn entirely new games — 'Hoist the Green Flag' and 'Cowboys and Indians'. We didn't play that kind of thing in the country.

Back to her rural origins. Peggy Walker, in 2008, outside Cairnfechel, the cottar house near Udny Green, where she spent much of her pre-Aberdeen childhood.

At her post-war marriage to Aberdonian David Walker.

Two country quines: Peggy seated with sister Bunty, 1932.

Dad didn't come out of hospital till the end of January; he'd been in it for five months. But we never went without. My mother was a very good manager, and Dad, too, had always been very canny, and that's how we managed to survive that time. Dad then became a tram driver. We got a house in Bedford Place, a house with a garden. I always remember it was £1 a week rent and Dad's earnings came to £2.4.7d. Then he got a plot of land and started to grow vegetables. He used to sweep our own chimney and soon other people would come up to him to do theirs. He used to tie his brushes to his bike and off he'd go. And he did gardening for people. Really, he just set to and used the skills he had – just as he had done in the country.

I was happy in my new environment despite the great changes. It's a case that as a child you adjust and don't really think about it. If the family unit is sound then you can put up with a lot. There was no real problem about being accepted into the town – there can't have been; after all I'm still living here, 70 years later!

Peggy Walker. b. 1924. Tarves and Kintore Place. Interviewed 2003.

Only the strong survive!

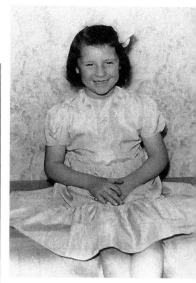

Before the big move north: Meg Forbes during her Denny girlhood.

When I was 12, the family moved up from Denny, near Falkirk. My mother had qualms about the whole thing. The journey in those pre-dual carriageway days took up to four hours by car; Aberdeen seemed very remote and far up to the north. It also had a reputation for being very cold and for housing 'funny folk'. I remember one teatime just before the move, her asking Dad quite anxiously, 'Is Aberdeen really going to be all right for us?' and my father replying, 'Oh yes, Aberdeen's a place where the strong live and the weak die off – we'll be fine!'

Life in Aberdeen has, on the whole, been good to me and for me. One of the differences I could point to when I compare the culture of the North-east with the Central Belt one I left at the age of 12, is an attitude towards education. My immediate family was always keen on my going on to take my Highers and earn qualifications, but that was not the universal attitude in the communities we left.

People down there then were more inclined to enter a life of acting as working fodder. I had cousins who simply left school at 15 and wouldn't have dreamt of staying on. Yet in the Aberdeen I encountered, there were the daughters of mothers who'd been working as fish filleters and who were determined that their own children would have a better future than they had had, and were prepared to make the sacrifices to ensure it. That was a contrast to my early Denny days. An old school friend's cry of, 'Nobody told me that I was allowed to stay on at school!', haunts me yet.

Margaret (Meg) Forbes. b. 1944. Denny and Northfield. Interviewed 2015.

A cold but friendly place

She survived – and as a student and teacher played a committed role in city life. Here Meg is rattling her can for Charities Week in 1962.

I was born in Belfast in 1948. My father had a job as an inspector with the Ministry of Agriculture in Northern Ireland. Our home was in Maghera, a market town in County Londonderry, but I spent my summer holidays in Uist, where my granny and her brother lived.

By the time I was due to leave school, I knew what I wanted to do with my life; it clearly had to be something involved with living things. My first thought was to go to Agricultural College; I then had a flirtation with physiotherapy. While I was dithering I came across, out of the blue, an advert in a newspaper which had been sent to us by our Scottish relatives. This was the *Stornoway Gazette* and there, in black and white, was the information that the Department of Agriculture & Fisheries was inviting applications for the post of a scientific assistant in their laboratory in Aberdeen. I hadn't a clue about Aberdeen itself, but the position appealed and I went for it.

I was invited to attend for interview at the Marine Laboratory, Torry. I took the ferry, then a train from Glasgow, and finally arrived in this Aberdeen late at night. The next morning, I took the bus over to Torry and went into the Lab, only to be told that they were running late and that I should come back later. I took a stroll up Victoria Road and

John Dunn celebrating his birthday in company of the younger generation – 'a young lady whose curiosity about the world is only matched by her unconditional affection'.

into St Fittick's and sat by the little granite building there and gazed out over the harbour. It was an impressive sight: what I saw was the exodus of trawler after trawler sailing out to sea, an assortment of craft, some of which were spick and span, others old rust buckets. I was aware of the smell of sea, oil and fish, so different from my own inland Northern Irish home. I found the whole scene stirring. In the distance, I could hear the din coming up from the shipyards, the clang of metal, and the noise of the rivet guns firing off.

I returned, had my interview, got the job and settled down to life in my adopted city. Aberdeen struck me as a cold place, certainly nothing like as mild as my moist and temperate Irish home. However, it was also drier and that first winter in the late '60s was unusually severe. I was aware of how clean and scrubbed the city was, that shopkeepers made the effort to wash down their frontage. I was also taken by the granite tenements, which were so different to the sandstone Glasgow ones, with their tiled entrances and their high ceilings. Above all, I found Aberdonians to be a friendly and welcoming people.

My previous experience of cities had been Belfast and Glasgow and I welcomed the more secure ethos that my adopted Aberdeen could offer me. One huge difference was the complete absence of sectarianism. In Glasgow you were always aware of it as an undercurrent and that, beneath the bonhomie, there was a strain of violence. I remember my uncle took me to see the running of the last tram in Glasgow and how, for me, the scene was marred by the way in which people made it an opportunity to get drunk. I was conscious of swarms of folk reeling about the streets, swearing and slurring their words and lurching into reach other. I know that drink is one of life's pleasures, but to go out like that to get deliberately hammered seemed to be a sad abuse. There was much less of that in the Aberdeen I was getting to know.

John Dunn. b. 1948. Maghera, Northern Ireland. Interviewed 2016.

I feel British but I also feel Polish

After the war I couldn't return home. Poland was now under a Communist regime. I came to Aberdeen by chance. When I joined the Polish army this is where I was posted.

When I demobbed I met my wife at Durris. She is Scottish. She died in 1977. She was ill for 23 years before that and in a wheelchair. I was talking to my grandson, who is eight, about all that and he said he would write to the Pope to make me a saint because I had stayed with my wife all through the long years of illness. I told him, 'Look I married for better or for worse – simple as that! In any case your plan has a flaw: you have to die first before you can be made into a saint'. 'Oh, in that case, I'll just wait a little longer.'

I found that jobs were limited for us Poles. We were restricted to jobs in coal mining, the quarries, the fish. The trade unions wouldn't have us. It was a question of job protectionism. This led to a lot of bitterness: during the war we had been welcomed with open arms, but in peacetime it was a totally different matter. If you were in uniform out

on the streets you were liable to be attacked.

There were 200,000 of us Poles in the UK after the war. Some did go back; some went to the USA, some to France. When we left the army, our priority was to get a job, to see to the essentials of life. We weren't looking for handouts. For us that would have been a great social stigma. Personally, I can't say I was made to feel very welcome. Most Poles would say the same. The media didn't help. The attitude was created that we were taking the jobs of the local people.

By sheer hard work and determination I got a Law degree and in 1954 qualified as a lawyer. Now I feel quite integrated. My clients are Scottish and other British. I have Scottish friends. I have noticed that although there might be resentment of the newcomer to start with, once they get to know you and find that you are a decent chap then they will accept you. It's the person, not the religion or the nationality, that counts in the end – but it does take time.

I brought my children up the way I was in Poland. Someone once asked how I managed to adjust from Poland to here. I told him my aim has always been to hold on to the best from my Polish culture and to acquire the best from my new one. I'm not prepared to overthrow what has been good about my upbringing in Poland.

There has been a distinct Polish community in Aberdeen. There is the Polish Association, which caters for the younger generations and for anyone interested in things Polish. That has 50 members. We have special church services, at St Francis in Mannofield. A Polish priest comes up from Glasgow to take the services.

It's difficult to tell you what nationality I now feel I am. I feel British, but I also feel Polish – it all depends on the situation. I now think in English, even dream in the language. After all, I've lived here for 60 years, compared to only 18 in Poland. But Poland is my roots and there is always something that draws you back to that. Nationality is where you are born; it's citizenship that expresses where you come to have your allegiance.

William Pyka. b. 1926. Poland and Leggart Terrace. Interviewed 2005.

William Pyka
There is an extensive Polish community in Aberdeen. The Polish Association join in the Celebrating Aberdeen march in 2016.

A site with potential: Silvia Quarantelli's parents, Mr and Mrs Guilianotti, outside their Rendezvous Café soon after its opening in 1933.

Before the war clouds broke: The Guilianottis behind the counter in 1939.

I have the best of both worlds

I was born in 1939 in Forest Avenue, just above the family shop there. My family was the Guilianottis and we owned shops on both sides: 'Piccadilly' and the 'Rendezvous'. My parents ran a shop, which in those days was known as a 'confectioners'; they made their own ice cream and some of the sweets. Both my parents' people had originally come from the same part of northern Italy. But my father – Attilio – was actually born in Peterhead in 1907. Peterhead was a real centre for Italian immigration; they were attracted because the herring fishing was doing well and there were opportunities to open up food and confectionery businesses.

That's how a lot of the Italian community started off over here. One person would come over, see an opportunity, build things up and then send word back for other members of the family to come and join him. Since then we've built up quite a network of cousins, uncles, aunts: I must be related to about three-quarters of Aberdeen's Italian population. They socialise together: dances, gathering at places like Kippie Lodge.

When people ask me whether I feel Italian or Scottish I usually answer, 'Both. I have the best of both worlds,' and that's true but, when I think back to the war years in particular, I appreciate that my background has been very different from most Aberdonians. Soon after war was declared and Italy came in on the German side, Churchill issued the order: 'Collar the lot' and this suddenly turned us into aliens. Thousands of immigrants were rounded up and interned.

My father was sent to prison. I was a babe in arms at the time. The policeman who came to arrest him was well known to the family; we called him 'Uncle Jack'. A lot of the police around there had got into the habit of dropping in to the Rendezvous. We were open all hours, often well into the night, making the ice cream for the next day and so on. The police would call in, check that everything was all right, go round the back and get a cup of coffee. And now our own Uncle Jack was coming to take my father away! He said, 'I'm very sorry Tonio – none of them could pronounce 'Attilio' properly – but I've got my orders'.

I was an only child. My mother was determined that we would not sink into poverty. She was really the dominant one in the family. She had started up a place at the Beach – the Washington Café – and she insisted that it should be done in style, with the girls all dressed in white pinafores and smart uniforms. Then she branched out to the Holburn Café. But that didn't satisfy her; she wanted something in the West End. She would walk up Forest Avenue and noticed that that was the terminus for the buses. She also saw the playing fields all around, at Harlaw and Rubislaw, so she got the idea of setting up a kiosk to sell ice cream. Then she decided to do the thing properly and to set up a shop. She sold the Holburn to her brothers, Alberto and Julio, for £1,000. This was in the 1930s.

When my father, in 1939, was incarcerated under the 'collar the lot' policy, he ended up on the Isle of Man. He and the group he was with called it 'Collegio'. Most of them were also from the catering trade and their incarceration together gave them the opportunity to exchange ideas and to scheme new projects for after the war so, in many

ways, it was a kind of education for them.

I remember the day my father finally came home. I stood on the pavement outside the shop, waiting. I saw this figure coming slowly up the road in a brown raincoat, carrying a brown suitcase held together with string. He'd caught the tram up from the station and now he was walking the last yards up the street.

Back in Aberdeen, my mother kept the business going. She was lucky: the district we were in was full of nice people who remained friendly. My mother was a hard woman in many ways, but you only had to tell her a hard luck story and she would be ready to listen and to help. She was good to people and most of them were good to her and to the business.

My mother took me over to Italy. A young man put a ring on my finger. This was Danilo, who later became my husband, but at that point I was only 17 and not ready. I gave it back and returned to Aberdeen. Danilo was studying to be a vet. We wrote to each other. He was just about to take his final exams when we decided to marry.

Danilo came over and we were married. In the family business we had to work very hard. Before I was married I didn't get any payment, but afterwards the wage was £8 a week of which I had to hand over £2 for lodgings. We stayed above the shop. The hours were long: we were open till 11 at night and afterwards there would be all the cleaning up and preparation for the following day. We made our own ices and lots of novelty items – snowballs, nougat wafers, ices in the shape of ducks and fish. All this had to be made ready for the next day. One of my jobs was to carry the ices through to the cabinet at the back on a tray. Once the trap door was left open and I didn't see it. Down I went, but all my mother could cry was, 'Oh no – the ices will be ruined!'

We worked night and day, all this in an atmosphere in the café thick with smoke and the scents of lime and lemon and orange juices. The work was hard, but my parents also knew how to entertain. Many a night my father would push back all the furniture, leaving just one long table. The home would become full of guests and there would be music and stories. Not all of the guests were from the Italian community by any means. During the war the Rendezvous had become a popular meeting place for all sorts of Aberdonians: women whose husbands were away in the Forces or soldiers back on leave.

I've been fortunate in that I've not really suffered the prejudice that some have. My approach has always been to laugh off any insults. When I've been called 'Dingo' I've simply said, 'Oh I think you mean "Wop", not "Dingo". But we never had any difficulty with our neighbours. We were well respected by them.

The North-east of Scotland is my home. I decided a long time ago that when I was getting old and the question would be raised, 'Do I go back to Italy or not?' I would stay here. It's where I've been born and where I've grown up. I'm both an Aberdonian and an Italian. That gives me the best of both worlds.

Silvia Quareantelli. b. 1939. Rendezvous Café. Interviewed 2006.

The son: Bob Meconi's father, Amadeo jnr, poses outside a Meconi shop, 1920s.

He spent all the hours of the day building up the family shops

I am of Italian descent; my grandfather came from a small town in Tuscany called Diecimo. He came over at a time when many rural Italians were emigrating in order to escape the hardships of their struggles to eke a living out of their fairly backward lives. My grandfather, Amadeo (snr), was supposed to travel only to Dundee, but he missed the stop and landed up in Aberdeen, the terminus. He immediately walked over the road to a shop beside the Tivoli Theatre, only to discover it was being run by Italians. The result was they got speaking and he ended up with a job.

But my father, Amadeo (jnr), never spoke much about any of this. In fact, while I was growing up I hardly ever saw him; he spent all the hours of the day building up the family shops. My granda had been determined to make a go of life in his new country and that is exactly what he did. Research has shown me that he managed to put together a small empire of several shops: in Torry, in St Andrews Street – which was probably his first one – and in Marischal Street.

These were confectionary and ice cream shops, though the St Andrews property was a chipper. I remember people would pop in straight from the fish houses with fish and ask him to fry it for them.

My grandfather lived from 1879 to 1937. He put his back into building up a successful business, but the real driving force was my grandma. He was a quiet man, rather the gentleman in his dress and his manner – he loved to go about in stylish clothes and was something of a dude. His wife, however, was a down to earth grafter and the real boss in the household. She was Scottish – Margaret Herd Gabriel was her maiden name. They had four sons.

Meconi's ran the very first chip van in Aberdeen, in the '50s. Their beat was the Hilton, Cove, Northfield and Mastrick areas, schemes which had just been built and were

The Meconi who started it all: Granda Amadeo snr outside his Torry shop, 1905.

still lacking in amenities, so their business prospered. Apparently, they would drive this large van, which had a funnel sticking out of its roof, the smoke streaming out behind him just like a trawler out at sea. They did the frying in the van itself, using coal as fuel.

The family worked round the clock. First Granda, then Roberto, used to go down to the fish market, then come back to the chipper, where my father and Roberto filleted the fish themselves, while my father's job was to peel the tatties and cut out their eyes. He would slog away at this till noon, come home for his dinner then return to it, till deep into the evening.

My wife, Heather, found her introduction into the Meconi family life something of an experience. She came from Bankhead, a normal Aberdeen background, and she just couldn't believe what she was landing among; her new family treated rows and dramatic shouting matches as the norm. They were constantly falling out and storming off. It was the same in the shops – they had no sense of discretion at all and would carry on their noisy disputes even when customers were about. Aprons would be torn off and thrown on the ground – just because my father was using Bertie's pans, that sort of thing. But they were also very welcoming and generous. When Heather was a hairdressing lecturer at the Technical College my father would love to boast about her success.

By this time, the family owned four shops: two in St Andrews Street, one on the corner of South Esplanade East and another at 21 Victoria Road in Torry. That's how I came to be a Torry loon. My early life was spent at 57 Grampian Road. I was expected to work in the shop but, instead, chose to do a couple of other jobs before becoming a

Aberdeen's first chip van: The Northfield travelling chipper in 1950.

Entry into Italian life: Bob with his Aberdonian Heather in 1967.

fish porter at the harbour, starting in 1972.

The Meconi shops were sold off; the business really died with that older generation. I speak no Italian and would regard myself as a Torry loon, but I remain proud of my Italian heritage. I am the third generation of a hard-working immigrant family, which slaved away to make something of their lives and which served the Aberdeen public well.

I know that there are still a number of Italian style organisations in Aberdeen but, on the whole, my generation has been happy to amalgamate into the wider society of the city. I have a photo from the time when they were still newcomers, attempting to make their way and to better their lives. It's dated 1925 and shows all the prominent Italian businessmen in the city, all 60 of them. They look a smart and gentlemanly bunch, obviously keen to show Aberdeen how fortunate the city was to have them.

Robert (Bob) Meconi. b. 1945. St Andrews Street. Interviewed 2016.

My arrival was scarcely propitious

I was born in Kathmandu, Nepal in April 1945. After my preliminary education there I went to India to train as a medical doctor. I did this under an international scholarship which I had won. As a stipulation of the award was that I would return to Nepal to work, I served in my native country, usually being posted to rural parts, for seven years. I then came to the UK and trained further in cardiology and then specialised in geriatric medicine.

I joined NHS Grampian as a Consultant Physician and the Medical Faculty in Aberdeen University in 1988 as a Senior Lecturer in Medicine in 1988. I have settled here and regard Aberdeen as my permanent home.

I retired as the Lead Clinician in our department when I reached 60 years of age. I have devoted my time since then in studying the language, philosophy, history and culture of my native land. With my wife we have founded an educational foundation there. I visit Nepal regularly.

I come from a well-educated professional background. My father was a civil servant and eventually retired as Governor of the Central Bank of Nepal. I was brought up in a loving and caring environment. During the first 33 years of my life,, Nepal was a totalitarian, repressive regime, completely under the thumb of the monarchy. Everything that the king, Mahendra, and subsequently his son, Birenda, who succeeded him, said, along with his courtiers, acted as the law. This system had held sway for generations and only changed in 1989 when a revolution overthrew the monarchy. By that time I had become naturalised in the United Kingdom.

The regime operated through patronage and nepotism. My father was a highly placed civil servant. He was an upright, honourable man, who refused to enter into the prevailing system of corrupt deals, and this meant that, from time to time, he fell out of favour. Consequently, my whole boyhood and beyond was lived under a constant fear of

> My father was a highly placed civil servant. He was an upright, honourable man, who refused to enter into the prevailing system of corrupt deals.

arrest and incarceration. There was a system of extensive secret police and spies were everywhere.

Although my school education necessarily followed traditional lines, education was seen as the escape route from this stifling atmosphere. If you seemed to follow the regime and had talent you could get on. I won my international scholarship and was able to complete my medical education in India. Even so, I was regarded with suspicion and that's why I was posted out into rural parts, to keep me out of harm's way.

Before coming to UK, I spent seven years as doctor in Nepal – Kathmandu, Jumla in the western province and then Dahran. In the foothills of the eastern mountains. Jumla is 105 miles from Kathmandu and is a remote, mountainous area with five months of snow. Houses were little better than mud huts, with the ground floor occupied by cattle; the family would sleep around a fire on the first floor. And the roof had a hole to allow smoke to escape.

We had to get water from a stream in buckets. Electricity was by generator, but intermittent and unreliable. And fuel was wood from forests. There was so little power that when you saw light bulb actually lit up, you thought it must be the sun.

A typical Nepalese rural house of the 1960s/70s. The ground floor is given over to animals.

People there were ruled by tradition and superstition. My job as a doctor was made difficult because of tensions with local faith healers. My attitude was to respect them – after all, there are psychological benefits from traditional faith healing.

As the only two doctors serving a population of nearly 50,000, we used to be available 24 hours a day. We lived in a bungalow within the premises of the health centre, although it was designated as a

Zonal Hospital. We had to get water from a stream in buckets. Electricity was available by a diesel generator for the telegraph office only. The fuel was mostly pine wood from the forests.

Two-thirds of our dwelling were given over to the surgery. The roof was made of compacted soil and often leaked, in which times you had to walk around indoors with an umbrella! We had two rooms and a kitchen with a pit-hole latrine. There was a shortage of basic medicines – sometimes not even an aspirin. There was neither a laboratory nor any x-ray facility. We had to depend upon our own clinical acumen to make a diagnosis. Much improvisation was needed.

The villagers helped to build a hospital while I was there. We ended up with four nurses, 10 orderlies and two doctors. After 28 months we were transferred to Dahran, which was more modern, but still with little in the way of diagnostic facilities.

After working like this for seven years, I decided to obtain specialist training in the

The villagers built their own hospital. The opening, with Prasanna Gautam standing at the front.

Treating an outpatient at Dharan, 1970s.

UK, arriving here in the Queen's Silver Jubilee year and when Virginia Wade won Wimbledon. I worked in several hospitals in England for four years, passed the higher specialist examinations, became a member of the Royal College of Physicians, UK, and eventually got a post as a Registrar cardiologist in Liverpool. I later decided to specialise in Geriatric Medicine.

Once I had received my full accreditation from the General Medical Council, I began to look around for senior posts as a Consultant Physician. I was short-listed for interviews in Warrington, Manchester, Abergavenny – and Aberdeen. But this was 1988 and there was a postal strike in England to protest at the plans to privatise the Royal Mail. This led to the postponement of the other three interviews. That left Aberdeen – so you could say that I am here because of Mrs Thatcher and her drive for privatisation!

My arrival in Aberdeen for the very first time was hardly a propitious one. I had been working till five in the evening in Sunderland and then had to get up to Aberdeen for an eight o'clock meeting – a pre-interview assessment really – the next morning. It was late October; it was dark; I was dead tired and it was raining. I got to the city at two a.m., in the bucketing rain. I had no idea as to where my hotel was, so I went up to a taxi rank in Union Street and explained my predicament. 'Look, I'm just about to clock off – it's the end of my shift', came the answer. But then, 'I can take you to the Marcliff on my way home.'

I followed him to what was then the old Marcliffe Hotel in Queen's Road, he refusing to accept any money for his trouble. The Marcliffe was then a small hotel without a receptionist at night, but the doorman took me to the room and rustled up some food. He then presented me with a half bottle of whisky to warm me up – completely gratis!

So all the negative things I'd heard about the meanness of the Scots had been completely blown away in my first 24 hours in Aberdeen. And it had stopped raining too! My meeting went well. I had to return to Sunderland that same evening, but had time to look around a bit. I drove to the beach and along the promenade. I immediately fell in love with that wide open bay of sand, with the North Sea rolling in. Today I still like to go to the beach for a few moments of tranquillity and long walks of contemplation.

A few days later, in spite of the traditional, rather parochial, system of appointments for senior jobs prevalent in the old Grampian Health Board at Albyn Place, it was gratifying to be appointed by unanimous decision of the committee to this prestigious post. It was, however, one of the most difficult interviews I had ever faced.

I was then tasked with caring for the elderly patients of Grampian, along with five other physicians. All of us colleagues worked hard to make the Department of Medicine for the Elderly at Woodend Hospital the most modern and user-friendly health service for the elderly in Scotland. I set up a specialist system of providing post-operative care and rehabilitation for patients with hip fractures. Subsequently I set up specialist clinics for medical management of adult patients suffering from urinary incontinence. I loved teaching medicine to the undergraduate medical students and junior doctors in training.

My grandfather was an esteemed scholar of the ancient Sanskrit literature and was my

Part of the Aberdeen scene: Prasanna in 2019, sporting his Bon Accord Probus club Past President's tie.

guru in my school days. I have resumed my interest in ancient history, philosophy and Sanskrit literature in my retirement. I have translated from Sanskrit into English the ancient Rig Veda. This is a compilation of a series of Mantras, or formulae, dating back more than 4,000 years. This is regarded by UNESCO as a 'world heritage', it being the oldest intact literature which has survived the vagaries of time. The texts deal with profound philosophical thoughts, the very history of Indian civilisation and, in addition, cover a wide spectrum of subjects such as science, history, medicine, religion, philosophy and astronomy.

Nepalese society has now changed and is much more democratic and open. Its history is a deeply rooted one. Now in my retirement, I have been working to establish an academy of ancient studies in an attempt to bring the world's attention to the rich heritage of my native country, hitherto not easily available to many.

So I certainly have no regrets in journeying from Kathmandu to make Aberdeen my home. I like the city; I have found it to be a clean and safe place. I feel privileged to have served the elderly patients of Grampian whose appreciation of my endeavours has been a constant source of inspiration to me. I have lived in the same house for nearly 30 years and have acquired a network of friends and social activities. I have joined local clubs and am involved in local charities, as is my wife, Leela, who is also a qualified doctor. Our son and daughter have married locally.

Aberdeen is my home, Nepal my roots.

Prasanna Gautam. b. 1945. Nepal. Interviewed 2015.

In addition to his work on the Rig Veda, Dr Gautam has written a number of other published books, including an account of his experiences as a doctor in rural Nepal: *I Will Need To Break Your Other Leg – Tales Of Medical Adventures And Misadventures.*

The NHS would collapse without people like me

> Aberdeen has changed since I arrived here. It has become much more cosmopolitan.

I came to the UK in 1986 when I was 26 as I could see no future for me in Pakistan and I had family in the UK. I have made my medical career here in the UK. My own children were born and brought up here and I have become thoroughly assimilated. I have grown to love Scotland and now regard it as home. After I'd passed my exams and was registered with the General Medical Council, in 1991, I got the chance to become a research fellow to Sir Graeme Catto, in Aberdeen, and have been in the city ever since. My work has been in renal disease. I then became a lecturer at Aberdeen University in its Medical Faculty and since 1996 have acted as a consultant in NHS Grampian.

All I knew about Aberdeen before I arrived was that it was the oil capital of Europe. But I have always believed that if you decide to settle in a place, then you should make the effort to find out as much about it as you can. So I have developed a great enthusiasm for Scotland, its history, its politics and its landscape. I have also read extensively in Scottish literature.

I think Aberdeen is a fantastic city to work and to live in. It has helped, of course, that I have thoroughly enjoyed my work and that my wife has been able to develop her own business as a purveyor of traditional Indian sauces to local delicatessens and food fairs. We have made many friends, drawn from a wide spread of Aberdeen society.

One of the great benefits of my work is that, through it, I have come into contact with all manner of North-east people. I have come to admire their character. Judging from what I have seen among my patients I would say that North-east folk are more stoical and resilient than most; that they keep their feelings to themselves and are loath to express pain or grief. I should imagine that all this springs from their background among the hardships of farming and fishing life.

This is very admirable, but I do sometimes wonder whether they wouldn't be better letting some of their feelings out rather than striving so hard to contain them. On the other hand, being their doctor and tending to people when they are in medical need, has brought me into intimate contact with their hopes, their fears and their characters. Patients will confide in you under those circumstances. It has been a very great privilege for me to have been able to get to know the people of the North-east in that intimate way.

Aberdeen has changed since I arrived here. It has become much more cosmopolitan. Of course, there are times when we are still regarded as incomers and from a foreign and hot land. My wife, even after 30 years of getting used to it, will on occasion be asked as to how she is bearing up under the cold.

But attitudes have changed. I can tell you a little anecdote to illustrate the point. Not long after I arrived, I had to treat the granddaughter of a member of the Aberdeen aristocracy. She had taken an allergic reaction to a drug and it was straightforward enough to administer the antidote and to put everything right. The lady was grateful, so much so

that I overheard her informing my consultant: 'Do you know, that coloured doctor was rather nice with our Jenny!'

Now, that kind of attitude and the use of that term could be regarded as inappropriate. I didn't take offence; I understood that the lady was from a generation when it was quite normal to approach a member of a different race with a certain amount of wariness, even condescension. She belonged to a different and passing age, one that was rooted in Edwardian mores.

When I arrived here, it was rare to find a non-white face at Foresterhill; now, from registrar and consultant level to nurses and to porters, you see them everywhere as valued members of the medical team. Indeed the NHS would collapse without them and that is widely recognised.

Izhar Khan. b. 1960. Karachi and Aberdeen Royal Infirmary. Interviewed 2016.

Aberdeen people are the very best

I was born in Pakistan, in 1971. My family lived in a rural area, about 18 miles from Islamabad, the capital. My dad was a farmer, never very well off but always anxious to give us all the very best start in life he could. I have five brothers and two sisters, and we have all done well – largely thanks to the brilliant upbringing we enjoyed. I married a

Izhar Khan
Part of local life:
Izhar Khan with the Golden Spurtle he won as 'the world's best porridge maker', in the 21st World Championships, 2014.
(IMAGE BY KIND PERMISSION OF ABERDEEN JOURNALS)

Tauqeer Malik Councillor Tauqeer Malik , 2018.

I played cricket for Mannofield. In 1991, I was about the only Asian in the Grades. Now they have reached such a representation that you could say it's the Asians who keep local cricket going.

young British Pakistani woman. We met when I was 20 and moved into the UK, to her own home city of Glasgow. At that point, I had been leading my own business, dealing in marble from local quarries for use in the construction industry.

Aberdeen is a particularly tolerant and welcoming city. The oil, catering and the University, as well as the NHS, have brought a sizeable number of us here, happy to make our lives as Aberdonians and to assist in the welfare of the city. There are now some 5,000 of us. I had no fears about coming here. My parents taught me to have confidence and self-belief.

How we ended up in Aberdeen, rather than stay in Glasgow, is because my brother-in-law was already here and spoke so highly of the city and its people. My wife was keen to come. She has always been a great support to me.

When I first arrived in Aberdeen, I was working in a video shop – the hiring out of videos was very big business then and our shop would often attract queues at weekends. Then I worked for the Royal Mail.

To start with, I played cricket for Mannofield. At that time, I was about the only Asian in the Grades. That was in 1991; a couple of years later, the number of Asians playing began to take off and now they have reached such a representation that you could say it's the Asians who keep local cricket in the area going.

My cricket career has been a great success. As a captain of Bon Accord I have played a full part in the local Grades scene. I was the first Asian to captain a Grades team; better than that, I have now become the longest-serving captain of the Grades Select team. I have been in this role now for 15 years; I have offered to stand down to give someone else a chance, but I have always been prevailed upon to keep going.

I was always anxious to open my own business. I spotted an opportunity when a shop in Springbank Terrace came on the market. It was a run-down place, but I put my energies into it and turned it round. I was there till 198I and worked at it seven days a week, all round the clock. That was for seven months of the year at least; come the summer the weekends belonged to cricket!

I was living in the Bridge of Don, still on the lookout for further retail opportunities. It came with the sale of a shop in Culter and with it a three-bedroomed house. The shop did well; we built up a mass of regular customers. Now, my wife is an expert curry cook and soon our customers were remarking on the enticing aromas around our place. So that gave me the notion of branching out into the curry business and so I opened a take-away. It has done very well. The secret is not simply good produce; it is, above all, in creating good customer relationships. I have always treated each of my customers as a good friend and have laid special emphasis on personal service. That has resulted in a loyal following.

But it has never been enough for me to simply act as a successful businessman; I firmly believe that you must play a full part in the life and welfare of your community. I have always gone out of my way to help people and, if anyone came to the door seeking donations or publicity for a good local cause, I never sent them away empty handed.

My desire to work for my community is what led me into local politics. I decided to apply to become a Councillor. I gave careful thought as to which party I should join and finally decided it had to be Labour as they were the most devoted – in my view – to social justice and committed to a diverse society in which everyone must be given an equal chance. I stood in the Bridge of Don ward in 1999 but lost.

I took advice from people in the Party; Frank Doran M.P. was very helpful to me. It was felt that my best opportunity would be in the George Street-Harbour ward, since this had the greatest concentration of Asian immigrant population. I stood – but still I lost. However, the whole experience was valuable and I discovered that canvassimg was something I really took to. I thoroughly enjoyed knocking on doors and engaging the public in friendly debate.

So I certainly wasn't going to give up. In 2012 I decided to stand for my own Lower Deeside constituency. I was advised against it and was told to stick to the George Street-Harbour area. The history of Labour in that ward was against me; even during the nationwide Labour landslide of 1997 the Party only received 150 votes. But Lower Deeside was my home ward; I knew the people there; I had become part of their community. When I was canvassing with Anne Begg [the then local MP] she was astounded at the local knowledge I had built up and the doors I could go to with a knowledge of who lived there.

There is always time for cricket: Tauqeer Malik at a presentation marking yet another successful season in the Aberdeenshire Grades, 2014. Lord Provost Barney Crockett and Councillor Alison Evison are with him.

The result was that in 2012 I was elected. I have tried to work hard for my constituents and to serve them all, whatever party they supported. I have made a point of always being available. At the 2017 election, my own vote stood up well. Lower Deeside is the eighth most affluent ward in the whole of the UK and yet it has given me, a Labour man, this great vote of confidence. I feel very honoured to have won the trust of them all. But then I have never had anything but a wholehearted support from the people there. I am very grateful for the way in which they, and Aberdeen as a whole, have taken me to their hearts. I can honestly say that I have never experienced anything that could be described as racial or cultural prejudice – my experience is that Aberdeen folk are simply above that sort of thing.

In fact, I would say that Aberdeen people are the very best! They are generous and welcoming. But, then, the city has become a very diverse one, the most so in Scotland. More than a quarter of its inhabitants are of immigrant stock and yet the city has succeeded in creating a harmonious and safe environment in which everyone is given an equal chance to get on and flourish. Now, when people ask, 'Where are you from?', I can quite proudly answer, 'Aberdeen' and when they ask me what my nationality is I can tell them, 'First Scottish, then British, then Pakistani'.

Tauqeer Malik. b. 1971. Pakistan and Culter. Interviewed 2018.

THE ARTS

Professor Paul Mealor conducts the University Choir outside King's College, Chapel, May 2017.

Charles Hemingway was an accomplished artist as well as being a memorable teacher. This is *Brig of Balgownie,* an early water colour of his.

VISUAL ARTS

He opened up our minds to what art could be about

Then there was Charles Hemingway, the Art teacher, an extraordinary teacher, a bit crazy. He would go off the deep end very easily; he would blow up and his face would turn puce. But he was also very influential. He terrified us to death – but he did teach us about the moderns. For all his strange behaviour he was trying to interest us in the Cubists and other aspects of contemporary art – the Russians and all sorts of exotic names. He tried to din them into us and although we were somewhat unwilling conscripts he did leave his mark on us. He would write up all these strange names on the board and then show us examples of their work.

He gave us an awareness that painting did not have to be like the usual stuff we'd got – the pre-Raphaelites, Constable. He gave us an awareness that there was something called 'modern art', that here was something from our own age, something for the future. Picasso, Matisse… he helped me to break into areas of art which I'd never thought existed. He left me with a taste for new areas of art, opened up my mind to what art could be all about. How you had to look at things and not just accept things for what they seem.

Peter Murphy. b. 1932. Aberdeen Grammar School. Interviewed 2002.

Aberdeen was an extraordinary place for art back then

For a working class family we were unusually interested in the high arts. We'd play at toy theatres: that and music and reading filled our lives. Looking back, I realise I had a very rich upbringing. I was always drawing and was always at the Art Gallery on visits. My grandfather loved painting too. The Art Gallery was very important to us all.

When I was young, the city was my world. Later, with holidays on the farm, my acquaintance with the country did develop and I have always found the transition from the urban to the rural a fascinating spectacle. But I've never really been much of a country person. The seashore has always attracted me for that very reason. Painting it is like painting the town. The shore is like the street and the cliffs are its tenements. The gulls and the waves fill it with endless noise and there's all that debris constantly being washed up on the shore. For me, it's a dynamic, perpetually noisy and changing place, not at all like the countryside.

One of the four ABBO Group of Aberdeen artists during the 1950s/60s. Bill is, 3rd left, with Eric Auld, Bill Baxter and Donald Byres. At the opening of the first McLellan exhibition, 1960. The acronym is made up of the first letters of their surnames.

And Aberdeen was an extraordinary place for art then. The Sculpture Court at the Gallery – gone now – was a marvellous thing. All those wonderful casts of the Elgin Marbles arranged around the entrance court, the whole history of Western art laid out before you.

My own family was a literate and a musical one, one which valued the arts. There were other working-class families with like aspirations. You'd recognise the signs when you went into their homes: the houses would be just that little bit quieter and more ordered, with some books and maybe scores of music on show. The people in them would talk in quieter, more serious voices. So I wasn't so very unusual in that respect in 1940s Aberdeen. Families like mine were in a minority, but it was a significant and recognisable one.

There was a lot of artistic enterprise in Aberdeen. There were individuals like Alexander Macdonald – he created the Alexander Macdonald Bequest collection – who worked to promote art in Aberdeen. It has been a very ambitious city in that respect. The whole construction of the city – think about Union Street or Union Terrace with its monuments and its gardens, think of the Athenaeum Reading Room, the concert halls and the Gallery. For me the whole ethos of the place was part of my education.

Aberdeen in the '40s and '50s was a wonderful place to grow up in. There's this myth that this was the era of austerity, a terrible grey and cheerless time of rationing and of restricted lives. Not at all! Really it was a time of expansion and of hope.

It has been a fertile ground for me and the great thing is that it is there for everybody.

With his wife, Helen, on honeymoon, London, 1963.

Bill's first teaching appointment was at the Nicolson Institute, Stornoway, 1950s. He is 2nd row from top, beside woman in white blouse.

At ease in his Muchalls garden.

Contemplating his next step: Sandy in his studio, 1980s.

The Art Gallery certainly was; the theatre always seemed to be full, the concerts well attended. It had a fine Central Library which was always well used.

Aberdeen has been a rich environment for me. One of the good things about it is its size. It's a city in which you could reach people. It's big enough to hold within it a range of interesting people, to give them jobs when they leave university, yet small enough to be intimate and knowable. I still love to go into the city. I like to park my car at the top of the Bon Accord Centre; I do a lot of sketching round there – I love it: the rooftops, the spires, the various heights and shapes. I think of it as my city still.

William (Bill) Ord. b. 1929. Ruthrieston Circle. Interviewed 2003.

For me being an artist is the most natural thing in the world

I can't say I came from an artistic background. My father was a trained mechanic who, after the war, worked for Charles Alexander's haulage company. There was little in the way of beauty in those Ashvale Place tenements. The stairs had only plain glass windows whereas the tenement blocks round the corner in Great Western Place were of higher quality and had stained glass on their stairwells and some mosaic work too. There were also trees lining its pavements. I was aware of this difference and came to understand that whatever our own surroundings looked like, something a bit better was possible.

To move on from Aberdeen Grammar School to the Gray's School of Art seemed a logical progression. The teaching at Aberdeen Grammar school under the Bush [Charles Hemingway] was nothing if not thorough. He succeeded in impressing upon us that 'art' was something to be taken seriously, that it was a matter of disciplined craftsmanship and not simply some form of self-indulgent expressionism. But I can't say I ever got to like the man. He could be fierce and overbearing, but I have to thank him for the rigorous training he gave us. He was never one to mince his words. When an exam came round he placed me near the bottom of the group. When I challenged my lowly placing he let

Acting out his own picture: Sandy Fraser with daughter Tracy.

At work in his garden.

me have it. Apparently everything was wrong with my effort; I'd got the proportions all wrong; I hadn't kept my eye on the finished product.

All this training has left its mark on me. Although my own career has been in art I wouldn't consider myself as an 'artist' so much as a teacher of art. Much of my work had been a matter of using the disciplined training I was given so as to experiment with a range of styles and topics. My work has been marked by a series of gradual shifts of styles; what happens is that I try to master one style, then move on to another one.

The city is often represented as a tableau of black and white images – all that granite, all those old photos of the harbour

With his family at home in Muchalls. Left to right – son Gavin, wife Helen, daughter Tracy.

packed with trawlers and of buildings stretching up Union Street. Yet the city is really much more colourful than that. I can't say, however, that cityscapes have been a prominent part of my oeuvre. I did once decide that I would take my easel out and pitch it just in front of where the Art College then was – that small triangle of grass and trees and Gordon of Khartoum's statue by the Cowdray Hall. I was looking up Rosemount

Alexander Fraser's *A Muchalls Garland*: The figures are arranged in a circle like a garland on the woman's head. The village in the background is his home of Muchalls.

> It's not a matter of inspiration, of waiting till some shaft of insight suddenly strikes you; no, it's a matter of doing a job properly.

Viaduct and attempting to engage with its great stretch of granite tenements. I was working away when I became distracted by this man circling round me with a large camera – the sort that press photographers use. Finally, he came up to me and asked, 'Have you seen an eagle round here?' It transpired that someone had seen me and my easel and had phoned the P&J to alert them to a possible story. However, the message had been misheard and this photographer had been sent out in pursuit, not of a man with an easel, but of a man with an eagle!

Whether this tells you anything about the respective importance Aberdonians place on eagles as opposed to art, I couldn't comment.

Cityscapes have never really been my thing. You see, to me art is a private activity, one which begins with my own personal absorption with shape and colour and dimension and positioning. I will begin by rough charcoal drawings on a canvas and that will be the raw material from which I will make a composition. That's the stage I really enjoy: the plotting out of figures on a canvas, then adjusting and shifting them around so as to arrive at a grouping that is balanced and whole. It's not a matter of inspiration, of waiting till some shaft of insight suddenly strikes you; no, it's a matter of doing a job properly, of bringing a basic idea to a finished state.

Of course, ultimately what starts out as a private activity becomes open to public view. But although I do appreciate the possibility of a good sale, my real public is the fellow artist. If I can produce something which will earn the respect of other artists, then I know that I have done something good. But once the work is finished and framed then it no longer is mine; it belongs to the wide world and I can feel quite detached from it. My interest will be in the next task to be done, not in what is now past.

So it's all about the basic ingredients of composition, of shapes, of positions, juxtapositions, sizes, the mix of cool and warm colours. It's about – to use a term much in vogue when I was a student, – 'plasticity', that is of working on a subject that you can remake into something that is really yours.

The other day I had to go to the dentist. As I was about to climb into the chair, the new dental assistant looked at me and asked, 'Are you the artist?' I am always startled that members of the public seem to think you are something special if you are entitled to wear the heading of 'the artist'. For me being an artist is the most natural thing in the world.

Alexander (Sandy) Fraser. b. 1940. Gray's School of Art. Interviewed 2015.

I still like to do my work on paper

My birth place was in a tenement block known as Black's Buildings – number seven. My bedroom was in a second floor flat at the back; from it I could overlook the actual stage door of His Majesty's Theatre. At night I was allowed to read in my bed by candle for half an hour and afterwards I would often creep out of my bed and, kneeling, peer through the window at all the comings and goings at the theatre stage door. I found it a constant source of fascination.

It was a working class area. I was born illegitimate and was looked after by my granny and mother. My granny had, in class terms, married down in that she was closely related to Thomas Bunting, a distinguished 19th century water colour artist – I was named after him. I've got some examples of his work on my walls – fine water colours.

My mother was what was called a 'mistress' at the Broadford Mills. This meant being in charge of a team of girls at the looms. She was in her twenties when she had me. My father – as I discovered later – was an expert in the use of belt-driven saws and the felling of trees in Canada – a saw doctor. The two families had a disagreement when my mother fell pregnant; his decided that their son shouldn't be allowed to marry down into the working class. But I was told none of this till much later.

So she had to go out to work and leave me in the hands of my granny and, on occasions, a wee woman – Mary Cave – who also lived in number seven. Granny was a tiny woman, but very capable. She was a great theatre goer and was particularly fond of revues at the Tivoli and light opera, ballet, Gilbert & Sullivan and quality musicals at HMT. We would often have sing-songs round the wireless set which my mother had

Tom Gibson
Near Black's Buildings. A very young Tom Gibson with his uncle Dougie in Union Terrace Gardens.

Tom receives The City of Aberdeen Medal for Civic Architecture from Lord Provost Sir Tommy Mitchell, 1956.

won in a competition.

When about nine, I started going over to Affleck Street on a Saturday morning to run messages for my two aunts. For this I would be rewarded with a half crown. I would spend one shilling of it at Taylor's Arts Salon in Schoolhill, usually on wax crayons and paper; sixpence would get me into the news cinema in Diamond Street and the remaining shilling was handed over to my gran.

I entered Aberdeen Grammar School as one of two free place bursars in 1946. I've a lifelong love of drawing and design. That's why I took to the Art Department at Aberdeen Grammar School. The Head of the Art department was a Mr Hemingway – the 'Bush', a very powerful and inspiring teacher. I know that the Bush could be a bit of a bugger – more than once he would explode with rage and you'd see a tin box of paints go flying across the classroom. But he knew his stuff all right.

Another source of early inspiration was the Art Gallery, which was close at hand to Black's Buildings. I would pop into it, partly to enjoy the paintings, partly as a quiet refuge. In those days art galleries, like libraries, were to be enjoyed in silence and I found that soothing. To begin with, the appearance of a lone working-class kid attracted a certain amount of wariness among the staff and I would be followed around by one of the attendants. But once I got to the Grammar and could go in clad in my uniform, suspicions melted away.

After the Grammar School I decided to make a career in architecture. Chance played a part. My mother spotted an advert in the P&J for a position in Bob Hendry's practice. I went along to his

KING'S COLLEGE CHAPEL + TOWER, OLD ABERDEEN.

'I still like to do work on paper': A fine depiction of King's College Chapel.

offices in Union Terrace, had an interview and was accepted. Bob Hendry only employed apprentices and young technicians and he did the training of them himself. You had to learn from scratch and from example. He embarrassed me when I first entered the office: 'Look at this new lad,' Bob told the others, 'he's got five Highers and that'll be more than the rest of you put together.'

To begin with I was on ten shillings a week, rising to a pound in my second year, and

Tom surrounded by family and friends
– including grandchildren – at his Ferryhill home, 2010.

from that I had to contribute half-a-crown for my National Insurance.

Bob Hendry's practice was in two rooms, with him and a lassie in one and us apprentices and technicians in the other. I started out with lettering work – very boring. But soon I was involved in his mainstream work of designing extensions and conversions and lots of farm building work. It was a great introduction. You'd do as he told you and look in the drawers and consult technical books. You'd go out on site visits, take your measurements and put down the detail in your sketch book. We didn't use cameras; it was all a matter of using your eyes and hands. I still like to do everything by sketch work on paper even though computers are now available.

The camaraderie in that office was a constant source of fun. We always got the work done, but we would also find time for diversions. We got up games of cricket in the office, using the gas fire filaments as wickets, a ping pong ball, and a rolled up piece of stiff cardboard as a bat. Occasionally a big hit would send the ball flying through the open window which looked on to Union Terrace and then one of us would be sent down to retrieve the bouncing ball before it got mashed up beneath the wheels of a passing tram.

By the end of my second year I was the leading apprentice; you'd spend one day a week at the School of Architecture as well as evening classes. Then I became full time at the architecture school, first at Schoolhill and then a sixth and final year in the new Scott Sutherland School of Architecture at Garthdee.

After qualification I moved into a big practice – Allan, Ross & Allan in Bon Accord Square. This was in 1957. In my National Service years – 1958-60 – I served as a Sapper in the Royal Engineers. I could always draw, always had a strong visual memory.

I have a liking for big cities; cityscapes fascinate me with all their various shapes and dimensions, jostling together to make up a whole. I love a city like Barcelona, Boston or Budapest and I'm proud of Aberdeen, although it is in sore need of care and attention

A man who enjoys the varieties of life: At Murrayfield after the Ireland game, with his wife Paula, 1999.

I'm not convinced that Aberdonians appreciate their cultural inheritance.

these days. There are still some lovely buildings around – take the top of King Street with its mix of John Smith and Archibald Simpson buildings. But so much has been neglected. The Castlegate should be a hub as it used to be, not just as a visual centrepiece, but as a gathering place for people as it was in my boyhood with its trams and buses and toilets and markets. We should try to make it a place to meet in once more, with outdoor seating and thronging pavements and a bit of greenery.

It's sad to see how my own Black's Buildings have been torn down and replaced by grass mounds and roads. During the drive for inner city clearances of the late 1950s, the '60s and the '70s my old home came to be regarded as a slum, yet these solid, decently constructed, granite-built tenement blocks could have been refurbished, the granite washed and rehabilitated to remain a thriving residential area. And that could have set the tone for the rest of the city centre too. All those fine buildings in Union Street could be homes in the storeys above first-floor floor levels and the people brought back into the heart of the city.

I've never seen the sense of tearing down perfectly sound granite buildings. I'm not convinced that Aberdonians appreciate their cultural inheritance.

Thomas (Tom) Gibson. b. 1934. Black's Buildings. Interviewed 2015.

Art acts as a healing therapy for me

My creative expression has always been through art. My mother had a talent for it and she would draw us all in charcoal. She was forever sewing things and embroidering cartoon figures around them.

Art has always been a source of sensory pleasure for me. More than that, it has also become the means by which I can work out and resolve my own fears and difficulties. Through the magic of composition I have found, too, that it is the gateway into the world of the unconscious. Dream figures and archetypal images have always played a strong part in my work. Art acts a healing therapy for me.

During my early childhood we didn't seem to have any permanent home and we spent several years just dotting about Scotland. But then my father got a post in the Music Department at the University and we were able to move into a university house in Tillydrone.

But now came the great disaster of my girlhood: my mother developed cancer and was obviously going to die. Her decline was quite rapid. I dealt with the tragedy by adopting the public role of the sorrowful young lady; I would get off the bus at the bottom of Union Street and walk to my home, wearing a mournful expression on my face, revelling in the huge tragedy that was now entering my life. This was really just a form of teenage exhibitionism, but it did help me to deal with the situation.

I was 16 when she died. The event has left a great mark upon my life and the way in which I have tried to cope with everything. I took to going into Seaton Park by myself

Rosy Long contemplates her *Tree of Life,* part of a Breast Cancer Awareness Exhibition, 2014.

Rosy beside some clay plaques, as part of the Forecourt Art Group show at Blairs Museum, 2014.

and seeking solitude and peace among the trees and flower beds. I discovered that the world of nature could bring me a peace, which I have ever after sought out as an important act of healing in my life.

I went to Art College and became anorexic. The anorexia was my way of trying to gain control over myself. It was the founder of the North-east School of Music, Dorothy Hately, who came to my rescue. She persuaded me that I must leave home and find myself by myself. I rented a flat in Holburn Street and gradually came out of the eating disorder. But, really, it took me years to feel at ease with the world and with myself. I think it was only meeting my husband Bill and having a family of my own which finally saw me whole.

What I have learnt from my life and from my efforts to capture its inner meanings through my art is that it is quality not quantity that counts, that we are, even if surrounded by pain and conflict, still able to engage with the beauty of the world around us and to savour the richness of the moment.

A lot of influences feed into my art, some of them rooted in my own childhood as half-hidden memories, some from stories that have captured my imagination, some from events that are part of my present day life. But when I begin on a new work I am first of all the artist and at that level the decisions I make about how to fill my canvas are to do with proportion or depth or balance – with getting the composition right.

I don't go into a new work with any detailed notion of what it is to be about – my

At home in Muchalls, seated on a bale with friend.

'Where I ultimately find myself – it's frightening but rather beautiful.'

primary aim is to make a good picture. But as I go along, ideas do take shape and an overall theme might declare itself.

Dreams and forests and animals play a large part in the imaginative resources I bring to bear. I have a whole series of pieces on the theme of 'My Childhood Dreams'. Ultimately, my art is a means of working out my fears and searching for ways of replacing them with hope. The final picture in this series shows me walking along a lonely path within the depths of a dark forest. The trees are thickly entwined and the forest is haunted by gloom and by dark shadows. But note that what I am moving towards is the bright moonlight, which illuminates my steps. The branches and their leaves in the light become a lovely tracery and are no longer menacing and stifling. I am moving through my fears and out into the light. I am 'alone' but my journey has become one of hope and a discovery of beauty.

There was no definite moment when I decided that I would become an artist. When I expressed an interest in going to the Art College at school I was strongly advised against it by my art teacher. 'Miss Rosemary Barrett-Ayres', she told me, 'as soon as you get through the door of that place, trousers will come down and the pants will be off you in a flash'. The prospect scared me and so I embarked on a course of training as a nursery teacher, down in Bradford.

But I found I was miserable doing that and so I decided to ignore all warnings and return to Aberdeen and take a four-year course at Gray's School of Art. I loved it all. I met nice and interesting people.

I love the world around me. I sit here in my home in Muchalls, I look out of the window and I am at once entering a world of colour and blended contrasts. I mean, look at the way the land with all its subtle shadings of green and brown falls towards the bright glitter of that sunlit sea. Sometimes you can glimpse deer and foxes moving through the fields. Views such as that inspire me; I love colour, and my pictures are full of strong bright hues. This is partly because of my poor eyesight, but it is also because of my positive disposition.

Rosy Long. b. 1947. Muchalls. Interviewed 2015.

LURE OF THE STAGE & POWER OF THE ARTS

The best picture house violinist in town

Our flats were surrounded by the large bulk of Middleton's factory, which manufactured envelopes, calendars, jotters for the schools. My father worked in the factory as a skilled book binder and that's where he first came across my mother, who was there in the same department, as a book binder's assistant. You might have assumed that's where their courtship began but not at all. As my mother explained to me, he was a highly skilled binder while she was a mere assistant and in those days the factory hierarchy was such that they would never have deigned to get together, except on strictly professional lines.

But my father was also a very accomplished violinist and decided to leave Middleton's to accept a post as a full-time violinist. This was to lead the cinema orchestra at the Torry Picture House. As it happened, my mother lived in Menzies Road and when he left Middleton's he did mention to her that he was off to appear as a resident performer at her local picture house, where he not only led the orchestra, but played solos too. So, she decided to go along to hear him play and became a frequent habituée of the cinema. Those were the days of the silent films and musicians were in great demand to accompany the action on the screen with expressive music. Torry was simply one of many cinemas which housed its own orchestra and people regarded them as an essential part of the cinema-going experience.

So she would go along to hear him play; they would meet up afterwards to talk about the music and that's where the romance which led to my birth was kindled. Torry, however, had only what was known as a half orchestra and my father was too highly

The Torry Picture House where Bill Cooper's father played his violin as an accompaniment to the screen.

La Scala cinema, Union Street, where he was head hunted to play. The cinema was later demolished to make way for the construction of the Majestic Cinema.

thought of in the trade to stay there for long. When the prestigious new cinema at the west end of Union Street was opened, he was recruited to play a leading role in its full orchestra. It was known then as the La Scala and, when it opened, was regarded as the last word in cinema luxury. In those pre-television days, cinema going was immensely popular and queues would form which wound right round back up into Union Row to get in for the latest Hollywood blockbuster, and indeed for almost any new film.

La Scala later became the Majestic, a very distinctive art deco building – now, alas, knocked down to make way for modern retail units; Pret a Manger now occupies part of the site.

I was only five when he died and my brother two, so I have very little memory of him – and that sadly includes his violin playing. I regret missing out on this since, evidently, he had a marvellous talent. He had graduated up through one violin teacher in the city after another, always advancing up the scale of experts till he ended up with Wilf Smith, who was reckoned to be the leading teacher in the city. He developed a wide repertoire, anything from classical and operetta to the popular numbers of the day. He would also improvise according to the needs of the action on the screen. He became renowned as one of the very best of his type in the whole city. And whenever family members came on a visit he would always take out his instrument and offer them 'Just a tune before you go.'

William (Bill) Cooper. b. 1936. La Scala Cinema. Interviewed 2018.

Orchestra Stalls for snobs, Gods for tips

My first job on leaving school at 14 was to act as a page-boy in His Majesty's Theatre. The pay was poor but the tips could be good. My task was to usher people into their seats and then to keep a lookout during the performances for any messages they wanted, such as getting them sweeties or cigarettes. The best tippers would be found in the cheaper seats up in the Gods, never down in the Orchestra Stalls. That's where the richer folk would sit, the West End types who were used to the theatre, whereas up in the Gods you'd get those who were intent on making the most of a rare night out and that included sharing their pleasure with the page-boy.

David Allan. b. 1919. His Majesty's Theatre. Interviewed 2014.

Taking to the stage: the beginnings of a dramatist's career

Charles was for many years Head of the Drama department at Aberdeen College of Education. In this 1977 shot of his Drama graduands are (back row from left): Annie Inglis, Charles Barron, Nicky Triplett, Principal James Scotland, Phil McMillan, Derek Ross, Carol Strang, John Smith. Front: Alan Nicol, Magda Dey, Sue Davidson, Kate Martin, Barbara Smith, Sylvia Robinson.

For my Secondary I went to Robert Gordon's College. There were three elderly lady teachers at the school and one of them was Miss Herbert – Skinny Liz. She directed the first play I appeared in. The thrill of it instantly converted me to all things theatrical. I was given a part in the crowd scenes in the *Auld Hoose*, which told the story of the school through the years. Skinny was responsible for the crowd scenes. There was quite a lot of action, including a riot; there was no script, only improvised dialogue, but I was thrilled by the whole experience. I loved all that dressing up.

I was aware of entering a world, one that fascinated me, one that meant glamour. I went through a spell when I fancied becoming a film star or a radio actor. But these were always youthful dreams; I never seriously considered the theatre as a professional proposition. It was about this time, too, that I began to follow the careers of some of the actors of the day, Gielgud especially. The local actors I saw frequently on stage, and began to take a real interest in them. By my third year I was going to the complete repertory season, weekly. I can still remember a lot of the plays: *Black Chiffon; See How They Run*; a lot of Noel Coward, which I was very keen on. It was the typical repertory fare of the day. I financed all this by taking an early morning paper round. Then, as soon as I was 17, I got a holiday job as a bus conductor. While I was at University I was doing this for three months each summer. Another opportunity to dress up in a uniform and to play a part!

I knew that drama would be an important part of my life but only at the level of hobby. The thought of becoming a professional actor, with all the insecurity involved, never entered my head. I was looking to become a lawyer or scientist, good respectable

Charles Barron as Macbeth, Haddo House Hall, 1991

professions. Academically, I did well at school.

For English I had John Foster. He did no teaching whatsoever, but simply used the classroom as his stage and us as an audience for stories of his own life. He never used the blackboard or engaged us in questions. His real enthusiasm was for drama, but to do a play was simply his invitation to take all the parts and act them out for us. He was a very vivid presence in the classroom. It never occurred to us that he wasn't actually teaching us. And we did learn a great deal about life and about plays. I remember him saying that he expected to have a new thought about *King Lear* while he was shaving, every morning of his life. That has always made me feel rather inadequate!

I enjoyed University. I loved the History and the English. University also gave me the chance to develop my drama interests. Murray Copland, an old school friend, had gone up a year before me so when he directed a play for Freshers' Week, I found myself as a member of the cast. During my time at the University I took part in four Student Shows and 12 straight plays.

Charles with the cast of his play *Toulmin*, 2004. He is seated with Sheila Reid and behind l to r, are Scott Armstrong, Yvonne Morton, Ken McRae, Roddy Beg (director) and Jill Hay.

Then, in 1956, I wrote my first play. It was inspired by the Hungarian uprising of '56, an event that moved us students deeply. There were demonstrations; it seemed natural for someone like me to stage something that would express the general mood. The Mermaid Society put it on, in the Students' Union. I didn't manage to get any tanks on stage but it did have a rather good torture scene, of which I was quite proud. Needless to say, I wrote, directed and acted in it. The work actually got quite a lot of publicity, locally at least, because of its topicality and because it was unusual then to have a new play written by a local person appearing in Aberdeen. The local press gave it quite a splash.

When I started my year at the 'TC' [later Aberdeen College of Education], the first person that was waiting for me on the doorstep at St Andrew's Street was Annie Inglis. She had known I was coming and was eager to enlist me into her various drama projects. She mounted *Hamlet* specifically to get me involved. I felt that the part was what I had been waiting for all my life. It was my first real leading role, and what a way to start.

This was the production that the High School for Girls attended and more or less mobbed. We did matinée performances for the schools and several hundred pupils came during the week. The girls and the boys were kept apart and came to separate performances. The one for the Grammar School boys was pretty hopeless: I couldn't even hear my fellow actors on the stage; the audience was making such a din among themselves. They just weren't interested. But the girls were completely different. They saved their riot for the final curtain. The fact that I was surrounded by young females who had to play the soldiers' parts also helped. Before I appeared, the stage had been occupied by two girl actors in knitted armour; well, I couldn't help but look manly and striking in contrast! Then, too, the time was right for these young girls in the audience: they were exactly the right age to be thrilled by a play that featured a lone, melancholy youth; it was the age of James Dean, don't forget.

Anyway, that Hamlet was my big moment. I could feel like a real star for a while. But I wasn't deceived. The whole occasion had somehow worked, but I realised I wasn't a particularly outstanding actor, nor especially handsome. But my involvement in drama had been sealed.

Charles Barron. b. 1936. Aberdeen College of Education. Interviewed 2005.

Charles Barron went on to sustain a distinguished career in Aberdeen, as Head of the Drama Department at Aberdeen College of Education, as an actor, and as a prolific playwright, especially in the Doric.

I loved putting things on the stage

I was brought up on music, songs, reading and telling stories. My sister Olive was very artistic and would have gone to Art School if the family budget at the time had allowed. Every Friday, she and my other sister, Helen, would make me a red crepe paper skirt and would sit, watching me dance to the 'Swedish Rhapsody'. We had a windy-up gramophone and would listen to plays and music on the radio. My mother loved the big choirs, especially the Glasgow Orpheus. She sang like a lintie and she, and my brother Jim, would harmonise at all the family parties – and there were lots! Jim has the most beautiful tenor voice and still sings in choirs and as a soloist to this day.

All this stood me in good stead when I became a teacher. At school we would put on dramatisations of events such as the Tay Bridge disaster. We would have performers, but also sound effects team and writing teams. I was brought up on music and songs and telling stories.

It also fitted in with my other great interest: performance and the theatre. I had always loved going to the movies and I now began to fall in with a group who were making their own films- the '67 Group. I wrote a couple of scripts and did some directing with them. At the same time, I was busy doing tapes in my school; I found that was a wonderful way to encourage children to learn. Here I was at Smithfield, which is a really tough area and where many of the children led hard lives.

Although I couldn't describe my own Torry background as well off, we had always felt secure and cared for. These were things you could no longer take for granted at

Before I appeared, the stage had been occupied by two girls in knitted armour; well, I couldn't help but look manly and striking in contrast!

'I fell in with a group making their own films'. Wilma Gillanders directing her own *Fragment* for the 67 Group, 1970s.

'A great trip':
Wilma with the
'Rockefeller Angels',
taken during a
Christmas season trip
to New York with her
daughter, Mairi, 2009.

Smithfield, my first school. But the school had Doreen Sim, who was a real dynamo of a teacher. We decided to put on a concert that would involve the children and their parents. We did the full thing, putting on a Black & White Minstrels show. I did the choreography and she played the piano. I found that I simply loved putting something on the stage, having my own cast to work with, seeing them gradually get it right. I remember this boy who came up to me, all dressed up in top hat and gloves and tails and saying to me, his face shining, 'Look Mrs Gillanders, I'm Burlington Bertie!' I thought to myself, 'Here's George, an ordinary kid from Smithfield and now he's been transformed into Burlington Bertie.'

Concerts became an annual inspiring event for pupils, parents and staff.

Then I moved to Quarryhill and I loved that too. We began, my classes and I, to view aspects of History as dramatised documentaries and produced audio tapes and slide presentations such as 'The Witch Burnings of Aberdeen'. It was a very powerful way to learn, and used the Expressive Arts to the full – actors, musicians, scriptwriters, sound effects teams. With the 'Tay Bridge Disaster' we actually won an International competition – not just the schools section but the all-category, prestigious 'Tape of the Year'. Lots of trophies for Quarryhill!

I was asked to direct *Iolanthe* for the Aberdeen Opera Company; I had done the choreography for two of their shows but this was a huge leap.

It was to be in His Majesty's Theatre, with 60 of a cast. The Scottish Parliament was then in its infancy and I hit on the idea of using that – politically active fairies (placards, saltire faces) and political party peers – many red ties, many yellow ties and one blue tie for the one Conservative. It worked well.

Since then I've carried on directing shows for the Aberdeen Opera Company; it's become a bit of a drug. It's the biggest toy in the world, to have all these different people and this empty stage to put them on, to bring it all together, to persuade

'My office'.

them into understanding what you want of them, to get them all to work together, under your direction.

The part I love most is when you are arranging the lighting. It's wonderful to have their trust and to bring something stunning to the stage. I enjoy the huge challenge and the chance to work with such talented people. During production, I make drawings of the action on the set and can then sit down with the lighting engineer and paint the show

With the prize-winning 67 Group: Wilma left with Cliff Stroud and husband Bob at front. Others featured include Hugo Gifford and Ken Hepburn.

with light. Take our most recent production, *Titanic the Musical*. For that we designed a set using scaffolding over 20 feet high; we used slides of the real ship and its story. It was epic: so moving, beautiful music and a fabulous, powerful show. It was such a joy and privilege to do all that on stage, here in Aberdeen.

Wilma Gillanders. b. 1944. Aberdeen Opera Company. Interviewed 2006.

We wanted to shake up society

The 1960s were a heady time for a crusading young student like myself. I remember the furore that surrounded the Lady Chatterley trial and my own efforts to procure a copy. I was a devout follower of The Beatles; I even took to the early Cliff Richard. Saturday nights would see me at the Beach Ballroom or at the Boys' Brigade dances at Skene Terrace. The King Street Church Youth Fellowship held public speaking events. Pink Floyd came to the Beach Ballroom and I was there.

We had a radiogram at home and then I acquired my own Dansette which I could play in the privacy of my own bedroom. I adorned the walls with posters of male pop stars, cut out from the centrefold of teen magazines. I even stuck up one of Cliff Richard, attired in an open neck blue and white striped shirt.

I joined the 62 Club in Summer Street. Many of those young folk, who accompanied me there, went on to do interesting and creative things in later life. We had a song writing group and a poetry one too. We were self-consciously arty and no doubt saw ourselves as something of a cultural elite, a bit like the Beatniks of the period and all those students who were demonstrating and campaigning about social justice and individualistic

A recent shot of Louise Baxter.

Still with energy to spare: Jumping for Joy, with Nick and Katharina Baxter, 2016.

self-expression in the States and France. I couldn't claim that our analysis of the social structures was very profound; we had a general desire to shake up a society, which we saw as conservative, capitalist and Establishment-dominated. All we knew was that we were young, we were full of energy and we wanted to push things in a fresh and different direction.

I am a firm believer in the power of the arts and of social action as keys to the good life for all. What we commonly term 'culture' should be far from some narrow elitist pursuit. Its practice has the ability to bring fulfilment to everyone; it nourishes the senses; its practice not only engages the whole person, but also brings a sense of control and confidence in the individual, along with a capacity to work with others.

I am sad to see the current diminishment in the role of the arts in mainstream education. The efforts of that well known Aberdonian, Mr Michael Gove, as Minister for Education, has led to a system of narrow target setting and so-called back to an academic rigour which treats children as examination fodder instead of attempting to open them up as confident, creative individuals. We live in a changing world which cries out for innovative thinking and not confinement within a regime that is really educating for yesterday's job market.

Not that I am pessimistic. In fact, the last few years have seen an upsurge in appreciation of the role of the arts in the life of the community. There's a huge amount of activity going on in the city, which most people are unaware of. The APA – Aberdeen Performing Arts – has given us a strong base. I am Chair of Castlegate Arts which runs the Arts Centre in King Street and am also on the board of a number of voluntary organisations which cover housing and health charity work, as well as cultural activity. I have been Cultural Co-ordinator of the Arts Education team at the Council and have now been appointed to the Chair of the Arts Centre theatre which intends to plant a number of tutors around the city in order to assist youth groups. Through all this I have become aware of just how vigorous the cultural life of the city actually is. Despite the current myth of an Aberdeen which is being outpaced by Dundee, we actually spend significantly more in this area than they do, while individual theatre attendance is superior to that of any other Scottish city.

Louise Baxter. b. 1948. Aberdeen Arts Centre. Interviewed 2015.

My main interest outside school was Aberdeen Children's Theatre

Generations of young Aberdonians have benefitted from the work of the Children's Theatre. Here is a shot of rehearsal for their 2013 production of *Les Misérables*.

My main interest outside school was the Aberdeen Children's Theatre and that was based up at the College of Education, run by Alan Nicol. I used to go up there every Saturday morning from 9 until 12 and it was great. We used to do an end of term thing when the parents were invited in one morning. I remember learning to sing, 'When the red, red robin comes bob, bob, bobbin' along'.

Then, when I went up to Secondary School, I went to the Children's Theatre, based on King Street next to the Aberdeen Arts Centre. I did that until I left school; I thoroughly enjoyed all aspects of that. You were taught everything, from the backstage stuff, painting scenery, making costumes, how lighting worked, make-up. But I always enjoyed the actual acting and in my final year there I won an award for the best all-round member. We did a show at the Arts Centre every year.

We did *Simon's Dream*. Then we did *Sweeny Todd's Shock and Roll Show*. In the fourth year, I had a speaking part where I played a life-size doll that came to life and was very outspoken and got to be cheeky to adults. That was the only time I had a speaking part; all the other times I was in the chorus – 'villager number three', 'third from the left', or something like that.

There was a huge amount of kids going to these theatre groups, and a good mix of boys and girls. They took us to see something at the theatre; I think it was something quite serious – something like Chekov. That must have been during the week and then on the Saturday, one of the actors came to speak to us about it and that was really quite exciting – especially when I was asked to give the vote of thanks. And I remember seeing that actor popping up in Eastenders a number of years later.

Dianne Morrison. b. 1967. Rosemount; interviewed 2015.

The Aberdeen Children's Theatre was established by the city's Speech & Drama Department under Catherine Hollingworth in 1959 – the first such in the UK.

MAKING MUSIC

The three future young Musical Milnes: From left; David (violinist), Aileen (pianist) and Martha (vocalist).

A faded copy of the press cutting from the time when the Musical Milnes were beginning to make their mark in Aberdeen, early 1950s.

The Musical Milnes

▶ **Facing Page:** A cast list for the 1968 production of *The Music Man.* Martha is listed as Mrs Paroo.

There was an article in one of the papers; they called us the 'Musical Milnes'. There's a photo of Aileen at the piano, me standing and David with his violin and I think that we entertained at every women's church guild in Aberdeen because once it was published, every guild wanted us to come. We were never paid for doing it, but my mother used to sit there in her glory and say 'That's my family'. David could make a violin sing; he had a touch with it that was unbelievable. He was playing a lot of

— PROGRAMME —

From MONDAY, 26th FEBRUARY to SATURDAY, 2nd MARCH, 1968

Nightly at 7.30 p.m. except Saturday when there will be two performances, at 5 p.m. and 8 p.m.

THE LYRIC MUSICAL SOCIETY

OF ABERDEEN

(An Amateur Company affiliated to the National Operatic and Dramatic Association)

presents

"THE MUSIC MAN"

by MEREDITH WILLSON

(By arrangement with Chappell & Co. Ltd.)

Cast in order   appearance:

Conductor	ANDREW GIBB
Charlie Cowell	ERIC COUTTS
Harold Hill	DONALD McLEAY
Mayor Shinn	ALEX GRANT
Ewart Dunlop	RON DUNCAN
Oliver Hix	ALASDAIR SMITH
Jacey Squires	*Members of the School Board* — DOUGLAS MOIR
Olin Britt	DOUGLAS KEITH
Marcellus Washburn	CHARLES MAIR
Tommy Djilas	JOHN BELKA
Marion Paroo	RHONA MARSHALL
Mrs. Paroo	MARTHA ALEXANDER
Amaryllis	HELEN WOOD
Winthrop Paroo	PETER KELLY
Eulalie Mackecknie Shinn	SYLVIA CONNON
Zaneeta Shinn	ALICE LOW
Gracie Shinn	CLARE WOOD
Alma Hix	CLAIRE URQUHART
Maud Dunlop	CELIA WALKER
Ethel Toffelmier	CATHERINE RITCHIE
Mrs. Squires	ROSE IRVINE
Constable Locke	RONNIE SMITH

Townspeople of River City—
Elizabeth Craw, Muriel Crichton, Alice Davidson, Olive Fraser, Margaret Gillan, Hilda Glennie, Helen Harris, Audrey Harvey, Margaret Hughes, Mary Kelly, Deborah March, Pamela Mavor, Jean Monro, Christine Repper, Margaret Robertson, Doreen Shepherd, Ethel Young
Eric Lawrie, Alastair McKelvie, Ian MacNay, James Munro, John Murray, Meston Reid, Robert Strathdee

Dancers—
Moira Hunter, Sheila Moncur, Kathleen Sim, Levena Taylor, Tommy Low, George Milne, Iain Reid

Children—
Carole Alexander, Fiona Alexander, Helen Belka, Nicola Connon, Roger Connon, Sheila Keith, Colin Morrison, Lorna Morrison, Tom Morrison, Elaine Smith, Alison Urquhart, David Urquhart

The Bon-Accord Silver Band   Conductor STEWART WATSON

The Boys of the Gang Show

301

A publicity shot, taken in the Duthie Park Winter Gardens, for the Lyric Society's production of *South Pacific*, 1974. Martha is second right.

Scott Skinner; he was playing classical; he was in the music festivals. I used to sing the Scots songs and arts songs and Aileen played.

David needed a new violin and the folks, of course, were hard up. My dad heard of this man that was going into a home, and had a violin. So Dad and David went and David got the violin. The man grew blind. We were out entertaining at Balmedie Eventide Home and this man turned to a woman and said, 'That laddie's playing my violin!' And he was right; it was David playing his violin.

When he had to do his National Service, he'd to go down to Aldershot and when they asked, 'Have you hobbies?' he'd written down that he played the violin. They must have got a violin from somewhere and made him play it and they said 'Right! Here's a travel warrant. Get up to Aberdeen and get your violin and come back; that's you in the Signals Orchestra'

Martha Alexander. b. 1937 Auchinyell. Interviewed 2015.

Music was a part of our daily lives

My mother was Isabella Littlejohn, and both sides of her family were musical. At one time there was a big Littlejohn band on Deeside. There used to be a photograph of them all in Ballater station, but I don't know where it's gone. Her mother's father, the king's ghillie and a dancing master, was known as Dancie Davie Rose. He used to go to Balmoral to teach the royal family to dance. He had made his own fiddle, an especially narrow one which fitted into his coat pocket. He travelled all over Deeside in a gig; he was known to like a dram, but could rely on his horse to see him home safely. He was drowned crossing the Dee in spate, and washed up on Ballater golf course.

Always part of her life: A young Lindy Cheyne appears at HMT in 1954. Left-to-right: Lindy Cheyne, Alison Mutch, Joan Gordon, Carol Waterhouse.

I inherited this music; it was the environment I grew up in. My three siblings, who were much older, sang in choirs and often the house was full of their singing in harmony.

I had a lot of contact with Deeside as I was growing up: I would say that that is where my heart lies. I was always pleading with my father to take a job in Aboyne. The countryside for me spelled freedom; I revelled in the smells and sights of it all and loved its animal life.

My mother was immersed in the oral tradition. She had been brought up in an environment of song, poetry and stories and she was always singing and reciting at home. She told the story of how, when she was a small girl, she joined in a poem the teacher was reading to the class. When the teacher asked how she knew it, she said that her mother read it to her. And when she went home and told her mother, she learned that the poem was familiar because its author was her mother's cousin – Charles Murray

Song was the natural accompaniment to our household tasks; doing the washing up,

> My mother's cousin, Geordie Rose, would come up from the Don Barracks and play his bagpipes. When I was about nine, I danced at the Aboyne Games to George's playing.

we would sing in three-part harmony. We had no record player at home; only a wireless. My uncle George stayed with us for a spell after he was demobbed and he bought a piano. Jess's husband would place brass ashtrays on the strings and play boogie. Then there were cousins bringing their instruments with them when they paid a visit. Best of all, perhaps, was when Mum's cousin, Geordie Rose, came up from the Don Barracks and played his bagpipes. I took dancing lessons with Eileen Ewen and when I was nine I danced at the Aboyne Games, to George's playing. My first stage appearance was at the age of three, as an Eskimo in Miss Ewen's show.

I went to the High School for Girls, and at the age of seven I was taken in hand by the eccentric Mrs Cruickshank (*née* Nan Davidson) who gave me piano lessons in a music room on the ground floor. She had silver hair in a wispy roll, with escaping tendrils. She had white skin and blue eyes and wore blues, pinks and lavenders; her room had vases of hyacinths. I adored her. She had a glorious voice and regularly sang and played piano at the BBC studios at Beechgrove. I had a good ear and could usually pick up new pieces without making an effort to read the music. She put a stop to my laziness by placing a sharpened pencil under my chin so that I couldn't see my hands and had to look at the music. I was taken to the BBC to sing for Children's Hour when I was about 13.

I was never really into rock and roll and the pop music of the '60s. When a friend enthused about some group called The Beatles I had to ask who they were – and this was in 1962! I loved madrigals and early music, and sang with guitar in folk song clubs and various venues. I have met so many wonderful people through music. I love traditional music and Bach alike. It's an important part of my life.

Rosalind (Lindy) Cheyne. b. 1943. Rosemount and Deeside. Interviewed 2016.

Where else can women get the chance to express their inner music?

I have always been acutely aware of sounds and the music of the human voice. When I was a young girl the family would travel in from our the home in Midmar each Sunday to the Church of Christ in Aberdeen and those services left a great impression on me. Although they contained plenty of hymn singing, the big feature of that church was the complete absence of any instrumental accompaniment. I was fascinated by the way in which the human voice on its own and in the company of other voices could make wonderfully rich music. There was no need for any organ or piano, not when the people around me in the congregation could work out their own harmonisations.

So I grew up, steeped in the a cappella tradition and loved the subtle variations that the challenge of seeking harmony from the input of various tones and pitches could achieve. We were always a musical family. Although I had little in the way of any formal musical education, music was all around me.

After the High School I went to the College of Education and qualified as a Primary

teacher. There was plenty of music and theatre around me. I took part in the Student Shows at HMT and at the College we put on a number of reviews directed by the inimitable Annie Inglis. Later I joined the Attic Theatre and took part in their regular pantos and summer shows.

Then my husband got a job in Libya and so I moved out there, first to live in Tripoli and later Ben Ghazi. Many of the wives out there with their husbands were looking around for things to occupy themselves with and so the notion of putting on shows took root. And so, because I'd had some sort of a career on the Aberdeen stage, I became the director! I fell pregnant and came home to have my baby delivered – only to discover that the baby was going to be twins! When I was in hospital I was visited by an old friend, who enthusiastically told me about this choir she had recently joined. It was called the Sweet Adelines; really, I simply must go along to it too. But first I had to return to Libya.

We finally came back to Aberdeen in 1985 and at last I could find out what these Sweet Adelines could be all about. They were holding an open evening so I went along, I must admit with a certain amount of foreboding. All those women and no men, what on earth could they all sound like? However, as I sat there listening, I knew I'd found something I would just love. So I took my two pieces along to an audition and was accepted in.

The Aberdeen chorus was started by a group of American oil wives in the early days of the oil industry, back in 1978, becoming officially registered in 1980. A chorus has to support a minimum number of 20; in Aberdeen we operate at about 80 members, of which 60 will be regular participants. We are termed 'chorus' rather than a 'choir' and this is to make the point that we sprang not so much from a church choir background as the barber shop glee tradition. So you mustn't picture us as ladies attired in black with books in front of us and standing still in lines, but rather as singers who wear flamboyant costumes, performers who gesticulate and move about.

I became a keen member, so much so that, when in 1995 our director fell ill and was forced to retire, I was invited to take over. So for the last 20-plus years that's what I've been doing, although I'm happy to say that since 2014 I've been assisted by a young co-director who is a youthful 25.

'A world of colour, melody and movement': The Sweet Adelines in typically exuberant pose.

Performing at Aboyne, 2014: Gwen Topp seventh left.

Always ready to sing for a good cause: At Hazlehead Park, 2015, in aid of Alzheimer Scotland.

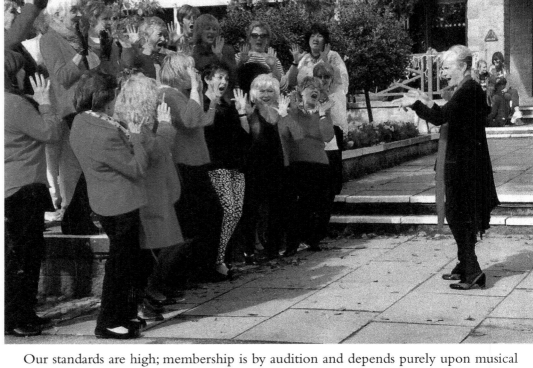

Once a week we can offer to take people out of their ordinary humdrum existences and invite them into a world of melody, of colour and of movement.

Our standards are high; membership is by audition and depends purely upon musical ability and commitment and in no way reflects social status. You can find a dinner lady singing alongside a CEO. And it's not only the music which keeps us together; there's all the banter and companionship too.

That's a good job because the fact that the Sweet Adelines is powered by regular competition means that we have to do a lot of travelling together. The rule is that a chorus must compete at least once every three years, the aim being to maintain high standards. Medals are awarded and I'm glad to say that we have been more than able to hold our own. Over the years we've netted six Golds, three Silvers and a lot of Bronzes.

All this reflects a great deal of hard work. In the competitions you only have your seven minutes on the stage so everything has to be spot on. You are required to perform two numbers: a ballad and then an 'up-tune' – something with a bit of uplift about it and the opportunity to accompany it with some smart choreography: music with motion. That's why costumes play a big part; we pride ourselves on presenting an eye-catching and colourful line up. It's important to hit that stage with something of a smile and a splash.

For me, the Sweet Adelines has been the perfect outlet for my love of music and that has been the case with the other members too. Our repertoire is mostly drawn from the era of the great melodies and witty, clever lyrics like those given to the world by such as Cole Porter, Rodgers and Hammerstein, Jerome Kern. It's music that goes with a swing and that's what we have to do too – go with a swing. Our standards have to be exacting but, with music like that, rehearsals are pretty lively affairs. You have to make things fun, to be serious but not solemn about it; you have to give people an enjoyable experience.

That, I think, is one of the great attractions of the Sweet Adelines. Once a week we can offer to take people out of their ordinary humdrum existences and invite them into a world of melody, of colour and of movement. It's also a place where all sorts of different folk can meet and can make something good together – and form lasting friendships. We work hard at what we do, but we also have lots of laughs. The great thing is we are all in it together. People come to us with a good voice and an ability to hold a tune, but often with a load of inhibitions. In our part of the world, especially, they will have grown up in a culture of reserved behaviour and warnings about the perils of showing off. But then they see other women, much like themselves, actually daring to move about and to give full throat to their voices and they realise that, yes, they can do a bit of showing off too.

I mean, where else can you create an atmosphere which gives women, who might have come from the stiff discipline of an office or the dull rounds of the kitchen where they have been essentially at the service of others, permission to come out of themselves and to express their inner music? Not so many, and certainly not in Aberdeen.

Gwen Topp. b. 1949. The Aberdeen Chorus of Sweet Adelines . Interviewed 2016.

I'd always fancied the pipes

I started the pipes when I was about eight through the Scout Pipe Band. A Mr. Mitchell was the Pipe Major at that time and we used to train in the school in Summer Street. We marched up and down the gymnasium and we had a chanter table and a table for the drummer boys as well. I had always fancied taking up the pipes and I liked Scottish music.

I thoroughly enjoyed my two years of National Service at Kinloss. Being in the pipe band was very good and there were lots of places we got to play at. The RAF knew I was a piper from my application form, but it never occurred to me that this might be the

Ken Raitt as part of the RAF Pipe band, at Kinloss, 1959. Ken is to be seen immediately behind the Pipe Major's left shoulder.

basis for a posting to Kinloss. The Warrant Officer at Kinloss, the Pipe Major, had asked to be notified if anybody had piping ability or was keen on piping. This was so that he could ask for them to be transferred from whichever station they were at to Kinloss to keep the pipe band going. There was only the one pipe band throughout the RAF at that time. I was quite happy to do piping rather than continue wholly in office work.

The pipe band played at different Highland Games where we were invited to represent the military. We were quite a spectacle in the 1960s, the RAF Pipe Band all dressed up in its gear – a well-turned out and smart band. We had about 20 pipers and maybe eight drummers – so it was quite a sight when we came down a main street. We went as far as the Channel Islands, for about a week. You were playing more or less all day, utilised for different things and sometimes we were out entertaining in the evening and gathering money for RAF associations or the Benevolent Fund, playing outside different pubs. One of the highlights for me was marching through the archway into the arena when our band once played at the Edinburgh Military Tattoo.

Ken Raitt. b. 1939. RAF Pipe Band. interviewed 2016.

I just have to keep on playing

Music has been at the centre of my life. I'm still teaching and performing even though I am now well past the age of official retirement. This is something I can trace back to my family life as a child. My mother had five brothers and one sister and they would sing together. One of them could play the piano by ear and that has been my gift as well. Right from my first encounter with the instrument I found I could pick up any tune and play it.

There was no television back then and people looked to make their own entertainment in their own homes. We had family sing-songs and because I could play the piano we would be invited to other people's homes, where I would play for them all. In those days, a piano in the home was quite a common feature. As I got older I would find myself being invited to play at engagement parties and at wedding present showings. I would play the popular music of the day, dance band numbers – that sort of thing.

Music was part of a formative experience in which rhythm, social activity, personal expression through words, movement and voice were at the heart of our growing up. I have taught at some 18 different schools, many of them in the poorer parts of the town, and I have always seen how the Expressive Arts can lift pupils, can bring them together in a sense of common purpose and, generally, brighten their lives.

In addition to my classroom duties, I have always looked upon myself as an entertainer. That is how I became involved in Jack Sinclair's Band. It started in the mid-1960s at a time when my husband was working as a compositor at a firm in Market Street. One of the travellers who regularly came into the firm was Dave McIntosh and he sang with Jack Sinclair. He was called 'the Singing Coalman'. Now, my husband and this Dave

A well merited recognition: Eileen Pike at the time of the award of the BEM for her services to music, New Year 2019.
(IMAGE BY KIND PERMISSION OF ABERDEEN JOURNALS)

McIntosh used to chat away and so he heard about my piano playing. Eventually he asked if he could have a tape of my playing. The next thing I knew was a phone call from Jack Sinclair himself asking me if I could come down to the Station Hotel. I was thrilled; the Station Hotel then was the place for dinner dances, an occasion when people would turn out in their tuxedos and their long dresses.

Then, when I was at a conference held at the old College of Education building in St Andrews Street, I suddenly was aware of the figure of Jack Sinclair standing at the door, gesturing me over. 'Look, I need to speak to you.' He told me his regular pianist had been struck down with an aneurysm and he was asking me to fill in. 'We're due at Inverurie tonight – can you make it?'

And that was the start of my long association with Jack Sinclair and his band. In those days he was always in great demand, both on TV and at events throughout the North-east. We were on the road night after night, even though we all held down regular day jobs. I was a teacher, Dave McIntosh a traveller and Jack himself was a legal executive at Ledingham & Chalmers. It was a hectic life; I had to get used to dashing home after a day in the classroom, having a quick shower, changing my clothes and then into the van which Jack drove to take us to venues all over the country. We would go up as far as Aviemore, the Black Isle and Inverness. We would act as the resident band at city hotels at the weekend.

We performed at local concerts held in halls or schools; we did parties, dinner dances and large family celebrations. We put on a real programme. One regular format was to divide the evening into two halves, the first of which consisted of a series of popular numbers, some purely instrumental. Then in the second half we might appear with a linked programme. One of our most popular ones was 'Hits from the Blitz', when we would come on in uniform and Jack would tell a story to join all the numbers together, even using recordings of Churchill speeches to add to the atmosphere.

We were also in demand by the Royal Family and must have played at Balmoral Castle

At the heyday of their success the Jack Sinclair Showband – with Eileen Pike at the piano – was in great demand, both on television and in the recording studio. This is the cover of one of a series of the popular collections brought out during the 1970s.

We would be up in the Musician's Gallery, 20 steps above the ballroom; down below the Royals would be dancing away.

some 30 times. There was always a wonderful atmosphere there; we would be up in the Musician's Gallery, 20 steps above the ballroom, and down below the Royals would be dancing away. They all knew their Scottish dances and joined in. The dances would include estate workers, guests, and policemen from the Met who were up on security duty. And to start the event off, the pipers in their Balmoral tartan would play the Royal Family down the two staircases and into the hall. The guests would be waiting for them there and the family would go round greeting them all.

The band kept going till the mid-90s. But as I say, I haven't stopped. As well as my teaching, I have been at work extending my repertoire. My latest development is jazz piano; I have been studying and taking exams in it, I have now earned my Diploma.

So music has been at the heart of my life and is what I am. I have been blessed to have this gift, one which has not only given me enormous satisfaction, but has also, it would seem, brought a lot of pleasure to others too.

Eileen Pike. b. 1940. Jack Sinclair's Band. Interviewed 2015.

Eileen Pike was awarded the BEM in the 2019 New Years honours list for services to music.

We were a top notch choir

My father was a well-known piano tuner. His main job was to act as Head Piano Tuner for J & A Marr in Bridge Street. This was the leading music store in Aberdeen then and had a whole team of piano tuners. My father was a real expert. If prospective buyers came into J and A Marr's he would demonstrate the pianos in the shop.

He was once invited to play for the great Italian tenor Gigli, I think in 1938. This was at a private concert in the Cowdray Hall, attended by Winston Churchill and the King, George VI. The Provost, Tommy Mitchell, was also there as were a number of other local dignitaries. Gigli's regular pianist was taken ill so Father was asked to step in.

He was terrified and not just because of the status of his audience; he'd received wounds in the war and was afraid they might interfere with his playing. Not only that, he hadn't got the full evening dress, a suit with tails. But the concert went off well; afterwards the King

'A real expert': Anne Russell's father at the organ of West Ruthrieston Church, 1947.

went up to my father and congratulated him on having given them all a lovely evening. Gigli approached him with a cheque, but my father waved it away, telling him that he had been delighted to play for the honour of accompanying such a great artist.

I started in the church choir at the age of nine. My brother and I both sang in choirs, while I took up the clarinet. My brother learnt to play the trumpet and the cornet. We

' A top notch choir':
The Arion Junior Choir
at the Music Hall,
1962.

would hold music evenings around the piano. The university Master of Music lived just across the road and more than once we'd get a knock at the door and the comment 'So and so is off-key.'

I joined the Aberdeen Arion Choir as an original member. The choir performed to a very high standard; in Scotland only the Glasgow Orpheus could come anywhere near us. Our greatest exploit was to enter the Festival of Britain choir contest in 1951. We were the sole Scottish representatives and there were 16 choirs from all over Britain.

It was a great adventure, going down in the sleeper to the capital. We all wore kilts and performed our piece – *The Maid Peerless* - unaccompanied and with a smile on our faces. One wrong note and the whole effort would have been ruined, but we did well and got a great ovation, though it was a Welsh choir that won. Hopes were high when we set off and the P&J gave us a big splash, with a headline telling the world that we were carrying the hopes of the whole of the North-east with us. We got a big send off at the station, but when we returned there were only two people there to greet us – my father and another father. They gave us a good cheer and gradually the rest of the passengers on the concourse joined in.

We were a top notch choir; the Brand sisters were part of our 24 members. We all blended in well. Although we failed to carry off the trophy, the King presented us all with commemorative plaques – I've still got mine; it's such a proud and treasured possession.

Touching the heights: Anne parachuting at Aldershot 1950 as part of an Industrial Medical degree course.

Anne Russell. b. 1932. Arion Choir. Interviewed 2015.

Poor Miss Auchinachie used to go about off her nut at these kids eating sweeties during choir practice.

The schools then were full of music

School was different then because there was a big emphasis on music. Now my mother had been brought up in the infamous Black's Buildings where, as we were told, if they went out the back, they were at the stage door of His Majesty's Theatre. And my Mother was always fascinated by theatre things and she wanted her kids to get a chance, so Aileen went to piano at school, I went to piano and David went to violin. It was five shillings a quarter.

And there was Miss Auchinachie, who came to do specialised work with the classes, and she had a choir and she used to pick kids for this choir that was held on a Saturday morning. And, of course, Joe Soap here was picked for it and really enjoyed it. It was held in the Middle School and what I remember was going over to Courage's sweetie shop and you could get a penny of mush that we'd buy before we went in, then sit and suck it and, oh dear, poor Miss Auchinachie used to go about off her nut at these kids eating sweeties during choir practice.

There were five violin teachers that used to come to the school. There was Peddie Willox, his wife, Andrew Davidson, his wife and I cannot remember the other one. So the schools at that time were full of music and some of the schools had their own orchestras. It really interested me the other week when watching the 'Last Night of the Proms' and the conductor said that every child in Brazil gets music. But the music seems to have gone here; it's the first thing to be cut in education. And for me, if I hadn't had music, I'd be lost.

When Scottish Opera started they didn't have a chorus [of their own] and I was auditioned and selected for the chorus in Aberdeen. The three operas we did were, during the week, *Don Giovanni, Madame Butterfly* and *Boris Godunov.*

The lad that trained us for the Scottish Opera was a university lecturer and he had one of the big houses down in the Old Town. He would put us outside and he would open his window and he would play his grand piano and make us walk up and down singing outside his house to practise. And when the professionals came, they turned round and said, 'Of the three choruses we've had that's the best one of the lot'. And I'm sure it was because he made us walk, up and down, to keep the movement.

Martha Alexander. b. 1937. Charlotte Street. Interviewed 2016.

Not the Stones or the Beatles – it was Schoenberg and Stravinsky for me

My father was an English teacher at Robert Gordon's College. He was regarded as a colourful and somewhat eccentric figure in the classroom and was famed for his devotion to drama and especially the works of Shakespeare. My mother came from a musical family, of German extraction. Her maiden name was Ludwig. She played the piano to a high standard. We had plenty of classical music at home and

Under Charles Foster
The Kincorth Waits
developed a nation-
wide reputation.
Shown here playing at
Bristol, 1983.

listened to concerts regularly on the Third Programme.

At school, namely Robert Gordon's College, my first taste of taught music started as early as 'Kindergarten 1' and progressed into Primary 1. We sang songs to the piano. In 'Kindergarten 2' we formed a class percussion band and I got the part of the cymbals player; I loved the power that clashing the cymbals gave me.

When we moved up to P3 we got a specialist music teacher. Lessons consisted mostly of belting out patriotic songs to his piano playing – *Rule Britannia*, the *British Grenadiers* and the like. Then came auditions for the choir. For my solo piece I chose Thomas Arne's *When Daisies Pied*, whereas the other boys opted for *Scots Wha Hae*. Their choice was considered the manly one and even though all that most of them could do was to drone it out in a monotone, they felt entitled to jeer at my efforts to master Arne's more delicate piece.

None of this was good for my image at an all-boys school and that was something I had to get used to as I moved up through the years. I remember our music teacher got us to sing a folk song to the tonic sol-fa rhythm and only three of us could do it effectively. The others all had to be punished for their failures. This consisted of being invited out to the front and then placed over the teacher's knee whereupon they received a spanking. All of them were wearing short trousers except for the boy who had on his kilt. So when he came to receive his chastisement, the teacher lifted up the back of his kilt but then, out of decency, replaced it before administering the punishment.

Every morning we started off the day with Assembly. Many of our morning hymns had a strong temperance message. One of the most joyful was the end of term, 'Lord dismiss us with thy blessing' and one of the most doleful was the 'Lord behold us with thy blessing', which signalled the start of another term.

When I reached the Senior School the music became decidedly better. At 13 I took up the trombone and got into the school orchestra. Playing it gave me a real sense of power and superiority; with it I could make a louder noise than anyone else in the orchestra. I was fortunate to receive lessons from a top class player who had been in the Halle Orchestra and who came up to play at HMT from time to time.

So I passed through my schooling as a bit different from the herd – no sport, classical music, not manly – but none of this really bothered me. While the rest of my generation was becoming crazed by the Rolling Stones and the Beatles, I was chasing avant-garde music – Stockhausen, the later Stravinsky, Schoenberg – and ordering discs from Bruce

> When our food was served up we discovered that we were not to receive any share of the feast that the guests were enjoying and we ended up with tinned meat and salad. Coarse language was involved.

Miller's so as to develop tastes that I knew were somewhat esoteric.

I was also appearing as a trombone player at a spread of venues throughout the North-east. I started playing in the Haddo House Concert Orchestra at the age of 17. I'd also started with the Aberdeen Opera Orchestra at age 15.

At Aberdeen University I began to study Moral Philosophy and Logic, taking Music as an outside subject. But I enjoyed this so much that I converted to a full-time Music Degree. This was a time in my life when I felt truly happy, most especially since a fellow student was Winnie, who is now my wife. After graduating with First Class Honours, I signed up for a PhD. My chosen subject was the 'Serial Music of Igor Stravinsky' but after several months I realised that I was no longer enjoying it. Instead, I decided to devote myself to instrumental music and became a Brass Instructor in Aberdeen City, a position which I held for 36 years, mainly at Aberdeen Grammar School.

I became especially interested in early 16th century material and was a devoted listener to the inspiring 'Pied Piper' programmes on the radio by David Munrow, who brought mediaeval and renaissance music and its instruments to a wider audience and did so with enormous enthusiasm. I decided to follow David Munrow's lead and form an early instrument group in Aberdeen from a set of local musicians. We called ourselves 'The Early Music Group of Aberdeen' and travelled around the North-east, putting on concerts. This was successful and we began to be in demand. But it all came to a stop when we were commissioned to put on a concert at Elgin.

We were meant to accompany a mediaeval banquet and we were promised suitable refreshment. But when our food was served up we discovered that we were not to receive any share of the feast that the guests were enjoying and we ended up with tinned meat and salad. This incensed some of the more hot-headed members of the group who began to make their displeasure known and to do so loudly. Coarse language was involved; insults were hurled at the banquet's organisers. The sackbut player was heard to yell, 'We don't dress up like this for pleasure – we're here for the food!' The upshot was that I broke up the group, which never appeared in public again.

One of the schools where I taught brass was Kincorth Academy. Winnie was a class music teacher there and we decided that this would be fertile ground to form another Renaissance music group, this time consisting entirely of school pupils. She assisted me in training the musicians, as well as making period costumes for all 15 members of the group. We received excellent support from the Head teacher, Alistair Urquhart, and from the Head of Department, Dr James McCloy.

We called ourselves 'The Kincorth Waits' and had many successful years. We attracted national attention and were invited to perform at the Albert Hall in the Schools' Proms. When we were down in London, we were invited several times to appear on the famous Children's TV programme, *Blue Peter*.

Part of my ambition was to demonstrate that a housing estate school like Kincorth was as capable of achieving high musical standards and of mounting concerts as any West End establishment and I think we fully succeeded in this. The school regarded us as a real asset and the parents took pride in what we were doing within their community.

Acquiring authentic instruments such as sackbuts, cornets, crumhorns and gemshorns was a problem to begin with. This wasn't the sort of stuff you could pick up in any of the local shops so I had to order them from a specialist firm in Bradford. This was an expensive business, so I realised that I would have to learn how to make the instruments myself, in my workshop here at home. I wrote around to various museums for the specifications and gradually, by trial and error and using the correct sycamore and boxwood, I mastered the procedures.

In the 1990s, I was happy to be commissioned by the Mary Rose Trust to make playing replicas of all the wind instruments which were retrieved from Henry VIII's flagship. At this time I also started researching early Scottish music manuscripts, and was delighted to find instrumental music by the 16th century Aberdeen composer, John Black – although I did have to reconstruct the missing parts in order to create performing versions. *These Fantasies* were published and have been recorded by top Early Music groups in both London and New York.

John Black was employed as 'Maister of the Sang Schule of Sanct Nicholace Paroche' and in 1992, Aberdeen City council decided to re-instate this post. I was duly appointed to form a choir of young people and to research the history of the Sang Schule. This worked well for seven years, progressing into a full four-part chorus, but as it was considered too elitist, funding was withdrawn in 1999. In 1994, I was also the recipient of an Honorary Doctorate in Music from Robert Gordon University for my work in Early Music.

The Kincorth Waits was disbanded in 2000 and again it was a misfiring mediaeval banquet that led to our demise. The Aberdeen University Alumnus Association invited us to perform at the Elphinstone Hall. We agreed to settle for only half our normal fee and looked forward to sharing in the good fare on offer. We were especially enticed by the fact that the surviving one of the 'Two Fat Ladies' team was to be preparing the food.

However, when the time came for us to receive our reward we found that, while the guests were being sumptuously fed, we were expected to settle for mere nibbles – sausage rolls and crisps. What made matters worse was the spectacle of mounds of left-over food being taken off, no doubt to be dumped somewhere as waste. Such lack of appreciation in our own city convinced me that the Waits was no longer worth the hassle and the decision was made to bring its life to an end.

But I've had a most enjoyable career and have never regretted spending it in Aberdeen or in teaching at the schools of the city. I also realise that I was fortunate to be involved at the time when music was expanding as a subject and as a source of enjoyment and personal fulfilment among the young people of the city. There's still a plethora of activity, but in the schools themselves resources have grown more and more scarce and the peripatetic instrumental tutor is expected to spread his or her work over a greater number of hours and pupils. There's also pressure to devote energies to putting on parent-pleasing shows.

Charles Foster. b. 1945. Kincorth Waits. Interviewed 2016.

Margaret Preston, a student of Charles Foster, seen here playing a Renaissance Flute, 1996.

SOME NOTABLE LIVES – 3

The rural roots: Wedding at Meadowley, Tarland, August 1900. David Middleton weds Elizabeth Bruce. The couple on the groom's side are John Middleton and his wife, Sarah Craib, Sheena Blackhall's great-grandparents, who had been married at Strathmore Farm, 1864. Alexander Middleton, the groom's brother and Sheena's grandfather, is 2nd from right, back row. The minister, behind the wedded pair, is the Reverend John Skinner.

'Just a humourless Kraut'

Something for the teacher? Bill Nicolaisen off on his first day at school, Freimfelder Volkschule, Halle/Saale, 1933.

At work on his PhD, Tubingen, 1954.

I was born in 1927, in Germany, at a place called Halle, in Saxony. My father was in the university department of Agriculture. My own career has involved the study of names. I once prepared a paper on all the various names I have been known by in my life. They amount to some two dozen. My first name was 'Putzy' – the name the family used in my early childhood.

Then, just on the eve of going to school, I announced, 'From now on Putzy will be called Willy'. I obviously felt that Putzy didn't possess enough grown up status for someone who was now to go to school. The family all obeyed and from that day onwards I was known as Willy. Names, you see, have power and are a means of declaring your identity to the world.

I started school the year that Hitler came to power, 1933, at my local Elementary school. But then the war intervened. I was now in Kiel and there were regular air-raids; as a very important naval base, Kiel came in for a lot of treatment by the RAF.

I remember being confirmed in the Lutheran church in May 1942. In fact, the church has gone on to be a life-long commitment for me, but that was an unusual step by then: although not expressly forbidden, it was frowned on by the Nazis. I recall one of the teachers at the Oberschule lining us up on the Monday and asking whether any of us had been confirmed that Sunday. Four of us stepped forward; he shook each of us by the hand and congratulated us on our courage. I also remember my mother saying that she wanted nothing to do with the Hitler Youth – she was quite capable of bringing up her own children without that kind of thing.

Exactly one year later, March 1943, everyone in my age group was called up to serve in the anti-aircraft batteries. In the meantime, my father was awarded a professorship in East Prussia and so the family moved there. I was transferred to an anti-aircraft battery in Konigsberg. By the time I left Kiel, that city had already suffered 270 raids and we now thought that we would be getting some respite from all that. East Prussia up to that point had been out of range of the RAF. But then it happened: the RAF managed to extend its range and within a couple of nights a city which had been unscathed was reduced to rubble.

By now the Russians were advancing on us. I remember the day – 25th January 1945. You could actually hear the Russian tanks in the distance getting nearer. We were at our usual family meal when our next-door neighbour burst in on us. He told us he had learned that there was a boat in the docks that would be able to evacuate us.

He took us down to the docks. It was a terribly cold day and some people just slipped on the ice at the water's edge and got drowned. We embarked and one of the engines packed up. It was decided to take us to Danzig. But the harbour there was absolutely full of ships and wouldn't take us in. That was a great blessing in disguise because the SS were waiting there and were taking all males over the age of 14 and simply stringing them on posts at the side of the road.

We were then directed to a large naval base on the Hel peninsula, a much better

destination. The navy still maintained its own traditions and was regarded as the senior service. I doubt whether it had many party members among its personnel. We were looked after while the ship was being repaired. Then it was announced that there was a large cruise ship lying off Hel and that a tug was available to take anyone over to it. My mother had had enough, so she and my younger brother got onto it while I stayed behind to look after the luggage. But the tug returned with them on it: the seas had been too high for any embarkation. My mother was absolutely depressed – but the next day the news came through that the ship had been sunk; another blessing in disguise.

We then took the train to Stettin, where there were people that we knew. After a few days my father turned up; his hair was completely white. I went to Lindburg to report to the Army offices there. I served in a unit near Leipzig.

But then the Russians came. They were coming from the south-east so we started moving towards the north-west. We'd get to a village, stay overnight and then move on. Gradually we got to a place near the Baltic called Schwerin. The Russians were behind us, the Americans before us. The Americans captured 50,000 of us in one day. So I became an American prisoner of war. We dug holes in the ground and took shelter in them. There was a school nearby; we removed its doors and used them to provide cover for our holes. We were there for three weeks. We found out that through the Yalta agreement the area was due to be placed under the Russians. We were scared that the Americans would leave us behind, but they packed us all into freight trucks, stuck an engine in front and took us into an area of Schleswig-Holstein that was British. We were handed over to them.

Now, I came from an agricultural background. Through my father's work, I knew a large farm in the area of Flensburg, so together with another POW, we knocked on the door and asked for work. We were very fortunate: we were allowed to sleep in the attic, we got our meals and we worked on the farm. Up to then we'd been starving – neither the Americans nor the British had been able to cope with the feeding of the 50,000.

I became a full-time farm worker. I stayed there for 18 months, as an apprentice. I acquired all the certificates – in milking, in sowing, in ploughing with horses. That was one of the most satisfying tasks I ever undertook: at the end of each day you knew exactly

Yet more letters to put after his name. Bill Nicolaisen M. Litt, D. Phil, Professor of English, on being awarded the degree of Doctor Honoris Causa, by Aberdeen University, 2006.

With his daughter, Fiona, Edinburgh, 1959.

Head of Scottish Place-Name Survey, Edinburgh, 1956–69.

The woman who had been running the survey had walked out in high dudgeon. He offered — I can still recall his phrase — 'to let me loose among her slips'.

what you had achieved. We would start in the middle of the field with a very small plot and gradually circle out to cover the whole field, with not a bit of it untilled; very satisfying.

But the war ended and I could now go back to my education. A lot of schools were arranging special courses for returning POWs. That's how I finally got my Abitur, in May '48. The winters of '47 and '48 were really bad but we were fortunate: because of my father's work he could always get enough oil seed to barter against clothing and so on. All through these terrible times we went to school and followed our studies; we did our best to carry on.

In October '48 I returned to Kiel to go to the university. I followed four subjects – English, German, Folklore and Comparative Linguistics. All through my career I've had a number of people to help me on my way. One of them, at Kiel, was Dr Fritz Braun. He was an Austrian Jew who had spent the war in England and had built up a lot of academic contacts in Britain. I went down with the worst flu I've ever had and found myself laid up in bed, sweating and running a high temperature. As I lay there, the landlady came to the door and said, 'Dr Fritz Braun is here to see you'. He didn't come in; he just stood at the door and said, 'Do you want to be the Assistant Lecturer at Glasgow next year?' I replied, 'Yes'. The Professor of German had written to Braun, enquiring if he could recommend anyone for a post that hadn't been filled since before the war.

So in 1951/52, I found myself teaching Phonetics and the German novella and holding conversation classes with students in Glasgow. That was the start of my academic career. But before I actually took up the position I went to Tubingen to discuss the topic of my dissertation with the Professor there. He told me, 'I'm interested in early river names – I think you should investigate whether or not they exist in Britain'. So I began my studies into the river names of Great Britain.

From '54 to '56, I was in Glasgow researching for a B.Litt. It was then that I came to realise how little had been done on the place names of Scottish rivers and that the field was wide open. Around then, I heard that the School of Scottish Studies in Edinburgh was carrying out a place name survey. I approached them to see if they had anything that would be useful to me. I went to see the man in administrative charge to be informed that the woman who had been running the survey had walked out in high dudgeon over something and that work on the survey had currently stalled. He offered – I can still recall his phrase – 'to let me loose among her slips'. They hadn't been able to find any replacement for the Survey – would I be interested?

The work at Edinburgh was enjoyable, but at the School my prospects were limited; after 13 years and being now 42 I needed a new challenge, so after much deliberation we decided to accept an offer to work in Binghamton, New York State. My time there opened up all sorts of opportunities and contacts for me. Over the years I became the President of nine societies in my field. Even when we came back that didn't stop. In Britain I became President of the Society for Place Names.

So how did I land up here, in the North-east of Scotland? Well, again it's contacts and fortune at work. My wife is Scottish; she's from the Glasgow area; my four daughters were each born in Edinburgh. Scotland was the natural place to come back to. The Aberdeen bit came about this way. In the '70s, I started my work on the Dictionary of Scottish Place Names. I saw that the Carnegie Trust was offering grants to support research on specific projects.

The grants were awarded through the universities by rotation and the following year it was due to be the turn of Edinburgh. I went along to the Trust and discussed my project with them; they were very keen and assured me that the

The 60th birthday: With wife May and daughters Fiona, Kirsten, Moira and Birgit, 1987.

Dictionary was exactly the sort of work the Trust would wish to support – but, in the event, Edinburgh failed to pursue the matter. Later, at a conference I ran into Tom Crawford from Aberdeen's English department. I told him my story and he immediately said, 'Oh, we must do something about this!' It was Aberdeen's turn the following year. So in '78/79 I found myself here for the year.

That was the start of my connection with the city. I returned through the '80s for a further couple of sabbatical years and most summers the family would come and I would spend the vacation months here. So when the time came for retirement, when I was 65 in 1992, I came back here, to Aberdeen. I'm still busy.

I never thought I'd still be actively engaged in academic work at the age of 76; this is my 53rd year at it. Back at the end of the war, when I was travelling across northern Germany looking for a secure place, with the Russians roaming around and the concentration camps just opened, I was taken by a newly-released inmate, who obviously had no love for Germans like me. He thrust me up against a tree and brandished a knife. He took my watch and then shoved the knife at my throat, letting it slide by at the last instant into the trunk. And since that second of May 1945 every day has always been an additional blessing for me.

So I've been fortunate. My life has taken many twists and turns. Yes, 'tributaries and rivers', has become more than just my dissertation topic. The flow of events has constituted my life. And we are very happy here. I have a room in the English department. I now write a regular series for the *Leopard* and have come to know 'Leopardland' and all its places and names very well.

We've now lived longer here than we have in any other part of Scotland. And we like Aberdeen. We like the fact that it is located on the sea. We like the size of it: it's not too large, yet it is big enough to support all the amenities that you would look for in a city. It has a football club which at least has the potential to win something. I like Aberdonians.

I find the Doric particularly interesting. Whatever people may claim – that it is only a dialect – I think of it as a language. I tell such people of the occasion I was in Bruce Miller's, waiting to be served behind a couple who had obviously come in from the country. They were asking for a certain tape; the assistant went off to consult with her boss. She reported back, 'Sorry, but it's all sold out'. The husband immediately responded, 'It's aa' selt oot, is't?' Now that's a real language shift, something more than a mere dialect.

So we are happy here in the North-east. And I can recognise the claims made about its people – honesty, thrift, directness and the rest. I'm glad to be here, but I'm also pleased that we have lived in other places and that each Christmas we receive some 270 cards from all over. I'm often asked about the differences between Scottish and American students.

What I say is that while a Scottish student will think first and then sometimes speak, an American will speak first and then think – sometimes. Of course, when you are asked to sum up such complex matters you can only resort to facetious simplifications of this sort. I should know all about the limitations of stereotyping – after all, I'm just a humourless Kraut, aren't I?

Wilhelm (Bill) Nicolaisen. b.1927. University of Aberdeen. Interviewed 2004.

I've always had a sense of God in my life

I grew up in Bucksburn. My father worked at Mugiemoss Paper Mill and Mum was a nurse at ARI. I was an only child of parents who were that bit older than the norm. They placed a great emphasis upon good manners and respect for one's elders – no first names, but always 'Mr' this or 'Mrs' that. I was expected to be neatly dressed – even when I went to a Secondary School where no uniform was in force my mother flatly refused to allow me to go in jeans.

As an only child, the Church gave a centre to my life socially. I loved the Boys Brigade and would look forward to a Friday night with an excited longing. For me it meant activity, games, learning, and, above all, camaraderie. It was at the BB that I encountered one of the formative influences on my life – Jack Dickie, who was the BB Captain. He was on the same shift at the paper mill as my father, so he inhabited the same working class world as we did. But he carried with him a real sense of moral authority, a palpable wisdom. He was a man who expressed his Christianity through his every word and action. He became a role model, a man who had a deep influence upon me.

I've always had this sense of God in my life, this personal spiritual awareness. I can't explain it, perhaps because it is inexplicable, something deeply instinctual within me. Along with this heightened spiritual interest there was also a burning desire to ask questions about the meaning of life, about how things worked and why things were as

Photograph to announce his induction as Minister at Queens Cross Church, 2009.

A man of both learning and God. Scott Rennie in church and with book in hand.

they were. I've always been absorbed by science as well as religion, seeing each of them, together and in their own ways, as containing the answers to our most pressing questions. I'm a rationalist and have never been happy with the pat answer. There's always been this tension between my faith and my rationalism, so that I have been left with a strong desire to see how the two of them fit together.

I loved both school and university. Secondary schooling was at Bankhead, a very different sort of establishment under its progressive Head, David Eastwood, to the traditional Primary at Bucksburn, where you had to wear the uniform, stand up when the teacher entered the room and say the Lord's Prayer every day. At Bankhead there was no uniform, no prizes, and no competitive sports.

I also got involved in local politics and was drawn to the Liberal Party. I am naturally distrustful of the extremes, either in nationalism or in the Left-Right divide and so a middle of the road party appealed. I detest dogma and instinctively feel that solutions must lie in the centre ground, in a willingness to compromise and to adjust. For me, politics and religion are inextricably linked; they are each of them about the human condition and the search for a better life, one founded on social action. Jesus Christ was a radical thinker, who resisted the orthodox dogmas of his time and invited us to be ready to turn things on their head and to reject those who simply exploit religion to pursue a self-interested cause.

University opened things up for me. I took a Geography degree before I moved on to Theology and preparation for the ministry. I deliberately avoided the Christian Union because, for me, it was dominated by a brand of fundamentalism which was at odds with my liberal outlook. I was still going to church, but even here I could suffer disappointment. One minister I had to listen to based his sermon on a rejection of evolution – here I was having to endure such anti-scientific bigotry while at the university I was studying palaeontology.

But it wasn't all bad. When I started on my theology course I attended the lectures of William Johnstone, the Professor of Hebrew Bible. The very first words he uttered were, 'We are going to study "Exodus" and what I must tell you is that you will discover that it is both more than history and less than history'. 'Thank goodness', I thought, 'This is

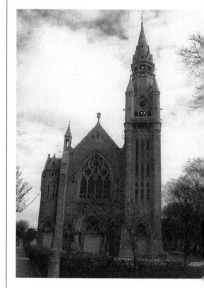

Queens Cross – that well established West End city church.

Scott in preaching mode.

what I am after – an opening of the mind and not some literalist interpretation'.

From the time I was 14, I also knew I was gay. In the end I did come out and then I discovered that the hardest person to come out to is yourself. I grew up 30 years ago in a much more hostile world than it has since become. There I was, a closet homosexual, surrounded by the acculturated homophobia of my fellow adolescents, with a working-class father who I felt didn't understand me. And on top of all that I wanted to enter the ministry!

No wonder I felt I had to keep my own sense of sexuality to myself. I secretly was more attracted to boys and yet I was in a culture which insisted I should be fancying girls. So I tried to do just that. I told myself it was something I would grow out of, that I just had to meet the right person and all would fall into place. And to some extent that's what did happen. I met my wife and fell in love with her. We married and had our daughter. Like a lot of gay men I made a decent fist of denying my nature and trying to conform to society's assumed norm.

In the end it was too much and the marriage broke down. But there were other issues too; she hated the life of the manse and the expectations which attended being the wife of the minister. I feel sorry she had to be subjected to that way of life. As it is, we still have a lot of feeling for each other. I have our daughter up here frequently and we are still close friends. The tragedy is that I could never give my whole self to her.

Scott marries David Smith, university lecturer, Aberdeen Registrar's, Office 2015.

This was while I was in my post at Brechin. I had every faith that God was no homophobe, that He is love and would accept me the way He had made me. I came out gradually. I let my closest friends know, I allowed myself to be seen in the company of men going to the cinema, and I invited my partner, Dave, who was teaching at Montrose Academy, to stay in the manse with me. I had been a hard working parish minister and had given myself freely to the Brechin community and so they adapted to my change in circumstance with ease, because they could look upon the whole person and not just regard me as some sort of issue.

Through all this, I had my faith in people enhanced. I had never held the traditional Calvinist view that people are fundamentally bad, that life is a constant round of vigilant judgement on each other. One of the huge privileges in being a minister is that you see the best in people; you come to know what ordinary people are capable of in the extremities of suffering. I have visited spouses forced to care for a partner who is in the final stages of dementia or parents whose child is suffering from a major disease like cystic fibrosis and, always, I come away, blown over by the uncomplaining devotion with which they attend to their task. To be a minister is to be daily moved by the depths of love that people show to their fellows.

All this has enriched my understanding of my faith. I was brought up to regard God in traditional terms as an all-powerful being up there, looking down upon his creation from on high, as King, a sort of super politician. But now I see Him in people, down

A lovely shot of Scott with daughter Rachel, Aberdeen Beach 2017.

here on earth, working through us in our daily lives. If you want to see God then you will find Him most truly present within people and not above them. To be a Christian is to be on a pilgrimage towards being fully human. That is why I cannot subscribe to any traditional dichotomy of the flesh and the spirit. For me, they are intertwined and to deny either is to reject our own humanity.

My first permanent parish was Brechin. I enjoyed my time there within an entirely supportive congregation. But I stayed for 10 years and at the end I considered that I was getting stale and needed fresh challenges. This was the time when Bob Brown, the minister at Queen's Cross, after being there for 25 years, retired, so my application was the obvious next step.

Queen's Cross had always acted as a liberal and radical voice. It had been founded back in the 19th century by a set of Free Church thinkers who shared a desire to embrace and not to reject the new spirit of biblical criticism which was sweeping in from the continent. Since then Queen's Cross has had a sequence of free thinking, bold ministers.

Inevitably, however, my application as an openly gay man living with a male partner created something of a furore, not so much at Queen's Cross but in the wider Presbytery. I dealt with it all by seeing the opposition as a test of my charity and my commitment. It wasn't a battle I would have chosen, but once it was declared I knew I had to confront it. I saw myself as the one picked out to fight for the inclusiveness of the Church and that I

Still smiling in the face of defeat. Scott and Rachel at the Burnley match which ended in a 3–1 loss for the Dons, 2018.

Go down to the General Assembly and you will see that there is now a lively group of younger clergy who are unafraid to speak up

would win because you can't turn back the tide of history. And although my appointment raised a heated opposition within the Church as a whole, the congregation at Queen's Cross was highly supportive.

This is progress. But I did recognise that on the wider front of sustaining the church's position in our national life we are faced with what can seem like an inexorable decline in its support. The data point to a drastic drop in membership and attendance since my own boyhood days. In the Scotland I grew up in it was clear that the Church had passed its peak in influence but that it still maintained an honoured role in society. My parents, for example, were typical; they might not be faithful Sunday attenders any longer but they held on to their membership and did respect the Church as a valued part of their heritage. The Church was still seen as an integral part of Scottish identity.

That, however, appears to have been supplanted by a wave of secular materialism which has now reached such a pitch that people can grow up and think of religion as an irrelevant relic of a bygone Scotland. But it's not all bad. One of the most heartening experiences of recent years has been to encounter other energetic voices within the Church. Go down to the General Assembly and you will see that there is now a lively group of younger clergy who are unafraid to speak up for the sort of reformist policies which we must embrace if we are to have any relevance in the 21st century. My personal fortune is that my own congregation at Queen's Cross shows little sign of flagging energy. I am determined that whatever might happen elsewhere, this church will continue to act as a progressive Christian voice for the North-east of Scotland – even if it is the last one!

Scott Rennie. b. 1972. Queen's Cross Church. Interviewed 2016.

From Ballater to the West End and back: The progress of a North-east writer

The family home was 15 Albert Terrace, Aberdeen. I know that nowadays this address is described in estate-agent spik as 'a charming period home' and all very West-end, but I must say that I don't feel I'm a West-end person.

My grandfather had been a master mason at Aboyne. My father was manager of Strachan's Buses that ran up Deeside. He would have left school at 13. He'd been brought up on East Mains Farm, Aboyne, but latterly took over the management of Strachan's Buses. His sister was Mrs Strachan, the owner of the firm, and her buses ran on Deeside from Braemar to Aberdeen. So, we spent every summer out at Ballater.

We also had, on my mother's side, my grandmother who lived with us. My grandfather ran a dairy-farm and owned several outlets about the town. My mother went to Garlogie School, but was sent into the town to Desswood Place with her grandparents – above the dairy that the family owned. She didn't get much of an education really, up to office work standard just. She could code switch easily, from Doric to Standard English. My father could never do that.

The female line: Lizzie Philip, Sheena's grandmother, at Glen Muick.

Sheena's parents: Charles Middleton and Winifred Booth at their wartime wedding.

The language at home was Scots. I suppose that the main influence on me as I was growing up was not my parents but my grandmother. When my parents married they bought the house at Albert Terrace with the money from the farm, so that was also a place for my granny. She had her own room, but I had to sleep in it too. She was fond of stories; all the time that we were together we'd speak in Scots.

You're speaking here about a family where you don't realise that you are living in a West-end house, you're just in a hoose. Life was quite isolated. Father left each day by seven o'clock to drive over to Ballater for his day with the buses. We were only together in the summer months when we were all out at Ballater. And for the first 16 years of my life all the speaking there was in the Doric, broad Doric. At the back of the garage there was this place called the 'shack' that my aunt owned. We just bade there.

For the rest of the year my mother insisted we got a good education, so we were back at Albert Terrace. It was like living in a Victorian time warp. The dykes were high all around; there was no community in a street like that. You just went into your front door and that was you. It was a sealed capsule, especially for a five-year-old. I would have been sent to children's parties, but I found that intensely stressful because otherwise you never saw any of these craturs. You had to put on a nice frock and say 'Thank you for inviting me to your nice party'. And all the time you'd be thinking, 'fan's this gaun tae stop,' ken? I usually sat on the stairs until it was all over and I could go back home.

In the town I had an insular life. Relatives came to visit, but no outsiders. My father was not the man to encourage any of that. He was a manager, but a hands-on manager – you've got to mind that here was a man who had left school at 13. He was highly intelligent, a great reader, a man for crosswords. But Mrs Strachan, his sister, was widowed young; her husband crashed into a tree and killed himself and three or four others at the same time, including a couple of my uncles. My father brought us up, but he also had to spend a lot of time out at Ballater with his sister.

At Ballater life was completely different: chalk and cheese. In the town I never got

The young Sheena Middleton – later Blackhall, at Glen Gairn.

Outside the depot 1926

out; the door was locked at six: 'Ye'll bide in and dae yer hamework!' But Ballater was completely opposite; the doors were aye open. I used to take a packed lunch and away. I would wander around till tea-time. I spent a lot of time up in the hills by myself. But we were never seen as central to Ballater life. 'Oh yer in-an-oot folk, fa cam here fer the summer jist!' That suited me fine, I was never in search of others for company. But I'd be going from one extreme to another, from this Dickensian town house to an old shack with a couple of rooms and complete freedom. But my real home was Ballater – that's where my heart-home was: Ballater.

My brother went to the Grammar and I went to the High. I didn't go to the High originally. At that time you weren't allowed into the High unless you'd passed this test. At the start of the IQ test we had to name beasts which were farm animals. Now, I'd spent plenty time when my uncle was farming at my granny's farm out at Hillhead, Cairnie. There I'd be in the byre, at the milking, watching it as I was o'er young to do it. But I'd be helping with the hens and other beasts. So here I was presented with this list of beasts, but I'd aye been tellt that you didna spik to strangers.

At the time of the IQ test for the High it was decided I was completely moronic. What did the wifie say…' Show me a haawse'. A horse! I mean, a sheltie, a cuddy – to me she was speaking a foreign language. 'Show me a sheep'. A yowe, a lammie… I could do nothing. I wet myself, I do remember that. That was the end of it.

PROPERTY TO LEASE

Category B Listed Town House
15 ALBERT TERRACE, ABERDEEN

That desirable West End property: Solicitor's publicity for Sheena's girlhood home, 15 Albert Terrrace.

It was all so alien. I was not supposed to speak to strange people and she was very strange. And she was using this foreign language, and here I was in a totally strange place. So I had to go to Mile End. My dialect was well enough received. We sang Scots songs in the choir, and on Fridays for a treat we were read *Wee MacGregor* by J. J. Bell, where the dialogue is dialect. 'My God, here's somebody's writing in the language I spik!' We got stuff out of the *Scots Reader,* which every Primary then had. I remember saying 'mannie' when 'many' was written up on the board and everyone laughed. But all she said was, 'Oh no – it's 'many'. It wasn't something I was ripped to shreds for.

Mile End was all right for me. I used to sit in at playtimes; I liked to do that. I was told, 'Well, if you don't want to go out and play with the others, you can just stay here in the classroom'. So I did – and I used to write. I wrote this great long story about my dog. The teacher was impressed. She asked the Head Teacher, Mr Ross, to read it. So he came in and read through it. He picked up his hand and hit me so hard across the ear that I just about fell off my seat. He told me I'd been changing tenses and that's what the smack was for. So I'd written this story and all I got for it was a skelp across the lug! He'd assumed that he'd been called in to spot the glaring mistake and what he came up with was this change in tenses. The teacher was shocked and so was I. I didn't write for a very long time after that.

I knew by the time I was 11 that I didn't want to go to the High School. But my mother was set on it: 'Say what you like about my bairns, they're nae feel.' I didn't pal about with any of the academic crowd. I tended to be friendly with my cousins in the country and they left school early to get jobs in hair-dressing and garages. I found them easier to speak to.

Really, I was content to live inside myself. My imagination gave me my companionship. And I was sharing my life with my grandmother. She was the one I'd come home to with my stories. Father would come home late in the evening from the buses. But I do remember phoning him when the results of the 11-plus came out. The head of the office, George, was there and he said, 'Ach weel lassie, ye'll hae tae learn English noo. Ye'll be wi aa the snobs noo. Ye'll hae tae change yer wyes; ye winna get aff wi spikkin like that at the High.' Which, of course, was very true.

I decided early on that if I was to be a teacher I'd be an Art teacher. I drew a lot. I won prizes. I once won the complete works of Shakespeare through a Brooke Bond Tea Competition.

I'd spent the whole summer out at Ballater and that had reinforced my Doric, so when I began the High I was even broader than usual. They all just laughed when I opened my mouth. But if you're at all bright, you just adapt. Sink or swim. I became ultra-English.

But I was not a success in the English class. The teacher was horrible. She used to read out the essays, and hold them in her two fingers like they were a little piece of dung. She'd say, 'Would the person who is responsible for this please come out here and take it back. I think she will know who she is'. Then she'd drop it on the table like a wee piece of dirt and you had to walk up past everybody and get it.

She got a hell of a shock when I got an A in my Higher English. I was chuffed about that. It wasn't at all what she had been expecting.

I left at the end of my fifth year and went to Gray's School of Art. The Head at the High, Miss Macnab, told me, 'Oh dear. What a shame you didn't come from the right sort of academic background – you might have done quite well'.

What did the High contribute to my development as a writer? Bugger all, I would say.

The High School pupil: Sheena in her Fifth year, shortly before she became a victim of Aberdeen's typhoid epidemic and her long stay at the City Hospital, 1964.

The head of the office said, 'Ach weel lassie, ye'll hae tae learn English noo. Ye'll be wi aa the snobs noo. Ye'll hae tae change yer wyes.'

Young Sheena with brother Ian.

My father didn't have much time for the place. The only time he was at the school was when I applied to Gray's and the teacher ripped the application form up in my face and put it in the bin. 'Why do you want to go there?' she asked. 'They'd have the skirt off the likes of you within five minutes flat!'

They were right, as it happens. I only got one year there. When I left Gray's I had no intention of going into teaching. But I had to do something. I remember Jimmy Scotland [Principal of Aberdeen College of Education] saying, 'The bottom line is, do you like children?' I found telling lies difficult, but on this occasion I did lie. 'Yes', I said. 'Well', he said, 'I've looked at your record and it seems to me that you'd be ideally suited academically to our B.Ed. course'. I didn't want any of it, but my father looked at the prospectus and told me that there was Art on it. 'Look', he said, 'You'll get to do lots of art'. Carrot, carrot!

At TC I did get Art. I also had Ian Munro in English. He was my tutor and he gave us Lewis Grassic Gibbon. And I had Bill McCorkindale and that's something I would not have missed. I got his lectures on poetry. That was my introduction to modern poetry. I read it with great enjoyment. He was truly inspirational.

It was Ian Munro who spoke up for me and saved the day. My last teaching practice was at Hanover Street. I was getting consistently high marks on the academic side, but my teaching was hopeless. I couldn't keep discipline. Kids will always sense your fear – and I was afraid. At Hanover Street I had this class of Primary 7 and there was this highly disturbed pupil in it. There had been a famous murder in Aberdeen when a man had twice killed children. He was caught after assaulting another one, who got away – and this disturbed pupil was the survivor. He just went around smashing things and attacking the other kids.

That was the finish as far as I was concerned. But Ian Munro stepped in. He told me, 'Right, if you promise me you'll complete the course, you can do a bit of practice at this nice rural school. Do that and I'll see you pass'.

After TC, I taught at Easterhouse, Glasgow. Glasgow would take anybody then. There, the worst students were sent to the worst schools – like Easterhouse. The Head Teacher looked at me and said, 'Right. Primary 2'. 'But I'm not trained for that.' 'Oh yes you are. Here's the book'. He handed me this scheme of work with 'Glasgow Corporation Education Department' stamped across its front. It laid out what I was to do. That was my training.

I wasn't happy there at all – it was even grimmer than I had feared it would be. My father spoke to his local councillor and he said, 'Look, the City isn't accepting anybody else at the present time, but the County is. Join up with County and she can get back into the City through the back door'. So I did some months at the Central, Fraserburgh; but I was just marking time till I got a post at Inchgarth, back in Aberdeen.

The language issue in Aberdeen was interesting. There was this girl at the college who invited me to her home. We'd both been at the High and we spoke to each other in English. Before we got to the house she told me that there was something she had to

The Gray's School of Art student: Sheena attends the wedding reception at the Victoria Restaurant, 1965, of George Wallace and Madeleine Angus. The figure to the left is Bill Gibb, later to become a famed fashion designer.

warn me about her father. What could it be, I wondered – drink? But it turned out that what she had to tell me was that her father always spoke in Scots. So I immediately spoke in Scots to him, and she was shocked. I got on great with him; he was a distant relative of Charles Murray, I discovered. He was as broad as you like. His wife was from Braemar and she spoke in English. But their daughter had gone to the High at age five and only ever spoke in English.

For myself, I found it so much easier if I just compartmentalised it all. Home was Scots, school English; Ballater was Scots, college English. I kept the two languages apart; I found that much easier than trying to build a bridge between the two.

But the language issue is not an easy one to resolve. For me it has to be one or the other. I'm not comfortable when in mixed company, in a mixed situation where some speak English and some Scots. When I married I made a conscious decision to marry someone as close to my parents as myself. Same speech, same customs. I thought that life would be much easier for me that way. That was my theory – to replicate my own background. But it didn't work and I was left with four kids, who, ironically, all went to Harlaw Academy [the renamed High]. So I saw the school in a different light, as a parent and as a member of a different generation. But that's all another story….

Sheena Blackhall. b. 1947. Albert Terrace and Deeside. Interviewed 2003.

A prolific story teller and writer, both for children and adults, and in both Doric and English, Sheena Blackhall has been responsible for over 130 poetry pamphlets, 15 short story collections; four novels and two televised plays. She has also translated *Jane Eyre, Dr Jekyll and Mr Hyde, The Wizard of Oz, The Gruffalo, The Gruffalo's Child, Of Mice and Men* into Doric, two children's books (published by the Reading Bus) and two *Legends & Urban Myths* collections (History Press). She has been active in children's education, bringing the joys of literature and language(s) to many North-east schools.

If you went to the dancing and a guy might say, 'Can I see you home?'
And you said, 'Aye, okay.' 'Far d'ye bide?' 'Northfield. 'Oh, aye, okay.
See ye later.' And off he'd go.   — Kathleen Porter (*née* Hay). b. 1932

COMMUNITY LIFE

Celebrating Aberdeen, Union Street parade 2018.
(IMAGE BY KIND PERMISSION OF ABERDEEN JOURNALS)

THE
COMMUNITY
IN ACTION

Round the corner from Nellfield Place: Sandy Gallacher's mother in Holburn Street as the girl in white dress at front taken during the General Strike, 1926.

Live and let live

The earlier part of my boyhood was in Nellfield Place in the 1940s. The following episode gives an indication of the way in which our community operated. Like most working class areas of that period, we had what was known as a local bookie's runner. This was before the days when the Government realised that it could make money by licensing betting shops in every High Street. The bookie's runner stood at the corner of a street and collected bets, usually on horse racing.

He would take in the money in the morning and then take the bets to either Dan Flynn or Farquharson for Fairness, which had offices in Bridge Street.

Winning bets would be paid out the next day. These turf accountants were licensed to take phone bets and this was the only legal way to bet, unless you were at the race course itself. Phones were unknown in working class homes in the 1940s.

Every so often the local constabulary would make a half-hearted attempt to apprehend a bookie's runner. What happened in Nellfield Place was something like this:

When spotted by the local bobbies the runner would be chased up Nellfield Place, where he would run into a tenement on the right hand side of the street and then, before the bobbies reached the tenement, he would have been welcomed into one of the ground floor flats. The bobbies, on entering the tenement, looked up and down the stairs and out at the back and then, on not finding their quarry, would go on their way, visibly assuring the good folk of Nellfield that everything was in order.

Our man knew the district well and after exiting the flat, where he was given refuge, went out the back way, climbed over the wall separating the Nellfield tenement from the Holburn Street tenements, strode out through the common lobby and so out onto Holburn Street and to safety.

It was generally accepted that both the bookie's runner and the police had their functions in society and people were happy to let them get on with it. It was also well known that in the Abergeldie Public House, further along Holburn Street, at closing time – 9.30 in those days – two measures of whisky were placed on the outside sill of the

The nearby school
– later burnt down shortly after the war – Holburn Street Primary. Sandy is centre back row.

A Nellfield gathering , 1947: A young Sandy at front left with friend Peter Kerr, with neighbours and parents behind.

gents' toilet at the rear of the premises and the front door would be locked. These glasses would be returned to the bar after the local bobbies had passed by on their nightly stroll around the area. This permitted the locals to finish their evening drinks, unhurried.

Alexander (Sandy) Gallacher. b. 1941. Nellfield Place. Interviewed 2015.

We used to share what we had

Smithfield Nursery was run by the Council and was attached to the school – but it's no longer there. It was excellent. Everybody in the community could take their kids to that nursery. It was to let mothers out to work.

A few of us mums were in the same boat – and we used to share what we had. 'I've got plenty of tatties; do you want some?' 'I've got plenty of bread…' And that's how it worked because we all had children – and we shared. Then we started fundraising for the nursery because they were good to us and we thought we'd do that back.

Marion Douglas. b. 1948 Northfield. Interviewed 2016.

The respectable poor

E rrol Place was the sort of street where everyone knew everyone else. An early memory is of a neighbour, Mrs Marsh, running up the street with her customary flowery apron over her head, shrieking out, 'The King's deid! The King's deid!' and all the other neighbours hanging out of the windows trying to take the news in.

It might seem to have been a solid working class neighbourhood, but there were subtle strata within it. The head of one family was a hopeless alcoholic – he was forever trying to cadge drinks off my father after hours at the club – and he was looked down upon by all and sundry. This was a great shame as his daughter, Gina – a girl with lovely long blond hair – was a great friend of mine, and yet I was warned not to mix with the 'likes o' her'. She carried the stigma of being a good-for-nothing drunkard's daughter. I remember coming back from my Sunday school and seeing her father lying insensible by the side of the road. My impulse was to try to get help for him, but when I approached a woman with the news that 'Our neighbour was in need of our help', her reply was, 'He's nae ony neebor o mine – he jist bides near me, that's aa!'

So there was a sense of being divided into the respectable poor and the undeserving poor. Values such as the work ethic, thrift and respectability were deeply held and in some ways it acted as a supportive community. Whenever someone died, the hat would go round to collect money to help defray the funeral expenses – but if someone fell short of the hardworking, respectable norms then they were likely to be ostracised.

Our neighbours worked in the shipyards, at the fish market or at the laundry. The street resounded to the sirens at Hall Russell's, at one o'clock, marking knocking off time while the great chimney at Stevenson's Laundry was a notable landmark. The steam from the laundry seemed to hang in the air, so the scent of washed linen and cotton impregnated my childhood.

Louise Baxter. b. 1948. Errol Place. Interviewed 2015.

Louise Baxter with parents, 1954.

Everything was at hand

E verything was very local to you. There was the shop that did the papers and the morning rolls; then further down the road, the delicatessen on the corner of Forest Avenue and Strathdee, the baker. Then round the corner from that was the butcher. So everything was at hand and you would often get sent to the shop to buy things. My mum smoked and I remember being sent to the shop with your list including however many cigarettes you'd to buy. Running errands were responsibilities that you had back then, but you don't do that with young children now.

Somebody came round selling the *Green Final* on a Saturday and there was the Cream Boy who came round selling cream; that was on a Friday. There were the Ale Boys, from Bon Accord Lemonade who'd come round with the different types of drinks for sale.

There was a fishmonger who would come round once a week. He would go in front

Ashley Road Primary School Country Dancing: Wendy as a member of the 1982 team – at a time when almost all of her classmates had local roots.

and pull down the counter once he'd got behind it. He would always give my sister a couple of grapes for free; they were always expensive. His fish, fried in Ruskoline, was another meal we would often have. So everything that you needed was around and everything was cooked from scratch; there was never anything really fancy.

People were happy. I don't think there was so much emphasis on what possessions people had; everybody was much the same.

Wendy Bradford b. 1972 Forbesfield Road. Interviewed 2016

LOCAL IDENTITIES

A great view along the Viaduct

At the front we enjoyed a great view right along the Viaduct with all its shops and constant coming and going of vehicles and people. There were shops all around us. Everything in those days before the fridge entered the home had to be brought in daily and so I would often be sent up the road to get the messages – but you never had to go more than 50 yards to find what you wanted. There was the Co-op, a fish shop, Rennie's the grocer, the Dairy for your milk. To the right hand side of our entrance there was Anderson's, the cycle shop, and to the left the fish shop. Anderson's was where you had to go each week in the days when we were still in the lower floor flat and without electricity, so as to get the batteries for the wireless recharged – the 'accumulators'. Then there were haberdashers, greengrocers, which had fruit on one side

In heart of the city:
The Skene Street corner tenement block where David Brown lived out his early life. His home was on the second floor next to the church tower; the bay window was the 'front room' and his bedroom the smaller window to the left.

Off to the Cubs at Beechgrove Church – the 25th Aberdeen – in Aberdeen Grammar school uniform.

In the prefab back garden with friend Jane Galbraith.

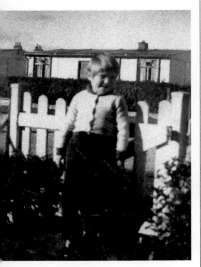

The young Dorothy Dunn at the gate of Redmoss Crescent

and chocolate on the other, a china shop and a post office.

Best of all, the Cinema House was just across the road at the corner with Skene Terrace. There was the excitement of seeing the van delivering the reels of film twice a week and gazing at the stills on the boards outside. Mrs Nelson, down the stairs, loved the pictures and she would take me twice a week to see each film that came out – Westerns, cartoons, romances, early technicolours.

Then there were Union Terrace Gardens just round the corner. There always seemed to be something going on then: the great draughts boards where you could watch the old men moving the pieces back and forward with long hooked poles, the ornamental Victorian toilets, and the weekly pipe bands and people leaning over the walls of the Terrace to watch the spectacle.

So everything was on our doorstep. To me our flat was a cosy place to come back to, a sort of refuge, after the bustle and the noise of the street outside. Not that the constant din of the traffic ever bothered us; I remember when we moved out to the Bridge of Don how uncanny I found the silence.

David Brown. b. 1946. Rosemount Viaduct. Interviewed 2014.

Redmoss – a good place to grow up in

My first home was in Redmoss Crescent at Nigg. These were prefabs which had been built after World War 2 for incoming workers. My parents were English: my dad was from Honley near Huddersfield and my mother was from Frizington in Cumbria. After the war my father was offered a post at either Coventry or Aberdeen – he opted for Aberdeen simply because he thought the housing situation would be easier.

With her parents and older sister, Pauline. The girl on the left is a friend.

We lived in the prefabs at Redmoss till I was eight. It was a good place to grow up in. The Gramps were more or less at the top of the road and I could jump on my bike and cycle for miles in complete freedom.

The Tullos area wasn't built up as it is now and there were plenty of open spaces with farmland and wooded areas all around. Jimmy Milne, now the owner of the Balmoral Group, was then a teenager, working on his father's farm at Greenbank Road. His father gave him a shed in which he grew mushrooms and my sister would go around with him in his van to sell these mushrooms to a grocer in Menzies Road, Torry. Across from us was a big house, Tullos House, with a long wooded drive leading up to it. We used to play along it but, Mrs Innes, who lived there, was forever shouting and chasing us out of the woods. It was later demolished to make way for the industrial estate. As long as we turned up for tea-time we were given absolute freedom to bike and to go anywhere we pleased.

Dorothy Dunn. b. 1953. Redmoss. Interviewed 2016.

'Enjoying' a Sunday stroll: in the centre of town with her father.

Those prefabs were so well designed

L iving in Torry was fine, but as we grew up it was obvious that we were becoming overcrowded. So an application was made to the Council and we were given a prefab home at Nigg. They had originally been built to house the workers for the Consolidated Pneumatic Toolworks Company when it set up a plant in Aberdeen. They were built to very high standards. They might have looked small from the outside, but they were so well designed that each one held two bedrooms, a kitchen, complete with fridge, a bathroom and each had a garden with its own shed. Compared to what we had come from, our prefab was positively luxurious.

My parents were very hospitable and loved entertaining. Mother was a great baker and sometimes there would be so many visitors to our prefab that if you were standing in the living room with a cup of tea and needed a spoonful of sugar, it was easier to go out the front door and go round to the back door so as to get into the kitchen – there was no chance of pushing a way through the great crowd of folk.

Margaret Mann. b. 1941. Nigg. Interviewed 2015

Margaret Mann: 'those prefabs were so well designed'.

A 1900s shot of a **tram** rattling round the bend at the Fountain, just outside the site of Jim Couper's boyhood bedroom.

Woodside was quite distinct from Town

Ours was a three-room flat just beside the Woodside Fountain. No bathroom and with a toilet outside. We had a kitchen with a bed recess, a bedroom and then the room which was kept strictly for visitors. However, as I was an only child we didn't feel crowded. We lived above an electrician's shop; the upper floor was the plumber's workshop and below was the coal cellar and washhouse. In the backyard was what had been a mill. Above this building there was a big local feature – the Woodside Lum. This had been attached to a mill. It stood out; we maintained that the German bombers used it to line up their raids.

Our neighbours tended to be hard working, skilled people – trawlermen, railwaymen, shopkeepers, plumbers and electricians. Woodside was a distinct shopping area with a great variety of stores running along Great Northern Road. There were the two butchers, two bakers, fish and chip shop, a large Co-op store, with its grocery side and its butter side. There were two chemists, a couple of banks – the Clydesdale and the Savings – a shoe shop and so on. Just about the only time we felt a need to go into the centre of town was when it was 'divi' time and my mother would take me to the Co-op in Loch Street to get kitted out with new clothes.

Woodside in those days was very much its own area, quite distinct from the town itself. It had a real sense of community. People would meet each other as they went about their affairs, which were entirely local.

People found their work in the area and did their shopping locally and on a daily basis in those carless, pre-refrigerator days. My mother would meet familiar faces each day as she was about doing her shopping and invariably that would be the cue for chat and an exchange of news. Leslie Russell, who grew up to become Head of R.E. at Hazlehead, was also brought up in the area and we were both handed down tales of how the two mothers could hold a conversation across the Great Northern Road – there was so little traffic in those days.

But there were the trams and they would have to negotiate the sharp bend by the Fountain. This was just outside my bedroom window and more than once I could tell

A recent photo of Jim Couper.

from their noise that they were going too fast and might not make it safely round the 'bend'. This could result in the odd derailment. And in the '40s there were still quite a number of horse-drawn carts about: there was the daily milkman and a vegetable cart which came to us from across the river. Peter Tortolano would push his barrow from Causewayend up to us at Woodside, sell his ice creams and then push it all the way back.

The most obvious change since those days is the way in which the road has been widened to accommodate its status as the trunk route northwards out of the city. The older houses on the east side have all been swept away, including the one I was born in. I accept all this as an inevitable aspect of progress. The traffic simply could no longer be accommodated.

But there has been a loss to Woodside's sense of distinct identity. I remember this old lady, Nan Sutherland, who always talked of going to Woodside as 'going up to the village', as a place separate from the city. It's interesting that Woodside has a series of street names which replicate those in Aberdeen – Gladstone Place, Canal Street, King Street, Queen Street, Don Street – showing that at the time they were laid out Woodside was still regarded as its own place which was free to use any names it liked for its streets.

But much of the economic reasons for it have disappeared too. When I was a boy the local Grandholm wool mill and the paper mill were big employers, as were the many shops. Now the works have closed down and people go off in their cars to the supermarkets so the inhabitants regard Woodside as a place to sleep in rather than to lead their whole lives in.

Jim Couper. b. 1935. Woodside Fountain. Interviewed 2014.

> In the '40s there were still quite a number of horse-drawn carts about: there was the daily milkman and a vegetable cart which came to us from across the river.

You could live in that street without going out of it for your shopping

The street that I lived in was off Crown Street, with College Street at the other end. It was a street of tenements on both sides and you could live in that street without going out of it for your shopping. There were shops in the whole street; all kinds of shops.

There was a mixed merchant's shop at one end and, coming up from it, there was a butcher and opposite there was a fish and chip shop at the corner. And moving along the street, you came to a house, number 18, and that's where I was born. Then up again was the licensed grocer and next to that was a barber, across the road was another mixed merchant's shop and moving up again you came to what you called a cobbler – a shoemaker and repairer. And then next was an upholsterer, then a dairy, then a chemist and on the other side, a draper – all in the one street. And that was it; you could have practically lived there without going out of it for your shopping.

Jim Butler. b. 1923. Marywell Street. Interviewed 2015.

Jim Butler with his sister, 1926.

A new house and car to go with it: Alex Rae (right), aged 10, with a cousin, proudly leaning against his father's Austin.

Mastrick was a different world

When we moved from Torry to Mastrick it was a different world – a place to play. In the early days at the top of the road there were the remains of ack-ack batteries; they'd been put up there – where the television tower is now –- to protect Dyce Airport in the war. The guns were gone but the emplacements were still there and we used to run in and out of these things like madmen – great fun.

There were open fields. Slowly, the houses were built all around, but part of it remained rough ground for a long time and we used to play up there. There wasn't much housing and you could see right into Dyce and you could see the airport away in the distance. There were kids all around; every household had kids. It was built for families, and they were all round about the same age, the immediate aftermath of men returning after the war. I had happy days in Mastrick – it was a good place to grow up.

Alex Rae. b. 1947. Mastrick. Interviewed 2016.

A marvellous place to grow up

With the money from my father's estate, my mother bought a bungalow high up in Kincorth, overlooking the Dee. For me, this was a marvellous place to grow up in. You could open the curtains and there before you lay the great spread of the city. Below the house the fields stretched down to the banks of the Dee; on its far side you could see Duthie Park and watch the trains as they drew in from Ballater, speeding down the incline alongside Allenvale Cemetery. Not only see but hear too, because at this point the driver would shut off the steam and allow his engine to coast down towards the Joint Station. The 'clonk, clonk' echoed right across the river to where our house stood. Then you could see right over to the high ground beyond Aberdeen, right up to the trees at Whitestripes. At night the lights sparkled and in the day time the skyline was filled with the spires of the city.

Yes, a marvellous place to grow up in – except for the fact that I could go weeks without meeting anyone of my own generation.

William (Bill) Brown. b. 1929. Kincorth. Interviewed 2014.

A young Bill Brown enjoys a round on the putting green at the Bridge of Dee, 1930s.

An outing to 'Corbie Tap', Echt: A 1926 shot of the Smiths with their friends the Forbeses. Pat's father has the sandwich, her mother has the hairnet and sister Ruth is the infant.

It used to be a happy neighbourhood

My childhood was in a lovely neighbourhood full of good folk and happy children. I could have gone down the whole street and named everyone in it and knocked at their doors and known I'd get a welcome. And now the whole community has been swept aside and broken up. In 1980 the City made a compulsory purchase of all these properties so that they could drive their dual carriageway through them. This was part of the grand plan to have a dual carriageway all through the town from the harbour up to the A96 and what has

A 1947 family grouping: Young Pat is right, father and mother to her right with brother David; includes sister Ruth and her husband Andy behind.

happened? You go to the top of what was once our road and find that this grand new road peters out and there's a line of traffic waiting at the lights!

And what was worse is that the price they were forced to accept was just peanuts, certainly nowhere near enough with which to purchase a new home. They all had to accept a council house. That whole happy neighbourhood has been destroyed.

Patricia (Pat) Brown (née Smith). b. 1940. Powis Place. Interviewed 2015.

> Aberdonians are a race apart. It's something to do with the Doric. It's our own special language.

THE CHANGING SCENE

I hate what the oil is doing to Aberdeen

Bob Gibb, oil specialist, at the height of his journalism career.

Aberdeen is a very special city. I've travelled the world and I think that Aberdonians are a race apart. It's something to do with the Doric. It's our own special language. Look at our reputation for being mean. We cherish it – because we know it isn't true. We are an honest people. Ask an Aberdonian his opinion and that's exactly what you will get – straight and direct. Yet Aberdeen welcomes people, it takes them to itself. My wife's a New Zealander and she thinks there's nowhere else like it. For her it's the most wonderful place in the world – and above all, Torry is. When you cross that bridge you are entering a different community. For us Torry is 'town', not Aberdeen.

But I hate what the oil industry has done to Aberdeen. When they discovered oil in the North Sea, I was the first journalist to break the story – in the Mearns Leader where I was editor in the early '70s. But I remember standing and looking at the new Aberdeen and feeling anger at what the oil was doing to the place.

I've become involved in the oil and the gas industries; that's now my specialism as a journalist. But I hate the damage the oil has done to the culture of Aberdeen. It's changed our outlook on life, our basic attitudes. It's also created the impression that all Aberdonians are rich. But that's a myth. Sure, there are many rich people in Aberdeen, but the money hasn't gone back into the city for everyone. For many it's just dragged prices up. I accept that something had to happen to replace the collapse in the fish and in ship-building and that the oil has given Aberdeen the opportunity to become the world centre for all the associated technologies, but the oil has done great damage too. The old Aberdeen had a uniquely close relationship with its rural hinterland and that's all gone now. We've become a different sort of city.

Robert (Bob) Gibb. b. 1932. Torry. Interviewed 2004.

No shops in Garthdee at that time

I remember the Ingin Johnnies coming from France with the onions on their bikes. They used to come round Garthdee. And there was Gordon: he was a sort of a Veggie Man and he used to come round. A baker used to come round. There were no shops in Garthdee at that time. You had to go into town to get the shops.

There used to be a slaughter man; my dad always called him 'Esson', and, if he was busy, my father would help him and he got what was called the slaughterman's 'slug'. My dad would come home with liver and meat from the cheek which my mother used to mince. Liver and back vein fried together: absolute bliss! If my mother had too much mince, she'd make it into parcels and send us to give some to the neighbours. The neighbours would give you a sixpence but you'd to hand it over to Mother.

There were message boys on the buses and my mother would walk up to the bus with a parcel; the message boy would take it and would then go on the Torry bus and take it to my grandfather's house. And my grandfather did the reverse: if he got a bit of fish he would put it on the bus and the message boys would deliver it to our house. But, of course, all of that has gone; now there are no message boys.

Martha Alexander. b. 1937. Garthdee. Interviewed 2015.

Martha Alexander, aged 12, in front of her wooden clad house Auchinyell Gardens.

I mostly remember the poverty

That's one of the things I remember most: the poverty. They were very poor in the '20s. And if a man wasn't very good at his job he was just sacked because there were four or five waiting to take it. I can remember the men standing at the corners as I went to school – standing at the corners of every street. I think they gathered there for company for one another. They used to stand there with their hands in their pockets.

They each had a little pin somewhere about their person; if they had a jacket on, it would be in their lapel and if they found a big tab of a cigarette in the gutter they'd pick it up and stick this pin through it and they'd get a few puffs from it. They were poverty-stricken but they all smoked – even if it was the tab of what somebody else had smoked. I think it was escapism: 'Oh, at least I can manage to have a cigarette'.

The men used to go about in spats and I'm sure it was because they had no heels to their socks. I know my father put on a pair of spats because he had only one pair of socks and there was a hole in them.

The Brig of Balgownie was a favourite spot for Aberdonians that wanted to commit suicide. My mother told me once about a young serving lassie who ran all the way along King Street with her little white apron on; she was expecting a baby and she wasn't married. And she ran all the way out to theBrig o' Balgownie and jumped and at the court hearing the presiding magistrate said, "If only someone had put out their hand and said, 'Where are you going, lassie?' that would have stopped her.

There are these huge, fancy gravestones – angels and all that sort of thing, big obelisks. If you read them… '9 year old', 6 year old, 3 months'. Of course it was dirt; just infections.

I can remember there was a place in Harriet Street, off Schoolhill and that was Mitchell & Muil's shop for getting rid of their bakery that they hadn't sold the day before – and it was half price or less. And there used to be great queues waiting there before eight o'clock in the morning.

Another thing, now, was if you had a job, and you were off sick, you couldn't be out after six o'clock at night; a man had to be in his house – and they used to send people round to see and if you were out after six o'clock your benefit was stopped. I remember a lady saying that she saved up and bought a second-hand sewing machine – her husband was unemployed – and she started making pillow cases and she charged seven pence a pair for them. And then a neighbour reported her to the Parish and the Parish came down and stopped his money because she was making money and she said she was maybe making a shilling a week, that was all, but her Parish money was stopped. You only got so long of unemployment benefit and then it was Parish and they were very strict.

My mother-in-law had two girls and two boys. The youngest one was a boy, Tommy. He was such a happy boy, singing *You Are My Sunshine*. He was three. He took meningitis and they had the doctor and then he needed a specialist and the unmarried sisters, or the unmarried brother, I'm not sure, gave them money for a specialist: two guineas – which was wealth then, and especially when the specialist came in and just looked and said, 'Oh no, there's nothing can be done.' Tommy died at three-year-old – and she mourned him.

I remember another child stayed down the road. I can't remember what was wrong with him, but they didn't get the doctor and the bairn died. What I do remember is my sister and a few of the other kids went round and asked if they could see him. They got taken in to be shown him and Nancy said he was dressed in a little sailor suit. That stayed in her mind.

Death in children, I think, was accepted. To prove the point, you've only got to go to the upmarket cemetery where the business people buried their dead – is it Springbank? Now there are these huge, fancy gravestones – angels and all that sort of thing, big obelisks. If you read them… '9 year old; 6 year old; 3 months'. Of course it was dirt; just infections.

Neighbours would stand at the window and say 'Look at that washing!' – I can remember, my grandmother, 'Look at that washing! That's nae very clean. She disna need tae be like that.' They lived in a small world; what went on, what the neighbours did you just watched, but you didn't speak. You didn't let them know anything about your business. She would have never spoken about her family or anything like that and Mrs Davidson downstairs wouldn't have spoken about hers either.

People didn't see a lot of their doctor. The chemist did well – because you went to the chemist for everything. I can remember going for fourpence of syrup of squills, fourpence of ipecacuhana and fourpence of something else. That was a shilling, and spent at the beginning of every winter for the coughs and the colds, etc. And then, if they had a boil or anything like that, they went to a chemist at the bottom of Schoolhill and bought a tin of Fisherman's Ointment; he made his own then. There were so many fish workers got bones in their fingers and things like that. It was very good for anybody that got a boil; kids got a lot of boils because they didn't have enough vitamins in their bodies. If you'd picked a nail and got a whitlow or something like that the kids were all taken to the chemist. The chemists really were very good, because they knew that people didn't have money. I think it was three-and-six for a doctor's appointment.

Gladys Morrice. b. 1920 King Street Interviewed 2016.

A sense of making a fresh start

'I saw the community growing up around me': Northfield takes shape, 1948.
[IMAGE BY KIND PERMISSION OF ABERDEEN JOURNALS]

When I was four we moved over to a brand new council house in Northfield. I can remember getting off the bus with my mother and having to trek through the mud, with all these new, half-completed houses going up around us, up from Springhill Road to our new home. And that is where I stayed till I left to get married 20 years later. I saw Northfield grow up all around me.

Life changed considerably during that time. We lived on a 200-yards-long road and when we moved in there were no more than three cars in the whole street – and now

Alistair McRobb enjoying the Northfield life, early 1950s.

there can be that number to one house. So many of the gardens which were looked upon as a proud possession have now been covered over as off-road parking.

With so little traffic we were free to play out in the streets. We'd chalk up a set of stumps on a lamp-post and have games of cricket. Being outside was our default position. If the weather was fine, and we were stuck inside with our heads in a book, our parents would tell us, 'You've plenty of time for that later. It's a nice evening so outside and play with your friends.'

It was an exciting time. The whole community was new and everyone who had moved into it, usually from inner city tenement flats with no separate bathroom or toilet, was conscious of being there at the start of something fresh and welcoming. Many of them were young families so there was a youthfulness about the place, a sense of making a fresh start. We certainly found it all new and exciting, having our own front door, our own toilet and being able to walk straight into our own home without having to clamber over other people's stuff left in a common hallway.

People came together in their effort to create a new community, one in which we cared for each other and showed respect for our neighbours. I remember when a neighbour, a painter by trade, across from us died and how all the adults from round about went to the house to view the body and to spend an evening sharing memories while we children were all herded into another neighbour's house to be looked after by an older school pupil.

Alistair with parents and sister in front of their new house in Northfield. The lamppost on which he and his mates would chalk a set of cricket stumps for a street game is behind them.

I also remember the buzz of a wedding at the church. This was opposite the G. M. Fraser Public Library, a favourite haunt of mine. I'd go there, sit poring over a book, but keeping an eye open for the emergence of the wedding party from the church. The groom would scatter coins and we children would rush out to grab a few of them; on a good day you might emerge with six or seven pennies – enough back then for a feast of sweeties.

There was a community centre attached to the library and later an extension was built that became the home of the Beehive Club. This was a mecca for us youngsters, one that became so popular that a waiting list had to be drawn up. There would be dances in the gym at the weekends. The church played an important part in our lives. I attended the Sunday School and at that time it was the largest one in the whole of Scotland with some 1,500 members.

Northfield had a great sense of togetherness in those early days of its existence and the church was at the centre of it all. If a snowstorm struck then you'd see three or four elders out on the streets digging out tracks and seeing that the old folk were getting home safely.

Alistair McRobb. b. 1946. Northfield. Interviewed 2015.

There have been a lot of changes

There have been changes in the people – the young ones and their impudence. Everybody has changed. Long ago when you went to the dancing, you could come home at one o' clock and quite openly walk down Union Street, comfortable that nobody would accost you. But you daren't do that now because you'd be terrified that somebody is going to jump out on you. I say to my daughter that she shouldn't come home herself but take a taxi if she's out late. It scares me to death.

If I wanted a change to go on a night out, or a pair of shoes, I'd have to save up. I'd go into a shop and pay them up over a period of weeks. Let's say they cost £4. So every week I'd go in with 5/- until £4 was paid and then I'd get the shoes. That was a common way. It was the same with the Provident and other money clubs that people had when they had no money. They'd maybe get a Provident cheque for £10 that would allow them to buy clothes, or something for their house, and then a man would come every week and collect the money until they'd paid the loan back with the interest.

The standard of living is better now, but I don't know if people are any happier. I used to know everybody wherever I've lived and would have been in everybody's house round about me. But now, you don't know anyone. Where I live now there are 12 different flats and I only know two people in one of the flats. Not like it was in the old days!

Kathleen Porter. b. 1932. Northfield. Interviewed 2016.

Kathleen Porter
– here aged 18 – found that living in far-flung Northfield was a potential impediment to romance, despite her evident good looks. See p332

A bath full of coal or salmon

My family, when I was growing up, didn't have very much. Kids now want for nothing at all; everybody's got a phone nowadays. Shoplifting was quite rife when I started in the Police. In my early days in CID the shops would maybe complain about £3 worth of groceries being stolen. There wouldn't be time now to tie up a policeman with the likes of that.

A lot of folk back then were struggling to survive. I mean Castlehill Barracks and such places were pretty dire. I've been into houses where there are not even skirting boards

because they've used them for firewood. Doors have gone into the fire as well. The bath, for example, if they did have a bath and a bathroom, would either be full of coal stolen from Ellis & McHardy or full of salmon from the Dee, all poached.

Ken Raitt. b. 1939 Holburn Street. Interviewed 2016.

Castlehill Barracks:
The notorious Castlehill Barracks housing scheme being demolished 1965.

> Aberdeen is just about the most ethnically diverse city in the UK. We have 15 different faiths and 42 different languages.

Aberdeen always had a radical element

I now find it difficult to count up all the organisations and initiatives I've become part of in the city. Currently I'm Deputy Lieutenant to the City; I'm Treasurer to the Lord Provost's Charitable Trust. Then I'm a Director of Aberdeen Performing Arts; I'm on the University Court; I'm Chair of the University Students' Affairs Committee and am also Chair of the Friends of the University's Elphinstone Institute. I'm President of the Alumnus Association, a Director of the North-east of Scotland Music Society and I'm on the Project Board for the new Students' Union at the University; I'm involved with the Rotary Club – oh, and I still play the piano for the Anchor Boys, as I have done for over 50 years, at High Church Hilton.

Sometimes I find myself battling against an overfull diary but, really, I wouldn't have it any other way. It's the pessimists and the fatalists who provoke me. You can't simply stand around and wait for others to do things. I think that's one of the reasons I enjoy working with young students: their minds have not yet become closed to all the possibilities.

In some ways I'm trying to fit into the inheritance of the city; Aberdeen has always had a radical, campaigning element to it – think of Lady Tweedsmuir, of Robert Hughes, of Tommy Mitchell, of Alec Collie – all politicians who were ready to speak up for the city as a whole. Think of the spirit of 'Britain in Bloom', of David Welch.

All this points to a city with a civic conscience. But I'm no longer sure that ethos is still intact. We used to be a city with a radical heart, but something of that reforming energy, that collective drive has been weakened – maybe despite the political rejection of her, we've all become infected by the spirit of individual acquisition and to that extent are Thatcher's children. We might like to think this has only happened down south – but just think of Scottish bankers!

Nor can you say that the city is what it used to be. Aberdeen has always been a distinctive entity, geographically isolated and self-sufficient, pursuing its own progressive path, anxious to preserve its very own independent character. Social justice and the commonweal were at the heart of its sense of itself. But then came the oil and an enormous influx of various people and corporate interests. Now, in many ways this has all been to the good: the arrival of such a range of people injected fresh life into the old place. The result is that Aberdeen is just about the most ethnically diverse city in the UK. We have 15 different faiths and 42 different languages. To begin with it was the Italians, followed later by the Chinese, the Indians and the Pakistanis: those concerned with the catering industry. Many of these families are now into a third generation and have become thoroughly settled in the North-east. Then the oil brought in the Indonesians, the Malaysians, the Scandinavians, the Americans, the French, and the Dutch – so we have become a melting pot of various peoples.

As Deputy Lieutenant I am involved in the citizenship ceremonies and there are no less than 11 of these per year. Each one includes some 30 to 40 adults who are there to become British citizens. The last one had 54 adults and 14 children, from 19 different countries – Chinese, eastern Europeans, Phillipinos, Malaysians, Nigerians, an American.

Jennifer Shirreffs with husband Murdoch: Two photos of her receiving the MBE in 2008 'for voluntary services to the community of Aberdeen'.

All this has the potential to open up the city to fresh ideas and a collective, enterprising spirit. But while the composition of the city has changed, Aberdeen itself has not succeeded in adapting to these fresh possibilities. We have reacted rather than been proactive. We've concentrated on housing the influx and so treated the city as a dormitory for workers; we've tagged these new people onto the existing physical structure and not attempted to enlarge our own mental horizons.

Mr and Mrs Aberdeen, the folk I encounter as I travel around with my bus pass, seem to be less than enthused by all the great opportunities which the changing composition of the city has brought in. All you hear is a moaning to each other as they sit on the buses: 'Look at this! Look at that! What a mess the city has become!' Oh we're so very good at moaning. What are the staple items of our conversation? Why, the impossibility of the Haudagain Roundabout, the parking situation at Foresterhill, the run-down state of Union Street. The great enterprising spirit of the last century and of the immediate post-war period seems to have got swamped by the sheer scale of change which oil has visited upon the city.

Yet I'm glad I've never moved away; I'm happy to be an Aberdonian. Beneath all the grumbles, this is a city which still has a lot going for it. What is needed is an influx not just of people but of a get-up-and-go spirit. It's the creed by which I've tried to steer my own life. I know that to some I'm just a scary wifie with a loud voice and a habit of treading on toes. But I believe that there is no such obstacle as a glass ceiling, that if you want to rise up then you can. On the other hand, I also understand that many find for whatever reason – circumstances, inherent limitations, bad fortune – it difficult to do that. People like me have been favoured in life and so it's payback time; we have a duty to do what we can for the commonweal.

Jenny Shirreffs. b. 1949. Aberdeen City. Interviewed 2014.

Sir Tommy Mitchell
as Lord Provost of the
City, escorting the
Queen Mother during
a war time visit to
Aberdeen.

A CITY TO BE PROUD OF?

Some local heroes

My career was in the fruit trade. After the war, when produce began to reappear, was an especially exciting time. The '50s and '60s were decades of ever-growing prosperity and it was good to be involved in all that. We had built up good contacts with the main British suppliers and growers and were confident of our business. The stuff, like the apples and the pears and plums from the Kent growers, would come up in box carts by rail.

We also used the local lorry firms which were rapidly expanding. The great name here was Charlie Alexander, a remarkable, self-made man who had started off as a simple ploughman. By iron self-control and hard work he developed a huge business. Starting off with the one lorry, which he drove himself, he built up a great fleet. His lorries would take fish down to Glasgow and Edinburgh; there they would be washed out and cleaned, loaded up with fruit and vegetables and brought back up to Aberdeen in the early hours of the morning. By seven a.m., a Charlie Alexander lorry would be sitting in the yard complete with your load for the day.

Then there was Tommy Mitchell who started out as the illegitimate son of a kitchie deem and who rose to become one of Aberdeen's best loved Provosts and to receive a knighthood. He was farmed out to a decent cottar couple who saw that he was well brought up. They apprenticed him to a local baker. He worked hard, learned his trade and saved up his money. Eventually he had enough to open his own baker's shop in Aberdeen. He joined the Seven Incorporated Trades and became Deacon of Bakers. He got elected as a councillor and then as Lord Provost. He served three terms; nobody cared

In full flow: Sir Tommy addressing the British Medical Association. Another Aberdeen great man, Lord Boyd-Orr is to his right.

Demonstrating his rapport with the younger generation. Sir Tommy receiving a cheque for the Spitfire Fund from a Westholme Avenue group.

to stand against him. He was always the same: a small, pawky figure, thrifty yet kindly in his dealings with others. I suspect he could ham his own ordinariness up a bit, but he was nevertheless a genuine man and a great servant of the people. As an Independent, his simple aim was to do what was best for the city, not to score party points.

I remember when as a young man I once found myself trading with the great Sir Thomas. This was 50 years ago and he was by then an old man. He came to the warehouse to buy half a dozen cases of oranges. He spent 20 minutes haggling with me over the price. He whittled me down till I had no profit left, and then he demanded a further discount for paying in cash. But the oranges were not for himself, but for children's hospitals and were to be his own gift to them. He was a wonderful, thrifty old man, who was determined not to waste a penny in a good cause.

Francis Clark was another great local character. He had been a junior doctor alongside my sister when she was a senior one. He decided to move into fish when he came to the conclusion that there was more money to be made there than in medicine.

When I was established I would go along to the University Club for my lunch where a lot of these marvellous local characters held court. You could listen to the stories of their early day exploits for hours. It was there that you became aware of a definite pecking order among the professions. At the top was the upper crust of Aberdeen lawyers, the Collies, the Williamsons, the Ledinghams. All of them had a tale to tell. I'm probably the last man alive in Aberdeen who was told how to get a band of Gordon Highlanders through the Khyber Pass safely.

One of our band was Harold Esslemont, notable for his two bowler hats which he always wore: a grey one for winter, the brown for summer. These were men who had made it and who were at ease with themselves and their position on the local scene. They could afford to take leisurely lunchtimes and the time to regale us with their stories. It was the oil boom and the more hectic days and changes in personnel that brought those sessions to a close. Everyone then seemed to become too busy.

Malcolm Sutherland. b. 1934. College Street. Interviewed 2004.

Tommy Mitchell who started out as the illegitimate son of a kitchie deem and who rose to become one of Aberdeen's best loved Provosts and to receive a knighthood.

The City's radical tradition

Powis was a fine area to grow up in, a place with a real community feel to it. Most of our neighbours were young families so we played together and grew up together. People looked out for each other: if someone was ill then it was the natural thing to make a pot of soup for them and if someone had a big fry of fish then that would be shared around. It was a working class community: neighbours had jobs in the fish market, in transport or, with 1,000 council homes being constructed each year in the city, in the building trade.

I was brought up in the culture and faith of the Labour party. My father was a longstanding member of the Independent Labour Party which he had joined in the Jimmy Maxton era, while his younger brother, Bob, eventually became a commissar for the International Brigade and fought in the Spanish Civil War against Franco. Bob lived his whole life with an unswerving commitment to the cause and was a communist till the day he died.

As a laddie I cut my teeth on delivering party pamphlets for our local Labour councillor, Billy Rose. When I had my year at the College of Education in 1965, the way in which the vacations fell gave me the opportunity to act as a sub-agent for the election of Donald Dewar in Aberdeen South, where he managed to overthrow Lady Tweedsmuir for Labour. In those days an election campaign still involved public meetings and I spent many a day pounding the streets to deliver flyers for meetings in Rosemount and in Kincorth.

I formally joined the party in 1966 and was a faithful presence at branch meetings. It was suggested that I put my name forward as a candidate for the city council and despite an initial reluctance I stood and was elected.

The work has been deeply satisfying. Basically it's all about social justice which, at grass root level, means helping people to claim what is rightfully theirs and thus to enjoy a better life. Often this is taking a quite basic step on their behalf. You find someone who has been existing in a council house which has a hole in its kitchen – simply because there was once a leak and the floor boards gave way. You can point such people in the right direction, make the necessary phone call, pull the appropriate strings.

What you are really doing is to give people a voice and you, with your confidence, your experience and your know-how can ensure that they are heard.

Aberdeen has a long history as a centre of radical thought. The first female strike in the UK actually took place at the Broadford Works back in the 1830s when the lassies engaged in the flax spinning had to endure horrible working conditions at the wet rollers, a system which left them soaked all through their 14-hour shifts. A hundred years later, Mosley's second in command, Raven Thomson, used to claim that Aberdeen was just about the toughest challenge for the British Fascist movement to tackle in the 1930s. They never did succeed in setting up a branch here though they had one in Glasgow.

So Bob Cooney, my uncle, was the inheritor of a fine tradition. He was gifted as a fine natural orator. He became one of the leading lights in the International Brigade which

> People complain about the run-down state of Union Street – yet don't seem to accept that, with so much of the street in private hands, there is little the council can actually do about it.

went out from this country to fight for the socialist cause in the Spanish Civil War. Aberdeen contributed 19 residents to that fight, plus a handful of others who had city connections.

So I am aware of a proud heritage as a Labour Party Cooney in Aberdeen. However, whereas Bob Cooney was very much a revolutionary socialist and a confirmed Stalinist to the very end, my own approach has always been a much more moderate, evolutionary one.

There is no doubt that the city is facing difficult times. The cuts in public finance and the freeze on council tax rates have presented us with an ever declining treasure chest.

I am well aware of the criticism which the Council's apparent stewardship of the city's fabric is attracting. People complain about the run-down state of Union Street – yet don't seem to accept that, with so much of the street in private hands, there is little the council can actually do about it.

The biggest controversy is over Marischal Square. Of course, it would have been nice to have been able to turn it into a fine open public square and so maintain an unimpeded view of Marischal College. However, the city finances are such that we simply couldn't give away such a prime money-earning asset. We felt we had no alternative but to maximise the income of the site and that could only be done by attracting a complex of revenue-yielding retail, office and recreational units.

Councillor Neil Cooney receiving the Britain in Bloom award on behalf of the city from Princess Anne, 1990.

In this way the intention is to bring in sufficient income through rentals to underwrite the essential services such as education and social care. And it's not true that we are neglecting the city's future. In fact, a lot of investment has been attracted to the city and this can be seen in the plans for the new conference centre, the much needed refurbishment of the Art Gallery and of the Music Hall. The hope must be that the exploitation of the Marischal Square site will act as a catalyst for further development in that end of the city, in the old Esslemont & Macintosh building and the Woolmanhill sites and thus complement all the building that is going on in the west end of Union Street.

I think I saw the best of local government, starting when Councillors were not paid and not potential careerists. It was a time of debates and cordiality between different groups. Sadly, these days now seem gone.

Aberdeen has a rich history, one that I am proud that my own family has played a part in – but we must strive to ensure that after the oil has finally gone, it will have a rich future too.

Neil Cooney. b. 1943. Powis Circle. Interviewed 2015.

'People should notice such things' – a Victorian pillar box, just 250 yards from Aberdeen Grammar school.

We learned to notice things

We learned to look at things. At the school, as a teacher, I would batter away at the importance of looking about you and noticing what was there. Local history.

I remember at the Grammar School recently I was talking about the Victorian age. Now the whole area around the school was developed during that period. The streets have names like Victoria Street and Albert Street. I was asking pupils to give me the names of the streets they passed on the way to school each morning and most of them hadn't a clue. 'Look,' I said, 'Where's Victoria Street?' Somebody said that it was in Torry – but that's Victoria Road.

They hadn't noticed the post boxes or the dates on the houses. If you look upwards you can see, in Aberdeen, the most wonderful decorative finishes to the chimneys, the gable ends and the windows – but nowadays people just drive through with their eyes on the road, or walk about and only see what is directly in front of them – or on their mobile phones.

For me, this interest started when I was a student teacher at the Middle School in the Gallowgate. There, I was having to teach stuff to kids who had no real interest in it – yet who were surrounded by streets with the most vivid names: Gallowgate, Netherkirkgate, Upperkirkgate and so on. They might not have much to say about the ins and outs of the Tudor dynasty, but their own immediate local history did strike a chord. I found I was able to teach through local history. Almost every aspect of the Industrial Revolution is visible here in Aberdeen – the canals, the textile works, the transport system.

We could talk about the development of Union Street and compare it to the New Town in Edinburgh. I was able to discuss the comparison that, whereas Edinburgh grew by building a new town on the other side of Princes Street, Aberdeen did it by building over the top of the old town. I asked them to notice what happens when you walk from the Art Gallery up Belmont Street, how the road first dips down then climbs up again; and when you cross Union Street, how you have to go down steps to get to the Green. Union Street is really a series of viaducts – the natural lie of the land is to continue to slope away from north to south, but Union Street was engineered as a straight central road for the new city. It's important to open people's eyes to what's around them, to show them that you can build up a picture of their city's past from what you can see every day.

Arthur McCombie. b. 1928. Aberdeen Grammar School. Interviewed 2005.

We're still backwards at coming forwards

I don't like people knocking Aberdeen; I'm a very proud Aberdonian. I think I can knock Aberdeen and criticise the City Council, but I don't like other people – outsiders – saying anything bad about Aberdeen. I think it's a great place to live. I'm always wanting people to see Aberdeen in a good light. I suppose it's just that when I was growing up people thought it was a remote place in the North of Scotland. I think Aberdeen is now much more on the map and that's a positive from the oil industry. We probably have services in Aberdeen that we wouldn't have had. I know it's not a huge airport, but it wouldn't have been as international an airport if it hadn't been for the oil industry. We certainly wouldn't have had the service industry that we have – hotels, restaurants and the like.

We are still backwards at coming forwards, I think. Possibly the City is still not promoted as well as it could be. I think it is a Scottish trait – 'dinna get ower big for yer boots' – and I think there is that built-in reticence to brag about what Aberdeen's good at and what we do well. I think we focus too much on the negative like how much in debt the Council is and the decisions about Union Terrace Gardens – and I sometimes think 'Give them a shake!' But then it's always the bad news that makes the headlines.

I like Aberdeen because it's a city but not a metropolis. You can walk down Union Street on a Saturday afternoon and you'll very rarely come home without having bumped into somebody that you know. I think there is still quite a community feel to Aberdeen. I don't feel that I'm just another person, another ant, but that I do belong somewhere.

So Aberdeen is a nice size of a city, but it has got a lot to offer, with lots of great cultural venues – the Theatre, the Music Hall, the smaller venues like the Arts Centre and the Lemon Tree. There are lots of nice places to go and eat. It's a safe city and in this day and age that's not something to be taken lightly. You don't have to go too far to be out into the countryside and then there's all the history there.

Whatever your interests are, Aberdeen caters for you. If you are a great outdoors person then you don't have far to go to be able to climb a Munro; if you are a gentle hillwalker there is that as well. If you're into water sports there's the beach, surfing, windsurfing – all that is here. Yes there are things that the city of Aberdeen does that are wrong, but other places do the same. There is, however, a lot that we do very well.

Dianne Morrison. b. 1967. Rosemount. Interviewed 2015.

Another example of Aberdeen being 'knocked'? A typical picture post card from the 1930s mocking the city's reputation for meanness.

To ignore the past is to repeat its mistakes

In 2007 I was persuaded to stand for the Council. I have always been a Nationalist so I stood for the Rosemount/Midstocket ward on the SNP ticket. It was very gratifying to be elected and not only on the back of SNP voters, but through support from right across the political spectrum.

One of my motivations has been a profound interest in the environment around me and the history that has produced it. My belief is that to ignore the past is to repeat its mistakes. Yet it's clear that this is exactly what often happens. Aberdeen has a wonderfully rich heritage, yet lacks a proper regional museum to celebrate it. We have become fixated on the immediate short-term future and have neglected Aberdeen's rich achievements in other fields such as medical, marine and nutritional research. How many

'I've always been a Nationalist': SNP councillor John Corall with Nicola Sturgeon, 2013.

Receiving the Samurai award, 2017, commemorating Thomas Blake Glover, an Aberdeen pioneer of 19th century Japanese development.

'A good place to live': John enjoying life at home, 2019.

young Aberdonians, for example, know of Boyd Orr's Nobel Peace Prize-winning work at the Rowett Institute on nutrition, of Richard Synge's research in biochemistry for which he also received the Nobel Prize, also while working at the Rowett, or of Professor John Mallard's development of the MRI scanner?

We have become obsessed with oil and have neglected the fact that Aberdeen has been at the centre of great industries such as granite, textiles, paper manufacture, not to mention the fish and agriculture, as well as medicine, engineering and the work of the Torry Marine Laboratory. One small example: Aberdeen had a world-leading granite industry and actually constructed the very first granite statue since the days of the pharaohs right here in Aberdeen – in Golden Square. But do we ever mention this achievement or even know about it?

I know this sounds a bit pompous, but I've always felt that there has been a strong streak of philistinism running through the North-east character, a kind of hardness. Whenever something visionary and new is mooted then the cries of 'waste of money!' will be raised. Then there's the well-known North-east distaste for self-promotion, a pouring of scorn on innovators as getting above themselves by having such fancy, airy-fairy notions.

Our future is going to be very rough unless we embrace the newer technologies. For the last two generations we have immersed ourselves in the oil industry and have developed pace-setting expertise in that area. But the oil is now running out and the future belongs to the new fuel-efficient and renewable energy developments. Yet we are merely tampering around the edges of it.

We are victims of short term thinking, of going for the quick and immediate buck and ignoring both our history and our possible future. So much of what is of value about our past has been torn down in the pursuit of a form of progress which has actually been counterproductive. Take the destruction of Loch Street and the blocking off of George Street so as to erect a pretty bog-standard shopping arcade, the Bon Accord Centre. This not only destroyed some fine granite buildings, but it also removed any possibility of introducing a one-way road system. The result is that we have stifled any question of effective traffic management in the city.

Then there has been the wanton destruction of the Green area. The Green was once the very heart of the city; Windmill Brae acted as the principal entrance into the city and ran into it. But now it's a poky, hemmed-in area overshadowed by the hideous concrete block of the New Market which replaced the fine old Archibald Simpson building. The rot set in when the Council allowed Littlewoods to build their extension at the back; I can remember one councillor rubbing his hands with glee and boasting that they had sold Littlewoods fresh air at a tidy profit – typical of the short-sighted, anything goes as long as money is involved attitude that has so blighted our city during the last 40 years or so.

Then we have Union Square. As a shopping mall it is very successful – the most frequented for its size in the UK. But that success has come at the cost of destroying local businesses and the role of Union Street as the city's premier retail strip. Union Square is

stuffed with well patronised eateries, but they are all branches of national chains and so the money goes out of the city while local eateries elsewhere languish.

As for Union Street itself, it will never return to its old shopping glories; I think we have to accept that much of it will have to revert to residential use plus a number of small niche market boutiques and specialist shops. A major problem is that so many of the properties are owned by outsiders who have little commitment to Aberdeen and are simply land-banking. It is the site they are interested in holding on to, not any business it could support. I know that people complain about the decay of the roofing and the vegetation growing out of guttering and so on and through the Aberdeen City Trust we have tried to counteract this by offering to carry out inspections and offering grants for improvement. But many of the owners simply aren't bothered; in fact in some cases the access to the upper stories has been blocked off and the spaces beneath the roof have been abandoned to nature and to deterioration.

But do I regret living and working in Aberdeen? Of course not. Despite all its problems it remains a city to be proud of, one with a rich past and a future that can still be full of possibilities.

John Corall. b 1946. Aberdeen City Council. Interviewed 2016.

Acting as an ambassador for the city: John in tartan trews at front as President of the Aberdeen History Society with hosts and fellow members; to his right, wife Kit, Isabelle and Sandy Wiseman and Dennis Scott, on a visit to twin town Regensburg, Germany, 2017.